Of Critical Theory and its Theorists

When the power of synthesis vanishes from the lives of men and when the antitheses have lost their vital relation and their power of interaction and gain independence, it is then that philosophy becomes a felt need.

G. W. F. Hegel

Of Critical Theory and its Theorists

STEPHEN ERIC BRONNER

BLACKWELL
Oxford UK & Cambridge USA

First published 1994

Blackwell Publishers
238 Main Street
Cambridge, Massachusetts 02142
USA

108 Cowley Road
Oxford OX4 1JF
UK

Library of Congress Cataloging-in-Publication Data

Bronner, Stephen Eric, 1949–
    Of critical theory and its theorists/Stephen Eric Bronner.
        p.   cm.
    Includes bibliographical references and index.
    ISBN 0–631–18737–5 (alk. paper). – ISBN 0–631–18738–3 (pbk.: alk. paper)
    1. Critical theory.   2. Philosophy and social sciences.
I. Title.
B809.3.B76   1994
142—dc20   93–30889
                                                                    CIP

British Library Cataloguing in Publication Data

A CIP catalogue record for this book is available from the British Library.

Typeset in 10 on 12pt Bembo by Photoprint, Torquay, Devon
Printed in Great Britain by T.J. Press, Padstow, Cornwall
This book is printed on acid-free paper

Contents

Acknowledgments

There are many people who have played a role in this enterprise. Luis Eduardo Mendieta generously offered his time, enthusiasm, and invaluable commentary on every phase of the enterprise. Samuel Assefa, Edmund Arens, John Ehrenberg, Michael Forman, Micheline Ishay, Kurt Jacobsen, Christine Kelly, Douglas Kellner, Eva Grunstein-Neuman, Jose Maria Rosales, Honglim Ryu, Manfred Steger, and F. Peter Wagner also provided me with their insights on various chapters and Alison Truefitt was exceptionally helpful in preparing the manuscript. I should also take this opportunity to thank Simon Prosser of Basil Blackwell Publishers for his commitment to the book, and also my wife, Anne Burns, for her patience and support. Finally, however, I would like to recall the memory of two very different thinkers who personally inspired my interest and commitment to the critical project: Ernst Bloch and Henry Pachter.

1

Introduction

Twenty-five years ago, when I first became interested in critical theory, it was the preserve of a small group of intellectuals. Journals like *Telos* and *New German Critique* had just formed and most academics in America had never heard of critical theory or, with the exception of Herbert Marcuse, its leading figures. The legend that critical theory inspired the movement of the 1960s is, certainly in America, misleading; its major works were translated only in the 1970s. Now, however, things are very different. Jürgen Habermas is everywhere legitimately recognized as a giant of social theory and there is hardly a literary critic who is unaware of Theodor W. Adorno or Walter Benjamin. Critical theory has invaded the most prestigious academic journals in disciplines ranging from anthropology and film to religion, linguistics, and political science. In fact, given the new stratum of technical experts and intellectuals concerned with normative and empirical disputation, it has arguably become a feature of the very society its proponents ostensibly challenged.

Reconstructing the radical aims of the critical project, evaluating its inadequacies along with its legacy for the present, is the purpose of this book. It is not meant to provide a detailed chronological history. Excellent histories have been written like *The Dialectical Imagination* by Martin Jay and, more recently, *The Frankfurt School* by Rolf Wiggershaus; important general works have also appeared such as *Introduction to Critical Theory* by David Held and *The Frankfurt School* by Zoltan Tar along with often magisterial biographies by scholars like Susan Buck-Morss on Walter Benjamin, Daniel Burston on Erich Fromm, Douglas Kellner on Herbert Marcuse, Arpad Kadarkay on Georg Lukács, and

Gillian Rose on Theodor W. Adorno. Nevertheless, an inquiry into the relevance of the tradition via a critical analysis of its major figures and basic themes is missing.

Of Critical Theory and its Theorists will employ the emancipatory imperative of critical theory against its predominant forms of expression. Space constraints have prevented the consideration of every important figure in the critical tradition. It would have been interesting to consider the work of important members of the younger generation like Oskar Negt, Claus Offe, and Ulrich Preuss. It also was not simply for want of interest that the contributions of Leo Lowenthal and Siegfried Kracauer to the sociology of culture or Otto Kirchheimer, Friedrich Pollock, and Franz Neumann to law and political economy, have been omitted. But the point was to deal with the classical formulation of the project and setting priorities became a necessity. The standing of any particular figure or idea was not decisive in making the choice of what to include or exclude. It was rather a matter of deciding upon what best fit my particular concerns and most contributed to the sketch of the general enterprise.

Critical theory is not a system nor is it reducible to any fixed set of prescriptions. Every major figure in the tradition of critical theory, perhaps for this very reason, employed the essay as a stylistic vehicle. The essay, with its inherently unfinished quality, is the logical form for generating anti-systemic claims and fostering the exercise of reflexivity. A certain logic always tied together the essayistic efforts of critical theorists from the past and that is also the case here. The contributions of one thinker are treated in one way and those of another are dealt with differently. The point is not to offer a neutral set of judgments or assess the importance of each thinker within the tradition equally. Each chapter provides a new and distinct interpretation of its subject matter. But themes carry over and new ones emerge. There is an open quality to the work, a space for the subject to develop connections, which probably reflects the condition of philosophical inquiry in general and the state of critical theory in particular. Indeed, if the essay is consonant with the spirit of the critical enterprise, so is the hope that the whole will coalesce into more than the sum of its parts.

Of Critical Theory and its Theorists seeks to reinvigorate the interdisciplinary character of the original enterprise and discussions will touch upon fields ranging from philosophy and aesthetics to politics and anthropology to theology and history. Any work on critical theory must also recognize its fluid character, the fact that it is no longer identifiable with any "school" or tendency, and that its continued relevance depends upon the willingness to confront old assumptions from the standpoint of new conditions. None of this, however, justifies the refusal to offer a general definition or understanding of the tradition. A stance of this sort can only feed obscurantism. The present volume is thus an attempt to present critical theory as a *cluster of themes* inspired by an emancipatory intent.

Critical theory, from the very first, expressed an explicit interest in the abolition of social injustice. The point was to show how repressive interests were hidden by the supposedly neutral formulations of science no less than ontology and, in this way, the movement always retained a commitment to the sociology of knowledge and the "critique of ideology" (*Ideologiekritik*). This internal or immanent encounter with the existing order, however, retained a transcendent or utopian component. A commitment to the integrity of the individual, and freedom beyond existing parameters, became perhaps the motivating factor behind the entire enterprise. The equilibrium holding between the immanent and transcendent elements of the project was always tenuous at best. The extent to which one or the other is given more or less weight is an interesting way to consider the development of critical theory and judge individual theorists in relation to one another. But even the balance between these two concepts shifts within the different works of any given theorist, and neither is ever sacrificed entirely. The intent is thus to preserve in reality the tension on which dialectical thinking can feed.

The objective was to foster reflexivity, a capacity for fantasy, and a new basis for praxis in an increasingly alienated world. Critical theory, in this way, stood diametrically opposed to economic determinism and any stage theory of history. It sought to examine the various "mediations" between base and superstructure. It engaged in a revision of Marxian categories and an anachronistic theory of revolution in order to expose what inhibited revolutionary practice and its emancipatory outcome. Critical theory wished to push beyond the stultifying dogma and collectivism of what became known as "actually existing socialism." The ideological and institutional framework of oppression was always thrust to the forefront and made the target of attack. This is what fed critical theory's concern with utopia and its unyielding commitment to experiment with new forms of experience and analysis.

The cluster of themes defining critical theory thus retains a certain integrity and coherence. It also emerges from a distinct historical context. World War I and the Russian Revolution provided the context in which new departures in dialectical thinking took place. The identification between technology and progress, science and moral development, collapsed in the trenches. Liberalism lost its allure; reform and good will had apparently proven useless. One apocalypse had been unleashed and another seemed on the agenda. The "betrayal" of proletarian internationalism by social democracy in 1914 along with the seizure of power by the communists, and a spate of proletarian uprisings throughout Europe in the aftermath of the war, thus provided the impulse for a critique of orthodoxy and the standard "materialist" interpretation of Marx.

Orthodox Marxism may have anticipated these events, but its belief that capitalist crises in the economically advanced world would automatically build the future of socialism in the most advanced nations obviously did not conform with the revolution in economically underdeveloped Russia, which Antonio Gramsci initially termed a "revolution against *Capital.*" Emphasis on the objective development of productive forces and bureaucratic forms of mass organization, which viewed republicanism as a prerequisite for socialism, gave way before a new concern with "consciousness" and the most radical possible transformation of society. A new concern with the connection between revolutionary theory and practice made itself felt. Thus, the relation between marxism and philosophy became a matter of importance.

Critical theory is usually associated with various members of the Frankfurt Institute for Social Research like Max Horkheimer who became its director in 1930; Leo Lowenthal who joined in 1926; Theodor W. Adorno who began to participate in 1928, but only became an official member ten years later; Erich Fromm who started his nine-year collaboration in 1930, Herbert Marcuse who joined in 1933, and Walter Benjamin who never officially became a member at all. But, in fact, it was spawned by a set of unorthodox thinkers more or less associated with the left wing of the communist movement who represented what Maurice Merleau-Ponty would call "Western Marxism." This tendency with its opposition to mechanistic materialism and all ahistorical forms of interpretation, its emphasis on the dialectical method and the importance of the idealist tradition for Marxism, its concern with consciousness and overcoming alienation, turned its thinkers into far more than merely the precursors of the "Frankfurt School." *Of Critical Theory and its Theorists*, for this reason, opens with chapters treating the contributions of Karl Korsch, Georg Lukács, and Ernst Bloch.

All had an extraordinary influence on the development of critical theory. Interpreting ideology as a "lived experience," rejecting rigid disciplinary constraints, seeking to reconstitute the connection between theory and practice, Korsch employed the insights of materialist dialectics to criticize the increasingly petrified forms of Marxism embraced respectively by the social democratic labor movement and the communist party. Historical materialism truly became historical. The critical power of the dialectic was directed at those who considered themselves its guardians. His relentlessly immanent confrontation with reality, however, does not deny transcendence. Freedom is never identified with any given form or system by this theorist who was finally expelled from the Communist Party and helped develop an "independent" Marxism.

Georg Lukács, who ultimately recanted his heresies in order to remain in the communist movement, contributed to this trend as well. His approach would prove a milestone in developing the sociology of knowledge. At the same time, however, it was far more metaphysical than that of Korsch. Orthodoxy, for Lukács, was a matter of method grounded in the categories of totality and mediation. He employed it both to analyze the discordant relation between "bourgeois" theory and practice as well as develop interpretations of issues like alienation, which would profoundly influence the future of critical theory. "Reification and the Consciousness of the Proletariat," which is arguably the seminal work of the entire tradition, makes this clear. It provides the frame of reference no less than the categories in which even the most adamant of Lukács' dialectical adversaries would operate. A critical commentary on this essay, which illuminates its anticipation of future issues and trends, thus seemed useful and appropriate to include.

Ernst Bloch was the greatest of utopian philosophers and his work blended historical materialism with the anthropological, religious, and existential questions deriving from a variety of different traditions. Marxism assumed a new apocalyptic form in the thinking of this maverick intellectual who would provide a radical criticism of stage theory and innovative analysis of fascism even while identifying himself with the communist movement. His influence on liberation theology became profound after World War II. Only now, however, is he becoming well-known in the United States. And that is strange. He had already been famous in Europe for decades. His utopian philosophy grew from the same soil as Korsch's concern with workers' councils and Lukács's emphasis on class consciousness and the abolition of all alienated social relations.

All of this, however, makes it clear once again that the owl of Minerva only spreads its wings at dusk. Korsch's *Marxism and Philosophy* and Lukács' *History and Class Consciousness* both appeared in 1923. This was the year in which the possibility of an international revolution was finally laid to rest. It was also the year in which the Institute for Social Research was founded in Frankfurt am Main. The initial research program was developed under the stewardship of Dr Carl Grünberg. It centered around the labor movement, the capitalist economy, and the new experiments with planning in the Soviet Union. Korsch exerted an important influence during this period and among the important scholars were Fritz Sternberg, Henryk Grossmann, Friedrich Pollock. Many members were aligned with the communist movement and its perspective on the state and monopoly capitalism even carried over into certain important writings of the 1930s. Nevertheless, a fundamental shift in direction took place when Max Horkheimer became director in 1930.

He coined the term "critical theory." He also used the *Journal for Social Research*, which would serve as the public forum for the Institute, to set the new agenda with its emphasis on a far broader cluster of issues ranging from psychology and aesthetics to philosophy and the critique of technology. "Horkheimer's Road" is an attempt to explore the various phases of his career, the contributions and limits of his thought, and certain assumptions behind the enterprise of what would come to be known as the "Frankfurt School." Indeed, especially given the lack of any major biography in English, this chapter assumes particular scholarly importance.

Horkheimer juxtaposed critical theory against all "traditional," metaphysical, and materialist forms of theory. His purpose was to highlight the manner in which critical theory militates against all attempts to construct a fixed system and every attempt to identify the subject with the object, whether conceived in terms of social institutions or the "covering" categories of philosophy. Ontology and instrumental rationality, which respectively either identify subjectivity with certain prefabricated categories or dismiss it entirely, would bear the brunt of his assault. I included, for this reason, one essay dealing with the relation between politics and philosophy in the work of Martin Heidegger, who would play such an important intellectual role in the 1930s, and another concerned with analytic Marxism. Both employ critical theory to contest alternative frameworks. Their relevance, however, also becomes evident in a different way.

Just as the quality of a great painting becomes clearer when surrounded by competing works of the period whose styles it radically contests, a particular theory assumes sharper outlines when contrasted with the philosophical positions it opposes. And, in the 1930s, the critical rationalism of the Institute gave it a unique position. This was a decade in which all hope for the future seemed lost. Walter Benjamin, who would become one of the most prominent literary critics and philosophers of the century, sought to save it by recapturing "the glow of the profane." He evidenced an extraordinary commitment to freedom, individuality, and philosophical experimentation during the time in which totalitarianism was on the rise. His attempt to construct a negative philosophy of history, substitute a less rigorous constellation for the classical Hegelian concept of totality, and emphasize the particular would ultimately lay the basis for transforming the entire critical project. Nevertheless, while most interpretations stress or even glorify the fragmented quality of his thinking and insights, this one will view those very qualities making for his current success as compensations for his failure to fuse the messianic with the materialist.

Walter Benjamin was an enthusiastic supporter of modernism like virtually every other major figure in the critical tradition. He viewed surrealism, with its emphasis on the transformation of everyday experience, as an essential component of the revolution. His own radicalization, in fact, occurred through his relationships with outspoken critics of bourgeois cultural traditions like Ernst Bloch, Bertolt Brecht, and Asja Lacis. With the extension of support by Stalin to the Popular Front in 1936, however, expressionism and modernism came under attack in favor of "realism." A debate took place in which Lukács, who had openly retreated from his youthful avant-gardism in order to propound a standpoint in conformity with the new communist line, set the stage for a debate in which Bloch and Bertolt Brecht offered the most important responses.

"Political Aesthetics in Retrospect" provides the background for the "expressionism debate" and a quick summary of the principal arguments. But it also confronts them in order to move forward. An emancipatory aesthetic for the contemporary era cannot remain stuck at choosing between realism or modernism. Arbitrary constraints of this sort are anachronistic. New categories are necessary to evaluate diverse artistic contributions, the ambivalent character of mass culture, the relation between representation and mimesis, and that is precisely what this essay seeks to offer in a preliminary form.

Exile, however, was the real theme of the 1930s and 1940s. The Institute of Social Research and most of its members, seeking to escape Hitler, ultimately relocated in the United States. There, in collaboration with Theodor Adorno, a brilliant musicologist and philosopher, Horkheimer wrote *Dialectic of Enlightenment*. This marked a significant shift in the direction of critical theory. No longer was the proletariat seen as the revolutionary subject of history, no longer were teleological notions of progress taken seriously, no longer was the liberal enlightenment legacy taken for granted, no longer was it merely a matter of redirecting technology towards new ends. The critical theory of society surrendered to a more directly anthropological form of inquiry. The possibility of revolutionary transformation was seen as fading in the face of an apparently seamless bureaucratic order buttressed by the "culture industry" and intent on eliminating subjectivity and the reflexive sources of opposition to the status quo. A certain cultural elitism took shape. For the proponents of critical theory, working within the dialectical framework of Hegel and Marx, it thus ultimately became a matter of recruiting Schopenhauer and Nietzsche in their battle against the collectivist strains within advanced industrial society.

Theodor Adorno was perhaps the most talented proponent of this new turn in critical theory. He and Horkheimer would become linked and, following the return of the Institute to Frankfurt in 1947, they would become the most important academic mainstays of the enterprise. The only real disciple of Benjamin, the inventor of "negative dialectics," Adorno's works show a genuinely remarkable range and quality; indeed, they include what is arguably the most important work on aesthetic theory written in this century. It is with Adorno, however, that the relation between theory and practice most nearly verges on disintegration and the connection between immanence and transcendence appears most tenuous. "Dialectics at a Standstill" will analyze his rescue of utopia through an "inversion" of reality and his redefinition of critical theory as an anti-systemic metaphysic lacking any criteria with which to justify its claims or articulate its aims.

Concerns of this sort are often reflected in the attacks on the difficult style employed by critical theorists. The heritage of dialectical philosophy surely had an impact; the complex use of complex concepts often justifiably demanded a complex style. Especially in the ideologically charged postwar context, however, members of the Institute also employed an "Aesopian" form of writing; indeed, often from fear or self-serving purposes, they wished to hide their Marxism and used the highly abstract Hegelian language for that reason. But there is also a theoretical justification for their abstruse style. Even while concern was expressed with fostering enlightenment attitudes in works like *The Authoritarian Personality*, which was directed by Adorno, the famous analysis of the culture industry implied that popularity would necessarily "neutralize" whatever emancipatory message a work retained. Nevertheless, there was nothing ambivalent about the willingness or the ability of Erich Fromm to engage the public.

No one was more popular than this great neo-Freudian psychologist. He was surely the most succinct and lucid stylist to emerge from the Institute. He was also perhaps the most loyal to its original purpose. Fromm was, originally, one of its most influential members and a close friend of Horkheimer. His concern was with social psychology and its relation to political and clinical practice; indeed, this would continue to serve as a point of reference even in his later attempts to link Freud with Marx. For this reason, when Adorno first insisted on developing the critique of anthropology from the standpoint of Freud's instinct theory, he clashed with Fromm. The dazzling newcomer won the battle. Fromm divorced himself from the Institute and proceeded to write a number of bestsellers including *Escape from Freedom*. Quickly enough, in fact, he was condemned for the "superficial" quality of his writings. Nevertheless, "Fromm in America" will explore his significance and the important influence he exerted on postwar intellectual and political life in the United States.

Critical theory reached its zenith in the 1960s and 1970s. Its emphasis upon alienation, the domination of nature, the regressive components of progress, the mutability of human nature, and the stultifying effects of the culture industry and advanced industrial society made the enterprise relevant for young intellectuals. Radicalism in theory, however, betrayed what was ever more surely becoming a conservatism in practice. New stalwarts of the establishment like Max Horkheimer and Theodor Adorno, for example, were essentially appalled by the movement their own writings had helped inspire.

Herbert Marcuse, however, remained faithful to the original practical impulse of critical theory. He self-consciously employed it to inform the rash of new movements. He also provided, whatever his work's other failings, a positive utopian response to what he termed "one-dimensional society." Pessimism concerning the future of a society in which all ideological contradictions were being flattened out combined with the commitment to a utopian vision. It was a perspective, viciously criticized by Fromm, which was predicated on confronting "progress" and the anthropological condition of humanity. His perspective sought to fuse the anthropological insights of the young Marx with the "play" principle of Schiller and the metapsychology of Freud. His concerns derived from those articulated by Adorno in the 1930s and, probably for this reason, Marcuse was viciously attacked by Fromm among others. Nevertheless, Herbert Marcuse was the thinker who really introduced critical theory to America and the attempt to illuminate his extraordinary influence led me to include the text of a short speech commemorating his death as the prelude to a critical examination of his utopian theory entitled "The Anthropological Break."

The passing of the radical wave created a new set of issues for the new generation of critical theorists. Taming its utopian excesses, mitigating its subjectivism, affirming its connection with the Enlightenment, establishing its relation to the empirical sciences, providing its normative concerns with philosophical legitimacy, and infusing it with insights from different traditions, all became matters of concern. Every one of these problems was confronted by the most brilliant modern representative of critical theory, and one of the pre-eminent philosophers of our time, Jürgen Habermas.

He was always concerned with "undistorted communication" and an emancipatory interest capable of informing the rational adjudication of grievances. He has also become a prominent "public intellectual," who has dared to take a stand on the most important political and philosophical issues of the age. Perhaps this is part of the reason why he retreated from his earlier methodological commitments to epistemological forms of inquiry. Habermas made a "linguistic turn," which was inspired by his new interest in pragmatism and analytic philosophy. Critical theory had originally viewed these philosophical standpoints with contempt. But, according to Habermas, the normative claims of critical theory would now finally receive justification. They would become grounded within the inter-subjective construct of language itself and, in this way, he believed that a new discourse ethic might prove useful in informing a host of essentially liberal perspectives on law and politics. But there are lingering questions concerning the character of this new system, its connection with the critical tradition, its claim to provide a "postmetaphysical" philosophy, its ability to deal with questions of material interest, and its relevance to political practice. Indeed, these issues are at the core of "Jürgen Habermas and the Language of Politics."

Critical theory projected an emancipatory promise and a new inter-disciplinary perspective seeking to inform the struggles of the oppressed. Martin Jay was thus correct in suggesting that the questions raised by the proponents of Western Marxism and critical theory were the right ones even if the answers they offered were not. The continuing relevance of the project thus depends upon the willingness to make good on that original promise and refashion various categories and assumptions in order to confront new conditions. But, in my opinion, this can only occur insofar as new developments in critical theory challenge its identification with both "negative dialectics" and discourse theory. Highlighting its political impulse, affirming its practical character, and beginning the sketch for a new critical theory of society is the purpose behind the last chapter of this volume.

"Points of Departure" will deal with issues ranging from the preoccupation with foundations and the totality to the status of utopia and the critique of ideology; it will emphasize questions dealing with solidarity and the domination of nature, class and cosmopolitanism, interests and autonomy, reification and aesthetics, the constraints on democracy and the need to contest the arbitrary exercise of power in both existing political institutions and the accumulation process. Confronting these questions will, furthermore, occur from a standpoint willing to identify critical theory with the democratic and socialist variants of the enlightenment tradition. The ambivalence concerning its connection with the enlightenment has become ever more wearying and ever less productive. Critical theory must now, once again, situate itself and make explicit its aims. Immanence can no longer be played off against transcendence;

emancipatory critique can develop only by reaffirming the connection between the two. This last chapter in *Of Critical Theory and its Theorists* seeks to contribute toward that end. It is thus less a conclusion than the attempt to provide a new beginning.

Stephen Eric Bronner
New York City

2

Karl Korsch: Western Marxism and the Origins of Critical Theory

Karl Korsch has traditionally been associated with Antonio Gramsci and Georg Lukács. It was they who originally crystallized what would become known as "Western Marxism" from which "critical theory" evolved. Even within this intellectual tradition, however, Korsch's work has been overshadowed by that of his two contemporaries. He too viewed Marxism as a theory of praxis, emphasized the importance of Hegel, attacked economism, and placed decisive emphasis on the role of consciousness. He also never identified the interests of workers with any party or embraced a rigid teleology. But his output was neither as suggestive as that of Gramsci, as dramatic as that of Bloch, nor as prolific, wide-ranging, and sophisticated as that of Lukács.[1] Nevertheless, when he died following a long illness in 1961 at the age of 72, Korsch had articulated a cogent and inherently self-critical perspective on Marxism informed by a radical notion of proletarian democracy.

His radicalism developed gradually and consistently.[2] An early member of the free student movement, he studied philosophy and received his law degree from the University of Jena in 1910. Then, in 1912, he went to England and encountered the Fabian Society. While skeptical of its bureaucratic and reformist politics, he was none the less influenced by its anti-metaphysical and "practical" conception of socialism. The Fabians also rejected the fatalistic determinism of orthodox Marxism and, given his early encounter with German Idealism, it makes sense that Korsch should have developed an emphasis on consciousness and other "subjective" factors with respect to the working-class struggle.

Such concerns were only reinforced by the Kantian socialist perspective of Kurt Eisner who became close to Korsch when the young man formally entered the German Social Democratic Party (SPD).

Interestingly enough, with Korsch, the materialist and idealist traditions were never seen as antinomial. Emphasis on the one over the other may have shifted during his career. Just as the emphasis on consciousness always retained an empirical referent in the early work, his later and more "positivist" writings were always informed by a normative commitment to the empowerment of workers. Anticipating the problems of verification and grounding normative claims, which would arise once the validity of the method became divorced from the truth or falsity of the conclusions reached,[3] Korsch always sought to retain an objective referent for his subjective claims along with a connection between theory and practice. Nor was he willing rigidly to juxtapose the dialectical "method" of Marxism against its "scientific" character. He often ignored the tensions between them and never systematically articulated the connection between social scientific inquiry and the approach of the natural sciences.[4] The entire thrust of his undertaking, however, suggests that the Marxian "science" would retain an inherently critical dimension. Thus, putting the matter somewhat provocatively, it is possible to consider his interpretation of Marxism as a "science" of class consciousness.[5]

In any event, however, the political development of Korsch was radically affected by World War I during which he served as a military officer before his expression of anti-nationalist views led to a reduction in rank. Disillusioned by the opportunism of the SPD, both during the war and in its immediate aftermath, he joined the dissident, pacifist, and revolutionary Independent Social Democratic Party of Germany (USPD); indeed, Korsch stayed with the left wing of that organization when it split to help form the German Communist Party (KPD) in 1919. And, rising quickly through the ranks,[6] he became the editor of the party's theoretical journal *Die Internationale*. Then, in 1923, *Marxism and Philosophy* appeared and Korsch became Minister of Justice in the revolutionary councilist government which briefly controlled the German province of Thuringia.

An "ultra-left" aura was thus cast over the first outspokenly Marxist professor in Germany. It was, however, less his philosophical "heresies" than the failure of this disorganized uprising and the shifting of political winds in Moscow that led to his condemnation by Zinoviev in the famous "professor's speech" at the Fifth Congress of the Comintern in 1924.[7] The complexion of the Comintern changed in that year which, soon enough, led to the "bolshevization" of the KPD under the leadership of Ruth Fischer and Arkadij Maslow.[8] In the process, Korsch became one of the party's most berated figures and the victim of a smear campaign which would culminate in his expulsion in 1926. It was only then that his "ultra-left" bolshevism began surrendering to anarcho-syndicalism.

This turn grew more pronounced as the SPD and the KPD gained an ever stronger monopoly on the organizational apparatus of the Left and, in the years following his expulsion, Korsch's influence was basically confined to left intellectuals, representatives of the councilist movement like the philosopher Anton Pannekoek or Rosa Luxemburg's old friend Henriette Roland-Holst, along with a few sectarian ex-communists like Amadeo Bordiga and Lucien Laurat the editor of *La Révolution Prolétarienne*.[9] He had his own study group which included important ex-communists like Manabandra Roy, social revolutionaries like Isaac Steinberg the one-time Minister of Justice in Lenin's government of 1918, artists like Bertolt Brecht and Alfred Döblin, as well as a number of young intellectuals like Erich Gerlach, Heinz Langerhans, and Henry Pachter.[10] Still, Korsch also tried to expand his contacts with workers and workers' movements. He thus maintained his friendship with Richard Müller, former president of the syndicalist German metal workers' union, and rendered what support he could to the International Workers of the World in the United States and the Spanish anarchists following his exile from Germany.[11]

It was already before the appearance of *Marxism and Philosophy*, which was ultimately published in a series edited by Carl Grünberg, that Korsch came into contact with Felix Weil. Grünberg would serve as the first director of the Institute for Social Research while Weil would finance this center for what would come to be known as the "Frankfurt School." In 1921 Korsch published the latter's study of socialization in his series entitled *Practical Socialism*, modeled after the educational undertakings of the Fabians, wherein his own important contribution "What is Socialization?" also appeared. Afterwards, along with Weil, Korsch served as the guiding force behind the first "Marxist Work Week" which would bring together Lukács as well as Karl August Wittfogel, Friedrich Pollock, Horkheimer, Paul Massing, Julian Gomperz, and others who would play such an important role in the development of the Institute and critical theory.[12]

Korsch, however, would ultimately play a minimal role in the what would become the "Frankfurt School." His unrelenting concern with the proletariat, his contempt for metaphysics, and his desire to maintain the connection between theory and practice placed him at odds with those who were content to "work but little, and talk a lot."[13] Korsch exerted his influence as a genuinely independent Marxist committed to promulgating a "revolutionary" perspective. Thus his development is indeed connected with the "revolutionary historicism" supposedly defining his thought.[14]

A certain concrete historical logic, willing to judge the value of a given theory or practice purely with respect to its immediate relevance for the class struggle, is generally seen as defining his worldview. And he was attracted to Leninism not because of its abstract "theoretical" superiority, but because he believed that it was expressing the most radical revolutionary possibilities of the working class in the wake of World War I. In fact, if it is somewhat of an exaggeration to link Korsch with the positivistic historicism of Leopold von Ranke,[15] the historicist perspective informs all of Korsch's work including his classic *Marxism and Philosophy*. Strains of pragmatism also become evident. Nevertheless, all this is infused with the need to maintain a consistent relation between theory and practice.

Philosophy is subsequently not seen as a wasteful exercise in metaphysics or an autonomous realm of intellectual endeavor. It is rather, according to Korsch, a "moment" within the existing "totality" of social relations. And so, in keeping with Hegel, he viewed philosophy as "comprehend[ing] its epoch in thought." The relation between theory and practice thus takes center stage. Admittedly, without explicitly formulating the undertaking, Marx had already employed a similar perspective in analyzing the bourgeoisie. But Korsch was the first self-consciously to employ "the principle of historical specification" in critically evaluating the theory and practice of the working class.[16] Rejecting the abstract standpoint of "pure theory," he proceeded by analyzing the historical practice of a class in terms of its own self-understanding. Thus, applying "the materialist method of history to the materialist method of history itself,"[17] Korsch was able to formulate a critique of Marxism from within the theoretical construct of Marxism itself.

According to his analysis, there are both progressive and decadent periods in the history of a class which reflect themselves in the particular modes of thought which arise.[18] The philosophy of a class on the rise will justify its activities by articulating transcendent aims while in a decadent period, when a class has already established itself, these goals will contract as existing contradictions become frozen and projected into the future.[19] The future itself will thus appear as nothing more than a mechanical elaboration of the present.[20] Indeed, all this becomes particularly evident in the fate of Hegelian philosophy in the modern epoch.

Korsch, no less than Gramsci and Lukács,[21] believed that the goals of the revolutionary bourgeoisie attained their most explicit articulation in the speculative philosophy of the young Hegel. Through Hegel's projection of freedom beyond the existent, and the inherently "critical" character of his thought, he was seen as making "self-conscious" the most radical possibilities and contradictions of his own class. Its political decadence during the latter half of the nineteenth century, on the other hand, is reflected in the attack on historical thought by abstract metaphysicians and a triumphant positivist materialism. Korsch views the situation with "Marxism" as essentially no different. It too, as Engels recognized, was the product of a class at a given stage of historical development; it too would experience the introduction of "dialectical" laws along with positivist forms of economic reductionism precisely when the actual, historical possibilities for revolution began to dim.

Korsch saw Marxism as falling into three relatively distinct phases and defined by a particular form of practice.[22] During the first period, from 1843–8, Marx was still in the process of giving his theory a critical shape which, in turn, reflected the conditions of a proletariat constituting itself in social and political terms; the "Marxism" of this period, with its decisively Hegelian influence, is subsequently seen as as projecting a set of radical goals capable of informing revolutionary practice. This, however, was far less the case with the second phase, extending from the failure of the Revolutions of 1848 to the close of the century, in which Marx and Engels' concern with developing a "scientific socialism" set the stage for the positivist interpretation of their work by Karl Kautsky and the foremost thinkers of social democracy; it was they who, while attesting to a formal orthodoxy, created a split between the revolutionary implications of the original theory and the reformist practice of their movement. The third phase would thus result in trade unionists rejecting the orthodox theory of social democracy while embracing its practice, and Bolsheviks maintaining – in Korsch's view – a too strict commitment to the "scientific" character of the theory while attempting to formulate a new practice.[23] Indeed, this analysis would lead Korsch to claim that during the "long period when Marxism was slowly spreading throughout Europe it had in fact no longer any practical revolutionary task to accomplish."[24]

Korsch may have retained elements of the materialist and the idealist in his theory. But his criticisms of metaphysics and positivism, when seen as independent systems of thought, informed much of what would become "critical theory."[25] His willingness to view philosophy as an immanent "moment" of the totality, and so as a form of practice in its own right, was also decisive for its early partisans. Korsch's contribution to "critical theory," however, extends beyond the historicism informing his work. There is also a positive *transcendent* element within his critical historical view of philosophy as an *immanent* moment of the social whole. This component of Korsch's thinking may not have been epistemologically articulated in an explicit fashion. Still, his theory presupposes the need to posit an alternative order. Consequently, though from a somewhat different vantage point, Korsch's thinking offers an emphasis on historical reflexivity similar to the one that would define the difference between "traditional" and "critical" theory in Max Hork-heimer's famous essay of the same name.

The existence of this transcendent component in Korsch's thinking itself has historical roots. A misunderstanding of the Russian Revolution occurred which informed the political thinking of Korsch as well as many of his radical humanist and anarchist contemporaries in the Weimar Republic. The revolutionary essence of 1917 was seen by them less in terms of the actually existing dictatorship than the theoretical emphasis on proletarian self-administration and the idea of soviets articulated by Lenin in *The State and Revolution*.[26] Soviets or councils arose throughout much of Europe in the aftermath of World War I. They seemed the new organizational form capable of overcoming "alienation" by fusing political with judicial and economic decision-making. A commitment to proletarian empowerment through this institutional arrangement informed Korsch's later criticisms of the communist move-ment, which even produced comment from Stalin in 1926, no less than his periodic calls for the revolutionary "restoration" of Leninism during the dark days of the "counter-revolution" from above.[27] But the fact is that, even during the "heroic" phase of the Bolshevik Revolution, the soviets never ruled Russia or anywhere else for an extended period of time. Consequently, in this instance, Korsch's critique of bolshevism stems less from actual historical practice than from an unrealized transcendent idea within Lenin's writings and those of the ultra-left within the communist movement.

A caesura between theory and practice, which became ever more pronounced as his sectarianism evolved, subsequently existed at the heart of Korsch's "revolutionary historicism" from the very beginning. No wonder then that the original denizens of the "orthodox" social demo-cratic movement like Rosa Luxemburg, Karl Kautsky, and Leon Blum – rather than he or his ultra-left and "Western Marxist" comrades – should have been the ones to provide the earliest, most politically concrete, and prophetic analyses of the Revolution. It would similarly only make sense from the standpoint of his own historicism that, in the wake of the revolutionary thermidor in the USSR during 1923–4, the majority of the European working class should have returned to the social democratic movement, or what Leon Blum called the "old house," from which it might at least derive some practical benefit.

But he did not return; not even when he was expelled from the communist movement. Social democracy appeared an atavistic relic rather than an alternative to the new authoritarianism. Its proponents could only point to the liberties offered by bourgeois democracies which, from a councilist perspective, were mainly seen as honored in the breach and employed to keep the working class from assuming substantive power. Proletarian "self-administration" (*Selbsttätigkeit*) was a concept for which they seemingly had as little use as the communists. In fact, excluding a few mavericks like Rosa Luxemburg, social democrats had nothing to say about transforming the production process; instituting new values of solidarity; extending the limits of a purely formal set of bourgeois democratic freedoms; curbing bureaucracy; overcoming a stultifying division of labor; creating new forms for empowering workers; or confronting the instrumental logic of capitalist accumulation which turned them into a mere "factor of production." Social democracy, in short, lacked a radical perspective on freedom with which to confront either capitalist or communist forms of exploitation.

And so Korsch remained on the outside. His commitment to a councilist system continued long after the actual historical possibility for its establishment had passed in the mid-twenties. The question is: what justified maintaining that commitment? The belief in a looming crisis? Perhaps. But Korsch always maintained that, if surrendering all belief in economic crisis turns the quest for socialism into a purely moral demand, theories postulating an "iron logic" for capitalism's demise are pseudo-scientific.[28] Opposed to both the exaggerated faith in crisis theory exhibited by orthodoxy, and the optimistic assumptions of reformism, Korsch was content to assert the need for revolutionary preparation without reference to the political form through which this should occur. And, as a consequence, his transcendent commitment to preparing for a future crisis had nothing to do with the actual crises with which the working class was confronted. It chose sides in the Popular Front, the Second World War, and the East–West conflict. But all this seemed essentially irrelevant to Korsch; only the Spanish Civil War – and for good reason – captured his imagination.[29] Thus, he was ultimately left with nothing more than the correct theoretical claim that a "crisis" – as against (say) a mere "recession" – demands the subjective response which will recognize it as such.

"Revolutionary historicism" is useless in understanding any of this. A different perspective is necessary. And such a perspective must confront the fashionable assumption that a historicist perspective is inherently critical; it is rather the genuinely critical perspective that is inherently historical.[30] Korsch recognized this in his own way and, if the insight helped make for his practical impotence, it also turned him into a theoretical forerunner of the Frankfurt School. History opposed his vision and, ultimately, he was forced to choose between the ideal and the real. And the result of that choice flies in the face of dominant interpretations. Indeed, it was not the historicist understanding of reality that would immanently produce the commitment to a particular set of radical ideals; it was rather the transcendent commitment to an un-realized idea of freedom that, for better or worse, would inform the historicist understanding of reality.

And reality took its revenge. As the idea of soviets became ever more abstract, Korsch's disillusionment grew. Some critics have suggested that this led him to totally abandon Marxism in his later years.[31] At the time of his death, in fact, Korsch was working on a biography of Bakunin; he no longer had much faith in the teleology of Marxism any more than the attempts to link theory and practice through some particular organizational form of working-class politics.[32] Anticipating the thinking of critical theorists in the 1930s, no less than the radical students of 1968, he was consistent in arguing that the "totality" stood in need of transformation. The emphasis on revolution, councilist demo-cracy, and proletarian empowerment remained; the transcendent perspective from which he sought to confront the degeneration of the proletarian movement never changed. By the same token, however, Korsch was always unconcerned with attempts at "dogmatic calculation [regarding] how the different versions of Marxist theory correspond to some abstract canon of 'pure and unfalsified' theory."[33] Orthodoxy was, for him, inimical to critical and historical thinking;[34] the real issue, then, is not whether Korsch abandoned Marxism. Indeed, one might as well ask whether Marx abandoned Hegel.

Korsch's criticism was always undertaken from within the dialectical method. Nor did he ever consider Marxism as a set of "iron laws." And the reason is quite simple. According to Korsch, from such a standpoint, it can never comprehend the society it wishes to transform.[35] Stuck at the level of appearances, unable to view its own assumptions and categories as historically contingent,[36] Marxism turns into a fixed and finished system.[37] Economic reductionism necessarily results when the unfolding of "objective" contradictions assumes primacy; the "ensemble of social relations" (Marx) disappears along with the ability to deal with the ideological and practical manner through which a class constitutes itself as such.[38] "Scientific Marxism" subsequently cannot serve as a theory of revolution precisely because it inherently neglects the political moment of action. Thus, even while viewing itself as a hard-headed analysis of reality, "economic determinism" or "vulgar materialism" loses that very relation to practice which, for Korsch, makes Marxism unique.[39]

Korsch argued that the decisive element within Marxism lay in its ability to recognize that all ideological, political, and economic phenomena were products of specific forms of social relations. Everything was thus a product of human activity and so open to critical scrutiny and transformation. Such was the perspective from which the reassertion of control by rational "subjects" over a historical "object" like capital, whose dynamics seemed to possess a life of their own, might take place. Indeed, it was from this perspective that Korsch developed his critique of "alienation" and the "inverted world" of bourgeois society.[40]

Marxism thus emerges as what Gramsci called a philosophy of praxis; its concern is with "revolution" and a commitment to proletarian empowerment whose possibilities for realization are continuously changing. The transcendent idea of revolution prevents Korsch's "historicism" from falling into a thoroughgoing relativism even while his commitment to an inherently unfinished notion of proletarian empowerment opens any existing political arrangement to critique.[41] His emphasis on the concept of "concreteness" [*Diesseitigkeit*], moreover, also led him to reject all ideological and practical justifications for oppression.[42] Just as materialism originally emerged from the critique of religion, so must the critique of capitalist (and even "socialist") ideology occur through the demystification of production relations.[43] And, at all costs, that criticism demanded the commitment to a concrete alternative: workers' councils.[44]

Arguing then that Korsch is engaged in a mechanistic "reduction" of theory to the class struggle, which leads "to the absence of a real critique of ideology," misses the point of his entire undertaking.[45] Exposing how Marxism was employed to veil an oppressive status quo and elaborating a critical historical method, immanently capable of questioning those uses to which it was being put, were the fundamental concerns with which Korsch was intellectually engaged. Nor did he ever view ideology as simply floating about in the superstructure as some reflex of an "objectively" constituted class struggle. Ideology was rather seen by him as a moment of the struggle itself. Thus, anticipating the thinkers of the Frankfurt School, Korsch could argue that it is incumbent upon "modern dialectical materialism to grasp philosophies and other ideological systems in theory as realities and to treat them as such in praxis.[46]

That was precisely what the economism of Kautsky and the "copy theory" of Lenin failed to do. "Truth," from such philosophical perspectives, lies only in the calculable realm of the economic "base" which directly and causally determines the "superstructure" of state activity and the various forms of ideological expression.[47] Perhaps political conflict can evidence a moment of "objective" truth insofar as it is directly interwoven with discernible and calculable economic interests. Ideology, however, is nothing more than "pure rubbish" (Kautsky) or simply "false consciousness" (Lenin) since it merely veils "objective" reality.[48] Thus, once Marxism is reduced to a "science" of economics, other dimensions of reality are either mechanically determined by its categories of explanation or simply ignored altogether.

Korsch, however, interprets Marxism neither as a theory of nature nor as a "science."[49] Instead it is understood as an inherently historical and value-laden approach which seeks to comprehend the existing "totality."[50] In keeping with this view, the attempt to fragment Marxism into a variety of disciplines denies its very purpose. Once an autonomous character is attributed to *any* single facet of the social totality its actual functioning, along with the structural interests it harbors, will prove impossible to define. Consequently, Marxism is "inherently bound to *praxis* (and self-consciously so) as a total system (*Gesamtsystem*). The critique of political economy is then intrinsically bound to the critique of ideology."[51]

Class consciousness remained decisive for Korsch along with a basic belief in the proletariat as the "revolutionary agent." With the collapse of the Weimar Republic and the Nazi triumph, however, the political paralysis of social democracy and the totalitarianism reigning in the USSR, it is no wonder that Korsch should have increasingly begun to concern himself with the notion of "counter-revolution."[52] In a counter-revolutionary period, after all, the proletariat will lack any forces with which to identify its revolutionary interests which, in turn, might offer a certain justification for Korsch's transcendent commitment to revolution in the face of historical reality. In any event Korsch refused to evaluate the counter-revolutionary development of the 1930s as a simple "betrayal" of the proletariat by the leadership of existing organizations precisely because "the fact of betrayal itself requires explanation."[53] And so, in attempting to analyze this "fact," Korsch began with the conditions which had fostered a reactionary international response to the Russian Revolution; it was a response, of course, which would ultimately infect the USSR itself.

Interestingly enough, like Lenin, Korsch was extraordinarily blind when it came to differentiating between existing capitalist regimes. Wishing to highlight the importance of the "critical" moment for Marxism, he never articulated how divergent institutional forms of bourgeois rule could affect the struggle of the working class or the importance of the radical democratic heritage for Marxism. Nor did he ever confront any serious criticisms of councils or the dangers of radically decentralizing power.[54] It was enough for him that the triumph of conservativism and fascism in so much of Europe had created a situation wherein the working class could not express its most radical possibilities. The thinking of the anti-philosopher thus remained, in Hegelian terms, hanging in the "abstract." And the abstraction of his commitment was only compounded by his belief that the proletariat should not put its faith in any major party to the conflicts of the thirties and forties since none expressed its real class needs or aims. Refusing to deal with the actual political and institutional choices of the time, no less than the later exponents of critical theory, Korsch relinquished his express concern with historical "specificity"[55] and proved unable to either theoretically or practically confront the "counter-revolution."

That, of course, was precisely his critique of the dominant working-class organizations. Korsch too divorced theory from practice in such a way that a fundamentally flawed view of politics and "the state" should have emerged. But given that both the communists and the social democrats had abandoned all revolutionary aims, as far as Korsch was concerned, their inability to develop a consistent theory of counter-revolution was logical and derived from the fact that they had themselves become part of what demanded criticism. While social democrats were employing Marxism as a purely formal theory, in order to promulgate support for bourgeois democracy and economic reform, the Soviet Union was using Marxism to postpone introducing the "realm of freedom" and justify the atrocious oppression "necessary" to achieve it.

"Progress" was thus uncritically employed by both organizations to justify themselves and their policies; it no longer had anything to do with the degree of empowerment which the working class had achieved.[56] But that was precisely how Korsch viewed "progress" and it is here that the "critical" element within his thinking becomes particularly evident. The lack of a coherent relation between means and ends within the two movements is exposed in his thought. Scientific Marxism loses its ability to illuminate changing revolutionary possibilities within a changing reality; it serves merely as a way of sanctioning the actions of parties which identify their own needs with those of the class they claim to represent. And that only makes sense since this "scientific" interpretation of Marxism places it in direct connection with the type of "contemplative materialism," inimical to a theory of practice, which was criticized in the *Eleven Theses on Feuerbach*. Indeed, Marx unambiguously maintained that the political consequences of drawing a sharp line of division between consciousness and its object are quite "real."[57]

The philosophical expression of the revolutionary working class, according to Korsch, should stand in a coherent relation to the most radical philosophical expression of the revolutionary bourgeoisie.[58] His thinking always placed primacy on the political and so, in a certain way, it makes sense that he should have adamantly opposed the Soviet Union in the Cold War. All the more strange then that he should have ignored the need to build upon the political legacy of parliamentarism inaugurated by the bourgeoisie. He was content to argue that establishing the purpose and meaning of a revolutionary project in the present will depend upon linking it to the unrealized "critical" impetus carried over from the past. Indeed, if the decline of class struggle is attributable to ideological as well as socio-economic and political factors, such a stance is theoretically logical.

Recognizing that "objective" reality is in part constituted by the particular "subjective" response to it, for Korsch, affirming the Hegelian heritage becomes a matter of practical importance.[59] No wonder, then, that *Marxism and Philosophy* should have ended with the famous citation of the young Marx: "philosophy cannot be abolished without being realized." Abolishing philosophy would involve institutionalizing direct democratic control by equal human "subjects" over a production process – or "object" – "alienated" from them. With the failure of the councilist movement, however, the possibility of actualizing that goal was lost. Perhaps, in contrast to Korsch, the later critical theorists surrendered his commitment to councils and emphasized the freedom of the subject in its unique individuality. But they too preserved the moment of transcendence embodied in philosophy from a dead historicism and a reality seeking to integrate its critical character. Philosophy, the tool of reflection and the expression of freedom, will thus – in the words of Theodor Adorno – "continue to exist because the moment for its realization was missed."

And Korsch's philosophy continued to exert an, admittedly subterranean, influence. He "believes adamantly in the new. So he loves the young," said Brecht, "and sees them rife in their possibilities."[60] An experimental, critical, and unfinished quality pervades Korsch's work. And undoubtedly for this reason it influenced Lucien Goldmann and the French group "Arguments" as well as Rudi Dutschke and Hans-Jürgen Krahl, Iring Fetscher and the journal *Marxismus-Studien* along with the Extra-Parliamentary Opposition (APO) and a host of young activist intellectuals in Germany during the 1960s; it even gained a certain notoriety in Yugoslavia, Hungary and Czechoslovakia where *Marxism and Philosophy* was distributed underground.[61] After all, from Korsch's exposition of Marxism, it becomes possible to question the Leninist vanguard no less than the social democratic or liberal notion of a political party in the accepted sense of the term. His theory militates against any stance seeking to transfer the old forms of radicalism into a new era and undercuts all attempts to employ Marxism as a tool to legitimate the existing order.[62]

Opposed to bureaucratic hierarchy, and supportive of all non-dogmatic attempts to enhance the self-administrative capacities of the oppressed, his approach suggests that there is not simply one adequate form of socialist organization nor one immutable theory that will forever inform a movement in terms of what it opposes and what it supports. Open to new categories and possibilities for radical action, whatever Korsch's own preoccupation with the traditional proletariat, his stance legitimated the concern with citizen initiatives and new social movements from a "Marxist" perspective. Nevertheless, the popularity he enjoyed was surely enhanced by the connection between his own political theory and the more general concerns of critical theory.[63]

Korsch's stance projects the need for a value-laden, critical, and interdisciplinary approach to social issues. Radicals in the European movement felt a kinship with his concern for transforming the "totality" and fusing the ideological, political, and economic moments of struggle in the revolutionary undertaking. They echoed his commitment to the political relevance of social and historical knowledge even as they recognized that socialism, as the emancipatory alternative to the existing order, could not be made by decree. Nor is it any wonder that, with the emphasis on participation and populist values, the councilist vision should have achieved a certain degree of popularity with radicals in Germany and Italy even as it prefigured the concern with *autogestion* in France. The radicals of 1968 agreed with Korsch that emancipation is a direct function only of the struggles in which the masses participate and that the critical theorist must expose, clarify, and project the most radical possibilities of the existent; indeed, with the emphasis on theory as a form of practice, yet another "elective affinity" (Weber) emerged between his mode of thinking and the student movement.

Karl Korsch's life and work is part of what Ernst Bloch termed "the underground history of the revolution." His isolation from the working class and its parties produced distrust and disappointment. Prizing the idea of revolution above all else, emphasizing the attack on the totality, Korsch saw politics as "all or nothing;" Brecht was indeed right in saying that, when framed in these terms, the world is always quick to answer "nothing."[64] The dogmatists laughed at his loneliness.[65] But, in refusing to compromise with reality, Korsch's thought maintained its integrity. He preserved the idea of freedom and socialism from the ways in which repressive institutions and philosophies claimed to have realized it. For that very reason, in contrast to those enamored with his historicism, the actual importance of Korsch's thought derives from its refusal to relinquish the speculative moment of theory to the dictates of historical necessity.[66] Indeed, that is what enabled him to treat ideas and institutions as contingent products of human activity.

Marxism in the hands of Korsch evidences its critical character and positive intent.[67] Stripped of teleology and scientific pretensions, however, the next step is to supplant it with a socialist ethic and transvalue the traditional view of the relation between theory and practice.[68] Korsch never took that step. Perhaps it was because he knew this would result in turning "revolution," the anchor of his worldview, from a strategic end into a tactic relevant under some circumstances and irrelevant under others.[69] But that remains an open question. Clear is only that Korsch was willing to make good on Engels' statement that Marxism is a historical theory and that loyalty to its founders lies not in the commitment to any particular set of propositions, concepts, or parties, but in facing its limits, mistakes, and anachronistic assumptions.

How to consider that legacy from the past? What holds for Marx, especially in this age of the reaction, holds for Korsch and those influenced by his thought as well. "The Moor has done his work. The Moor is gone." Or is he? The issue, of course, is no longer how an emancipatory struggle conforms to the dictates of a given thinker; it is rather, as Korsch already knew, a matter of what contribution a theory can make to furthering the current struggles for freedom. New norms and institutions remain necessary in order to confront history with its own unrealized possibilities. Critique has not yet lost its importance. And that is because, if the age of freedom has not yet dawned, the time of dogma is still far from over.

Notes

1   A bibliography of Korsch's writings can be found in *Jahrbuch der Arbeiterbewegung 1: Über Karl Korsch* ed. Claudio Pozzoli (Frankfurt, 1973).

2   On his early life, cf. Michael Buckmiller, *Karl Korsch und das Problem der materialistischen Dialektik: Historische und theoretische Voraussetzungen seiner ersten Marx-Rezeption (1909–1923)* (Hannover, 1976); on the later years, Gian Rusconi, "Korsch's Political Development" in *Telos* 26 Winter (1975–6).

3   Cf. Georg Lukács, *History and Class Consciousness: Studies in Marxist Dialectics* trans. Rodney Livingstone (Cambridge, Mass., 1970), pp. 1ff.

4   Martin Jay is correct in noting that "Korsch was clearly rejecting the idealist indifference to empirical reality that Lukács had defended immediately after his conversion to Marxism" in *Marxism and Totality: The Adventures of a Concept From Lukács to Habermas* (Berkeley, 1984), pp. 144ff.

5   "[Marx] created the theoretical-scientific expression adequate to the new content of consciousness of the proletarian class, and thereby at the same time elevated this proletarian class consciousness to a higher level of being." Karl Korsch, "The Marxist Dialectic" in *Karl Korsch: Revolutionary Theory* ed. Douglas Kellner (Austin, 1977), p. 136.

6   Note the historical introduction by Douglas Kellner to his edition of *Karl Korsch: Revolutionary Theory*, pp. 3ff.

 7   Note, for a more complete discussion, Andrew Arato and Paul Breines, *The Young Lukács and the Origins of Western Marxism* (New York, 1979), pp. 176ff.
 8   Cf. Richard Lowenthal, "The Bolshevization of the Spartacus League" in *International Communism* (London, 1960), pp. 23–71.
 9   For a historical overview, see Paul Breines, "Praxis and Its Theorists: The Impact of Lukács and Korsch in the 1920s" in *Telos* 11 (Spring, 1972).
10   Note the description of Korsch in the "Autobiographical Fragment" of Henry Pachter, *Weimar Études* (New York, 1984), pp. 1ff; also see the interview with Heinz Langerhans in *Jahrbuch der Arbeiterbewegung*, pp. 267ff. and his poem "Der Lehrer" in *Zur Aktualität von Karl Korsch* ed. Michael Buckmiller (Frankfurt, 1981), pp. 150ff; finally, in this regard, there is the insightful, touching, yet ironical piece by Bertolt Brecht, "Über meinen Lehrer" in *Gesammelte Werke* 20 vols. (Frankfurt, 1967), pp. 65ff.
11   On the influence which he exerted in the decades following World War II, cf. Frank Dingel, "Das Symposium über Karl Korsch vom 20 bis 21 Juni 1980 an der Universität Frankfurt" in *Internationale Wissenschaftliche Korrespondez zur Geschichte der Deutschen Arbeiterbewegung* (1980) vol. 16, no. 3, pp. 404–12.
12   Buckmiller, *Karl Korsch und das Problem der materialistischen Dialektik* (Hannover, 1976), p. 403.
13   Note his letter to Paul Mattick of November 20, 1938 included in *Karl Korsch: Revolutionary Theory*, pp. 283ff.
14   Kellner, *Karl Korsch*, pp. 33ff.
15   Jay, *Marxism and Totality*, p. 144.
16   Karl Korsch, *Karl Marx* (New York, 1938), pp. 24ff.
17   Karl Korsch, *Marxism and Philosophy* trans. Fred Halliday (London, 1970), p. 92.
18   An extension of this position appears in the view that modern philosophy is defined by three fundamental "moments" corresponding to the rise of the two dominant classes of the modern production process: that of Descartes and Locke, Kant and Hegel, and Marx. Intriguing is the claim that the attempt to forge a new moment of thought, while bypassing the dominant philosopher of the given moment, will necessarily result only in a retreat into the thinking of an earlier philosophical framework. Cf. Jean-Paul Sartre, *Search for a Method* trans. by Hazel Barnes (New York, 1963), p. 7.
19   "In the middle of the nineteenth century [the bourgeoisie] ceased to be revolutionary in its social *practice*, and by an inner necessity it thereby also lost the ability to comprehend in *thought* the true dialectical interrelation of ideas and real historical developments, above all of philosophy and revolution." Korsch, *Marxism and Philosophy*, p. 40.
20   An interesting example of this appears in the thought of Lukács whose *History and Class Consciousness* of 1923 forwarded a utopian conception

of subject–object unity and a radical attack on alienation and reification. These concerns essentially vanish from his uncompleted *Ontology* which emerges as an acceptance of the Soviet Union and its limits. Cf. Gáspár M. Tamás, "Lukács' Ontology: A Metacritical Letter" in *Lukács Reappraised* ed. Agnes Heller (New York, 1983), p. 155.

21 Cf. Russell Jacoby, "The Inception of Western Marxism: Karl Korsch and the Politics of Philosophy" in *Canadian Journal of Political and Social Theory* vol. 3, no. 3 (Fall, 1979), pp. 7ff.

22 For a critique of his historicist analysis, cf. Jay, *Marxism and Totality*, pp. 137ff.

23 For a differing interpretation of this development, see the preface to Stephen Eric Bronner *Socialism Unbound* (New York, 1990), pp. xiff.

24 Korsch, *Marxism and Philosophy*, p. 59.

25 Korsch, *Karl Marx*, p. 218.

26 Cf. Georg Bammel, "Vorwort zu *Marxismus und Philosophie*" in *Zur Aktualität von Karl Korsch*, pp. 71ff.

27 Note Korsch's essays "Lenin and the Comintern" as well as "State and Counterrevolution" in Kellner, *Karl Korsch*, pp. 149ff. and 237ff.

28 Cf. "Some Fundamental Presuppositions for a Materialistic Discussion of Crisis Theory" in Kellner, *Karl Korsch*, pp. 181ff.

29 Ibid., pp. 212ff.

30 Note the critique of Karl Mannheim's *Ideology and Utopia*, for its hidden metaphysical assumptions and relativism, by Max Horkheimer, "Ein neuer Ideologiebegriff" in *Archiv für die Geschichte des Sozialismus und der Arbeiterbewegung* (1930), vol. 15.

31 Some go so far as to say that "few doubts remain as to Korsch's total rejection of the Marxian perspective" in Leonardo Ceppa, "Korsch's Marxism" in *Telos* 26 (Winter, 1975–6), p. 118; also, cf. Paul Piccone, "Korsch in Spain" in *New German Critique* (Fall, 1975).

32 The central texts used to justify Korsch's abandonment of his old theoretical commitments is "The Crisis of Marxism" (1931) which was translated and reprinted in *New German Critique* (Fall, 1974), pp. 7ff and the "Zehn Thesen über Marxismus Heute" (1950) in Karl Korsch, *Politische Texte* ed. Erich Gerlach und Jürgen Seifert (Frankfurt, 1974), pp. 385ff. In the first piece, Korsch does say that "Marxism as an historical phenomenon is a thing of the past," but goes on to state that "Yet, in a more fundamental historical sense, the theory of proletarian revolution, which will develop anew in the next period of history, will be an historical continuation of Marxism" (p. 11). This, of course, stands totally in accord with the present interpretation. Although a similar mode of argumentation occurs, that is arguably less clear in the case of the "Ten Theses." In this regard, however, it is important to mention a conversation with Hedda Korsch shortly before her death. She told me then that the "theses" were less a reflection of her husband's own views than notes to spark discussion in a course for workers, which her husband was teaching in Zurich. Of course, such ad hoc information

is independent of their impact and relevance. Nevertheless, Hedda
Korsch requested that at some point I express her views for the historical
record, and I take this opportunity to do so.

33   Cf. Oskar Negt, "Theory, Empiricism, and Class Struggle: On the
Problem of Constitution in Karl Korsch" in *Telos* 26 (Winter, 1975–6).

34   Naturally, self-criticism need not take the form of Eduard Bernstein's
"revision" of orthodox Marxism into a theory of social reform. Still,
it is interesting to note that Korsch saw Bernstein as historically correct
in his attack on the Marxism of the Second International insofar as his
was the theory which the SPD was actually following in practice.
Meanwhile, in her famous debate with the revisionists, Rosa Luxemburg – who Korsch obviously found otherwise much more sympathetic
– is seen as neglecting actual practice and arguing purely on the level of
theory. Note his essay "The Passing of Marxian Orthodoxy" in Kellner,
Karl Korsch, pp. 176ff; also cf. Bronner, *Socialism Unbound*, pp. 50–2.

35   For "economic ideas themselves only appear to be related to the material
relations of bourgeois society in the way an image is related to the object
it reflects. In fact, they are related to them in the way that a specific
particularly defined part of the whole is related to the other parts of the
whole." Korsch, *Marxism and Philosophy*, p. 84.

36   "It might be observed that irrespective of whether or to what extent the
'unity of theory and practice' thus understood was a reality, [Marxist
orthodoxy] was quite compatible with the traditional or transcendental
conception of truth as consisting in the conformity of our judgment
with a state of affairs completely independent of our cognitive activity.
In other words, the unity of theory and practice, thus understood, did
not conflict with what Marx called the 'contemplative' conception of
knowledge." Leszek Kolakowski, *Main Currents of Marxism* 3 vols, vol.
3, p. 311. trans. P. S. Falla (New York, 1978), vol. 3, p. 311.

37   Cf. Karl Korsch, *Die materialstische Geschichtsauffassung und andere Schriften* ed. Erich Gerlach (Frankfurt, 1971), pp. 3–130.

38   Thus, Korsch can claim that those who dissociate the "truth" of
economics from the "falsity" of ideology will "universally transfer the
dialectic into Object, Nature and History and (so) present knowledge
merely as the passive mirror and reflection of this objective Being in the
subjective consciousness. In so doing they destroy both the dialectical
interrelation of *being* and *consciousness* and, as a necessary consequence,
the dialectical interrelation of *theory* and *practice*." Korsch, *Marxism and
Philosophy*, p. 117; he is subsequently not simply engaged in some
variant of "reflection theory," which is the position argued by Leonardo
Ceppa, in "Korsch's Marxism" pp. 96ff.

39   "[So] long as that material foundation of the existing bourgeois society
is only attacked and shaken, but not completely overthrown, through
the revolutionary proletarian struggle, the socially entrenched thought-
forms of the bourgeois epoch can only be criticized and not definitely
superseded by the revolutionary theory of the proletariat. The critique

of political economy, which Marx began in *Kapital*, can therefore only be completed by the proletarian revolution, i.e. by a real change in the present bourgeois mode of production and of the forms of consciousness pertaining to it." Korsch, *Karl Marx*, p. 157.

40 Rolf Wiggershaus, *Die Frankfurter Schule: Geschichte, Theoretische Entwicklung, Politische Bedeutung* (Frankfurt, 1988), p. 70.

41 For an alternative view, see Kolakowski, *Main Currents of Marxism*, vol. 3, pp. 308ff.

42 Korsch, *Karl Marx*, p. 84.

43 "*Materialistic criticism of religion* is aware of the fact that the ideological reflection of the real world cannot be totally dissolved until the practical conditions of every day life offer to the human beings concerned, a continuous display of perfectly intelligible and reasonable relations both between man and nature and between men and men. Similarly, the life process of society, i.e., material production does not strip off its mystical veil until it is transformed into the result of the conscious and self-controlled activities of freely associated men." Ibid., p. 161.

44 On the councils and their role, cf. Korsch's *Schriften zur Sozialisierung* ed. Erich Gerlach (Frankfurt, 1969) as well as his *Arbeitsrecht für Betriebsräte*, which appeared in a special edition by IG Metall under the title *Auf dem Wege zur industriellen Demokratie*, (Frankfurt, 1968).

45 Ceppa, "Korsch's Marxism," p. 110.

46 Korsch, *Marxism and Philosophy*, p. 64.

47 "Neither 'dialectical causality' in its philosophical definition nor 'scientific causality' supplemented by 'interactions' is sufficient to determine the particular kinds of connections and relations existing between the economic 'basis' and the juridical, political and ideological 'superstructure' of a given socio-economic formation." Korsch, *Karl Marx*, p. 227. For a sophisticated analysis of the relation between "base" and "superstructure," which builds on Korsch's perspective, see Franz Jakubowski, *Ideology and Superstructure in Historical Materialism* trans. Anne Booth (London, 1976).

48 In contrast to the "three-level" approach to reality offered by orthodox Marxists, Korsch forwards a completely different view. Roughly speaking, where certain sciences lie in direct immediate relation to material production, their relation to those means of production will necessarily be mechanistic. On the other hand, there are also sciences and processes which lie in indirect, mediated, relation to material production but which simultaneously lie in direct, unmediated relation to the production of social relations; these grow out of material production and in them material production itself extends – as in the case of the "culture industry." Finally, as with the fine arts, there are processes which do not lie in direct relation with either material production or with the direct production of social relations; instead, they only stand in direct relation with overriding cultural production as such. Thus, Korsch does achieve a certain differentiation of forms, even while – as is to be expected –

these interrelations can appear in qualitatively different combinations in differing stages of production. Cf. Karl Korsch, "15 Thesen über wissenschaftlichen Sozialismus" in *Politische Texte*, pp. 51ff.

49 No less than for Lukács, for Korsch, humanity is at once bound to nature and yet separated from it. Though it is possible to explain how scientific changes occurred and how science is employed from the historical perspective of social theory, this is not the same as saying that social theory has the last word in terms of the specific results achieved by a scientific formulation. Korsch warns against such vulgar misuse of social theory – which, for Marxism, can lead to nonsense like the "dialectics of wheat" – in his *Kernpunkte der materialistischen Geschichtsauffassung: Eine quellenmässige Darstellung* (Hamburg, 1973); Lukács also reacted against the attempt to present Marxism as a single unified theory of nature and society when he critically noted "that Engels – following Hegel's mistaken lead – extended the dialectical or socio-historical method to apply also to nature," which lacks all those reflexive aspects that "form the crucial determinants of dialectics." Lukács, *History and Class Consciousness*, p. 24. This point is badly misinterpreted by Kolakowski, *Main Currents of Marxism*, vol. 3, pp. 314ff.

50 Korsch, *Karl Marx*, p. 150.

51 Korsch, *Kernpunkte*, p. 9.

52 Kellner, *Karl Korsch*, pp. 232ff.

53 Note the essay "The Revolutionary Commune" in Kellner, *Karl Korsch*, p. 201.

54 Cf. Bronner, *Socialism Unbound*, pp. 172ff.

55 Kellner, *Karl Korsch*, pp. 232ff; also, cf. "Brief von Amadeo Bordiga an Karl Korsch" in Pozzoli, *Jahrbuch der Arbeiterbewegung*, pp. 243–7.

56 Cf. "The Idea of Progress in Marxism" in *Socialism in History: Political Essays of Henry Pachter* ed. Stephen Eric Bronner (New York, 1984), pp. 65ff.

57 According to Korsch, "vulgar" Marxism recognizes three "levels of reality." The first, the economy, is the only objective and totally non-ideological reality, while the second – law and the state – is somewhat less "real" or "objective" since it is clad in ideology. The third level, that of pure ideology, is putatively objectless and unreal or – as Kautsky would have it – "pure rubbish." ibid., p. 73. Kolakowski mistakenly identifies the position that is being attacked with the standpoint Korsch supports; cf. Kolakowski, *Main Currents of Marxism*, vol. 3, p. 313.

58 Korsch, *Marxism and Philosophy*, p. 42.

59 "In social affairs, the act of investigation coincides with its object – such is the Hegelian interpretation adopted by Marxism. From this point of view Korsch likens the Marxist theory of society to the view of Clausewitz (also a Hegelian) that the theory of war is not a matter of external observation but is part of war itself . . . The dialectic is not simply a 'method' applicable at will to any object. It would seem that in Korsch's view it is altogether impossible to expound the materialistic dialectic as a

collection of statements or precepts of investigation. As an expression of the revolutionary movement of the working class it is part of that movement and not a mere theory or 'system.' " Kolakowski, *Main Currents of Marxism*, vol. 2, p. 313.

60 Brecht, "Über meinen Lehrer," p. 65.

61 Note the fine essay by Michael Buckmiller, "Aspekte der internationalen Korsch-Rezeption" in *Zur Aktualität von Karl Korsch*, pp. 9ff.

62 Korsch, "Zehn Thesen," p. 386.

63 Oskar Negt, "Zurück zu Marx und Engels! Oder: Was können wir von Korsch lernen?" in *Zur Aktualität von Karl Korsch*, p. 39.

64 Brecht, "Über meinen Lehrer," p. 66.

65 The joke went around that, in the midst of an important political conflict, someone asked: "Where is Korsch?" Someone else then supposedly answered: "He is taking the correct position – while sitting in his room." Klaus von Beyme, *Theorie der Politik im 20. Jahrhundert: Von der Moderne zur Postmoderne* (Frankfurt, 1991), p. 107.

66 Negt, "Zurück zu Marx und Engels!," p. 43.

67 Korsch can thus note that, in contrast to the late Adorno, "Karl Marx was a *positive dialectician and revolutionary* and the magnificent character of his spirit is very evident in the *Critique*: he never allows his critical work to become a mere *negation* of the errors and superficialities analyzed . . . He always goes on to expound or briefly indicate the *positive* and *true* concepts which should replace the error and illusion he criticizes." Korsch, *Marxism and Philosophy*, p. 140.

68 Bronner, *Socialism Unbound*, pp. 167–8.

69 Ibid., pp. 176ff.

3

Philosophical Anticipations:
A Commentary on the
"Reification" Essay of Georg Lukács

Georg Lukács was still a communist when he died in 1971 at the age of 86. He had become reconciled to the limitations of the Soviet Union and his thinking had taken a conservative and ontological turn. All the more ironic that Rudi Dutschke and the intellectuals of the student movement should have resurrected his masterpiece, *History and Class Consciousness*, which introduced the two concepts most notably associated with critical theory: alienation and reification. The book offered an innovative foundation for the critique of ideology, generated a new concern with the "totality," and provided critical theory with a sense of radical purpose. It conceived of the proletariat less as an empirical than as a logical category whose ethical primacy derived from its role in thematizing the structure of capitalist society. His interpretation of alienation and reification transformed materialism into a theory of praxis. It ultimately deepened the understanding of revolution, highlighted the role of consciousness, resurrected the vision of utopia, and influenced any number of philosophical developments as well as the thinking of the New Left. No longer would Marxism prove identifiable with party dogma or arbitrarily chosen citations from Marx or Lenin capable of justifying any particular political exigency; orthodoxy became a matter of method.[1] Nor would dialectics remain a fixed system. It would now appear as a method capable of incorporating the insights of new thinkers and meeting the problems posed by new historical conditions.

History and Class Consciousness, contrary to myth, was not the first book to link Hegel with Marx.[2] But, in fact, it was the "charter document of Hegelian Marxism" and "almost single-handedly succeeded in raising [Marxism] to a respectable place in European intellectual life."[3] It was a remarkable philosophical achievement whose most ambitious, and ultimately seminal, chapter was entitled "Reification and the Consciousness of the Proletariat." The book, however, was marred in a number of ways. An adherence to Leninist principles, whatever the influence of Rosa Luxemburg,[4] led to the underestimation of civil liberties and hampered the development of a socialist theory of democracy. An exaggerated emphasis on consciousness also bred indifference to the specification of institutional constraints and the politics of power. Its voluntaristic radicalism, similarly, undercut the emphasis on historical determination while its utopianism burdened political action with a completely unrealizable set of expectations. Indeed, Lukács' preoccupation with the "identity" between subject and object created the conceptual framework wherein even staunch critics, like Theodor Adorno, would become defined by what they opposed.

Critical theory, partly for this very reason, never dealt concretely with the issues raised in the work. Both its positive and negative appropriation were informed by metaphysical prejudices. A more concrete interpretation was also hindered by the fact that Lukács himself used the terms alienation and reification interchangeably.[5] These concepts retain their relevance. But they call for reinterpretation in light of the teleological collapse, which has become evident to all except the most dogmatic partisans of the past. Differentiating alienation from reification is a matter of some importance. First, however, it is necessary to clarify their historical background and their traditional philosophical connotations. Only then will it become possible to confront their implications for modernity.

Alienation has a long history. Its most radical sense already appears in the biblical expulsion from Eden.[6] The story of paradise lost precedes the loss of objects to the world of exchange, which originally defined its social usage.[7] The biblical allegory justifies the fallen state of humanity and explains why people are condemned "to earn their bread by the sweat of their brow." It also shows why trust between individuals has been lost, nature appears as an enemy, and – interestingly enough – redemption becomes possible. Unity and harmony are forfeited and humanity is stripped of its organic connection to the world with the banishment of Adam and Eve. Human choice has produced the fall and, with the expulsion, the hope of recreating paradise. Prometheus seeks to make good on that hope, but he is thwarted for all eternity by a "wicked god" bent on condemning human hubris.[8] Hope becomes fused with the recognition that its fulfillment will never take place. Thus, utopia becomes the only response to alienation.

Alienation is the experience of "estrangement" (*Verfremdung*) from others,[9] and the intimation of an alternative. This becomes apparent in different ways in the *civitas dei* of Augustine and the *cur deus homo* of Anselm; alienation appears in Maimonides and Dante, the desire of Hobbes to escape from a condition in which "life . . . [is] poor, nasty, brutish, and short" as well as in the more beneficent conception of the "state of nature" offered by Locke. Nowhere, however, does this problem of alienation become more evident than in the early essays of Rousseau. Wealth and the creation of artificial needs corrupt the "natural" virtues like decency, simplicity, kindness and honesty. Civilization thus subverts the communal values that make life worth living. And so, if Rousseau had little use for the nobility or its trappings, he was also aware of the way in which the bourgeoisie was cutting people loose from the security of the past. The loss of tradition by "simple souls" was what rendered a radical response necessary. Science was as responsible as the arts, materialism was as much to blame as metaphysics, for fragmenting the community. Anomie no less than despotism or inequality thus generates the need for determining a "general will."

Society must prove reducible to the individuals composing it. Only in this way is it possible to restore the "self-respect" (*amour propre*) of the individual. Rousseau thus makes his plea for a small community of individuals with similar backgrounds and traditions in which authority is accountable and each has the right to participate in making decisions. No confrontation with provincialism or cultural prejudices, however, can really take place. Any such attempt would obviously usher in the conditions of alienation he so dramatically sought to mitigate. Cosmopolitanism and technological progress, individualism and occupationally differentiated notions of identity, become the enemies of an organic community. Rousseau would undoubtedly have identified with the critical tenor of the following lines from Hölderlin:

> You see craft-workers, but no people; thinkers, but no people; priests, but no people; lords and servants, youths and persons of property, but no people. Is this not like a battlefield on which hands, arms, and limbs of all sorts are lie strewn amid one another while their spilt life-blood runs into the sands?[10]

In this vein, especially with the irretrievable passing of the *ancien régime*, contesting alienation would ever more surely spur what the young Lukács called "romantic anti-capitalism." The first systematic encounter with alienation, however, occurred in the writings of Hegel. His concern is with how action occurs behind the backs of individuals; alienation exists insofar as their creations escape conscious control. World history is the stigmata suffered by the Absolute Spirit (*Geist*) whose goal is to reappropriate its "estranged" objectifications.[11] Alienation (*Entfremdung*), or the experience of this "estrangement" (*Verfremdung*) is overcome insofar as such an appropriation takes self-conscious form through the constitutive categories of the spirit's "absolute idea": religion, art, and philosophy. Liberation thus becomes a matter of domesticating the "cunning of reason" and empowering humanity over the world estranged (*verfremdet*) from it.

Alienation is the experience of a world beyond the control of those who created it. The concept initially is reducible neither to psychology nor economics. Claiming that the weakness of the concept derives from its narrow connection with production subsequently misses the point. The conceptual problem with alienation has less to do with any reductive definition than its all-encompassing character. Every form of objectification, according to Hegel and the Lukács of *History and Class Consciousness*, results in alienation. The spirit of freedom is estranged in the material world and only teleological faith in the possibility of cleansing the stigmata of history can bring about its ultimate recovery.

Alienation is experienced in every facet of the "totality" and, in keeping with the sources of the concept, the ultimate confrontation with it must thus prove total as well. Transcending alienation involves transcending objectification. And, for this reason, a new identity between subject and object must dissolve what Marx would later term "pre-history." New conditions of empowerment would subject the world to human control; its estranged character would vanish along with the experience of alienation. Utopian and anthropological preoccupations thus became elements of any response to alienation. Indeed, critical theory would embrace them even when its most formidable proponents no longer accepted either the teleological assumptions of Lukács or his view of the "totality."

Abolishing alienation is less a matter of overcoming capitalism than of redeeming the miseries of history; indeed, Hegel even conceived of history as the "Calvary of the absolute spirit." But, in contrast to Walter Benjamin or Ernst Bloch, he was no utopian. The act of cognition was, for Hegel, the culmination of a process wherein the universal implications of reason are actualized in a new state governed by the rule of law. A degree of existential alienation would remain even at the "end of history" insofar as individuals would always continue to face their own mortality. His political vision of a rationally ordered society, a state reproducing itself under the rule of law (*Rechtsstaat*), thus creates the space in which people can deal with their most private concerns free of external interference. In keeping the exploitative class relations of civil society intact while privileging an essentially unaccountable bureaucracy, however, subjectivity is withdrawn as individuals are treated philosophically as objects. Hegel may have taken bourgeois philosophy to its limits, but he never transgressed them.

A revolutionary theory of the proletariat, for Lukács no less than for Korsch, must stand in coherent relation to the most revolutionary theory of the bourgeoisie. Lukács, for this reason, sought to create a direct link between Hegel and Marx without reference to the impact of Feuerbach. He was already aware of Marx's comments concerning the "contemplative" character inherent within ahistorical forms of materialism.[12] Still, there is something ironic about the fact that Western Marxists could only highlight the revolutionary moment of historical materialism by emphasizing its idealist rather than its materialist roots. It is all the more strange since Feuerbach essentially criticized Hegel for ignoring the concrete source of alienation without providing anything other than purely formal ideas for its resolution.

Alienation, according to Feuerbach, derives from the externalization (*Entausserung*) of human powers and possiblities upon a non-existent entity: God. An imaginary other world comes into existence, which is the richer, the poorer this one becomes. Reality appears alien to the individual as responsibility for its genesis and progress shifts to an Other. God is thus the anthropological source of alienation, and atheism – insofar as it projects a certain *existential* empowerment – thus becomes the foundation for a new humanism. Feuerbach deals with the experience of alienation in a way that Hegel does not. His anthropological critique of alienation, of course, has nothing to say about practical empowerment; history vanishes and the human essence is comprehended in terms of a "dumb generality" which *naturally* unites individuals. Resurrection of the individual occurs through the contemplative resurrection of the species. Marx could thus correctly claim that Feuerbach failed to grasp the significance of "revolutionary" or "practical–critical activity" and that "the highest point attained by *contemplative* materialism . . . is the contemplation of single individuals in 'civil society.' "[13]

The *Eleven Theses on Feuerbach*, which Engels termed the "first document" in which the "germ" of a new worldview appears, were only published in 1888 as the appendix to *Ludwig Feuerbach and the End of Classical German Philosophy*. They mark the point at which Marx breaks with the abstract humanism and idealism of his youth, not in the sense that he simply abandons old concerns, but rather insofar as he will generate a new set of categories with which to interpret the logic of accumulation in an "inverted world."[14] The famous chapter on "commodity fetishism," which describes how capitalist production transforms subjects into objects for the accumulation of profit, is thus the real "materialist" source of "reification" (*Verdinglichung*).

Marx never used the word. He was content to differentiate alienation from objectification in the *Paris Manuscripts of 1844*.[15] But the problem is that Marx essentially derived alienation from the division of labor and its threefold estrangement of the individual from his community, from his product, and his own potential. Marx, of course, never published these writings. They only appeared in 1932 after being smuggled out of the Institute for Marxism–Leninism with the help of its director, David Rjazanov, who would later pay with his life for this and other acts of intellectual integrity. The early manuscripts became seminal to the thinking of the New Left and, before then, to the the development of critical theory. Nevertheless, for once, it is perhaps useful to consider why Marx might have chosen not to publish them.

He never retracted the democratic commitments expressed in the *Paris Manuscripts*. But their utopian bent and anthropological form of argumentation is another matter. The class categories, the logical rigor, and the institutional insights of the later works are obviously lacking. The thinking of Marx moves beyond Hegel and Feuerbach. He notes the role of wealth and, for example, how it can make smart the stupid and render beautiful the ugly. This insight is appropriated from Shakespeare, however, and the structure of capitalist production is never delineated. The response to alienation, furthermore, is left at restoring the "species being" of humanity or the wholeness repressed by the division of labor. An organic connection between humanity and nature, the individual and the community, is now projected into the future rather than conceived as having been lost in the past. The abolition of private property is highlighted. But the romantic impulse remains. The spectre of a "new man" presents itself as utopia is placed within an admittedly indeterminate end of history wherein the anthropological conditions of repression are abolished. Transcendence supplants immanence, speculation supplants the need for institutional referents, and voluntarism defines the teleology. There are thus good reasons why Marx should ultimately have moved beyond these legendary early works even as he began to contest all forms of "contemplative" materialism in 1845 with the *Theses on Feuerbach*.

What Marx in his later years might have deemed the failings of his youthful writings, however, seemed to fit the revolutionary mood during the years when *History and Class Consciousness* was being written. The messianic moment of redemption seemed to have arrived with the Russian Revolution, and the suffering endured by the masses during World War I and its aftermath seemed to prefigure the apocalyptic transformation of reality. Empires had crumbled, forty million had been slain or crippled, and now in the "heroic years" between 1918 and 1921 international revolution was apparently spreading throughout Europe. Councils were springing into existence with each revolt. Enthusiasts thought that "popular justice" was making legal institutions anachronistic and that money was being eliminated in the USSR. Cultural experimentation seemed ready to combine with the inexhaustible radicalism of a communist vanguard in expressing the general will of a "new man." This was the historical crucible in which the new revolutionary agent, the "subject–object" of history," was apparently taking shape; indeed, finally, it seemed possible to speak concretely about the abolition of philosophy.

Modern philosophy, according to Lukács, was preoccupied with one basic task: it wished to interpret the world as its own product rather than as an independent creation of God or some other-worldly entity.[16] The purpose was to render reality, or the object of cognition, open to knowledge. This could occur only insofar as the object was recognized as being humanly constituted. Lukács, in this vein, approvingly pointed to Vico who saw the difference between history and nature deriving from the fact that humanity had created the one and not the other. The material basis for the historical constitution of reality, however, was the barrier for this new philosophy. The source of its alienation from practice remained closed to investigation. Thus, employing the dialectical method, Lukács sought to show "the *connection* between the fundamental problems of this [modern] philosophy and the *basis in existence* from which [its] problems spring."[17]

The "Copernican revolution" of philosophy is where the analysis begins. Kant had, after all, demonstrated that the objective or scientific interpretation of phenomena presupposed the intervention of the subject.[18] It is a transcendental subject whose constitutive categories, time and space, make the perception of facts possible. These categories of transcendental apperception, however, remain closed to "pure reason." Subject confronts object and freedom stands opposed to necessity. The mind generates a set of antinomies whose resolution is precluded by definition.[19] Scientific rationality, which is the only source of absolute knowledge, is limited in its applicability to the analysis of *phenomena*. It hits against a "barrier," the "thing-in-itself," or the construct existing *a priori* through which any form of knowledge is made possible and from which the derivation becomes possible of those "ultimate" purposes for which scientific inquiry is undertaken.[20] Knowledge pertaining to such noumenal issues is necessarily normative and speculative. A division between fact and value takes place.

But, from the standpoint of a "critical philosophy," this is precisely where the problems begin. Kant had sought to protect scientific inquiry from the incursions of metaphysics. But, with the shift from a feudal to a capitalist society, it became a matter of protecting metaphysics from the incursions of science. The danger to critical thinking would, in fact, gradually become all the greater given the *inherent* inability of instrumental rationality either to contest the normative context in which it is employed or limit its own absolutist claims to truth. Science would thus come to treat all questions other than its own as "irrational" and deny its epistemological limits. Context would vanish in the name of the empirical fact and the "thing-in-itself" would appear, even in the thinking of Engels,[21] merely as a shadowy unreality standing "behind" the object like Plato's forms. "Pure reason" with its objectifying, transhistorical, and uncritical presuppositions thus turns into a self-generating and ever expanding system.[22] Nor is there a way to contest this development practically. Its evolution ever more surely becomes identifiable not only with that of philosophy, but of "progress" under capitalism.

The preoccupation with the subject by the proponents of critical theory, for this reason, was only logical. Kant, of course, had sought to preserve the integrity of the subject by developing an ethics predicated on autonomy and universalism. But the founder of "critical" philosophy, whom Moses Mendelssohn called the "ultimate destroyer" of all systems, recognized that it was impossible to overcome the barrier between subject and object through theory alone.[23] He was unwilling to surrender "practical reason" to the imperializing tendencies of science. Recognizing that freedom could not be proven, he was none the less willing to introduce it as a postulate for discussing human affairs in ethical terms. Even his categorical imperative, however, is predicated on intentionality no less than the weeding out of every subjective and anthropomorphic tendency and material interest; "it strives with ever increasing vigour to drive a wedge between the subject of knowledge and 'man', and to transform the knower into a pure and purely formal subject."[24]

Freedom is divorced from necessity as the contingent moment is subsumed by an ethic whose abstract categories cover disparate choices as surely as any "natural" law.[25] Formal laws make their appearance in the noumenal no less than in the phenomenal realms of existence. They give moral evolution a teleological underpinning even as they serve as a barrier to the understanding of crises or qualitative ruptures.[26] The genesis of contingent events is thus closed to rational investigation while the ethical decision remains contemplative insofar as it is ultimately predicated on the manipulation of universal claims. Form manifests an "indifference" to content,[27] which mirrors the fractured relation between theory and practice. The world becomes reified insofar as reality loses its dynamic qualities. Indeed, given the divorce between theory and practice, that is necessarily the case since "theory and praxis in fact refer to the same objects, for every object exists as an immediate inseparable complex of form and content."[28]

Only art offers the prospect of unity between form and content or theory and practice insofar as it projects a "purposeful purposelessness." This is experienced, according to Kant, by the individual. Schiller extends this idea through his concept of "play." Social existence is seen by him as having alienated humanity from the full use of its powers. It is now only in aesthetic "play" that one can become fully human and, in this sense, art renders whole what society has torn asunder. The political debacle of the French Revolution is salvaged in an aesthetic utopia wherein humanity is culturally molded into a "living shape." Harmony predicated on a new unity of subject and object defines the aesthetic Lebenswelt. Schiller's critique of alienation points to the totality. The resurrection of reality, however, occurs only in thought as an "illusion" (Schein) and the "new man" can arise only through a rupture with the world as it exists.[29] The origins of society no less than the formulation of a concrete response to it remain outside the purview of his argument: utopia contests the experience of alienation, but it leaves the reified world intact.

Nor is it much different with Fichte. He too considered it impossible to analyze the genesis of reality or the object from within the assumptions of idealism.[30] The real divorces subject and object and, as a consequence, the "space between projection and thing projected is dark and void." The only way to overcome this separation is, with Goethe, to emphasize *the deed*. Remaining within the boundaries of a philosophy committed to extend absolute knowledge, however, is possible only if the object is posited in the abstract by an equally abstract subject. An untraversable chasm thus divides the reality wherein subject is opposed to object from the intuitive grasp of the ontological situation wherein the object is the alienated expression of activity by an absolute subject. Overcoming alienation involves recovering the object or rationally and ethically empowering the subject with respect to its use. No determinations exist, however, and no constraints. Freedom remains the postulate of subjectivity. Nevertheless, it also remains impossible to derive categories for analyzing the constitution of the context wherein freedom is exercised. Its reified essence translates into its equally reified appearance.

Coming to terms with freedom concretely can, according to Lukács, occur only by using dialectics as a historical method. Categories of reflection must lose their permanency; the connection between essence and appearance must develop rather than remain anchored in an ahistorical abstraction. Thus, according to Hegel, "there is nothing in the essence of an object that will not become manifest in the series of its appearances." History becomes the teleological unfolding of all human potentiality within a context whose increasingly *determinate* definition marks intellectual progress.[31] The "thing-in-itself" is, in this way, finally rendered comprehensible since questions of logic and epistemology become grounded in the qualitative material nature of their content.[32] Insofar as this content needs definition, furthermore, the totality emerges as the "concrete concept" wherein links are immanently forged between form and content as well as between theory and practice.[33]

The content of the individual phenomenon is radically changed when seen from within the context of the totality. Subjectivity is no longer defined in terms of the isolated entity of bourgeois materialism or the purely formal subject of transcendental idealism. It is now conceived as sublated (*aufgehoben*) and mediated by the agent responsible for the unfolding of teleology. The new subject speaks to the reified totality in a way the individual subject cannot. Historical change is impossible if the empirical individual is the only agent. He or she, after all, must confront the world as a pre-existing complex of ready-made and unalterable objects. "For the individual, reification and hence determinism are irremovable. Every attempt to achieve 'freedom' from such premises must fail, for 'inner freedom' presupposes that the world cannot be changed."[34]

The individual ceases to serve as the measure of all things. Kierkegaard and Nietzsche, who so preoccupied the young Lukács,[35] give way to Hegel and Marx. Alienation as the inalterable condition of social existence becomes open to historical transformation. Hegel's "world spirit" (*Weltgeist*) might have been engaged in working its way to universal consciousness through the culture of nations. Now, however, the proletariat of Marx – as interpreted by Lukács[36] – will take on the mission of historical change and create something far more radical than a bureaucratic state under the rule of law or a *Rechtsstaat*.

The proletariat will usher a classless society into existence and serve as a new subject–object of history by bringing "pre-history" to a close.[37] The purpose of the proletariat is the same as that of the "world spirit." Both seek the abolition of arbitrary power and a world in which history is made consciously. The difference is merely that the proletariat of Marx and Lukács is material in the sense that it is generated by the production process and that a reified or alienated form of production itself becomes the object of transformation. Thus, Marx could write that "when the proletariat proclaims the dissolution of the previous world-order it does no more than reveal the secret of its own existence, for it represents the effective dissolution of that world-order."

The self-understanding of the proletariat, for this reason, is simultaneously the objective understanding of the nature of society.[38] It perceives the mediations, which differentiate the effects of a reified totality on different classes. The proletariat simultaneously rejects the determinism of orthodox social democracy and the moralistic "ought" of Kant; it overcomes the dualism by seeking to discover "the principles by means of which it becomes *possible in the first place* for an 'ought' to modify existence."[39] The revolution thus can no longer occur merely in thought even if its "objective possibility" is itself determined by thought. It becomes apparent that

> a *new* element is required: the consciousness of the proletariat must become deed. But as the mere contradiction is raised to a consciously dialectical contradiction, as the act of becoming conscious turns into a *point of transition in practice,* we see once more in greater concreteness the character of proletarian dialectics . . . [N]amely, since consciousness here is not the knowledge of an opposed object, but is the self consciousness of the object, the act of consciousnesss overthrows the objective form of its object.[40]

Lukács offers a new interpretation of Marx. Materialism is no longer seen as the antithesis of idealism. The greatness of Marx now appears in his synthesis of these two traditions, which is predicated on the claim of Hegel that dialectics must present itself as "the immanent process of transcendence." But there was still the matter of explaining why so much of the proletariat was incapable of recognizing the need for unity along with its revolutionary mission. Reference to its inherent economism, in keeping with Lenin, only begged the question. A given form of thinking with certain assumptions was involved even if it derived from a particular mode of productive activity. Making sense of this connection between theory and practice meant contesting not merely the experience of alienation, a world outside the control of those who had created it, but the logic informing its production and reproduction. Lukács, in this way, would take up the famous claim of Marx that "social life is essentially *practical.* All mysteries which mislead theory to mysticism find their rational solution in human practice and in the comprehension of that practice."[41]

The experience of alienation called forth the inquiry into the conditions for its production and reproduction: reification.[42] The unyielding emphasis on subjectivity and the unique experience by the modernist avant-garde was in part a reaction against standardization, mechanization, rationalization, and the leveling or equalizing tendencies of what would become advanced industrial society. Similar concerns appear in the work of the neo-Kantian philosophers in Germany.[43] Lukács was close to many of them including Max Weber, Georg Simmel, Wilhelm Windelband, and Emil Lask who helped inspire the concern with reification.[44]

Orthodox Marxism, however, was basically unconcerned with the extraordinary impact of the production process during the rise of monopoly capital. There was little discussion of the "inverted world" of commodity fetishism with its logic of accumulation whereby workers are considered, from the standpoint of capital, a mere cost.[45] Production was seen instead as a mechanical function of technology. Its deadening impact on consciousness and the creative interaction with nature was simply underestimated. The unrelenting development of technology would supposedly – of itself – increase competition among firms, mechanically increase the "industrial reserve army," depress purchasing power, and generate revolution.

Lukács wished to consider economic categories in terms of their political implications. And, in so doing, he transformed technology from a governing principle into the product of given social relations, which then defines them in turn.[46] Lukács' point is not that technology or the sciences are irrelevant. It is merely that bringing them under control must involve opening them to historical inquiry and revolutionary transformation from the standpoint of the totality. Both are expressions of the division of labor wherein subjectivity is fragmented through rationalization, and specialization of skill leads to the destruction of every image of the whole.[47] Overcoming the division of labor is therefore the only perspective with which to reassert a practical concern with the empowerment of workers, whose existence and consciousness are ever more surely becoming defined by the technological universe.

The division of labor, of course, preceded capitalism. Along with the commodity, in fact, it reaches back into the beginnings of the inter-change between humanity and nature. The division of labor is the material expression of a purposive rationality predicated on calculability and efficient routinization of tasks.[48] Calculability inherently involves transforming qualitative differences between objects into quantitative ones and, insofar as production involves the objectification of subject-ivity, reducing natural resources and people to the same mathematical units of analysis. Only with assumptions of this sort is it possible to conceive of selling commodities for more than the price of producing them and, for this reason, commodification retains an anthropological component. There is, for Lukács, no "pure" form of theory. Interests are always hidden in the assumptions of a particular conceptual framework.

But the logic of capitalist production and the manner in which anthropological tendencies of reification were brought to fruition never really became issues for orthodox Marxism. It was essentially content to criticize capitalism for its unequal distribution of commodities rather than for its production process; indeed, Marx himself had castigated the nascent social democratic movement on precisely this point.[49] The problem with capitalism was seen as stemming from an anarchic market erupting in periodic crises. Planning and nationalization, which the partisans of the labor movement would undertake within a parliamentary framework and use in conjunction with certain market mechanisms, basically defined "socialism" in the thinking of Karl Kautsky and the other dominant theorists of orthodox Marxism. Only Rosa Luxemburg and certain of her supporters ever really developed a more radical outlook. Even their criticisms, however, never really extended to issues concerning the division of labor.[50]

Lukács gave revolution, which he viewed as the categorical imperative for a theory of practice,[51] a new meaning by fashioning a dialectical link between anthropology and history. Confronting capitalism would now involve confronting history itself. Looking at Marx with the eyes of Hegel, breaking the identification of dialectics with the economic or technological determinism of Engels, Lukács introduced a messianic conception of teleology into a supposedly materialist worldview. Even before Fichte condemned his age as one of "absolute sinfulness," the followers of Sabbatai Sevi, the "false messiah" of the seventeenth century, believed that only after every sin was performed would the messiah come. In the same vein, approximately one hundred and fifty years later, Lukács would pronounce the proletarian revolution possible only once the the commodity form had become dominant. His *Theory of the Novel* had already displayed a preoccupation with the apocalypse and, inspired by Martin Buber,[52] sought to show that modernity had not dried up the "metaphysical source" of Judaism. Now, in *History and Class Consciousness*, only under the conditions in which subjects have been most fully transformed into objects by the production process can the abolition of reification occur.

Lukács, of course, did not mean that the revolution would have to await the moment at which reification defined every person on the planet. It was, following Hegel and Max Weber, a matter of *tendency* and an ability to recognize the point at which society is learning to satisfy all its needs in terms of the commodity.[53] It is no longer a matter of whether more or less commodities exist in capitalist society, but of determining whether the way in which they were produced dominates all other possible forms of production. Anthropological tendencies from the past are newly rationalized insofar as the ever more powerful market transforms the *subject* of production into an *object* for consumption.[54] The very "compulsion" towards objectification under capitalism makes it possible for a worker to become "conscious" of the class context. Indeed, this was why Lukács could claim that "the objective theory of class consciousness is the theory of its objective possibility."[55]

History and Class Consciousness provides a hermeneutic. The extent to which the worker recognizes his objective condition results in a change of that condition.[56] The method of historical materialism, for this very reason, must privilege the moment of consciousness. Later forms of critical theory would, in fact, retain this hermeneutical imperative even when the interpretation of the object became based on nothing more than the "constellation" in which it was subjectively situated. The ability to fashion this constellation, or exert the normative claims of reflexivity in comprehending the object, would also rest on resisting the identification of reification with progress. A theory self-conscious about its relation to practice is thus "essentially the intellectual expression of the revolutionary process itself;"[57] indeed, for this reason, "bourgeois" theory must stand in opposition to that process.

Explaining reification and the ability to deal with it thus become two parts of the same question. "Intellectual genesis must be identical in principle with historical genesis."[58] Thus, the dialectical character of Lukács' teleology becomes apparent. Capitalism with its commodification process generates two dominant classes whose symbiotic linkage in the experience of alienation is simultaneously denied by the conflict of material interest between them. It is thus the point of departure for developing the critical consciousness of the proletariat.[59] Or, putting the matter another way, meaning in history is dependent upon the action by a self-conscious proletariat born of processes intent on "disenchanting the world" (Max Weber).

Reification is the material expression of this "disenchantment." It is the framework within which facts gain their meaning and thus the barrier against which the variants of metaphysics and positivism constantly struggled. They both equated reason with natural laws capable of covering all empirical contingencies and, in this way, they relinquished any concern with the subjectivity of the subject no less than the material constitution of the unique event. Scientific rationality and metaphysics both veiled the contradictions of reality by focusing on either the phenomenal *or* the noumenal dimensions of reality. Both assume an abstract or "reified" character as content becomes divorced from form. Incapable of recognizing the framework in which the given fact gains meaning, seeking to isolate the datum from the conditions of its constitution, both prove incapable of contesting the reifying conditions in need of transformation.[60]

Understanding reification is possible only by bringing to bear those categories which reification denies. For this reason, according to Lukács, the materialism inherited from Marx must differentiate itself from all the older versions and, in keeping with the Hegelian notion of totality, contest the given system rather than its mere empirical expressions. Natural laws and the criteria of the natural sciences, which uncritically employ trans-historical categories and thus freeze reality, have no place in the historical inquiry appropriate to dealing with social issues. The point is no longer to "prove" whether a "transformation" of value into prices take place. The "labor theory of value" can now take phenomenological form,[61] and the empirical investigation into the commodity can dissolve into a critical analysis of the social relations "hidden" within it. Marxism thus becomes a critical theory of society grounded within a philosophy of history rather than a science based on fixed claims.

History and Class Consciousness is an attempt to subsume the empirical forms of capitalism within an analysis of its "real life-process."[62] The framework within which facts gain their meaning thus becomes the object of criticism for the new revolutionary subject. Reification defines that framework. It enters into each moment of the totality. The moments are not reduced to economic class interests, but rather become defined in their constitutive dynamics by the same form of economic and bureaucratic rationality. Max Horkheimer and Theodor Adorno could thus analyze the "culture industry" from the perspective of a rationality committed to producing increasingly standardized products for the broadest possible audience in order to maximize the largest possible profit.

Reification is seen as ever more surely reducing production to its constitutive elements and turning specialization into the principle of life. It increasingly turns the product into an "objective synthesis of rationalized special systems whose unity is determined by pure calculation."[63] Even space and time are reduced to a common denominator while the latter is "degraded" into a calculable dimension of the former;[64] indeed, from within what is itself a reified ontological framework, this is precisely what Martin Heidegger would so stubbornly seek to resist both in *Being and Time* as well as in his lecture given at Marburg University in 1924 entitled *The Concept of Time*.[65]

Interiority crystallizes into a fundamental concern. Subjectivity under reification, already assumed the externalization of the interior (*Entäusserung*) within an increasingly prefabricated and ever more deadening form of everyday life. Activity becomes the mere manipulation of abstract laws.[66] Personal responsibility or authority fades behind the network of institutional systems and sub-systems. No one rules even while all are ruled without genuine accountability or discursive determination of priorities. The person becomes a mechanical part of a mechanical system, which exists independently of him or her, and thus demands attitudinal or intellectual accommodation.[67] The fragmentation of the object is mirrored in the subject. Memory is endangered to the point where, paraphrasing Walter Benjamin, even the dead will not escape the grasp of the victor. The "second nature" of humanity, which is the anthropological product of reification, makes reflection on the mutability of the existing order impossible.[68]

Breaking that "second nature" is possible only through an act capable of providing a new and coherent definition for the relation between continuity and discontinuity or anthropology and history.[69] The position of the proletariat within the production process, its preconstituted existence as the revolutionary subject of history, anchors the moment of revolutionary transcendence within the production process and its immanent contradictions. With the integration of the proletariat, however, the moment of transcendence assumes legitimacy in its own right. An immanent foundation for contesting reification ever more surely vanishes from the work of the Frankfurt School. Affirming the sociological, for this very reason, becomes more important than ever before. The historical failure of the proletariat has not necessarily invalidated the need for drawing an epistemological connection between thought and action or consciousness and being. Investigating it remains as necessary as before even if the relation between theory and practice must take a new form. With the unqualified rejection of such concerns, in fact, philosophy retreats into forms of thinking associated with an earlier time. Ironically, this is the sense in which alienation remains what Lukács called "the specific problem of the age."

Alienation played a role in all the works of Lukacs. The search for salvation from "transcendental homesickness," the anxiety generated by the unyielding demands of society in conflict with those of the spirit, pervaded his remarkable *Soul and Form*. Despair over the cultural decadence of modernity in *Theory of the Novel*, the demise of the epic notion of life and its fragmentation expressed by the bourgeois novel, mirrored the descent into World War I. The apocalyptic strain, the obsession with a world on the brink, did not disappear in *History and Class Consciousness*.[70] Communism would end the era of "anarchic individualism" and recreate human society in the form of an "organic whole."[71] Indeed, this work faithfully reflected the thinking of the "ultra-left" of the Communist International during the "heroic" years of the Russian Revolution.

All things seemed possible. Only the proper consciousness of proletarian unity seemed necessary for the abolition of alienation and the introduction of a new world. But commitment to the revolutionary undertaking, even by the proletariat itself, was impossible to assume if ideology was indeed a "lived experience" (Korsch). Nor was unity a natural phenomenon for workers; a party seemed necessary whose legitimacy would rest on its ability to articulate and contest the constraints on the revolutionary enterprise.

Reification was such a constraint. Its specific impact on the proletariat turned it into *the* theoretical and practical barrier to action. The importation of consciousness "from the outside" (Lenin) thus becomes a logical consequence of the argument even though Lukács warned against the party acting as a "stand-in" for the proletariat.[72] Only a party of committed "revolutionary intellectuals," reflexively privileging the moment of transformative action, can contest the objectivity to which the working class is structurally consigned. The vanguard, for this reason, exhibits the "true" consciousness of the proletariat. It alone can confront the empirical interests of particular groups of workers, which are articulated by trade unions, no less than the utopian fatalism of the social democratic labor parties whose promises of "the day" – always in the future – on which a socialist transformation would occur rang ever more hollow in the years following World War I.

Lukács would, using his party name, forward the notion of a "democratic dictatorship" in the "Blum Theses" of 1928.[73] As a youthful bohemian, however, parliamentarism was anathema to him even before his association with the anarcho-syndicalist Ervin Szabo from whom he learned his revolutionary Marxism.[74] Empiricism and determinism were, in the same vein, seen as incapable of inspiring revolutionary action since they uncritically reflected the very reification in need of abolition.[75] Both tended to subvert the use of mediations. Fostering action, however, called for mediating the subjective and empirical interests of workers with their objective and scientifically predetermined mission which, in turn, made it incumbent upon the vanguard to "impute" a certain consciousness to the working class in the articulation of a program or a tactic.[76] The vanguard thus manifests an "aspiration to totality,"[77] which sets the framework for judging any particular action,[78] and renders it the actual subject–object of history.

Herein lies the totalitarian strain within *History and Class Consciousness*. The integrity of the individual subject is subsumed by the subject of history,[79] the working class, whose idea or consciousness of its mission is incarnated within the vanguard. Checks on its power are subsequently irrelevant by definition and its revolutionary character is presupposed. The vanguard need define itself neither by illegality or legality; its commitment to the goal teleologically justifies opportunism in meeting the needs of one exigency and then another as the organization sees fit. Necessity is turned into a virtue. The organizational question is thus resolved metaphysically; indeed, there is something quite legitimate about suggesting that Lukács "willingly asserts his idealism in order . . . the better to secure it against attack."[80]

Ethics surrenders to teleology which, in turn, becomes the preserve of the vanguard. A different interpretation of the relation between ethics and teleology in Lukács, however, is also possible. Aristotle had, after all, developed an ethics based on teleological assumptions. Uncertainty and contingency, which demand ethical choices, are not necessarily precluded by teleology. Teleology can, from this less dogmatic conception, presuppose an ethic. The "standpoint of the proletariat," itself teleologically generated by history, can subsequently turn into a universal ethical formulation intent on subjecting to criticism all institutions – including the vanguard party – seeking to constrain the freedom and capacity for self-administration of the working class. Class consciousness, in keeping with the thinking of Rosa Luxemburg, would thus turn into the "ethic" of the proletariat and this interpretation gains particular credence insofar as the vanguard party plays no role in the most famous chapter of *History and Class Consciousness*.

The method of Lukács, from this perspective, actually confronts his own political choices. In keeping with his earliest essays, which sought to balance the soviets with the party, the chapter on reification tends to militate against the totalitarian views articulated in other parts of the book.[81] The soviets, of course, had already lost even the semblance of independence when the book appeared in 1923.[82] But its "utopian surplus," to employ the phrase of Ernst Bloch, contested the authoritarianism of communist politics and the commissars sensed it; indeed, it was not merely because Lukács was aligned with the wrong faction at the Fifth Congress of the Comintern in 1924 that Zinoviev should have called for the censure of *History and Class Consciousness* along with the various Hegelian interpretations of Marxism by Karl Korsch and others.[83]

The decisions of this Congress reflected the end of the "heroic" phase of the Russian Revolution, recognized that proletarian revolution outside the USSR had failed, agreed upon the need to "bolshevize" the communist parties of Europe, and asserted that industrialization of the nascent state should take priority. The works of Lukács and Korsch, however, opposed the majority of the Comintern on every point. The conflation of alienation and objectification may have fostered authoritarianism by obscuring the delineation of criteria for differentiating the true from the false and the emancipatory from the repressive, but it surely harbored a concern for the integrity of the subject and the establishment of a utopian "realm of freedom" through the new unity between subject and object. The universalist radicalism of *History and Class Consciousness* also justified precisely the commitment to international revolution which the Congress wished to countermand. The transformation of Marxism into a critical method, a theory of society rather than a science, also constituted an obvious threat to the implementation of a new fixed and finished dogma by the Comintern. Where a new turn toward "productivism" was taking place, along with an uncritical admiration of technology,[84] Lukács maintained his belief of 1920 that "liberation from capitalism means liberation from the rule of the economy."[85] Finally, in seeking the abolition of reification, Lukács could build on the earlier essays comprising *History and Class Consciousness* and project a moral imperative for instituting new forms of "self-administration."[86]

Lukács' critique of reification is inherently threatening to any institution; it fosters the demand for empowerment. And this follows from the interpretation of Marxism as a theory of praxis. Materialism is now identified with deciphering the constitution of reality, the capitalist totality, from the standpoint of its historical potential for transformation. But, for this very reason, revolution becomes associated with a new set of expectations. Alienation defines every form of objectification. It is no longer a matter of one class supplanting another, or one form of state substituting for another, but of introducing a new form of life. Determinations vanish as "historical specificity" (Korsch) becomes sacrificed to what was actually a premodern, apocalyptic, conception of radical change. Thus, the theory of praxis ever more surely turns into its opposite: a purely contemplative radicalism.[87]

The failure of the proletariat to fulfill its role as a revolutionary subject not only strengthened this tendency, which reached fruition in the notion of "negative dialectics," but also shattered the symbiotic connection between the bourgeoisie and the proletariat on which the entire teleological conception of Lukács ultimately rested. The logic behind the philosophical development from the transcendental subject of Kant to the historical subject of Hegel and then to the proletariat of Marx collapses along with the promise projected by liberalism for socialism. Tradition loses its coherence; it no longer extends from the Renaissance to the Enlightenment to the proletarian victory. Universalist foundations lose their validity and the door opens to Nietzsche. The original conflation between alienation and objectification, without a revolutionary agent for transforming pre-history, will now create an abstract negation pitting the particular against the universal and a uniquely individual subjectivity against society.[88]

History and Class Consciousness, in highlighting the question of reification, anticipated this development. It generated a concern with subjectivity and the debilitating character of instrumental rationality and bureaucracy. Foreshadowing Max Horkheimer, and the "one-dimensional society" of Herbert Marcuse, Lukács even envisioned the possibility of a

> petrified factuality in which everything is frozen into a "fixed magnitude," in which the reality that just happens to exist persists in a totally senseless unchanging way precludes any theory that could throw light on even this immediate reality. This takes reification to its ultimate extreme: it no longer points dialectically to anything beyond itself: its dialectic is mediated only by the reification of the immediate forms of production.[89]

Dialectics is no longer, with Hegel, the immanent process of transcendence. Immanence and transcendence, unless anchored by the proletariat, lose their connection with one another. Utopia must now stand outside history. It can appear in the fixed presuppositions of discourse, which Jürgen Habermas can employ to counter the empirical "distortion" of language, or in the anti-systemic stance used by Theodor Adorno and Walter Benjamin to break any identification between subject and object. In either case, however, the critical theory of society and the political attempt to transform the structural imbalance of power will lose their primacy. Emancipation will leave the reified world intact and invariant.

Coming to terms with the practical effects of reification is possible only by questioning the assumptions underlying its definition and the manner in which both Lukács and the later proponents of critical theory sought to deal with it. Systemic forms of linguistic philosophy are incapable of developing any "principles of historical specificity" (Korsch) while the various versions of an anti-systemic "negative dialectics" are blind to the need for deriving determinate criteria for practical judgment; indeed, if Lukács was mistaken in equating praxis with the objectification of subjectivity, no other alternative approaches can really deal with labor as the historically mutable interaction of the subject with a pre-given object. Positive forms of linguistic philosophy and negative dialectics actually complement one another insofar as each is defined by what it opposes. Both are "one-sided" or, in Hegelian terms, "abstract." Reification thus invades the very theory seeking to resist its claims.

A new point of departure would suggest that just as alienation is different from objectification, so are both different from reification. All this, at first glance, is relatively simple. Marx himself had criticized the Hegelian attempt to conflate objectification with alienation by noting that, while the former is neutral and trans-historical, the latter is inherently negative and occurs only under distinct historical conditions. A non-alienated alternative to the status quo is possible for Marx and, in keeping with the refusal to reify theoretical concepts, it becomes illegitimate to naturalize existing social relations. Nevertheless, if non-alienated activity can occur only outside capitalist social relations, the ability to make judgments or employ "practical reason" in the realm of "pre-history" is severely compromised.

There is, however, a hidden truth to this error since alienation speaks not merely to rendering institutions accountable, or resurrecting the subjectivity lost in the assumptions of the existing accumulation process, but to what Walter Benjamin appropriately termed "the poverty of the interior." The allure of chiliastic and eschatological forms of thought lies in their promise to enrich it. But where messianic movements built on solidarity can compensate for given forms of identity deficits, none can ever completely eradicate the problems associated with the subjective experience of alienation. Even a new order in which "the free development of each is the condition for the free development of all" will not solve the problem. In fact, precisely insofar as social change seeks to bring this about, disorientation will necessarily occur and thereby generate new forms of alienation. Responding to alienation politically is far more difficult than rectifying the unequal distribution of wealth or existing conditions of linguistic distortion.

Alienation has an existential component. It is more than a reflex of "social conditions" and is irreducible to the division of labor. Intellectual works of the past show how the concept speaks to issues of loneliness, mortality, unrequited love, unfulfilled hopes, expectations denied and a host of other personal and communal concerns. The teleological belief that the contradictions of a given age will become resolved before the next epoch dawns is an illusion.[90] Unresolved religious and anthropological problems, what Ernst Bloch called "non-synchronous contradictions," have obviously been carried over into the "disenchanted world" of advanced industrial society. The past, in the words of Marx, still weighs like a nightmare on the living.

Alienation is an experience of society as other. It is obviously a historical product, but its non-linear character makes its theoretical reconstruction almost impossible. Alienation is inherently indeterminate and more than the sum of its historically constituted parts. It escapes every formula and reconstitutes itself with every piece of legislation especially since "progress" achieved in one arena of social life may produce regression in another. Thus, even if it is not considered an ontological category, alienation is surely part of humanity's "second nature." A group mediated by cultural myths, religious rituals, social customs, political institutions, and processes of production is never reducible to the individuals inhabiting it, even should a resolution of every determinate contradiction take place.[91] No "solution" to the riddle of alienation is possible without "society" changing its phenomenological character. That is why the legitimate response to alienation can offer nothing less than the utopian vision of a "home," without estrangement and grounded in real democracy, "which has appeared to everyone in childhood and which no one yet has visited."[92]

Utopia is kept alive by the persistence of alienation. No institutional arrangement or theory of action can promise to abolish mortality or introduce what Herbert Marcuse called a "new sensibility." All this attests to the unrealizable quality of utopia and the asymptotic relation of freedom to reality. There is no denying, however, the validity of authentically new cultural experiments seeking to transform the phenomenological encounter with the "world." Alienation is a *felt need*, which is not invalidated even when attempts to fulfill it are made in the most ideologically tainted ways.[93] It will continue so long as the subject engages in an externalization (*Entaüsserung*) of his or her subjectivity. But whether this externalization is estranged (*verfremdet*) will depend upon both the character of the activity and the manner in which it is interpreted. Consequently, following Ernst Bloch and Walter Benjamin, confronting alienation will demand a uniquely *utopian hermeneutic* capable of reconstructing the meanings of the past in terms of their relevance for an emancipated future.

Reification has no need of utopian hermeneutics in order to constrain its effects. It is inherently determinate and involves a certain "interchange" between humanity and nature. Reification is based on rationalization. The two concepts, however, are different.[94] Rationalization involves dealing with nature in an instrumental or mathematical fashion. Reification appears only insofar as purposive ends are denied and closed to critical scrutiny in the employment of such techniques. It is perhaps best illustrated by the "inverted world" of the commodity form wherein the subjects behind production are structurally turned into objects for the accumulation of profit while capital, which is ostensibly the object of the undertaking, is turned into the subject supposedly generating the process. Individuals are thus turned into "things;" their reflexive capacities are undermined along with their choices since concepts lose their historical character and assume a fixed and finished, or "natural," form.

Reification, in terms of this definition, was what Marx sought to confront when he subtitled his principal work the "critique of political economy." With Lukács, however, things are different. Legitimate concerns over the imperializing ambitions of scientific rationality, are conflated with an implacable opposition to every form of rationality unwilling to recognize the constituting character of subjectivity. Mitigating reification is rendered impossible by definition and, for this reason, Lukács is unable to develop a genuine theory of praxis. The theory of reification itself becomes reified.

None of this renders class or class or class consciousness irrelevant. Class alone still provides the structuring principle of the existing accumulation process and the conditions for its reproduction. A logical if not teleological reference to class consciousness thus remains unavoidable for contesting reification. *History and Class Consciousness* continues to provide a fundamental source of intellectual value. Employing class consciousness honestly, however, means stripping the concept of all teleological connotations and making its "ideal" character explicit and relevant to the exercise of ethical judgments concerning the accountability of all social institutions and the issues dividing working people.

But that is only possible by breaking the identification between reification and objectification. The point for a contemporary movement is not whether to employ instrumental rationality or the newest and most advanced forms of computer technology. It is now a matter of determining what priorities are privileged, how they were determined, and the extent to which accountability is being exercised. Exercising practical judgment in such matters, however, presupposes an ethical rather than a teleological perspective. Utopia no longer renders a regulative ideal of justice unnecessary. Karl-Otto Apel and Jürgen Habermas are thus correct in suggesting that this calls for distinguishing between utopia and a regulative ideal of justice derived from the proceduralist implications of a discourse ethic. Nevertheless, without even considering practical questions, exaggerating the *existential* benefits of such an ethic would prove a mistake.

Utopia may no longer be embedded within history. But concerns with the good life, the fulfilled existence, are still relevant. Neither liberalism nor socialism, nor the two in combination, offer a solution to the manifold problem of alienation. Even the most emancipatory practices inspired by these ideologies can merely inform institutions seeking to further the creation of universal conditions for an ever greater exercise of subjectivity. They cannot directly influence the existential meaning attributed to particular choices or phenomenologically alter the relation between the subject and the otherness of society. Indeed, following Hegel, emancipatory politics can only project the context wherein the more personal encounter with one's life can more fully take place.

Just as those committed to justice cannot dismiss the utopian concern with alienation, however, so must the utopians take seriously the confrontation with reification. The transformation of people into things is not a matter of theory; it occurs insofar as the logic of capitalist accumulation turns workers into a "cost of production" and political authoritarianism denies their integrity as subjects of law. Accountability and empowerment, concepts which underpin the notion of popular sovereignty and the extension of democratic principles from the the state into civil society, are the twin pillars on which a critical theory of society rests. An assault on reification occurs with every institutional attempt to realize these concerns. The moment of positivity, for this reason, cannot vanish from the critical method. Thus, even if many of the assumptions made by Lukács have lost their relevance, the future of freedom will still depend upon our ability to formulate a persuasive and plausible theory of practice.

Notes

1 "Let us assume for the sake of argument that recent research had disproved once and for all every one of Marx's individual theses. Even if this were to be proved, every serious 'orthodox' Marxist would still be able to accept all such modern findings without reservation and hence dismiss all of Marx's theses *in toto* – without having to renounce his orthodoxy for a single moment. Orthodox Marxism, therefore, does not imply the uncritical acceptance of the results of Marx's investigations. It is not the 'belief' in this or that thesis, nor the exegesis of a 'sacred' book. On the contrary, orthodoxy refers exclusively to *method.*" Georg Lukács, *History and Class Consciousness: Studies in Marxist Dialectics* trans. Rodney Livingstone (Cambridge, Mass., 1971), p. 1.

2 Cf. Max Adler, *Marx und Engels als Denker* (Frankfurt, 1972).

3 Martin Jay, *Marxism and Totality: The Adventures of a Concept from Lukács to Habermas* (Berkeley, 1984), pp. 84, 102.

4 Note the chapter entitled "Rosa Luxemburg and Western Marxism" in Stephen Eric Bronner, *Rosa Luxemburg: A Revolutionary for Our Times* (New York, 1987), pp. 96ff.

5 Lukács, *History and Class Consciousness.*, pp. xxiiiff.

6 Cf. István Mészáros, *Marx's Theory of Alienation* (London, 1970), pp. 28–33.

7 "The infinitive of alienation is an ancient word, which had a social connotation from the beginning. *Abalienare*, according to the Romans, meant to externalize (*entäussern*) oneself in something meant for sale. Grimmelshausen may have still called exchange the process of alienating (*veralienieren*). But, in contrast to French and English, this foreign word otherwise disappeared from everyday speech. It was almost the same with the German 'to alienate' (*entfremden*), at least in its original reference to the implications of exchange: people have alienated themselves from one another in the sense of becoming cool to one another." Ernst Bloch, *Verfremdungen* 2 vols, (Frankfurt, 1968) vol. 1, p. 81.

8 Cf. Paul Ricoeur, *The Symbolism of Evil* (Boston, 1980).

9 "The infinitive of estrangement (*verfremden*) is, however, not ancient. But it is difficult to translate. Remarkably, according to Grimm, Berthold Auerbach is the first to give it literary definition in his novel of 1842, *New Life*. There the parents feel themselves estranged, that is to say deeply hurt, because their children speak French, which they cannot

understand, in their company. Apparently the children are talking about them. They are absent and, like servants who are not supposed to listen, feel estranged." It is from the perspective of this original feeling of distance that Brecht would develop his "estrangement-effect" (*Verfremdungseffekt*). Bloch, *Verfremdungen* vol. 1, p. 82.

10   Friedrich Hölderlin, *Hyperion* in *Gesammelte Werke* ed. Friedrich Beissner (Stuttgart, 1957) vol. 3, p. 153.

11   Cf. Georg Lukács, *Der junge Hegel* 2 vols, (Frankfurt, 1973) vol. 2, pp. 826ff.

12   "The chief defect of all hitherto existing materialism – that of Feuerbach included – is that the thing [*Gegenstand*], reality, sensuousness, is conceived only in the form of the *object* [*Objekt*] or of contemplation [*Anschauung*], but not as human sensuous activity, practice, not subjectively." Karl Marx, "Theses on Feuerbach" in Karl Marx and Friedrich Engels, *Selected Works* 3 vols, (Moscow, 1969), vol. 1, p. 11.

13   Ibid., vol. 1, pp. 13–15.

14   Georg Lukács, *Der junge Marx: Seine philosophische Entwicklung von 1840 bis 1844* (Pfüllingen, 1965).

15   Cf. Note the comparison between Lukács and Marx by István Mészáros "Kontingentes und notwendiges Klassenbewusstsein" in *Aspekte von Geschichte und Klassenbewusstsein* ed. István Mészáros (Munich, 1972), pp. 124ff.

16   Lukács, *History and Class Consciousness*, p. 111.

17   Ibid., p. 112.

18   Ibid., p. 128.

19   Ibid., p. 134.

20   Ibid., p. 115.

21   Ibid., pp. 131ff.

22   "Thought regresses to the level of a naive, dogmatic rationalism: somehow it regards the mere actuality of the irrational contents of the concepts as non-existent . . . Alternatively we are forced to concede that actuality, content, matter reaches right into the form, the structures of the forms and their interrelations and thus *into the structure of the system itself.*" In that case the system must be abandoned as a system. For then it will be no more than a register, an account, as well ordered as possible, of facts which are no longer linked rationally and so can no longer be made systematic even though the forms of their components are themselves rational." Ibid., p. 118.

23   Ibid., pp. 122–3.

24   Ibid., p. 128.

25   "What is important is to recognize clearly that all human relations (viewed as the objects of social activity) assume increasingly the objective forms of the abstract elements of the conceptual systems of natural science and of the abstract substrata of the laws of nature." Ibid., p. 131.

26   Ibid., p. 105.

27 Ibid., p. 126.

28 Ibid., p. 126.

29 ". . . Either the world must be aestheticized, which is an evasion of the real problem and is just another way in which to make the subject purely contemplative and to annihilate 'action.' Or else, the aesthetic principle must be elevated into the principle by which objective reality is shaped: but that would be to mythologize the discovery of intuitive understanding." Ibid., p. 140.

30 Ibid., pp. 123–4.

31 Determination specifies the "conditions" by which an object or event is defined or created; indeterminacy is blind to such specificity and thus renders an object or event "unconditional" or hypostatized; the phenomenon appears abstract since it is closed to historical definition or creation. Hegel took over these terms from the close friend of his youth, with whom he would later split, Friedrich Schelling, in "Vom Ich als Prinzip der Philosophie" (1797) in *Werke* vol. 2, pp. 166ff.

32 "With this came the discovery of dialectics in history itself. Hence dialectics is not imported into history from outside, nor is it interpreted in the light of history (as often occurs in Hegel), but is *derived* from history made conscious as its logical manifestation at this particular point in its development." Ibid., p. 177.

33 Ibid., p. 142.

34 Ibid., p. 193.

35 Cf. Stephen Eric Bronner, *Socialism Unbound* (New York, 1990), pp. 6ff.

36 Lukács, *History and Class Consciousness*, p. 146.

37 It is only once society has become demystified or rational, which occurs through the extension of the commodity form under capitalism, that the rational reconstruction of the past becomes possible; indeed, Marx already knew that the human is incomprehensible from the standpoint of the ape and that the ape is only comprehensible from the standpoint of the human. This subverts the objection raised by Josef Revai who argued that, if the proletariat alone can "know" the conditions of its creation, it becomes impossible to speak of conscious historical agents in the past. Dialectical notions of history, after all, basically emerge with the entry of the bourgeoisie upon the world stage. See the reprint of the 1924 review of *History and Class Consciousness* by Josef Revai in *Theoretical Practice* 1 (January, 1971).

38 Ibid., p. 149.

39 Ibid., p. 161.

40 Ibid., p. 178.

41 Marx, *Theses on Feuerbach*, p. 15; Lukács, *History and Class Consciousness*, pp. 262ff.

42 Cf. Andrew Arato, "Lukács' Theory of Reification," *Telos* 11 (Spring, 1972), pp. 26ff; cf. Andrew Feenberg, *Lukács, Marx, and the Sources of Critical Theory* (Oxford, 1986).

43 Cf. Andrew Arato, "The Neo-Idealist Defense of Subjectivity" in *Telos* 21 (Fall, 1974), pp. 108ff.

44 Georg Lukács, "Emil Lask" in *Kant-Studien* (1917–18), pp. 349ff.

45 Cf. Karl Marx *Capital* 3 vols, ed. Friedrich Engels and trans. Samuel Moore and Edward Aveling (New York, 1973) vol. 1, pp. 71ff.

46 The critique of Nikolai Bukharin's *Historical Materialism*, written in 1922, would emphasize that "Technique is a *part*, a moment, naturally of great importance, of the social productive forces, but it is neither simply identical with them nor . . . the final or absolute moment of the changes in these forces. This attempt to find the underlying determinants of society and its development in a principle other than that of the social relations between men in the process of production . . . leads to fetishism." Georg Lukács, *Political Writings 1919–1929* ed. Rodney Livingstone and trans. by Michael McColgan (London, 1972), p. 136.

47 Lukács, *History and Class Consciousness*, p. 103.

48 Ibid., p. 94.

49 "Vulgar socialism . . . has taken over from the bourgeois economists the consideration and treatment of distribution as independent of the mode of production and hence the presentation of socialism as turning principally on distribution." Cf. Karl Marx, "Critique of the Gotha Programme" in *Selected Works* (Moscow, 1969) vol. 3, p. 20.

50 Class consciousness and "self-administration" (*Selbsttätigkeit*) were the goals she and her followers sought to further. Note in particular her reflections written in early February 1906 on the mass strike in *The Letters of Rosa Luxemburg* ed. Stephen Eric Bronner (Atlantic Highlands, 1993 2nd edn.), pp. 112ff.

51 Lukács, "Tactics and Ethics" in *Political Writings*, pp. 6ff.

52 Cf. Georg Lukács, *Selected Correspondence 1902–1920* ed. and trans. Judith Marcus and Zoltan Tar (New York, 1986), pp. 148 and *passim*.

53 Lukács, *History and Class Consciousness*, p. 91.

54 Ibid., p. 87.

55 Ibid., p. 79; also, cf. Iring Fetscher, "Zum Begriff der 'Objektiven Möglichkeit' bei Max Weber and Georg Lukács" in *Revue Internationale de Philosophie* 106 (1973).

56 Lukács, *History and Class Consciousness*, p. 169.

57 Ibid., p. 3.

58 Ibid., p. 155.

59 "If, then, the standpoint of the proletariat is opposed to that of the bourgeoisie, it is nonetheless true that proletarian thought does not require a *tabula rasa*, a new start to the task of comprehending reality and one without any preconceptions. In this it is unlike the thought of the bourgeoisie with regard to the medieval forms of feudalism – at least in its basic tendencies. Just because its practical goal is the *fundamental* transformation of the whole of society it conceives of bourgeois society together with its intellectual and artistic productions as the point of departure for its own method." Ibid., p. 163.

60 Instrumental rationality "by concerning itself with the formal calculability of the contents of forms made abstract, *must define* these contents as *immutable* – within the system of relations pertaining at any given time." Ibid., p. 143–4.

61 Cf. Isaak Ilych Rubin, *Essays on Marx's Theory of Value* trans. Milos Somardziga and Fredy Perlman (Montreal, 1982) and Roman Rosdolsky, *The Making of Marx's Capital* trans. Pete Burgess (London, 1977).

62 Lukács, *History and Class Consciousness*, p. 93.

63 Ibid., p. 88.

64 Heidegger would surely have agreed, albeit from an ontological perspective, with the claim of Lukács that "thus time sheds its qualitative, variable, flowing nature; it freezes into an exactly delimited quantifiable continuum filled with quantifiable 'things' (the reified, mechanically objectified 'performance' of the worker, wholly separated from his total human personality); in short, it becomes space." Ibid., p. 90.

65 Cf. Lucien Goldmann, *Lukács et Heidegger* ed. Youssef Ishaghpour (Paris, 1973).

66 "But Engels' deepest misunderstanding consists in his belief that the behavior of industry and scientific experiment constitutes praxis in the dialectical, philosophical sense. In fact, scientific experiment is contemplation at its purest. The experimenter creates an artificial, abstract milieu in order to be able to *observe* undisturbed the untrammelled workings of the laws under examination, eliminating all irrational factors both of the subject and the object." Lukács, *History and Class Consciousness*, p. 132.

67 Ibid., p. 89.

68 Ibid., p. 184.

69 Ibid., pp. 186–7.

70 Cf. Arpad Kadarkay, *Georg Lukács: Life, Thought, and Politics* (London, 1991), pp. 192ff; Michael Löwy, *Georg Lukács: From Romanticism to Bolshevism* (London, 1979).

71 Cf. Georg Lukács, "The Old Culture and the New Culture" in *Marxism and Human Liberation* ed. E. San Juan Jr. (New York, 1973).

72 Lukács, *History and Class Consciousness*, p. 327.

73 Cf. Lukács, *Political Writings*, pp. 227ff.

74 Cf. David Kettler, "Culture and Revolution: Lukács and the Hungarian Revolution" in *Telos* 10 (Winter, 1971).

75 The point was not simply to proceed without reference to the facts since ". . . what is decisive is whether this process of isolation is a means toward understanding the whole and whether it is integrated within the context it presupposes and requires or whether the abstract knowledge of an isolated fragment retains its 'autonomy' and becomes an end in itself." Lukács, *History and Class Consciousness*, p. 73.

76 Ibid., p. 71.

77   Ibid., p. 198.
78   "Every momentary interest may have either of two functions: either it
     will be a step towards the ultimate goal or else it will conceal it. Which
     of the two it will be depends *entirely upon the class consciousness of the
     proletariat and not on victory or defeat in isolated skirmishes.*" Ibid., p. 73.
79   Ibid., p. 171.
80   Kadarkay, *Georg Lukács*, p. 270.
81   Andrew Arato and Paul Breines, *The Young Lukács and the Origins of
     Western Marxism* (New York, 1979), pp. 142ff.
82   Cf. Samuel Farber, *Before Stalinism: The Rise and Fall of Soviet Democracy*
     (London, 1990).
83   Kadarkay, *Georg Lukács*, pp. 280ff.
84   "The foundation of our whole policy must be the widest possible
     development of productivity," it was already possible to claim in 1918,
     "everything else must be subordinated to this one task." Nikolai
     Bukharin and Evgenii Preobrzehnsky, *The ABC of Communism: A
     Popular Explanation of the Program of the Communist Party* (Ann Arbor,
     1967), p. 74.
85   Lukács, "The Old Culture and the New Culture," p. 5.
86   It is probably correct to suggest that in the 1920s, Lukács "incessantly
     tried to reveal the 'ideal type' of the system as opposed to its empirical
     reality, a procedure barely tolerated by the system itself (hence the
     constant conflicts between Lukács and the cultural bureaucracy, but this
     same procedure also entailed acceptance of the final principles of the
     regime." Ferenc Fehér, "Lukács in Weimar" in *Lukács Reappraised* ed.
     Agnes Heller (New York, 1983), p. 79.
87   Lukács, *History and Class Consciousness*, p. xviii.
88   Cf. Paul Breines, "Praxis and its Theorists: The Impact of Lukács and
     Korsch in the 1920s" *Telos* 11 (Spring, 1972), pp. 102ff.
89   Ibid., p. 184.
90   Cf. Ernst Bloch, "Aktualität und Utopie: Zu Lukács' '*Geschichte und
     Klassenbewusstsein*' " in *Philosophische Aufsätze zur Objektiven Phantasie*
     (Frankfurt, 1969).
91   Note the discussion of the "third," and the tensions deriving from the
     way in which the group is qualitatively different from the individuals
     composing it, in Jean-Paul Sartre, *Critique of Dialectical Reason* ed.
     Jonathan Ree and trans. Allan Sheridan-Smith (London, 1976), pp. 95–
     108, 345ff. and *passim*; also, *The Sociology of Georg Simmel* ed. Kurt H.
     Wolff (New York, 1950), pp. 26ff., 58ff.
92   Ernst Bloch, *Das Prinzip Hoffnung* 3 vols. (Frankfurt, 1973) vol. 3, p.
     1628.
93   "Religious suffering is the expression of real suffering and at the same
     time the protest against real suffering. Religion is the sigh of the
     oppressed creature, the heart of a heartless world, as it is the spirit of
     spiritless conditions. It is the opium of the people." Cf. Karl Marx,

"Toward the Critique of Hegel's Philosophy of Law" in *Writings of the Young Marx on Philosophy and Society* ed. and trans. by Loyd D. Easton and Kurt H. Guddat (New York, 1967), p. 249.

94 Jürgen Habermas, *The Theory of Communicative Action* 2 vols. trans. Thomas McCarthy (Boston, 1984) vol. 1, pp. 355ff.

4

Utopian Projections: In Honor of Ernst Bloch

> The true genesis is not at the beginning, but at the end.
>
> *The Principle of Hope*

Ernst Bloch is only now becoming known in the United States. Especially towards the end of his long life, however, he was one of the best-known intellectuals in Europe. His extraordinary literary output, which always oscillated between art and philosophy, was marked by a unique metaphorical and expressionist prose. His students revered him and, during the 1960s, he served as an inspiration. But, with the rise of neo-conservatism and the collapse of communism, his influence began to wane. Utopia became a word of derision. Nor is it legitimate any longer to speak of a "teleological suspension of the ethical" (Lukács). Alternative systems have lost their appeal; socialism and utopia seem ready for the dustbin of history. But there is no denying the existential price for the new philosophical moderation. People feel "hollow," as T. S. Eliot observed, in a modernity seemingly bereft of vision and purpose. Thus, it is still worthwhile to consider the thinking of undoubtedly the greatest of utopian philosophers who died in 1977 at the age of 92.

From *Spirit of Utopia* and *The Principle of Hope* to collections of stories, essays, and the last great works like *The Problem of Materialism* and *Experimentum Mundi*, one idea preoccupied Ernst Bloch: the "dream of the better life." The content of that dream, the goal inspiring human action, led to disquisitions on everything from reincarnation to alchemy. His "romantic anti-capitalism" was fundamentally premodern, cosmological and eschatological, and the attempt to fuse it with Marxism and the Enlightenment expanded the boundaries of emancipation more than any thinker before or since. Martin Jay was surely correct in noting how the philosophy of Bloch shows that Western Marxism was more than just Hegelian Marxism. There is also something strangely esoteric about his way of thinking. For all that, however, his basic ontological claim was simple enough: "everything existing retains a utopian glimmer and philosophy would be nothing were it not capable of furthering the intellectual solution to the creation of this crystalline heaven of a regenerated reality."[1]

Ernst Bloch was a prophet like Marx and Thomas Münzer. His restless life, always spent in exile, gave meaning to the identification of philosophy with "transcendental homesickness." His work, however, provides new content for an idea as old as humanity itself. Past utopias especially of the political variety were concerned with pacification, order, and symmetry; they were usually far more culturally conservative than most radicals would care to admit. But there was never anything boring about the utopian conception of Ernst Bloch. Its free-flowing quality became part of his expressionistic literary style. Its cosmpolitan character was reflected in his extrardinary intellectual range. Its inherently unfinished quality left open the new experience of tomorrow.

Just like the others, of course, his utopian conception retained residues of repression and confusion. Its teleological elements led Bloch to identify with Stalin and often to compromise his political judgment. Seeking to build on the example of Marx, he wished to make his utopian philosophy relevant for the present and a prefiguration of the future. But prophecy is not the stuff of politics; indeed, even with the benefit of hindsight, his lectures made it apparent that he had little real political insight and many contemporary attempts to somehow preserve him from his past are dishonest. There was nothing ambigous whatsoever about his support for the Moscow Trials.[2] Nevertheless, it was an exaggeration for Jan Robert Bloch to claim that the work of his father constituted nothing more than a "philosophical and propagandistic cover for Stalin's bloody terror."

Ernst Bloch knew that the value of a work is not exhausted by the politics of the author. And, in contrast to Martin Heidegger, there is a critical and reflexive moment within his philosophy, which *immanently* calls into question the particular judgments on policy he made. Bloch's thinking was genuinely that of a maverick. Oskar Negt might have called him the "German philosopher of the October Revolution," and Bloch's life-long admiration for Lenin was undoubtedly genuine, but most communists – in Germany no less than the Soviet Union – considered him an outsider and a mystic. Even within the Institute for Social Research, with which he was loosely associated, few took him seriously. Bloch's thought never jibed with the pessimism of Adorno and Horkheimer.

He was older. His philosophy harked back to intellectual tendencies existing prior to World War I when cultural radicalism was defined by a commitment to the "new dawn" foreshadowed by Nietzsche, the visionary communitarian socialism identified with figures like Gustav Landauer, the concern with reification and alienation exhibited by neo-Kantians like Emil Lask and Georg Simmel, the rebirth of interest in Jewish mysticism and Christian chilianism, and the manifold experiments of the modernist avant-gardes. Bloch's thinking incorporated elements from all these sources and others as well. Indeed, the result would prove uniquely his own and jut boldly into the future.

Utopia, in the thinking of Ernst Bloch, ceases to exist as "nowhere;" an other to real history. It is a constituent element of all human activity and, simultaneously, historical. It becomes manifest in the quest for meaning, the thrill of sports, the desire for love, the daydream, the wonder of a child, and the experience of lightness before a genuine work of art. Each is a dim prefiguration (*Vorerscheinung*) of its existence; the question becomes how to articulate and realize the hopes unconsciously shared by humanity. And here, whatever the influence of neo-romantic and mystical currents from the turn of the century, revelation is inadequate to the task at hand since "the forward glance becomes all the stronger, the more lucidly it becomes conscious. The dream in this glance seeks to make itself clear and the premonition, the right one, quite plain. Only when reason begins to speak can hope, in which there is nothing false, blossom again. The not-yet-conscious must become conscious in action, *known* in its content."[3]

Utopia is at the core of human existence. But humanity appears in a variety of forms and so it follows that utopia will receive articulation in a variety of ways. It is no accident then that the gaze of this most European of thinkers should have extended to Zoroaster, Confucius and the stories of the mythical Scheherazade. He retained what Kant termed a "teleology of hope," but considered material equality as the precondition for actualizing utopia. If this obviously led him to Marx, however, the recognition that various forms of experience provided a sense of the *novum* also led him to medieval mystics like Meister Eckhart, Jakob Böhme, and Paracelsus. A rationalist concerned with determining the "ratio of the irratio," the critical character of mystical experience, he undertook the construction of a "left Aristotelianism" extending from Avicenna over Giordano Bruno to Leibniz and Marx.

Ernst Bloch may have believed he was integrating the insights from this tradition into the "warm current," rather than the scientistic "cold current," of Marxism. Ultimately, however, he was engaging in a peculiar form of eclecticism. And so, it makes sense that he should have been criticized from virtually every angle. But Bloch was rigorous after his fashion. His cosmological theory of nature was built on a knowledge of physics and it anticipated what would become a new preoccupation with the "eco-system" and "animal rights;" indeed, his belief that human emancipation presupposes a new form of interaction with nature from the standpoint of its repressed subjectivity has now become a commonplace within the ecological movement. Nevertheless, many of the technical and political criticisms of his work remain valid.

His philosophical stance was never bound to praxis as he claimed and especially now, in an avowedly anti-speculative age, his utopian theory seems anything but "concrete." His Neoplatonic claims were too often asserted rather than argued and his categories generally lack precision. The theological strain in his work and its eschatological character call for a suspension of disbelief. Few criteria are provided for the formulation of ethical or aesthetic judgments. He has little to say about the constraints on revolutionary transformation, the structure of emancipated production relations, or the democratic institutions necessary for maintaining a realm of freedom. When analyzing death and resurrection, daydreams and utopian symbols, the line between fantasy and logic often becomes blurred.

His daring attempt to reintroduce a radical *telos* into dialectical thought and ground it within an ontology of Being, however, extends the tradition of natural law and Marxism beyond purely economic or even regulative concerns. In this vein, whatever his own political commitments, the philosophy was a response to the manner in which goals commonly agreed upon were displaced into an ever more distant future by the communist vanguard. There is an inherently critical element to his way of thinking, which rests on a positive vision of emancipation. Its sophistication and quality has little in common with the dogmatism promoted by the communist states he supported. Nevertheless, its willingness to unearth the moment of freedom and happiness in everyday experience also confronts what has become a deadening philosophical pessimism among Western intellectuals.

Ernst Bloch wished to provide an ontological foundation for utopia. His philosophy thus retained an eschatological view of history. But it was one without the certainty of salvation or redemption. Realizing utopia, according to Bloch, can occur only through the creation of conditions capable of guaranteeing humanity's reflection on what has been ignored.[4] It depends ultimately upon an act of will and the commitment to, in the words of his friend Walter Benjamin, "never forget the best." But categories for determining the "best" were, for Bloch, never forthcoming. It was enough to emphasize that the best will only appear where it is least expected. Tolerance and civil liberties are thus immanently demanded by the philosophy of the man who once defended Stalin's show-trials. Unacknowledged works by the most diverse cultures, "traces" (*Spuren*) of forgotten lives, fragments of historical production, retain untapped perspectives on the "best life," which never simply "vanish" (Hegel) into immediate forms of practice. Indeed, "the waking dream everywhere feeds on what has been missed."[5]

Realizing the utopian *novum* in the future depends upon tapping the potential from the past. And this, in turn, is dependent upon the degree of consciousness generated in the present. The future is thus no mechanical elaboration of the present; nor does it emerge from a series of "steps" or "stages" deriving in linear fashion from the past. The future is open; determining the "horizon" of the present is possible only through unearthing the "anticipatory consciousness" embodied in the cultural achievements of the past. Utopia is not an abrupt break with the past; thus, in contrast to critical theorists like Adorno and Horkheimer, history becomes more than the unrolling of "necessity" and "freedom," more than the affirmation of "negativity." That is why Bloch could say that: "To the *novum* there belongs, in order that it really exist as a *novum*. not only an abstract opposition to a mechanical renewal, but rather in fact a specific type of renewal: namely, the not-yet-realized total content of that goal which is itself meant and intended and processed out of history's progressive novelties."[6]

Of course, for all Bloch's claims to materialism, his remains a fundamentally idealist vision. The "objective contradictions" within the existing order are not entirely forgotten. But the essential point, important enough, involves a commitment to *de-ideologize* ideology and the articulation of a utopian hermeneutic capable of building the content and furthering the realization of a "realm of freedom." Having said that, however, the philosophy of Bloch harbors a unique view of ideology which flies in the face of Leninist orthodoxy. Indeed, whatever the attempts to employ the language of communist orthodoxy, it inherently rejects any mechanical distinction between "true" and "false" consciousness.

The thinking of Bloch also rejects the popular idea that the potential within any form of social practice is exhausted by examining the historical context from which it arose. A reaffirmation of the dialectical relation between immanence and transcendence occurs as cultural products become more than mere "artificial social constructs;" they can also "jut beyond" the historical conditions of their emergence. And Bloch draws the theoretical consequences. A perspective takes shape in which, against all dogmatic forms of dialectical stage theory, it becomes impossible to assume that a reconciliation of *all* the contradictions defining a given epoch will take place before the next appears on the scene.

Unresolved problems as well as unfulfilled hopes can carry over from one phase of history into another. And the form, no less than the function, of these "non-synchronous contradictions" will change within the dominant socio-economic and political structures of the new period. A single unresolved concern like salvation can manifest both positive utopian and negative disutopian characteristics in different ways in different historical epochs. The implications of Bloch's approach are important for analyzing manifold phenomena including racism, sexism, the "cult of the personality," and the role of atavistic classes like the peasantry and petit bourgeoisie. Indeed, even while Bloch considered the proletariat immune from "non-synchronous contradictions," the concept would prove crucial for his remarkable analysis of German fascism.[7]

Once again, however, the political underpinning of his argument was impractical. There was simply no serious possibility of developing a "triple alliance" of the workers, peasants and disgruntled petit bourgeoisie against the Nazis. This perspective obscures the mass base of Nazism and, mistakenly, tends to equate it with the interests of "monopoly capital."[8] There is also something questionable about the claim that Marxism was being stripped of its utopian ideals in the 1920s even while the Nazis were employing a corrupt notion of the apocalypse in furthering their quest for power. Nor is it ever really made clear, except when referring to the most extreme circumstances, how the categories of "false" and "true" utopia are ultimately grounded in anything more than good will.

In any event, the Nazis surely reaped enormous propagandistic value from mutilating the past and establishing their particular forms of utopian symbolism. This becomes as apparent in the marching songs as in the films of Leni Riefenstahl and the torchlight parades. Coincidence alone, according to Bloch, cannot explain why Möller van der Bruck should have taken the notion of a "third reich" from the humanist and utopian vision first articulated by the medieval philosopher Joachim di Fiore.[9]

Ideology thus becomes a fungible concept. It is neither fixed nor finished. Ideology may obscure and justify the oppression of the status quo. But, since human practice inherently retains a teleological component, it will also retain an emancipatory moment. A ruling ideology is for him, in more concrete terms, the ensemble of ideas of a ruling class. But a universal interest, generally articulated while a class is on the rise, can co-exist with a particular one in any given work. "Liberty, equality, fraternity" is an example; "we the people" or "the right to life, liberty, and the pursuit of happiness" is another. Every articulation of a universal interest projects the desire for justice, harmony, freedom, and the like. Most likely the dominant class will become alienated from the radical implications of its ideals by its oppressive activity. Without the existence of the utopian element in ideology, however, it becomes impossible to explain the allure of these ideals or why they can transcend the context in which they arose.[10]

Radical analysis is then not just a matter of sociological analysis or explaining the "immanent" historical roots of ideas. It is a matter of unearthing their "transcendent" potential as well. The ideology of a given period is subsequently never entirely "false," as in "false consciousness," since a set of "not-yet-realized" utopian possibilities remains "latent" and waiting for self-conscious appropriation. The new society, in short, will not just "objectively" appear. "Subjective" action is necessary to interpret the unfulfilled possibilities of the past and reshape the repressed needs of humanity as they appear in the manifold set of cultural products through which history is understood.

Gone is the determinism of "scientific socialism" and the willingness to ascribe an inflexible class content to a given idea or work. The "cold current" must give way to the "warm" one. The sober emphasis on modernization gives way before the mission articulated by the young Marx and the Lukács of *History and Class Consciousness.* Visions of anthropological transformation, the employment of dialectics as a critical method with a humanistic intent, the creation of a fuller, richer, more meaningful existence become the purpose of the socialist enterprise. The aim is "to lift the world and inwardness, in their new interaction, out of their alienation and reification. Marxism is thoroughly realistic, but definitely not in the sense of a banal schematic copy of reality; to the contrary, its reality is: actuality plus the future within actuality. Through its own concrete change, which it ever holds open, Marxism demonstrates: that there is still an immeasurable amount of unused dream, unfinished content of history, unsold nature in the world."[11]

Just this, the "unused," the "unfinished," and "unsold" – in its humanistic potential – is what critical inquiry must clarify. Grounding itself within the tradition of emancipation, in theory and practice, becomes a crucial concern. Reflection and critique never lose their primacy in the work of Bloch. But the importance of fantasy, and the experience which explodes the constraints of the given, is never lost either. Dealing with such concerns, in fact, becomes obligatory for the cultural critic. Aesthetic criticism subsequently cannot remain content with either political or sociological pronouncements. Nor will purely formal judgments get to the heart of the matter. Art, for Bloch, is a mode of enjoyment and of experiencing the world in a new way.

And the implication of his position is clear enough; chaining either cultural production or criticism to the traditions of the past is inherently illegitimate. Art, for Bloch, *must* experiment with new forms of expression which overcome the limitations of the past. The value of art, in fact, appears in its simultaneous ability to serve as a "utopian laboratory" and a "feast of elaborated possibilities" for the future.[12] There is no stasis. The possibilities of a work, in his view, change through its interaction with a changing public. Bloch subsequently considers it necessary to judge even "unpopular" works, which might initially appear as irrationalist and fragmented, with an eye on the new and the unexplored. Bloch thus does not see "decadence" in the surrealist and expressionist attempts to merge dream and reality, perceive the world in a new light through distortion, or juxtapose dissimilar objects through montage. He looks for more. He delights in the new color of the Fauves, the fantastic imagery of the surrealists, the irreverent fun of the Dadaists, and the free play of the expressionists. The Stalinist always remained a modernist. And he wasn't a snob either. Indeed, just as he took exception to the "realist" position favored by Lukács in the famous set of debates between them during the tail end of the 1930s, his interest in a variety of popular forms ranging from the detective novel to nursery rhymes placed him in opposition to the stance usually associated with the Frankfurt School.

Experimentation with new forms and the aesthetics of fantasy make for, in the view of Bloch, a "dream which looks ahead" (*der Traum nach Vorwärts*) and confronts the "way things are." This dream is not defined by a retreat into childhood fantasies. And so, in contrast to Freud, Bloch refuses to concentrate upon the "nightdream" whose truth emerges in memories of the past or the "no-longer-conscious." He instead emphasizes the role of the "day-dream" with its projection of the "new," the "not-yet-conscious," and its loose connection with the situation in which the individual finds himself. Hope appears in the "day-dream;" happiness is envisioned "as the shape (*Gestalt*) of things to come." The day-dream, for Bloch, is capable of surmounting the censoring qualities of the super-ego and thus inherently retains a utopian kernel.[13]

Arguably, in analyzing the subjective presentiment of utopia, Bloch ignores how social repression is introjected into the very substructure of the individual, and the freeing of rage that can occur once objective referents are exploded. Also, in his emphasis on the "anticipatory consciousness," the "day-dream," and the "not-yet-conscious," he rips the concept of possibility from any determinate analysis of existence and turns it into the property of pure consciousness. This would obviously place him in opposition not only to the followers of Marx and Lenin, but also to adherents of Martin Heidegger and Jean-Paul Sartre.

Phenomenology and existentialism had gained in popularity during the 1930s. They emphasized the "concreteness" of individual existence and drew a connection between the concept of "possibility" and death.

The central category of "authentic" experience was "anguish" or "dread." Bloch, was aware, however, that hope is as legitimate a fundamental mode of experience as anguish, once a "possibility" is encountered. With any "concrete" possibility, after all, there is the hope of its being fulfilled as well as the anguish at the thought of its remaining unfulfilled.[14] Death is unavoidable; only through a philosophical sleight of hand does it become a "possibility." And so, once again, Bloch draws the consequences. Real possibility, for him, "does not reside in any finished ontology of the Being of that which is already existent, but rather in that ontology of the not-yet-existent (*noch-nicht-Seiende*) which is continually grounded anew as it discovers the future in the past and in all of nature."[15]

An openness to the possibility of utopia remains. Bloch's ontology is neither fixed nor finished. And, precisely for this reason, the unfulfilled promises of the past and the untapped sources of consciousness in the present prevent any *absolute* denial of utopia in the future;[16] indeed, once again, a famous line from the "Theses on the Philosophy of History" by Walter Benjamin comes to mind: "every second of time is the strait gate through which the Messiah might enter." And so, a "militant optimism" comes to define Bloch's worldview. Optimism of this sort bears no relation to the passive and naive variant so often encountered. Rather, it assumes the existential commitment to make good on the "latent" possibilities existing in the present and help in actualizing a new world for the future.

Now, Sartre once wrote that the question of whether history has a meaning is foolish, for the real question involves what meaning is given to it. Perhaps Bloch was too quick in dismissing the contribution realism might make in determining the concrete conditions wherein the "new" can serve as an "interruption." But he was correct when he wrote that "man does not live by bread alone – especially when he doesn't have any." Idealism is essential for the emergence of any political movement. And the fact is that the idealism of the intellectuals and the masses has dissipated with the collapse of the communist experiment in the East and the simple identification of social democracy with technocratic reform in the West. The reaffirmation of ideals is no small matter in today's world.

But that does not call for the suppression of the unpleasant or a self-imposed blindness regarding the mistakes of the past. This was a point of which Bloch was aware; human nature may be malleable, but the evil runs deep. And yet, "in the negative there are also constructs of the unconstructable, the absolute question: there are unbearable moments of wonder."[17] A Kafka who describes the existential no less than the bureaucratic nightmare with such precision thus makes a utopian contribution precisely insofar he defines what must be overcome. Nor would his work lack an "anticipatory consciousness." Indeed, Brecht captured this when he said that Kafka "saw what was coming without seeing what was there."

Of course, it is highly debatable whether the "anticipatory consciousness" of utopia is inherent within every cultural construct. Bloch, in his ontological justification of aesthetic claims, may well have overstated his case. But he is willing to address the unacknowledged question. What is the worth of art? And his answer juts beyond the immediate effects of a work. He knows that every great work of art remains, "beyond its immediate manifestation, imprinted upon the latency of the other side; that is, upon the content of the future which has not yet appeared during its own time, if not upon the content of a yet unknown final state. For this reason alone, the great works of all times have something to say and, in fact, a far-reaching *novum* which is not noticed in any of them by the previous age."[18]

A project, inherently new, presents itself in the philosophy of Ernst Bloch. Embracing it militates against provincialism and against certainty. This project is founded on hope and a willingness to recognize that the potential for emancipation breaks the constraints of every fixed and finished system. It is the same with art and philosophy; of all the philosophers within the tradition of critical theory, he is the most generous when it comes to aesthetic experience and so perhaps best understands what it means to speak about the integrity of an artwork. His is an essentialism which does not exclude; it doesn't serve the purposes of sexism, racism, or any other form of oppression. His thinking refuses to accept anything as simply given; the articulation of what it means to strive for the "best life" can be found in a hundred rivers and a thousand streams. It calls for a cosmopolitan frame of mind and a refusal to chain the meaning of a work to any set of political aims or particular experiences. Critical interpretation breaks the chains of dogmatism and that enterprise, no less than the quest for utopia, is unending. Thus, following the African sages, Ernst Bloch would maintain towards the end of his long life that "if a story is nothing then it belongs to him who has told it . . . but it is when it is something that it belongs to all of us."[19]

Notes

1 Ernst Bloch, *Geist der Utopie* (Frankfurt, 1973), p. 217.
2 Cf. Ernst Bloch, "A Jubilee for Renegades" in *New German Critique* 4 (Winter, 1975).
3 Ernst Bloch, *Das Prinzip Hoffnung* 3 vols, (Frankfurt, 1973 ed.), vol. 1, p. 163.

4   Bloch, *Das Prinzip Hoffnung*, vol. 2, p. 620.
5   Ernst Bloch, *Verfremdungen* (Frankfurt, 1964), p. 181.
6   Bloch, *Das Prinzip Hoffnung*, vol. 1, p. 230.
7   Ernst Bloch, *Erbschaft dieser Zeit* (Frankfurt, 1962), pp. 104–60.
8   Note, for a more extensive analysis, Stephen Eric Bronner, 'Working Class Politics and the Nazi Triumph' in *Moments of Decision: Political History and the Crises of Radicalism* (New York, 1992), pp. 33ff.
9   Bloch, *Das Prinzip Hoffnung*, vol. 2, p. 590.
10 Ibid., vol. 1, p. 170.
11 Ernst Bloch, *Die Kunst, Schiller zu Sprechen* (Frankfurt, 1969), p. 67.
12 Bloch, *Das Prinzip Hoffnung*, vol. 1, p. 249.
13 Ibid., vol. 1, p. 101.
14 Ibid., vol. 1, p. 285.
15 Ibid., vol. 1, p. 274.
16 Ibid., vol. 1, p. 226.
17 Ibid., vol. 1, p. 351.
18 Ibid., vol. 1, p. 143.
19 Ernst Bloch, *Spuren* (Frankfurt, 1969), p. 127.

5

Horkheimer's Road

Max Horkheimer was born in Zuffenhausen, a suburb of Stuttgart, in 1895. Son of a wealthy Jewish businessman, his early school years were undistinguished and he left the *Gymnasium* to work as an apprentice in his father's textile factory. In 1911, however, he made the acquaintance of Friedrich Pollock who would become an important political economist, an early member of the Institute, and a life-long friend. It was Pollock who introduced Horkheimer to the world of the mind, travelled with him, and supported his desire to marry Rose Riekher, nicknamed Maidon, a non-Jewish woman, against the wishes of his family.[1]

Horkheimer, even in his youth, was influenced by a certain Jewish consciousness. But his views were assimilationist and critical which, in keeping with a certain enlightenment tradition of Judaism, he considered two moments in the same process of emancipation and allowed him to judge the existing order in terms of its own professed ideas of liberalism.[2] His interest in Kant, especially given the popularity of neo-Kantianism in Germany around the turn of the twentieth century,[3] thus makes sense. Horkheimer's dissertation would concern itself with the relation between teleology and the capacity for normative judgment (*Urteilskraft*) in the philosophy of the great Königsberg thinker. The young man would inherit the idea of freedom as pertaining to an individual subject resisting the encroachments of instrumental rationality, a fundamental commitment to reflexivity, and the skepticism concerning absolutist claims which defined Kant's "critical philosophy." Another thinker from the early days, however, would also exert an influence: Schopenhauer. His ethical emphasis on compassion no less than his hatred of violence fit with the historical experience of the Jews and would influence Horkheimer's entire intellectual development. Schopenhauer's *Aphorisms for Worldly Wisdom* had a pronounced impact on the early collection of jottings and impressions, published in 1934 under the pseudonym Heinrich Regius, entitled *Dawn*;[4] indeed, the aphoristic form would later become a hallmark of critical theory.[5] Schopenhauer's *The World as Will and Idea*, with its contempt for the most arrogant assumptions of rationalism, also affected Horkheimer's famous encounter with the Enlightenment. Finally, the striking pessimism of Horkheimer's later essays evidences the influence of the philosopher he already admired in his youth.[6]

Quite obviously, Horkheimer had his differences with both thinkers, and scholars differ over the respective degree of influence exerted by them. Probably neither had the decisive impact on him of Marx.[7] Kant and Schopenhauer, however, always remained with him; one gaining temporary predominance, the other never disappearing entirely. "Concrete" experience and the yearning for an inarticulable alternative seemed constantly at war with a commitment to speculative inquiry and fear of irrationalism.

During the 1930s, of course, Marx enabled him to surmount the limits of these two antinomial thinkers. But, especially following World War II, the tensions between them resurfaced in Horkheimer's worldview. Most interpreters suggest, in fact, that the later philosophical problems encountered by the Frankfurt School were directly related to the reliance on Kant.[8] Probably, the growing influence of Schopenhauer played an even greater role in leading the critical theory of Horkheimer into a *cul de sac*. But, either way, this oversimplifies the matter. Indeed, it was more a matter of his refusal to recognize the philosophical and political incompatibility between their respective approaches no less than those dividing the enlightenment tradition from that of its critics.

Attempts to construct new philosophical standpoints will, of course, always involve a degree of experimentation with the past. But there is a difference between integrating insights from different thinkers and seeking to conflate mutually exclusive assumptions or traditions. Kant emphasized reflexivity, the universal subject, republican values, and a "teleology of hope" while the philosophy of Schopenhauer was framed around intuition, subjectivity, elitism, and a profound pessimism. But, rejecting epistemology and all "systematic" forms of thinking, Horkheimer sought to embrace mutually exclusive assumptions and traditions. Thus, his theory manifested perhaps *the* crucial problem of critical theory.

His thinking changed over the years. But, Max Horkheimer never surrendered his commitment to critical theory. A concern with the negation of suffering and the emancipatory force of free subjectivity never left him. It stayed with him from the very beginning, even before he was drafted into war service where his time was spent in a Munich health clinic. There he heard of the Russian Revolution, experienced the disintegration of the monarchy following Germany's defeat, and anticipated an "association of free people" in the council movement. The war seemingly forecast the cataclysmic end of bourgeois society even while emancipatory hopes were becoming inflamed by the spectre of a new and militant Communist International. And so, for a while, the determinate negation seemed to supplant the indeterminate. The influence of Schopenhauer receded into the background as Horkheimer sought to forge a critical theory fundamentally committed to the idealist strain within the enlightenment tradition and Marxism. A metaphysical pessimism was being tempered by historical optimism. He saw the "objective tendencies" for transforming capitalist society. Nevertheless, even in the beginning, a lingering doubt remained over whether the transformation would ever occur.

It was in the aftermath of the war that Horkheimer, together with Pollock, returned to high school, received a diploma, and decided to pursue academic work. Following a semester at the University of Munich, Horkheimer transferred to Frankfurt where he studied *Gestalt* psychology, economics, music, and philosophy. Ultimately, after taking courses with Edmund Husserl and meeting Martin Heidegger in Freiburg, he wrote his rather routine dissertation – on Kant's *Critique of Judgment* – for Professor Hans Cornelius in whose seminar he also encountered his later collaborator: Theodor Adorno.

The crucial event occurred in 1923. Felix Weil, whose family had made its money as wheat merchants, had long been Horkheimer's friend and, in that year, he funded a new institute to study the history and theory of the workers' movement. Dr Carl Grünberg, a professor of law and politics at Frankfurt University, became its first major director following the death of Albert Gerlach who did not live long enough to make an imprint. *The Institute for Social Research* would become the first independent Marxist institute in Europe.[9] During the early years it reflected Grünberg's somewhat traditional Marxist emphasis on political economy. While Horkheimer worked on *Dawn*, a novel posthumously published as *Out of Puberty* (1974), and started on a book entitled *The Crisis of Marxism* which he never finished, the Institute committed itself to works like Henryk Grossmann's study on capitalist laws of accumulation and collapse, Karl August Wittfogel's inquiry into Chinese economics and society, and the first systematic study of Soviet economic planning by Pollock.

The focus would change, however, after Grünberg suffered a stroke in

1927. Pollock ran the Institute for a year. But the real shift from political economy to critical theory began when Horkheimer took over as director in 1930. That he should have been chosen for the post came as a shock. Horkheimer held no chair.[10] Also, outside of a few articles, very little of his work had by then appeared; in fact, it was only in 1930 that Horkheimer finally published the *Beginnings of the Bourgeois Philosophy of History*. But the only others who could have assumed a leadership role, Grossmann and Pollock, were preoccupied by their political activity with the Communist Party. Horkheimer, for his part, knew the Institute's administrative workings.[11] He had also already become a pronounced influence on the young scholars who attended Institute seminars and would ultimately serve as the core of the "Frankfurt School" – Theodor Adorno, Walter Benjamin, Erich Fromm, Leo Lowenthal, and Herbert Marcuse.

Horkheimer's inaugural lecture was published in the Institute's *Journal for Social Research*.[12] There he articulated the new philosophical and practical project of the Institute: its "supra-disciplinary" approach which, in fusing philosophy with empirical social scientific research, would produce a new materialist enterprise guided by normative assumptions.[13] Such a standpoint, which would inform the major undertakings of the Institute during the 1930s, presupposed a concern with historically situating phenomena as well as an awareness of philosophy's role in shaping the very society it seeks to describe. Positivism and all appeals to ontology, in short traditional philosophy, thus came under attack from the perspective of Horkheimer's new anti-philosophical critical theory.[14] And yet a commitment to the autonomy of theory beyond its relation to any particular worldview was retained as well as a utopian concern with the abolition of all repressive social relations. All this would receive further definition in a series of articles, also originally published by the *Journal*, which included perhaps *the* seminal work for the new philosophical enterprise: "Traditional and Critical Theory."[15]

Critical theory was originally conceived by Horkheimer as a materialist enterprise. But his version of materialism did not reject the moment of critique inherited from idealism. Aware with Marx that practice alone could evidence the truth content of philosophy, and that idealism veiled the practice of exploitation, he nevertheless recognized that the proletarian revolution had betrayed the truth it was meant to actualize. None of this, of course, is inimical to the method of Marxism.[16] And the fact is that Horkheimer was committed to the Communist Party throughout the 1930s and orthodox notions, like the mistaken belief that fascism was the product of "monopoly capital," would often appear in his writings. Nor did his early work evidence any antipathy to science or technology per se; it merely made the claim, quite radical at the time, that science was mediated by the contradictions of society at any given phase of historical development. It is true that, like Schopenhauer, he believed ethics should be grounded in "concrete" needs rather than universal precepts.[17] Nevertheless, the commitment to the enlightenment heritage became manifest in Horkheimer's famous claim that critical theory inherently involves the attempt to actualize the materialist content of idealist philosophy.[18]

"Critical theory," in this sense, was arguably itself a by-product of the theoretical innovations undertaken by Georg Lukács and Karl Korsch in the early twenties.[19] After all, they had already argued that Marxism was not some dogmatic form of economic reductionism with a catechism of theses and predictions. Rather, according to Lukács, Marxism was an inherently "critical" method dedicated to examining the "totality" of social relations and so, in the words of Korsch, committed to "the application of the materialist conception of history to the materialist conception of history itself."[20] Both thinkers had also provided a "dialectical" critique of "vulgar materialism," by which they meant empiricism and positivism, as well as a rejection of all fixed and finished philosophical systems. Then too, their historicist approach resurrected the connection between Marx and Hegel in the most radical terms and placed consciousness, as well as the practical role of ideology and reification, at the forefront of the theory. Indeed, while committed to a "ruthless critique of everything existing" (Marx), they also sought to influence political practice with an eye towards abolishing the alienating effects of the division of labor along with all forms of exploitation.

So where then does Horkheimer's philosophical contribution lie? Most importantly, perhaps, the critical method assumed a genuinely independent status. No longer tied to a party or a given institutional arrangement as a goal, surrendering any connection to teleology or ontological grounding, it brought the unrealized aspects of human freedom to the foreground and raised the question of "compassion" in terms of an anthropological ethic.[21] Horkheimer also sought to explore, without reference to the "privilege" accorded a supposedly preconstituted proletariat, the manner in which consciousness was the product of various practices connected with a broad definition of civil society in its historical unfolding. Of course, building on Lukács and Korsch, neither positivism nor a metaphysics based on the primacy of intuition were considered adequate as a fulcrum for defining truth claims.[22] Facts would now gain their validity only when historically situated and linked to the ideal of the "good society" as a standard with which to confront the present. Horkheimer's critical materialism subsequently anticipated what has now become known as postmetaphysical thinking.[23]

The "identity" between reason and reality, embedded within scientific rationality, became the enemy of this burgeoning "critical theory." And that is precisely because it sought to analyze the processes constituting the given totality along with its repressed possibilities for emancipatory change. Belief in the non-identity of subject and object would soon become *the* hallmark of critical theory and distinguish it, not only from orthodox Marxism, but from the thinking of Korsch and Lukács as well. Horkheimer's essays from the 1930s, materialist though they were, provide perhaps the best articulation of this commitment to preserve the freedom of subjectivity (*Selbsterhaltung*) and so anticipate what would later become the decisive metaphysical preoccupation of "critical theory."[24] He, no less than Adorno or Benjamin, refused to identify the freedom of the subject with any objective philosophical or social arrangement – whether the interests of a party or even a radically democratic system of councils.

This desire to protect subjectivity from an increasingly rationalized world of commodification and instrumental thinking would ultimately demand a new emphasis on the autonomy of theory from practice. But this new concern was a two-edged sword. Critical theory could now benefit from divergent philosophical perspectives, call "civilization" itself into question, and suggest that all citizens – rather than just workers – suffered from an "alienation" that retained a manifold set of social, psychological, and cultural features. The emphasis on the autonomy of theory would, however, also infect the entire enterprise with a basic indeterminacy. And so, without making reference to specific conditions or institutions, the proponents of the new tendency would ultimately criticize both reform and revolution in the name of a complete transcendence of the given.

The use of "critical theory" as a code word, which already becomes evident in Horkheimer's early writings, enabled a certain interpretation of Marxism to enter academic discourse.[25] But even that had its merits. Horkheimer's philosophical move anticipated a new set of conditions. A new age would witness emancipatory theory outstripping the establishmentarian practices of both traditional working-class parties even while the elite university of times past was turning into a mass institution with a new constituency ready to appropriate the insights of radical thought. Thus, the basis for the influence critical theory would come to exert.

As the 1930s drew to an end, a changing relation to even the most undogmatic interpretations of Marxism was beginning to make itself felt.[26] Political economy was being supplanted by social psychology on the part of Horkheimer and his colleagues if only because, in various empirical studies on the working class and the nature of authority, research had shown that only a small minority of members from the left political parties displayed a coherent ideological orientation and were disposed to revolutionary engagement.[27] Works of this sort were obviously meant to explore the conditions that inhibited the revolutionary process. By radically expanding the preconditons for genuine revolutionary action, however, they also gradually fostered a sense that an emancipatory transformation of the status quo was no longer possible. The original intention predominated, of course, so long as the proletariat was still considered the vehicle for revolutionary transformation. Nevertheless, the pessimistic tendency began to grow ever stronger with the soviet thermidor, Hitler's triumph, and Horkheimer's difficult attempts to relocate the Institute in exile.

For all that, however, it was during the 1930s that the Institute made perhaps its greatest contributions to the development of social theory. These were inspired by the work of Horkheimer. "Traditional and Critical Theory," along with a host of other philosophical essays seeking to delineate the stance of the Frankfurt School, were complemented by works like *Studies on Authority and the Family* (1936),[28] on which Horkheimer collaborated with Erich Fromm, as well as his own essays like "The Jews and Europe" (1938) and "The Authoritarian State" (1940).[29] The collaborative enterprise essentially argued that the transfer of socializing functions from the family to various political institutions produced an increase in sadomasochistic tendencies, and a loneliness that craved authority.[30] Inquiries of this sort were complemented by the analyses of how liberalism was giving way to authoritarian institutions and atavistic racism was emerging from capitalism. Each of these works subsequently explores a different dimension of repression. In viewing them as a whole, however, Horkheimer wishes to suggest that the traditional connections existing between civil society and the political realm are being destroyed while ideology is becoming a direct expression of the state. Thus, already in this period, Horkheimer is claiming that a form of unaccountable bureaucratic control is coming to weave all realms of public life into a seamless web of domination.[31]

What binds these works is the belief that liberal capitalism did not and cannot fulfill its emancipatory promise. The enlightenment notion of progress, implicit in Hegelian teleology and inherited by Marxism,[32] is thus called into question along with the ability of the proletariat to break from its ideological bonds and change matters. Qualitative differences between regimes and institutions subsequently begin to fade. It only makes sense, then, that the budding tendency to provide a "critique" of the "whole," without any "positive" institutional referents other than some passing references to the need for workers' councils, should lead to analytic trouble;[33] if socialism is merely the "negative reflection" of what it wishes to oppose, and fascism is a direct product of bourgeois society,[34] each is merely a structurally distinct version of the same authoritarian state.[35] Thus, Horkheimer would influence a new philosophical perspective in which individual freedom is inimical to the *form* of bureaucratic domination existing within advanced industrial society.[36]

Totalitarian society, in this way, became the basis for an analysis of modern society as such.[37] In the totalitarian world, the world of bureaucratic rationality run amok, the relevance of principles and normative concerns for judgment diminish. Such a belief was obviously buttressed by the Munich Agreement of 1938, which sacrificed Czechoslovakia to the Nazis in order to secure an illusory "peace with honor," and the Hitler–Stalin Pact of 1939 that would unleash the Second World War. Enemies became allies as political principle seemingly vanished before the overwhelming impact of political exigencies. Ideological differences between regimes seemed to give way before an instrumental willingness to deal with one another and sanction repression.[38] Ever more surely, along with the relatively uncritical perspective on the Enlightenment of earlier days, the once firm belief in the Soviet Union and the revolutionary mission of the working class fell away. Thus, the original commitment to emancipation became divorced from any concrete vehicle that might bring it about.

But in fact there was no longer such a vehicle. There were no historical referents and, under the circumstances, Horkheimer felt that he could philosophically maintain his commitment to emancipation only by turning away from the given historical reality. This is where the real break with the tradition of Hegel and Marx, the real beginnings of what Adorno would later call "negative dialectics" and what Herbert Marcuse termed "the great refusal" appears. Freedom, from this time on, will no longer appear as the "insight" into "necessity" or the attempt to confront a given period with a determinate, emancipatory possibility born of its own contradictions.[39] It will now become the rejection of "necessity" per se.

Seeking to preserve the lost moment of experience, the revolt against an all-encompassing reification and the implications of historical objectivism, Horkheimer collaborated in developing what might be termed a new "negative" philosophy of history. The historical character of the original "critical" enterprise thus gave way before an approach capable in a new way of differentiating between the "ought" and the "is" or the potentiality of freedom and the actuality of repression."[40] That is what received expression in *Dialectic of Enlightenment*.

Begun in the early forties, completed in 1944, first published in 1947, this book is surely the most important product of the Frankfurt School and the most influential work of critical theory. There is a lingering debate over who wrote what parts and the poor translation only increases its already high level of difficulty for the English speaking audience.[41] The work was essentially the product of ongoing debates between Horkheimer and Adorno, which were taken down in dictation. The book retains numerous unresolved contradictions and Horkheimer, in particular, was wary of republishing it after the Institute had moved back to Germany. It surely seemed too radical for him in retrospect. His activity on the project, however, was no aberration from his other intellectual undertakings.[42] Quite the contrary. Its most basic themes appear again and again; indeed, even if his prose is generally more lucid, the *Dialectic of Enlightenment* is not that alien to what Horkheimer employed in certain other works.

Debating who played the leading role is a matter of purely pedantic interest. It was ultimately a common effort and both authors must ultimately take responsibility for its content no less than a style in which loosely connected essays and cutting aphorisms eschew any systematic mode of presentation and brilliantly juxtapose insights from radically diverse fields. The purpose of the book, however, is clear. Horkheimer and Adorno wished to situate the critique of bourgeois society within an anthropology of domination ("*Urgeschichte der Herrschaft*");[43] they wished to show how progress resulted in barbarism and how the very mythology of domination the Enlightenment sought to destroy reappears as its own product.[44]

Metaphor illuminates a critical philosophy of history. Regression rather than progress is seen as defining human development so that fascism is understood as surpassing "the conditions that prevailed before its coming to power, not in a negative sense, but rather in their positive continuation."[45] All this emerges from a dazzling reading of *The Odyssey* where the "cunning" of instrumental reason is employed by Odysseus, who changes his name to "no one" in order to escape death at the hands of monsters. Sacrifice lies at the base of rationality; the repetition of sacrifice thus disempowers the gods it seeks to exalt even as it undermines subjectivity and freedom. Under any circumstances, *from the very inception of civilization*, an allegory appears in which individuals are condemned to preserve their existence by destroying it. Subjects are now, according to Horkheimer and Adorno, indeed interchangeable.

Nor is that merely the result of any particular social or political system. It is rather a product of the utilitarian attempt to dominate nature through instrumental rationality.[46] Myth had originally sought to control nature and now, in the age of full-blown barbarism, enlightenment would retreat into myth. This is the real if unacknowledged legacy of the Enlightenment which, according to the authors, extends from Kant over Sade to Nietzsche; after all, if Kant undercut the verities of all mythical or normative claims in the name of scientific rationality, Sade could take the next logical step and view all subjects as instrumental means for personal gratification even as Nietzsche, ruthless in the critical application of his skepticism, would ultimately become able to consider all of history and nature as subordinate to the arbitrary will of the subject.

Commodity production underpins this development and, insofar as its form of exchange value transforms qualitative differences into quantitative ones,[47] necessarily turns technical rationality against all forms of metaphysics and normative concerns. The exercise of arbitrary power complements a process which subordinates subjects ever more surely to the mercy of objective forces and strips them of the capacity to make normative judgments. The apogee of this development lies in anti-semitism and the gas chambers.[48] But the dynamic exists just as surely in the modern era with its conformist and profit-driven "culture industry," which seeks the "lowest common denominator" for its products, and subverts the very possibility of reflection or revolution. Thus, "humans pay for the increase of their power with alienation from that over which they exercise their power. Enlightenment behaves towards things as a dictator toward men. He knows them in so far as he can manipulate them."[49]

Dialectic of Enlightenment is clearly a critique of enlightenment undertaken from the standpoint of enlightenment itself; indeed, there is even a certain connection between this book and Adorno's later defense of metaphysics and its unfulfilled promises. The problem is one of thinking in terms of closed systems and dogmatism. Horkheimer and Adorno believed that, in jettisoning the speculative and reflexive component of reason, instrumental rationality actually wound up insulating itself from criticism and becoming a new dogma akin to myth.[50] It only makes sense then that their joint effort wished to preserve the reflexive moment of language from practice which, in turn, became the theoretical justification for the complexity and density of their prose.

In opposition to Nietzsche and the thinkers of postmodernism, however, Horkheimer and Adorno never collapsed cognition into power and consistently rejected a relativism which they saw as connected with historical positivism. They believed that enlightenment rationality violated the reflexive component of language and thus ineluctably aided in the creation of a totalitarian society. Deluded by assumptions of unilinear progress, the sentimentality of humanism,[51] intoxicated by scientific rationality, complacent in its utilitarian domination of nature, the proponents of enlightenment engendered precisely what they wished to suppress.[52] The resurrection of Schopenhauer's influence along with the new pessimistic strain in Horkheimer's thought is fundamentally tied to this new critical attitude towards the Enlightenment and a view which, in contrast to the earlier writings, holds that "technical rationality is the rationality of domination itself."

Horkheimer expanded on the consequences of this claim in *The Eclipse of Reason* (1947). Speculative philosophy might still hold out the idea of a final reconciliation between humanity and nature, the possibilities of the individual and a society that might actualize them. But he maintained that every object, including society, was increasingly becoming immutable and "self-identical" – or equivalent to the objective categories that define it – in the thinking of pragmatists and positivist successors to enlightenment philosophy committed to eliminating all utopian or speculative criteria of judgment and identifying technological progress with progress as such. Nor is idealism free of sin; viewing progress as a phenomenon of the mind, subordinating concrete experience to abstract categories and the theoretical imagination to fixed modes of thought, its metaphysical presuppositions led to the surrender of any power it might have had to protect concrete individuality against the incursions of instrumental reason. Indeed, these were the ways in which enlightenment turned reason into a "slave of the passions."

Dialectic of Enlightenment unquestionably remains a landmark in radical thought. Placing the individual at the center of a dialectical analysis, employing metaphor and rejecting positivist criteria of truth, Horkheimer and Adorno forwarded an anthropological perspective which revealed how the instrumental domination of nature expelled freedom from the historical process even as it threatened to invade the realm of the subject. Their analysis of the "culture industry" would profoundly influence the discourse on media and society. Horkheimer and Adorno turned conformism into more than a merely bohemian concern and the instrumental colonization of everyday life into a political issue. Then too, anticipating postmodern philosophy, their work is an assault on the need for epistemological congruence and shatters the complacency which the workers' movement traditionally accorded the Enlightenment. It also provides one of the earliest attempts not only to link Marx with Freud, but also with Nietzsche, and calls upon philosophic radicalism finally to surrender those traditional optimistic assumptions about civilization which it can no longer sustain. Horkheimer and Adorno, for perhaps the first time in the Marxian discourse, make plain that the price demanded by all teleological notions of progress is too high.[53]

Dialectic of Enlightenment, however, remains a *chef d'oeuvre manqué*. Nagging questions of even more fundamental importance, do not vanish. Is this work merely an extrapolation of conditions pertaining in the 1930s and 1940s into the future? Is the concept of enlightenment defined with logical precision? Did the Enlightenment really turn against itself or did the contradictions of capitalist society engender a reactionary response to it? Does a viable image of the Enlightenment emerge? Does this critical analysis subvert any emancipatory attempt to deal with the bourgeois past or the subsequent history of philosophy and political practice?

Horkheimer and Adorno viewed the Enlightenment as the most advanced ideological expression of a rising bourgeoisie seeking to establish a new production process and solidify its political control. But they also saw it as part of an anthropological assault on theological thinking and superstition. They never recognized, however, that it is more than either or the two in combination. Identifying "enlightenment" merely with a debunking of what stands beyond the scientific domination of nature and what Kant called "pure reason" ultimately results in the very reductionism and "reified" form of philosophical inquiry that Horkheimer and Adorno putatively sought to oppose.

Their image of the Enlightenment is arbitrary and one-sided. Emphasizing its connection with technological rationality, in fact, a genuine historical analysis is never undertaken.[54] Horkheimer and Adorno forget how the enlightenment concern with universality became tied to republicanism, socialism, and internationalism;[55] how the rule of law was designed to protect the individual and constrain arbitrary power; and how the commitment to scientific knowledge fostered tolerance and openness to change rather than mere contentment with the status quo. Enlightenment political philosophy was predicated on the accountability of state power while its greatest figures such as Lessing and Locke, Hume and Kant, Diderot and Franklin, were fundamentally committed to liberal beliefs. The claim that "enlightenment" gave rise to fascism is, in normative terms, simply wrong: there is hardly a single modern antifascist value which does not stem from the period of the great bourgeois revolutions that extended from England, to America, to France.[56]

Just as it is a mistake to locate the ideological source of fascism in the Enlightenment, however, so is it mistaken to view the phenomenon as a simple outgrowth of bourgeois civil society. Not only was fascism a self-conscious ideological response to liberalism and Marxism, democracy and socialism, but the atavistic anger of its mass base – located in *pre-capitalist* classes like the petit bourgeoisie and peasantry – was fundamentally directed against the two dominant classes of the modern production process: the capitalists and the proletariat.[57] Neither from the standpoint of intellectual nor political history, let alone class analysis, does the interpretation offered by Horkheimer and Adorno make sense. The tale of Odysseus, in which the destruction of subjectivity becomes the only way to preserve the self, thus ignores the obvious. It was not instrumental reason which brought about fascism and destroyed the ability of the individual to make normative judgments, but rather real movements with one set of values intent on eliminating those committed to *qualitatively* different ones.

The approach of Horkheimer and Adorno obscures this. For, even if historical reconstruction is inherently a hermeneutical project mediated by inherited guilt and allegorical or utopian modes of reasoning, it must still retain "objective" or institutional points of reference; indeed, without such referents, social interests become distorted and politics itself becomes a purely arbitrary enterprise. Horkheimer and Adorno, of course, were to offer a "radical" external perspective with which to contest all competing standpoints. But, from the start, the attempt to unify qualitatively different phenomena under a single rubric could only lead to pseudo-dialectical sophistry.[58] Communist theoreticians, interestingly enough, were always masters at this game. They liked to see fascism, committed to the destruction of parliamentary democracy, as the product of "monopoly capital" – which nevertheless putatively ruled the bourgeois democracies of the interwar period.[59] Then too, all "superficial" differences notwithstanding, such a stance allowed them to castigate social democrats as "twin brothers" of the Nazis in the years preceding the Popular Front of 1936 – which means nothing less than that Leon Blum and Charles Maurras or Rudolf Hilferding and Joseph Goebbels were "really" one and the same.[60]

Horkheimer, even after surrendering any lingering belief in the revolutionary character of the Soviet Union, provided a new twist to this former communist way of thinking.[61] The "integral statism" of his deeply pessimistic essay "The Authoritarian State,"[62] with its suggestion that socialism has lost its internal connection with historical progress and that a burgeoning bureaucracy is eradicating qualitative differences between governmental forms and ideologies, serves to justify the claim of *Dialectic of Enlightenment* that liberalism engenders fascism.[63] Historical analysis of the relation between liberalism and fascism, no less than any political discussion of the differences between them, vanish in favor of philosophical and anthropological abstractions.

And these are only reinforced by the decision of the authors to consider Sade, Schopenhauer, and Nietzsche as an extension of enlightenment thought.[64] Nor does it help to claim that Horkheimer and Adorno emphasized that "social freedom is inseparable from enlightened thought," for their real point was that a "self-destruction" of the Enlightenment took place."[65] The Nazis knew, of course, that both positivism and idealism were intrinsically connected to the liberal tradition and that, whatever the degree of purposeful misrepresentation, the roots of their own ideology lay in the vitalist critique of enlightenment thought by many of the same thinkers like Schopenhauer, Bergson, and Nietzsche embraced by Horkheimer and Adorno.

Whatever the "superficial" differences between thinkers, however, the authors of *Dialectic of Enlightenment* sought to demonstrate their claim by broadening the "Enlightenment" to include its greatest and most self-conscious critics. Remaining true to the thrust of this book, in fact, Adorno would later write that "not least among the tasks now confronting thought is that of placing all the reactionary arguments against Western culture in the service of progressive enlightenment."[66] Indeed, this would become crucial to the famous analysis of the "culture industry" offered by many of the most important proponents of critical theory.

Too often it has been forgotten that a critique can be leveled from different political perspectives and serve different purposes; indeed, for this very reason, situating it within a philosophical tradition becomes very important. Rousseau, Mill, and Gramsci all observed the trivialization of culture and – perhaps because they never lost track of their political projects – did not fall prey to elitism. The modernist critique of mass culture embraced by Horkheimer and Adorno, however, is not really indebted to them. It begins on the Right with Nietzsche and a host of anti-enlightenment critics who evidenced a peculiar brand of aristocratic radicalism. They too wished to preserve subjectivity from the "lowest common denominator" or a world increasingly dominated by crass materialism and technological rationality. No less than Horkheimer and Adorno, they expressed their contempt for democracy, "the masses" and "the herd mentality." They were also quick to note the false sense of immediacy produced by various fads and what was termed "the loss of *niveau*." No less than Horkheimer and Adorno, they despised the conformism of mass society and were obsessed by modernity's manifold threats to subjectivity.[67]

Of course, the authors of *Dialectic of Enlightenment* viewed cultural developments as interconnected with a given system of production. If they were critical of popular culture it was because they believed it subverted genuine autonomy and deadened the spirit of emancipation. Horkheimer and Adorno preferred "classic" and technically complex works.[68] But that was based on their belief that such works alone fostered the capacity for reflexive discernment and the remembrance of past horrors in the face of declining educational standards and perpetually changing fashions.[69] Artworks which seek to express radical political messages are seen as merely fueling the hegemonic power of the status quo by creating a false sense of liberty and fostering a relativism in keeping with what Herbert Marcuse would term "repressive tolerance."

Thus, the extent to which a work is made popular by the culture industry is the extent to which its critical or emancipatory potential is absorbed.

But is it really true that commodification exhausts the critical potential of an artwork? Is Charlie Chaplin merely an example of "affirmative culture"? Or is he no different than the Three Stooges? That Horkheimer and Adorno do not provide any categories for differentiating between works is a weakness of their social theory of culture. It is true enough that the public realm of discourse has narrowed, that there is a literacy crisis, and that the general level of cultural production has fallen. Horkheimer and Adorno were obviously correct in believing that most works produced by the culture industry deaden the intellect.

But their analysis always rests at the "form" of commodification to which they reduce all popular works; thus, in line with the philosophical thrust of *Dialectic of Enlightenment*, Adorno could write that "every visit to the cinema leaves me, against all my vigilance, stupider and worse."[70] A metacritique results. Without categories capable of drawing distinctions between popular works, ironically, the aesthetic vanishes within the sociological. Content to highlight the repressive character of mass culture per se, they ignored the restrictive and undemocratic conditions under which it is produced and the manner in which lowered cultural demands are generated by the current division of labor. It was enough for Horkheimer to note that, if the culture industry comes to define the public realm, then the moment of emancipatory resistance will enter the tenuous domain of a private experience constantly threatened by the extension of technical rationality.[71] Thus, interestingly enough, he was actually less sanguine about the emancipatory role of aesthetics than either Adorno or Marcuse in their later writings.

Talk about the "integration" of such works, however, only begs the question of whether they were really rendered impotent or whether they actually helped change the "hegemonic" system and were only then turned into museum pieces. Questions of this sort, however, are never entertained in *Dialectic of Enlightenment*. The whole is what counts and, increasingly, it is defined by a reifying form of instrumental rationality. Concrete attempts to transform the existing order and its network of significations, given the integrative propensities of the culture industry, become spurious by definition – always beside the point. Solidarity is conformity; enlightenment has become deception. A single option remains and Adorno embraced it with his claim that "only insofar as it withdraws from Man can culture be faithful to man."

Critique talks itself into exhaustion. It retreats into what Thomas Mann and then Lukács termed a "power protected inwardness." It reproduces the very conditions it claims to contest. Political judgments, from this perspective, can only appear ad hoc. Even the concept of utopia, from which critique ultimately derives its power, becomes subverted. Originally it retained a sense of the institutional prerequisites necessary for the construction of an emancipated order. It was as much a regulative idea for action as a vision of emancipation. Now, however, it can only appear as a reified other. Horkheimer will play a leading role in this respect. His later writings, in fact, transform utopia into a quasi-religious "longing for the totally other" (*das Sehnsucht für das ganz Andere*). Thus, with the actual possibility for emancipation precluded, his enduring commitment to the concept would become coupled with the most debilitating pessimism.

Horkheimer was scarred by the war and the revelations about the concentration camps. He had observed the weaknesses of Weimar; he had been exiled by Hitler and betrayed by Stalin. Ever more surely, in fact, he began to emphasize ill-defined concepts like "marginality" and "admirable small groups" whose irrelevance to the "apparatus of oppression" has made possible their "escape to truth." Solidarity would become universal by empathizing with "those standing outside" and, following Schopenhauer, compassion would become the foundation for ethics. This standpoint anticipated much of the social theory later elaborated by Herbert Marcuse. Nevertheless, insofar as the revolutionary vehicle became identified with the individual will rather than class, the notion of emancipation changed.

It is irrelevant whether some of his later speeches and radio talks had an optimistic ring, whether the totally administered society projects vague tendencies towards universal solidarity, or even whether the father of critical theory called upon the rebellious students of the sixties to recognize the freedom offered them by the West in contrast to the East.[72] His postwar view of advanced industrial society, even as it derived from the earlier collaboration with Adorno, lost its radical sense of purpose. His skepticism in the postwar era now extended to democracy itself. He may have continued to think of himself as "radical." But, in fact, he sought stability rather than revolutionary transformation or even structural reform. This hidden desire often gave Horkheimer's political admonitions in the years to come a sanctimonious and conservative quality.

His social position had also changed from the time he first left Germany. Horkheimer's academic standing in the United States increased after the Institute undertook to publish a five volume series entitled *Studies in Prejudice*, for which Horkheimer – collaborating with Samuel Flowerman of the American Jewish Committee – wrote the Foreword. The *Studies* would result in at least three classic texts: *Rehearsal for Destruction* by Paul Massing, *Prophets of Deceit* by Leo

Lowenthal and Norbert Guterman, and *The Authoritarian Personality* by Theodor Adorno and numerous other collaborators. It only made sense, then, that the newly constituted West German State should have eagerly sought the return of the Institute. The offer was generous and, after much agonizing and haggling, Horkheimer agreed. The Institute, amid a good deal of fanfare, relocated to Frankfurt in 1949.[73] Then, in 1955, Horkheimer and Adorno decided to publish the *Frankfurter Beiträge zur Soziologie*,[74] and thus made popular the previously unknown publications of the *Journal for Social Research*. They became major intellectual figures in the postwar order and Horkheimer, who ultimately became chancellor of Frankfurt University, collected a coterie of remarkably talented students which included Jürgen Habermas and Alfred Schmidt.

The influence of critical theory on even more radical intellectuals like Rudi Dutschke and Hans-Jürgen Krahl, two of the most prominent figures in the European uprisings of 1968, would also prove profound. They admired the stance which seemingly called upon them to contest both liberal reformism and soviet communism; they believed that the power exerted by bureaucratic rationality demanded a new emphasis on participatory democracy, normative judgment, and what Marcuse appropriately termed a "new sensibility." They saw the culture industry and its mode of manipulation as eliciting the need for a radical transformation of everyday life, a genuine "cultural revolution," and an openness to the contributions of the Third World in which various movements were undertaking the difficult struggle for national self-determination. They agreed with Adorno that "the whole is false."

But when radical students shouted slogans, like "Power to the Imagination!" or "Be Realistic, Demand the Impossible!", Horkheimer reacted angrily. Again and again, his *Notizen* evidence concern with the supposedly totalitarian threat engendered by the student uprisings and the fear of impending chaos brought on by excessive democracy.[75] A caricature of the movement appears in his writings. There is little enough said about the civil rights movement; about what Eisenhower himself saw as the threat from the "military–industrial complex;" about poverty; the dynamics that led to Vietnam; the tumbling of Pompidou; or the attempt to transform everyday life.

Horkheimer's arguments were actually no different than those raised by a host of less philosophically talented mainstream conservatives. They too warned of abandoning values; they too talked about political realism with respect to a foreign policy, a war, and a defense budget that made no sense; they too employed old-fashioned communist sophistry with their hysterical claims that the critics of the West, naively and unconsciously, served the interests of the East; in search of security they too raised the banner of family, religion, community. And, forgetting the criticisms that he himself had once leveled against these same ways of thinking, Horkheimer no longer wished to argue that "the critical theorist's vocation is the struggle to which his thought belongs. Thought is not something independent, to be separated from this struggle."[76]

It was as if, like Luther, he feared the practical implications of his own ideas. The critical perspective withered; the arguments sounded less and less original. And so the rebels could only shrug their shoulders when, in articles like "Critical Theory Yesterday and Today" (1970), Horkheimer claimed that a fundamental contradiction existed between the quest for individual freedom and the call for equality.[77] The more discerning knew that this argument had already been made – and made better – by the most important exponents of laissez-faire capitalism like Friedrich von Hayek and Milton Friedman. Nor were they misled. John Stuart Mill knew that the practical exercise of democracy is facilitated by economic equality and that freedom is not furthered by treating individuals as means to an end since inequality will then follow logically.

But Horkheimer forgot about Mill along with those other enlightenment thinkers like Locke, Kant, Jefferson, and Paine, who exhibited similar concerns. Schopenhauer could now take center stage; contradictions, such as that between freedom and equality, must prevent the new society from coming into being. Practice must now stand paralyzed by theory; conveniently, in complete agreement with the ultra-left, Horkheimer's stance allowed him to condemn all action by the Left as not radical enough. His own politics during the postwar era reflected the truth of his insight that *les extrêmes se touchent.*"[78]

Political conservatism became justified through philosophical radicalism. He maintained his hatred of nationalism and militarism, and there were still isolated moments of bravery; thus, in spite of his support for the state of Israel, Horkheimer never surrendered to the more extreme forms of Zionism and openly criticized the Eichmann Trial.[79] But, in keeping with his new prominence, his writings on returning to Germany generally adopted a decidedly cautious and anti-political tone.[80] He had little use for Marcuse's "marginal groups' theory," the "new sensibility" of the rebels, "surplus repression," or theoretical attempts to break with the "reality principle." Horkheimer neither embraced ontology, which explains his distance from Ernst Bloch, nor retreated into aesthetics in the manner of Adorno. Nevertheless, he was unwilling to abandon utopia and surrender the idea of a radical alternative to instrumental rationality.[81]

There is a sense, then, in which the end lay in the beginning. The moment of indeterminacy that had plagued critical theory from the first now reached fruition. And so too did the commitment to allegory. With all aesthetic and strictly philosophical avenues closed, remembering the betrayal of one revolution and fearing the next, with thoughts of Auschwitz and the atomic bomb indelibly etched on his consciousness, with progress still an illusion and subjectivity still endangered, only religion could keep alive the vision of "the wholly other." Such is the solution to the "enigma" of his final theoretical choice and his philosophical decline.[82] Horkheimer looked to the Old Testament which taught that, just as the attempt to portray God is prohibited, knowledge of the true and the good is inaccessible. The injunction against idolatry is an injunction against false idols; Horkheimer's theological stance thus retains certain elements of the demystifying and defetishizing stance originally associated with critical theory. Nevertheless, while the younger Horkheimer was too much the materialist to believe that a perception of the absolute is the condition for judgment, the old man now wished to employ the sacred to preserve a moment of hope from the profane.[83]

Yearning for God,[84] for the "wholly other," served as the foundation for a happiness denied by the world and the common interest of humanity in abolishing suffering. The social function of this theological standpoint was obviously to provide a new foundation for morality.[85] Solidarity, or perhaps a group of secular parishioners, would somehow translate into a "community striving for a better existence;" Horkheimer thus anticipated the concern of a contemporary communitarian theorist like Michael Walzer with establishing the "moral sentiment" and what Richard Rorty now conceives as a common desire to eliminate "cruelty." But Horkheimer's stance is more systematically elaborated and more existentially concrete. The image of the other, confirming the insight of Schopenhauer that earthly happiness always remains incomplete, both makes existence bearable and maintains the inability to end suffering in secular terms.[86] And so, where Kant postulated a God who justified hope given the limits of absolute knowledge, Horkheimer introduced an indeterminate yearning for an inexpressible alternative to provide the individual with consolation in an otherwise hopeless world.

The tension in the later work of Horkheimer derives from the fact that it must negate immanent, historical, social conditions and still contest the whole in the name of the other. He continued to reject all ideologies by which the individual would become reconciled to suffering and employed a notion of "complete justice" to challenge the reality of injustice. But, for all that, a profound pessimism obviously inspired the "negative theology."[87] His new morality never translated into an ethic capable of dealing with practical problems. There are no categories of judgment; it forwards no positive injunctions nor foundations for institutional criticism. At the same time, whatever its indebtedness to Judaism or Christianity,[88] the new standpoint offers neither the prospect of salvation nor the reality of community. Horkheimer's "negative theology," for this reason, can neither meet the existential needs of religiosity nor the secular demands of the dialectician.

Of course, his concern in the later writings is – formally at least – the same which inspired so much of his early work and Dialectic of Enlightenment: the preservation of the self under conditions of total administration. And the argument proceeds apace. For where there is barely a self to preserve and no historical or political vehicle to secure its happiness, dialectically – or better paradoxically – reason projects the need for faith. Only through faith can the victims of progress gain something for their sacrifice; only through faith is it possible to maintain the "yearning that the murderer not triumph over his innocent victim."[89] But this "yearning" translates into nothing concrete. It recedes behind the ontology of Bloch and the more radical utopian promise of Benjamin's negative philosophy of history. It loses the critical edge and, frankly, verges on the trite and the sentimental. The world is left as it is. Thus, far more than the philosophy of the Enlightenment, Horkheimer's critical theory with its initial commitment to reflection and emancipation ultimately turned into its opposite.

It is a mistake, however, to remember Horkheimer only by his later political and theoretical efforts. His influence was felt by every major current within critical theory as he championed the moment of negativity in transforming the understanding first of philosophy then history and then theology. His enterprise was marked by genuine cosmopolitanism, extraordinary intellectual range, and a profound humanism. He was among the first to confront the radical implications of the divorce between theory and practice in the dialectical project. He also drew perhaps the most radical consequences of Benjamin's insight that emancipation must involve a break with progress and history.

Even if others remained more true to the radical implications of the original project, Horkheimer always sought to delineate the correspondence between a historical milieu and its own delusionary self-understanding. He always hated authoritarianism and sophistry. He always prized the individual rather than an abstract revolutionary "subject" like the class or the nation. And, with this concern in mind, he employed the critical method to assault the shibboleths of enlightenment, science, the family, and the bureaucratic state. Willing to call the most basic values of modernity into question, both organizationally and philosophically, he helped create a framework in which intellectuals might further the original critical undertaking. Nor did he ever lose his love for the treasures buried in the great philosophical traditions of the past. And the commitment to an alternative, even when he could no longer find its secular anchor, stayed with him to the end. In fact, until his death in 1973, Max Horkheimer always sought to capture that speculative moment of knowledge which shows how reality falls short of what we can imagine and what the powerless so often unknowingly demand.

Notes

1 Helmut Gumnior und Rudolf Ringgüth, *Max Horkheimer: in Selbstzeugnissen und Bilddokumenten* (Hamburg, 1973), pp. 7–27; Rolf Wiggershaus, *Die Frankfurter Schule: Geschichte, Theoretische Entwicklung, Politische Bedeutung* (Munich, 1988), pp. 55–67.

2 Judith Marcus and Zoltan Tar, "The Judaic Element in the Teachings of the Frankfurt School" in *The Leo Baeck Institute Yearbook* (London, 1986), p. 344.

3 Andrew Arato, "The Neo-Idealist Defense of Subjectivity" in *Telos* 21 (Fall, 1974), pp. 108–61; also, Barbara Drygulski Wright, "Sublime Ambition: Art, Politics, and Ethical Idealism in the Cultural Journals of German Expressionism" in *Passion and Rebellion: The Expressionist Heritage* eds Stephen Eric Bronner and Douglas Kellner (New York, 1988), pp. 82–112.

4 Max Horkheimer, *Dawn and Decline: Notes 1926–31 & 1950–69* trans. Michael Shaw (New York, 1978).

5 "If today the subject is vanishing, aphorisms take upon themselves the duty to consider the evanescent itself as essential. They insist, in opposition to Hegel's practice and yet in accordance with his thought, on negativity." Theodor Adorno, *Minima Moralia: Reflections from a Damaged Life* trans. E. F. N. Jephcott (London, 1974), p. 16.

6 "Metaphysical pessimism, always an implicit element in every genuinely materialist philosophy, had always been congenial to me. My first acquaintance with philosophy came through Schopenhauer; my relation to Hegel and Marx and my desire to understand and change social reality have not obliterated my experience of his philosophy, despite the political opposition between these men. The better, the right kind of society is a goal which has a sense of guilt entwined about it." Max Horkheimer, Preface to *Critical Theory: Selected Essays* (New York, 1982), p. ix.

7 Horkheimer, especially toward the end of the 1920s, "understood himself as an advocate of Marxian theory in the sense that he viewed his position as an extension of a line that went from the French Enlightenment over Hegel and Marx." Wiggershaus, *Die Frankfurter Schule*, p. 66.

8 Frank Hartmann, *Max Horkheimers materialistischer Skeptizismus: Frühe Motive der Kritischen Theorie* (Frankfurt, 1990).

9 The idea for the Institute emerged from a meeting – "the first Marxist work week" – of about two dozen intellectuals who sought to determine the character of "true" Marxism in the aftermath of the war when new philosophical perspectives were emerging amid the more obvious

battles between social democrats and communists. Participants in this work week, nearly half of whom would later work with the institute in one capacity or another, included such prominent thinkers as Karl Korsch, Georg Lukács, Paul Massing, Julian Gomperz, Karl Wittfogel, and Friedrich Pollock. Ibid., pp. 23ff.

10   It is important to note that, from the beginning, the Institute was directly associated with Frankfurt University and the director had to hold a chair (*Lehrstuhl*). Grünberg's chair was given to the political economist, Adolph Löwe, while Paul Tillich used his influence to establish a chair in social philosophy for Horkheimer. ibid, p. 50.

11   In the final analysis, "institutionally and cognitively, Max Horkheimer occupied the dominant position within the circle . . . [N]ot every member could play an equally influential role within the group, suggesting an overall structure in which a figure of cognitive leadership systematically integrated the various disciplines. This group structure was in turn based on the Circle's institutional substructure – on the 'dictatorship of the director' that was anchored in the Institute's statutes and often invoked by Horkheimer." Helmut Dubiel, *Theory and Politics: Studies in the Development of Critical Theory* trans. Benjamin Gregg (Cambridge, Mass., 1985), p. 184.

12   For the text, see Max Horkheimer, "The State of Contemporary Social Philosophy and the Tasks of an Institute for Social Research in *Critical Theory and Society: A Reader* eds Stephen Eric Bronner and Douglas Kellner (New York, 1989), pp. 25–36.

13   "Horkheimer attempted to overcome the crisis of Marxism by attempting to link it to modern developments in the realm of 'bourgeois' science and philosophy. Max Weber's refusal to speculate about any predefined meaning for the world was combined with Heidegger's rejection of any trans-historical essence for humanity; the attempt by Lukács and Korsch to preserve the philosophical elements in Marxism were combined with [Max] Scheler's integration of empirical knowledge into philosophy." Wiggershaus, *Die Frankfurter Schule* p. 53; also cf. Alfons Söllner, *Geschichte und Herrschaft: Studien zur materialistischen Sozialwissenschaft 1929–1942* (Frankfurt, 1979), pp. 30ff.

14   Cf. Hauke Brunkhorst, "Dialektischer Positivismus des Glucks" in *Zeitschrift für philosophische Forschung* vol. 39, no. 3, 1985, pp. 353ff.

15   Also, for a basic analysis of the concept, cf. Herbert Marcuse, "Philosophy and Critical Theory" in *Critical Theory and Society*, pp. 58–73.

16   Cf. Douglas Kellner, *Critical Theory, Marxism and Modernity* (Cambridge, 1989), pp. 22ff.

17   In 1932, Horkheimer could also still see technological rationality as value-neutral. Crucial for him in overcoming the "crisis" brought on by the great depression is the need to redirect productive forces from the perspective of a new set of socio-political relations. Cf. Max Horkheimer, "Notes on Science and the Crisis" in *Critical Theory: Selected Essays*, pp. 3–10.

18 Horkheimer, "Materialism and Metaphysics" in *Critical Theory: Selected Essays*, pp. 45–6.

19 Leszek Kolokawski, *Main Currents of Marxism* 3 vols (New York, 1978), vol. 3, pp. 341ff; Dick Howard, *The Marxian Legacy* (New York, 1977), pp. 100–1.

20 Karl Korsch, *Marxism and Philosophy* trans. Fred Halliday (London, 1970), p. 92.

21 Note the essay of 1933 by Max Horkheimer, "Materialism and Morality" in *Telos* 69 (Fall, 1986), pp. 85–118; also, Herbert Schnädelbach, "Max Horkheimer and the Moral Philosophy of German Idealism" in *Telos* 66 (Winter, 1985–6), pp. 81–104.

22 Max Horkheimer, "The Latest Attack on Metaphysics" in *Critical Theory: Selected Essays*, pp. 132ff.

23 Jürgen Habermas, "Max Horkheimer: Zur Entwicklungsgeschichte seines Werkes" in *Texte und Kontexte* (Frankfurt, 1992), p. 92.

24 Cf. Heidrun Hesse, *Vernunft und Selbstbehauptung: Kritische Theorie als Kritik der neuzeitlichen Rationalität* (Frankfurt, 1986), pp. 137ff.

25 Howard, *The Marxian Legacy*, p. 91.

26 Kellner, *Critical Theory, Marxism and Modernity*, pp. 83ff.

27 Dubiel, *Theory and Politics*, p. 13.

28 Horkheimer, "Studies on Authority and the Family" in *Critical Theory: Selected Essays*, pp. 47–128.

29 These essays are translated and reprinted respectively in *Critical Theory and Society*, pp. 77–94 and *Telos* 15 (Spring, 1973), pp. 3–20.

30 A similar line of reasoning, stressing the weakening of the ego produced by the modern substitution of television for the patriarchal father, would reoccur in Herbert Marcuse, "The Obsolescence of the Freudian Concept of Man" in *Five Lectures: Psychoanalysis, Politics, and Utopia* trans. Jeremy J. Shapiro and Shierry M. Weber (Boston, 1970), pp. 44ff.

31 Following the seminal essays of Pollock, Horkheimer and Adorno could ultimately come to view "state socialism" as one variant within a broader trend towards bureaucratic domination and – with the belief that the preservation of profitable accumulation rested on the transformation of the state into a capitalist in its own right – an "economic justification for considering an economic analysis of society no longer necessary or even possible." Dubiel, *Theory and Politics*, p. 81. Also, Friedrich Pollock "State Capitalism: Its Possibilities and Limitations" in *Critical Theory and Society*, pp. 95ff; "Is National Socialism a New Order?" in *Studies in Philosophy and Social Science* 9 (1941).

32 "According to Hegel, the stages of the World Spirit follow one another with logical necessity and none can be omitted. In this respect Marx remained true to him. History is represented as an indivisible development. The new cannot begin before its time. However, the fatalism of both philosophers refers to the past only. Their metaphysical error, namely that history obeys a defined law, is cancelled by their historical error, namely that such a law was fulfilled at its appointed time." Horkheimer, "The Authoritarian State," *Telos* 15 (Spring, 1973), p. 11.

33 Thus, Horkheimer will compare the Western working-class organiza-
    tions with those of the Soviet Union, which is defined in terms of
    "integral statism;" the "integral state" was, of course, originally a
    concept employed by the far Right. Ibid., pp. 7–8.

34 Also, Herbert Marcuse, "The Struggle against Liberalism in the Total-
    itarian View of the State (1934)" in *Negations: Essays in Critical Theory*
    (Boston, 1968).

35 Admittedly, Horkheimer believes that the form of political regime
    matters to the individual and that the degree to which the state remains
    dependent on private capital is crucial. But actual criteria for *political*
    differentiation are external to the theory; they recede before the
    emphasis placed on bureaucratic rationalization and the belief that state
    capitalism is creating the conditions for its own demise. Interestingly
    enough, however, this same indeterminacy allows Horkheimer to
    envision a situation in which "two friend–enemy blocs of states . . . will
    dominate the world . . . and (find) in their reciprocal threat to each other
    new grounds for an arms race." Howard, *The Marxian Legacy*, p. 111.

36 Thus, for Horkheimer and other major proponents of the Frankfurt
    School, the fascist form of state capitalism merely completes the
    historical logic of late-capitalism, itself a product of liberal capitalism,
    and Hitler's Germany reflects the basic tendency inherent in all Western
    industrial nations. Dubiel, *Theory and Politics*, pp. 44ff and *passim*.

37 This definition of totalitarianism, as the absence of intervening institu-
    tions to protect the individual from the state, is already indicated in
    Horkheimer's "The End of Reason" in *The Frankfurt School Reader* eds
    Andrew Arato and Eike Gebhardt (New York, 1982), pp. 36–9.

38 Thus, in spite of his obvious anti-fascism, Horkheimer could mirror the
    sentiments of his circle for the duration of the war by writing on the day
    of its outbreak that "the frightful thing about this situation is that given
    the present constellations and rallying cries, there is not a single one
    toward which one could feel even distantly sympathetic." Cited in
    Dubiel, *Theory and Politics*, p. 76. Also, Horkheimer, *Dawn and Decline*,
    p. 152.

39 Horkheimer seeks to provide a material foundation for this claim by
    stating that "European history is finished and therefore positivism is
    right. There is no escape except machinery. All concepts that are
    irreducible to facts are meaningless." Horkheimer, *Dawn and Decline*,
    p. 173.

40 "The research program of the 1930s stood and fell with its historical–
    philosophical trust in the rational potential of bourgeois culture – a
    potential that would be released in social movements under the pressure
    of developed forces of production. Ironically, however, the critiques of
    ideology carried out by Horkheimer, Marcuse, and Adorno confirmed
    them in the belief that culture was losing its autonomy in postliberal
    societies and was being incorporated into the machinery of the
    economic-administrative system. The development of productive

forces, and even critical thought itself, was moving more and more into a perspective of bleak assimilation to their opposites. In the totally administered society only instrumental reason, expanded into a totality, found embodiment: everything that existed was transformed into a real abstraction. In that case, however, what was taken hold of and deformed by these abstractions escaped the grasp of empirical inquiry." Jürgen Habermas, *The Theory of Communicative Action* trans. Thomas McCarthy (Boston, 1987), 2 vols, vol. 2, p. 382

41 Cf. Robert Hullot-Kentor, "Back to Adorno" in *Telos* 81 (Fall, 1989), pp. 5ff.

42 Cf. Jürgen Habermas, "Nachwort" to *Dialektik der Aufklärung* (Frankfurt, 1986).

43 Söllner, *Geschichte und Herrschaft*, pp. 190ff.

44 It is important to note that the concept of "enlightenment" has two meanings. Horkheimer made this point clearly in his lectures of 1959–60 at Frankfurt when he wrote: "On the one hand, it means the philosophical tendencies in England, France, and Germany which developed a specific theory of knowledge in opposition to the dominant theological views . . . On the other hand, and more decisively, one understands under enlightenment the total philosophical thinking which, in contrast to mythology has led the battle to achieve clarity over its own ideas and make concepts as well as judgments visible to everyone. Clarity, hence the name enlightenment: philosophy as struggle with error and superstition is also and always enlightenment . . . Both meanings are bound with one another." Max Horkheimer, "Die Aufklärung" in *Gesammelte Werke* (Frankfurt, 1989) vol. 13, p. 571.

45 Dubiel, *Theory and Politics*, p. 71.

46 In a work written for Horkheimer's fiftieth birthday, *Dialectic of Enlightenment* is described as a "*dialogue intérieur* [wherein] there is not a motif . . . that does not belong as much to Horkheimer as to him who found the time to formulate it . . . in principle everyone, however powerful, is an object . . . [so that] with the dissolution of liberalism, the truly bourgeois principle, that of competition, far from being overcome has passed from the objectivity of the social process into the composition of its colliding and jostling atoms, and therewith as if into anthropology." Adorno, *Minima Moralia*, pp. 18, 37, 27.

47 Horkheimer's view thus comes down to the claim that: "Everything that is not reducible to numbers becomes illusion for the Enlightenment. This answer provides the unity from Parmenides to Russell. It stands on the destruction of the gods and qualitative differences." Predig Vranicki, *Geschichte des Marxismus* 2 vols (Frankfurt, 1974), p. 831; Horkheimer and Adorno, *Dialectic of Enlightenment* trans. John Cumming (New York, 1972), p. 6ff.

48 "Anti-semitic behavior is generated in situations where blinded men robbed of their subjectivity are set loose as subjects. For those involved, their actions are murderous and therefore senseless reflexes, as behavior-

ists note – without providing an interpretation. Anti-semitism is a deeply imprinted schema, a ritual of civilization; the pogroms are the true ritual murders. They demonstrate the impotence of sense, significance, and ultimately of truth – which might hold them within bounds . . . Action becomes an autonomous end in itself and disguises its own purposelessness." Max Horkheimer and Theodor W. Adorno, *Dialectic of Enlightenment*, pp. 171–2.

49 Ibid., p. 9; also, p. 87.

50 Note the seminal essay by Alfred Schmidt, "Aufklärung und Mythos im Werk Max Horkheimers" in *Max Horkheimer Heute: Werk und Wirkung* ed. Alfred Schmidt and Norbert Altwicker (Frankfurt, 1986), pp. 180ff.

51 "In the innermost recesses of humanism, as its very soul, there rages a frantic prisoner who, as a Fascist, turns the world into a prison." Adorno, *Minima Moralia*, p. 89.

52 "The permanent sign of enlightenment is domination over an objectified external nature and a repressed internal nature . . . Horkheimer and Adorno [thus] play a variation on the well-known theme of Max Weber, who sees the ancient, disenchanted gods rising from their graves in the guise of depersonalized forces to resume the irreconcilable struggles between the demons.' Jürgen Habermas, "The Entwinement of Myth and Enlightenment: Max Horkheimer and Theodor Adorno" in *The Philosophical Discourse of Modernity: Twelve Lectures* trans. Frederick Lawrence (Cambridge, Mass., 1987), p. 110.

53 Horkheimer summarized the position nicely when, in an aphorism from 1957–8, he wrote "the destruction of the inner life is the penalty man has to pay for having no respect for any life other than his own. The violence that is directed outward and called technology, he is compelled to inflict on his own psyche." Horkheimer, *Dawn and Decline*, p. 161.

54 Note the rather pale historical discussion of 1926 by Max Horkheimer, "Vorlesung der deutschen idealistischen Philosophie von Kant bis Hegel" in *Gesammelte Werke* (Frankfurt, 1990) vol. 10, pp. 12–23.

55 The claim that democracy and aristocracy are different possibilities for a republic ultimately becomes irrelevant with the self-conscious turn of the nobility against the Enlightenment after 1815 and the inherently democratic political implications of most enlightenment theorists. Horkheimer, "Die Aufklärung" in *Gesammelte Werke*, vol. 13, p. 593.

56 A very different view of the Enlightenment, which locates utopian resources in past philosophical traditions and movements seemingly leveled by an omnivorous instrumental reason, is provided by Ernst Bloch, *Natural Law and Human Dignity* trans. Dennis J. Schmidt (Cambridge, Mass., 1986).

57 Note the historical argument developed by Ernst Nolte, *Three Faces of Fascism* trans. Leila Vennewitz (New York, 1965); also, the philosophical argument, concerning the role of "non-synchronous contradictions"

in analyzing fascism, by Ernst Bloch, *Erbschaft dieser Zeit* (Frankfurt, 1973), pp. 45ff.

58 Neither Horkheimer nor Adorno ever took to heart the insight from Nietzsche with which they putatively agreed: "He who seeks to mediate between two bold thinkers . . . stamps himself mediocre: he has not the eyes to see uniqueness: to perceive resemblances everywhere, making everything alike, is a sign of weak eyesight." Cited by Adorno, in *Minima Moralia*, p. 74.

59 ". . . liberal theory is true as an idea. It contains the image of a society in which irrational anger no longer exists and seeks for outlets. But since the liberal theory assumes that unity among men is already in principle established, it serves as an apologia for existing circumstances." Horkheimer and Adorno, *Dialectic of Enlightenment*, p. 169.

60 The willingness to treat any opponent of the communist movement as providing an "objective apology" for capitalism or fascism, as the case may be, emerged during the infamous "third period" of the Comintern and became routine under Stalinism. See Georg Lukács, *Die Zerstörung der Vernunft*, 3 vols, (Darmstadt, 1962) vol. 3, pp. 196ff.

61 Note the somewhat questionable claim that, given how the argument highlights the question of "organizational form," it has little in common with the "social fascist" thesis of the Communist Party. Cf. Dubiel, *Theory and Politics*, p. 71.

62 Habermas, "Max Horkheimer," p. 97.

63 It is revealing that, in a commentary on Leo Lowenthal's *Prophets of Deceit*, Horkheimer could write: "I still do not quite understand your extreme caution about discussing the relation between democracy and fascism. Why should it be so daring to point to the trend of democracy towards fascism? In my opinion, this trend is one of the most important theses – nay, presuppositions – of any critical theory of present-day society." Cited in Leo Lowenthal, *Critical Theory and Frankfurt School Theorists: Lectures, Correspondence, Conversations* (New Brunswick, NJ., 1989), pp. 206–7.

64 Nietzsche will later be termed by Horkheimer "the most radical enlightenment figure in all of philosophy." And in the general indeterminate sense of the term "enlightenment," of course, that is arguable; in terms of the values and political ideas deriving from the specific movement of 1650–1830, however, it is obviously nonsense. Here, the unfortunate consequences of using one term in two ways become obvious. Cf. Horkheimer, "Die Aufklärung," p. 574.

65 Horkheimer and Adorno, *Dialectic of Enlightenment*, p. xiii.

66 Adorno, *Minima Moralia*, p. 192

67 Horkheimer and Adorno, *Dialectic of the Enlightenment*, pp. 120ff.

68 The notion that "high art" provided a critical and emancipatory alternative to that of the "popular" variety was already argued in the 1941 essay by Horkheimer, which anticipates much of the cultural

argument in *Dialectic of Enlightenment*, entitled "Art and Mass Culture" in *Critical Theory*, p. 273.

69 For two conflicting views, note the essay by Martin Jay, "Mass Culture and Aesthetic Redemption: The Debate Between Max Horkheimer and Siegfried Kracauer" in *Fin de Siècle Socialism and Other Essays* (New York, 1988), pp. 82ff.

70 Adorno, *Minima Moralia*, p. 25.

71 Horkheimer, "Art and Mass Culture," in *Critical Theory: Selected Essays*, pp. 274–8.

72 Horkheimer, *Dawn and Decline*, p. 230.

73 While Adorno, Horkheimer, and Pollock returned there were others like Marcuse and Lowenthal who decided to remain in the United States. "This permanently destroyed the possibility of re-establishing the sort of multidisciplinary research program begun in the early 1930s and continued to some degree or another in the 1940s. For, while Horkheimer talked in his inaugural address of merging American social science research methods with speculative social theory, the Institute undertook few multidisciplinary projects, and never really returned to serious work on developing a systematic social theory of the current epoch." Kellner, *Critical Theory, Marxism and Modernity*, pp. 119–20.

74 Max Horkheimer, et al., *Aspects of Sociology* trans. John Viertel (Boston, 1972).

75 "Democracy in the age of mass propaganda will not respect the constitution. Poor human rights that are anchored in it, poor freedom which democracy is meant to protect. But democracy exists for the sake of the majority, and human rights apply to the individual. Has there ever been a time when the individual was secure? Relatively so in the industrialized countries of the nineteenth century perhaps, but only perhaps. And freedom after all is the freedom of the so-called people, not of the individual. So don't worry as long as it is the majority that opts for constitutional change – change against the individual. That's why democracy leads to its opposite – tyranny." Horkheimer, *Dawn and Decline*, p. 159; also pp. 137, 141, 153, 179, 186–7, 233 and *passim*.

76 Horkheimer, "Traditional and Critical Theory," in *Critical Theory: Selected Essays*, p. 245.

77 Note the interview with Max Horkheimer entitled "Die Preis der Aufklärung" in *Gesammelte Schriften* (Frankfurt, 1989) vol. 13, pp. 225ff.

78 Horkheimer, *Dawn and Decline*, p. 225.

79 Ibid., pp. 193ff.

80 Wiggershaus, *Die Frankfurter Schule*, pp. 479ff.

81 "Philosophy is the futile attempt to achieve recognition for a kind of knowledge which is more than merely instrumental. It is the attempt to produce truth which not only has no practical purpose but cannot even be used in the ordering and application of the knowledge one has . . . Recourse to the immanent logic of the work of art is useless, for philosophy lays claim to a different kind of truth. What remains is

insight into the impotence of all that is spirit and is not content with mere power. That is the truth, and at this point materialism and serious theology converge." Horkheimer, *Dawn and Decline*, pp. 159–60.

82 "Horkheimer's theoretical and political decline represents one of the enigmas of the history of Critical Theory." Kellner, *Critical Theory, Marxism and Modernity*, p. 113.

83 The elder Horkheimer "begins with the assumption that truth cannot exist without an absolute . . . Without *ontological* anchoring, so he believes, the concept of truth must fall back into the innerworldly contingency of the mortal person." Jürgen Habermas, "Zu Max Horkheimers Satz: 'Einen unbedingten Sinn zu retten ohne Gott, ist eitel'" in *Texte und Kontexte* (Frankfurt, 1992), p. 119. A somewhat different view is offered in Max Horkheimer, *Sozialphilosophische Studien: Aufsätze, Reden, Vorträge 1930–1972* (Frankfurt, 1972), p. 143.

84 Max Horkheimer, *Die Sehnsucht nach dem ganz Anderen* (Hamburg, 1970), p. 70.

85 Hans Günther Holl, "Religion und Metaphysik im Spätwerk Max Horkheimers" in *Max Horkheimer Heute*, pp. 140ff.

86 "The state itself must regulate views and attitudes, must become totalitarian, for religion is finished. I mourn the loss of the superstitious belief in a Beyond. For the society that gets along without it, every step that brings it closer to paradise on earth will take it further from the dream which makes earth bearable." Horkheimer, *Dawn and Decline*, p. 223.

87 Max Horkheimer, "Die Aktualität Schopenhauers" and "Schopenhauers Denken" in *Gesammelte Schriften* vol. 7, pp. 136ff, 252ff. Also see Rudolf Siebert, *Horkheimer's Critical Sociology of Religion: The Relative and the Transcendent* (Washington, D.C., 1979); also Alfred Schmidt, "Aufklärung und Mythos im Werk Max Horkheimers" in *Max Horkheimer Heute* ed. A. Schmidt and N. Altwicker (Frankfurt, 1986), pp. 180ff.

88 Cf. Matthias Lutz-Bachmann, "Humanität und Religion: Zu Max Horkheimers Deutung des Christentums" in *Max Horkheimer Heute*, pp. 108ff; Joseph Maier, "Judisches Erbe aus deutschem Geist" in *Max Horkheimer Heute*, pp. 146ff.

89 Horkheimer, *Die Sehnsucht nach dem ganz Anderen*, p. 62.

6

Ontology and its Discontents: Unorthodox Remarks on the Philosophy of Martin Heidegger[1]

Martin Heidegger has been the subject of controversy since the publication of *Being and Time* in 1927. All members of the Institute for Social Research at Frankfurt, with the exception of Herbert Marcuse,[2] were skeptical of his work from the very beginning. But only Theodor Adorno, in *Negative Dialectic* and *The Jargon of Authenticity*, ever dealt with the ontology of Heidegger directly and even he did not offer a sustained immanent critique of the architectonic girding the original phenomenological enterprise. Nor has, more recently, Habermas.[3] The lack of such a critique is a matter of some importance. Heidegger is, after all, the most sophisticated practitioner of the approach most opposed to the anti-systemic and enlightenment impulses of critical theory.

Now, over the last few years, a new debate has centered on Heidegger's politics. Some have suggested that his biography condemns his work,[4] others have argued that his fascist political involvement had a defining influence on his thought,[5] while still others have maintained that his thought militates against the Nazi movement with which he was incontestably associated.[6] Even if Heidegger committed himself to fascism, and never expressed remorse for the extermination of the Jews, this still does not mean that his philosophy is reducible to his personal beliefs. Beliefs may play a role. Nevertheless, especially in light of the interpretations developed by Jacques Derrida and Jean-François Lyotard, it is obvious that the complicated language and anarchistic individualism of Heidegger do not exactly conform with the plebian tastes and totalitarian values of the Nazis.

Jürgen Habermas has taken a more judicious view. Even while stressing the moral culpability of Heidegger, especially after 1945,[7] Habermas considers it imperative to prevent criticism of his worldview from being allowed "to cloud our view of the substantial content of his philosophical work."[8] A connection between "work" and "worldview" exists. But, insofar as the conflation of "philosophical theory with ideological motifs" is seen as taking place only after 1929,[9] *Being and Time* is preserved from the atavistic and irrationalist developments of his later writings. Habermas has acknowledged the influence of this indisputable masterpiece on his early works like *Knowledge and Human Interest*; it also influenced important thinkers like Hans-Georg Gadamer, Herbert Marcuse, and others. Perhaps that is why, whatever the stinging character of Habermas's political condemnation, his philosophical criticisms of Heidegger are somewhat timid. His position, in the final analysis, is not very different from the one taken by Karl Löwith and Karl Jaspers.

It is necessary to approach the matter in a different way. There is no question of the crude nationalism, the irrationalism, and the unmistakable expressions of support for the Nazi regime after 1933. It is different in the early work. But the need for political judgment remains. External must give way to an immanent critique capable of exposing the assumptions buried within the ontological constructs. It becomes necessary to discover the *historical residue* within the language of philosophy and examine its hidden connotations.[10] Rather than rip this category or that phrase from its overriding construct, rather than remain merely analytic, criticism must deal with the normative implications generated by the internal logic of the original argument in *Being and Time*. Rather than ask whether the philosophy of Martin Heidegger is *fascist*, which immediately skews the argument, the real question concerns its *proto-fascist* character and how it fosters the climte in which reactionary values of this sort can thrive. Only in this way is it possible to bring together the strands connecting the phases of Heidegger's life and work.[11]

Various questions and concerns underpin a critique of this sort. Are the anti-democratic and neo-romantic sentiments of the 1920s, which Heidegger never retracted,[12] an intrinsic part of his philosophical construct? Does his phenomenology mystify both social relations as well as the self-perception of the individual? Is it legitimate to extol intuition over reflection as the criterion of judgment? Is experience safe from the incursion of ideology? Is any ontology really preserved from historical conditions? Is there a critical component with which the philosophy can contest the arbitrary uses to which it was put?

If questions such as these are not worth asking then a "politicizing" critique of Heidegger's phenomenology can indeed produce little more than a "scandal" from which publishing houses alone can profit.[13] If they are legitimate, however, then political critique must confront what Theodor Adorno derisively labeled the "taboo" against rational comprehension generated by Heidegger's language. The writing is complex and, in fact, he casts a mystifying veil over the propositions on which the ontology rests. Verbs are turned into nouns and then, in conformity with this reifying procedure, simply introduced as ontological categories. Heidegger tends to coin these words himself, which is not unnatural for a philosopher.[14] Too often, however, there is nothing except his own assurance that a new ontological dimension has actually been revealed. The result is a philosophical shell game, which is perpetuated by many of his followers. Thus, J. L. Mehta can write that "the basic precondition for an appreciation of Heidegger . . . is the realization that he cannot be interpreted, and therefore should not be judged in terms of the thought of any preceding stage of Western philosophy."[15]

Heidegger himself, quite consciously, sought to preserve his philosophy from "trivialization" by demanding that specialists interpret it only within the narrow bounds of the text. Critical analysis gives way before a self-referential textual exegesis. And this, in turn, creates the conditions for more popular investigations which, lacking a critical edge, only increase belief in the depth of the "secret" underlying the original argument.[16] In a very simple popular introduction to Heidegger's work, for example, Magda King can write that: "the first time one truly understands Heidegger's questions, one knows it by a cold shiver running down one's spine."[17] If this "shiver" isn't felt then, presumably, that's that.[18] Claims of this sort cater to the myth that has sprung up around Heidegger. They turn him into *the* philosopher whose thinking cannot be comprehended because it elaborates a "higher" truth.

Interestingly enough, however, Heidegger was actually quite direct in stating the goals of his undertaking. *Being and Time* was an inquiry into the nature of "Being as such," its modifications and derivations in terms of "temporality," along with that of the "being" capable of inquiring after its character. Seeking to confront the "functionalization" of thought, no less than its mechanistic assumptions, Heidegger wished to reassert the autonomy of philosophy. This meant confronting both nominalism and realism, idealism and materialism, subjectivism and objectivism.

"Being" would now become irreducible to any set of categories or social claims. His interpretation, no less than his new phenomenology, would subsequently rest on the "ontological difference" – itself ontologically grounded – between empirical or ontic and ontological forms of inquiry; indeed, this provided the basis for his claim that "every positive science is not only relatively, but rather *absolutely* differentiated from Philosophy."[19] Indeed, with its increasing commitment to what Nietzsche termed the "poetic" elaboration of philosophical claims, his later work would only radicalize this original assumption.

The point of his reinterpretation of Being was to overcome the distance between metaphysical concepts and everyday experience. It was for this reason that he turned back to the pre-Socratics in order to contest Plato and the entire Western tradition of philosophy. Being would no longer appear as "the most general notion," which "presents itself" in the generation of ever more particular metaphysical categories. It would instead become rendered "concrete" from the perspective of his new "fundamental ontology" (*Fundamentalontologie*) as "Being as such," or the "Being of beings."

"Being," in this way, turns into the highest and most particular concept; the most indefinable and yet the most self-evident of concepts. "Being is always the Being of an entity;"[20] even so, since it escapes objectification in any category, it juts beyond (*übersteigt*) all mere generalities and is irreducible to any particular entity. "Being" is subsequently "there" only in the temporality (*Zeitlichkeit*) of an "existence" (*Dasein*) capable of asking after its own "Being."[21] No *existenzielle* or ontic manifestation, no individual, can exist without an *existenzial* or ontological underpinning in "Being."[22] Thus, seemingly, philosophy is rendered "concrete."

A revolution is seen as having taken place. The distinction between subject and object, informing Western thinking since Plato, is surmounted by Heidegger in the category of "existence" (*Dasein*). Antinomies and conceptual oppositions collapse. Since the uniqueness of this "existence" is its ability to ask after its "Being,"[23] for example, the questioning of Being becomes part of existence itself. Consequently, in a radical philosophical claim, Heidegger can assert that hermeneutics is possible only on the foundation of ontology.

But, in fact, this ontological category of "existence" (*Dasein*) is nothing more than an intuiting subjectivity with decisionist inclinations. *Dasein* is not seen as equivalent with interiority,[24] for example, since it becomes manifest in space (*im-Raum-sein*). Space, however, is soon enough analyzed as irrelevant to the disclosure of meaning. The content of Heidegger's categories is always withdrawn after they are introduced. Thus, even though Heidegger considers discourse the defining characteristic of *Dasein*, the questioning of "Being" is later seen as capable of occurring only within a form of silence or inner speech since "everyday life" inherently threatens its "disclosure."[25]

The rational subject of western philosophy, in keeping with Schopenhauer and Nietzsche, is seen as sterile and abstract. But the reaction against reflexivity is undertaken in the name of "experience" by a categorically defined entity stripped of any empirical content. Whether any real advance on traditional philosophy has actually been made remains an open question. The usual criticism of the transcendental subject, after all, is that it cannot deal with genuine particularity or historical determinations. But neither can the categories of Heidegger since "Being as such" is, by definition, qualitatively differentiated from the "being" of any particular entity or circumstance (*Angelegenheit*). Closed to any form of inquiry other than the ontological,[26] in fact, concrete criticism cannot challenge the lack of concreteness generated by the "concrete" inquiry.[27] Nevertheless, Heidegger is incapable of justifying his claim that questions concerning an indeterminate "Being" are intrinsically more meaningful than those dealing with the determinate ways in which people exist, or even the manner in which they constitute their existence.

Nowhere does this problem loom larger than when Heidegger attempts to deal with a concrete issue: the nature and effects of technology. Why technology or science needs to be discussed in terms of some "lost" grounding for existence is never "concretely" justified. Nor are the problems immanently deriving from the contradictions of technology or the theories delineating its possibilities ever confronted. Normative and political concerns, which presuppose a genuine historical context, are less overcome than simply defined out of existence. It is enough, in keeping with the "ontological difference," for Heidegger to counsel: "We can indeed use technically created objects and yet, nevertheless, along with all appropriate utilization, keep ourselves free from them in such a way that we release them. We can make use of technically created objects in the way in which they must be made use of. But we can, at the same time, leave these objects as they are, as something which does not concern us in our innermost and authentic selves. We can say 'yes' to the absolutely necessary use of technically created objects and we can at the same time say 'no' in so far as we prevent them from laying exclusive claim to us, and thus warping, confusing and finally laying waste to our Being."[28]

Isolated from the reality it seeks to comprehend, grounded in the ontological difference, Heidegger's philosophy protects the authentic individual – if only by fiat – from the intrusion of the very technology he hopes to employ. There is no discussion of transforming technology or controlling it;[29] social interests and priorities stand outside the analysis. According to Heidegger, however, his analysis is not metaphysical.[30] The concrete philosophy is content to assert: "we" can have it both ways. "We" can say "yes" and "no" simultaneously. But the logic is clear. It makes sense insofar as Heidegger's philosophy denies any mediation between the ontological and the ontic, historicity and history, time and temporality.

The ontological difference suggests that, for all the talk of a concrete philosophy, an untraversable chasm continues to separate the two moments of the analysis. Metaphysics is not overcome; it merely assumes a different guise. An inquiry into the constitution of reality is discarded in order to generate meaning from the ontological foundation on which it supposedly rests; that is to say, in the ontological categories which, existing *a priori*, order the meaningless chaos of ontic reality. The stage is thus set for the individual to achieve meaning outside the meaninglessness of social or public life. An inversion of "concrete" existence results from this unacknowledged metaphysic which veils what the inquiry originally sought to expose: the "lived life" of the individual.

Heidegger apparently suspected a problem. In the 1930s, therefore, he embarked upon a "reversal" *(die Kehre)*. He reached the conclusion that *Being and Time* was still too informed by the metaphysical thinking he wished to surmount. His "reversal" led him to change his language and purify it of non-German characteristics;[31] the philosophical analytic of *Dasein*, framed in terms of a "fundamental ontology," now receded in favor of "existential" ontology, an even sharper emphasis on hermeneutics, and what became ever more "poetic" descriptions of the ways in which Being opened itself – to those who could still "listen" – in immediate experience. Academic philosophy is understood as giving way to a thinking beyond philosophy and argumentation.[32] What were existential constituents of *Dasein* now appear as products of a process coming from afar. A mystical "illumination" or "reminiscence" of Being is thus ultimately seen as supplanting the concrete experience of *Dasein* in its temporality as a "Being-unto-death" *(Sein-zum-Tod)*.[33]

The "reversal" caused a great deal of excitement. Heidegger was viewed by some as retreating from the philosophical contributions of his early work while others saw the change as somehow connected with his "new" association with the Nazis. Scores of commentators sought to differentiate between the early, apolitical, "rationalist," Heidegger and the late "quasi-fascistic," "mystical," and "irrationalist" philosopher. And, in a way, this only made sense. The paring down of language obviously increased its indeterminacy and the possibilities for communicative misunderstanding; it is also noteworthy that, during this same period, Hitler was equally engaged in "purifying" the German language of its "foreign" elements and reintroducing the old script. Nevertheless, from the critical perspective, this debate is of little importance.

Being and Time had already made clear that "existence," while always "mine," should not be understood in traditionally reflexive terms; nor is the difference between the "authentic" revelatory "disclosure" in the temporality of existence and later forms of "illumination" of particular importance except to "the clergy of Being" (Bourdieu). The vague and indeterminate categories of *Being and Time*, furthermore, make a move from the "I" to the "we" possible without any qualitative change in the declamatory form of argumentation.[34] An arbitrary self-judgment, which involves more than merely passing over what Ernst Tugendhat called "the problem of truth," always defined the individual in Heidegger's thinking. No matter what the particular changes then, from the present perspective, his own insistence in the *Letter on Humanism* that no methodological discontinuity existed between the early work and the later appears justified.[35]

Heidegger's philosophy always took the form of "religious atheism" (Lukács). And this rendered his ontological "revolution" suspect from the beginning. Heidegger's philosophy always prized what the Enlightenment always struggled against, which becomes particularly clear in his notion of "thinking." Such "thinking" is something very different from what is ordinarily considered as "thought." Intentionality no longer retains an object.[36] Thinking is stripped of any purpose or interest; it is "neither theoretical nor practical. It occurs in the face of this differentiation. This thinking is – insofar as it is – a thinking turned towards Being and nothing outside of that . . . This sort of thinking has no results. It achieves no effects. It is enough for its essence that it is. But it is in that it expresses what it has to say . . . Historically, only one [mode of] expression befits the subject matter of thinking: the one that accords with its content. Its contentual binding force is essentially higher than the validity of the sciences, because it is freer. It allows Being – to be."[37]

Dogmatism presents itself in the guise of tolerance. Against the imperializing claims of the sciences, without normative purposes or practical aims, "Being" makes its claim through "thought." Ultimately, however, such thinking is directed to the same "inner sanctum" so central to all religious experience.[38] The sole purpose of "thinking," for Heidegger, is to allow the encounter of "existence" (*Dasein*) with its objectively indefinable "Being" (*Sein*). It thus becomes clear why he is so stubborn in his insistence upon retaining the word "thought." Because, in fact, there is only one other word which approximates his concept: revelation.[39] A traditional concept of this sort, however, would contradict the self-styled revolutionary nature of Heidegger's philosophy. Better to engage in linguistic contortions, obscure the real issue, and claim that "the worst, and therefore sharpest danger is Thinking itself. It always must think against itself, which it is only rarely able to do."[40]

Thinking disowns its critical character. It has nothing with which to combat the ideology it claims to contest. Thinking turns into revelation. It is the "un-thought" that becomes the "highest gift" that thought can bestow.[41] Beyond all standards of judgment, devoid of self-reflexivity, "thinking" only "thinks" itself, decides for itself without any possibility of contradiction. No wonder, then, that Heidegger should have loftily refused to engage in debate concerning his philosophy or refute its critics. All of this, according to him, is nothing more than a "game of the small-minded." One "thinks" precisely what one wishes to think. Being is "let be." And that is that. Arbitrariness and a peculiar arrogance become intrinsic elements of the philosophy.

The concept of "thinking," however, is no less mystifying than other categories of the ontology with which it is linked. For instance, along with its derivative categories of "concern" (*Besorgen*) and "solicitude" (*Fürsorge*),[42] "care" (*Sorge*) is seen as a crucial *existenzial* component of *Dasein*. The concept of "care" serves Heidegger as a kind of equivalent for work and retains the twofold meaning of "taking care of one's needs" and "being anxious." It only follows from his notion of "thinking," however, that this existential-ontological concept should lack any creative overtones.[43] Now, when employed by St Augustine, *caritas* needed no "creative" dimension. Religious, premodern, the category not only linked the individual with others, but all with the God who "cares" for his creatures. For Heidegger, however, God does not assume center stage. Consequently, his use of this medieval concept constitutes less a serious encounter with modernity than a flight from it.

How to think about the concrete ways in which people "care" is never disclosed. It is actually little more than a dirty secret since concrete activity necessarily falls into the inauthentic realm of "public life." The situation is no different with Heidegger's concomitant notion of "concern." Hate and love are both manifestations of the concept. Qualitative differentiations, therefore, become obliterated in favor of what remains an abstraction. Ontology of this sort harmonizes in thought those very differences which champions of exploitation and domination would maintain in fact. It mystifies an understanding of the social processes actually taking place.

Many in the 1920s, when mass society and political conformism were becoming so dominant, believed that the philosophy of Heidegger offered a corrective by highlighting the individual. The actual threats to individuality, however, never receive attention. Nor is it really *individuality* that comes into play. His philosophy is concerned only with *individuation* and the subsumption of genuine uniqueness within formal categories capable of structuring meaning and purpose.[44] For Heidegger, after all, an individual can only relate to others insofar as *Dasein* preconceptually, or apodictically, is capable of confronting its own "Being" (*Sein*).[45] An essential (*wesenhaft*) characteristic of *Dasein* is, admittedly, its "Being-in-the-world" (*in-der-Welt-Sein*).[46] Neither social communication nor public activity, however, help the individual come to terms with what "concerns" him. "Meaning" is gleaned only from the experience of what is most unique to the existence of the particular individual. "Being-in-the-world" thus turns into its opposite or, employing the jargon, what might be termed a being-alone-with-others. This becomes evident through the *existenzial* categories by which the "Being" of *Dasein* is "authentically" revealed in-the-world: namely speech (*Rede*), an attuned attitude or "state of mind" (*Befindlichkeit*) and "intuitive understanding" (*Verstehen*).

These three categories arise simultaneously and, within them, *Dasein* finds itself in the world;[47] or, better, is able to comprehend its "fall" (*Verfall*) into the world.[48] This notion of "falling" is crucial to Heidegger's entire philosophical structure. For, in that "fall," *Dasein* is "thrown" into a situation in which it does not properly exist as a self. *Dasein* tumbles into "everyday life," the condition in which it mostly (*zunächst und zumeist*) exists: "the they" (*das Man*). This existence within "everyday life," this losing of oneself in *das Man*, is precisely what Heidegger considers as "inauthentic" (*uneigentlich*). Indeed, it is from such a mode of being that the "authentic" (*eigentlich*) individual must "wrench" himself.[49]

Now it has often been noted that the "indifference" characteristic of *das Man* has a "positive" character. This, however, is simply another example of Heidegger positing a term with a distinct connotation and then arbitrarily withdrawing its content. All the derivative categories of *das Man* have a negative ring and that is the case with "indifference" as well. "Indifference" to the question of Being not only characterizes the "averageness" (*Durchschnittlichkeit*), the "lack of need" (*Bedürfnislosigkeit*), the "nullity," and indecisiveness of *das Man*, but also the stasis of natural phenomena in contrast to people. Reality is also experienced by *Dasein* as confused, meaningless, and a "whirl" (*Wirbel*) in the "everyday life" dominated by *das Man*.

The confusion of the simple, introspective, sensitive young provincial in the jungle of public life is a staple of old-fashioned romanticism. Confronting the triumph of *Gesellschaft* over *Gemeinschaft*, using the categories of Ferdinand Tönnies, is the goal. A general concern with the rapid extension of industrialization, the explosion of technology, the growth of cities and the expansion of the proletariat, formed the socio-economic complex wherein Heidegger's philosophy took root. The material insecurity of the artisan, the peasant, the petit bourgeois, and a conservative academic aristocracy,[50] in the face of a production process dominated by workers and capitalists was only compounded by the "demystification of the world" (Max Weber), the "death of God" (Nietzsche), and the loss of traditional notions of "meaning."

None of this is external to the philosophy. Contempt for enlighten-ment values and the "functionalization" of thought constituted a res-ponse to the impact of modernity on atavistic groups in the years following World War I. Unique is only the manner in which their experience is provided with an ontological grounding. In rendering atavistic experience "higher" than rational inquiry and identical with the structure of reality itself, however, an ideological element enters the philosophy. No wonder then that virtually every positive example of work and worldview in the writings of Martin Heidegger derives from the life of the peasant, the craftsman, or the artisan. Their rejection of science and rationality as dynamics of modern life receives expression in the primacy of intuition and revelation. Their world is not that of republican democracy and mass culture. The only way to deal "authenti-cally" with the public realm is by embracing a simpler form of organic existence and the inviolability of one's "Being."

Hopelessness and pessimism pervade Heidegger's view of public life. Social reality is necessarily profane. There is only the self resigned to confront its fate. A fairly conventional form of the inner sanctum subsequently becomes the logical presupposition for "wrenching" one-self from the clutches of everyday life and *das Man*. This realm of "existence" (*Dasein*) threatens "authenticity" or that individual "possibi-lity" which no one else can ever experience in quite the same way: death.

Death became a cultural obsession following World War I. It would play a crucial role in Heidegger's ontology as well. Revealed within the experience of "dread" (*Angst*), whereby the "authentic" confrontation with existence is certified, death individuates *Dasein*; it becomes "*Dasein*'s ownmost possibility. Being towards this possibility discloses to *Dasein* its ownmost potentiality-for-Being in which its very Being is the issue. Here it can become manifest to *Dasein* that in this distinctive possibility of its own self, it has been wrenched away from the 'they' (*das Man*)."[51]

Individuality is discovered in the "extreme" situation. This would also become a dominant theme among right-wing intellectuals, no less than certain anti-fascists like André Malraux and Antoine St Exupery, in the aftermath of the war. Concern with the "extreme" situation is central to the cult of the "hero." Both become part of a tradition which extends from the romantics to Marinetti and Mussolini to Ernst Jünger and Gottfried Benn. No wonder then that Heidegger should conceive of "everyday life" as preventing the individual from "authentically" coming to grips with the "possibility" of death. Or putting the matter another way, if only because no one can experience "my" death for me,[52] *das Man* inherently interfers with the ability of the self to recognize its "own-most possibility." Here is the basis for that "shiver" caused by the philosophy of Heidegger. The ever-present "possibility of death" isolates the individual from immersion in "Being-with-others" and solidifies one's "own" experience of "Being," which now may be understood as a "Being-unto-death" (*Sein zum Tod*).

Death ceases to exist as a terrible certainty and is, instead, turned into a spiritual "possibility." The simple everyday horror of death appears as a "deficient modus" (*defiziente Modus*) of existence; after all, by definition, it exhibits fear of what renders the individual unique. A death-fetish results, which stands in accord with the ideology of National Socialism, wherein the individual must relate to the actual negation of existence as if it were an affirmation. Death supposedly rounds out what is always foregoing (as a "project") and fragmented. Only in confronting death can one step beyond "everyday life;" for, in falling back upon existence, death gives life its fullness in view of its end. Only through the comprehension (*Verstehen*) of death can the individual experience existence in its "whole unwholenesss" (*ganzes Unganzheit*).

Death loses its horror and gains a form of dignity. The response, however, is not difficult to formulate; indeed, when a student once remarked that Heidegger's greatness lay in placing man before death, Max Horkheimer replied that General Ludendorff had done that much better. Here, in the discussion of death, is an example of what Adorno called the "jargon of authenticity." And that jargon also makes its appearance in defining "dread" (*Angst*) as the "authentic" experience wherein one's existence as a "Being-unto-death" reveals itself. Martin Buber, Ernst Bloch, and others have noted how Heidegger hypostatized one moment of existential awareness and identified it with "authenticity." *Angst* assumes primacy by fiat and it is simply asserted that the particular "stance" (*Haltung*) taken in the face of death, or the "decision" made in advance (*vorlaufenden Entschlossenheit*), will determine the way one deals with the rest of life. The sense of solidarity or friendship evident in the "I–thou" relation, or the experience of "wonder," could just as easily serve as the foundation for a notion of authenticity. Heidegger, however, does not take "illuminations" of this sort into account.

Conquering death would logically liquidate authenticity. And, in this way, a curious inversion of utopian thinking takes place. The best becomes what toughens, tests, inwardly strengthens. The nihilism and the "hardness," emphasized by disparate right-wing intellectuals like Ernst Jünger and Carl Schmitt, is mirrored in Heidegger's thought. The individual is left with the truism that each will die, that no one can die for him, while the concrete manner in which each *dies* is left open. The values for which one lives are irrelevant. Death, now posited within existence as its "Being," assumes a stranglehold.[53] Avoiding it, preventing it, is no longer the issue. Nor is whether one dies of poverty or sickness, with friends or alone, in a hospital with a private nurse or on the street as a derelict. Ontic concerns of this sort are irrelevant for this philosophy in which life becomes the "shrine of nothingness."

The late disclaimer of humanism by Heidegger in his *Letter on Humanism*, where he seeks to differentiate his philosophy from all "isms," was already apparent in *Being and Time*. Associating life with dying is a short step from identifying death with the affirmation of life. Finitude becomes the content of *Dasein* while death serves as the fixed point from which everything else gains its meaning.[54] "Being" is thus revealed in its "temporality" (*Zeitlichkeit*) rather than clocktime (*Zeit*) which, in turn, subverts any notion of "history" (*Geschichte*). It is a different concept which assumes primacy since "authentic Being-towards-death – that is to say, the finitude of temporality – is the hidden basis of *Dasein*'s historicality."[55]

Heidegger's pessimism creates an inward turn. "Historicity" (*Geschichtlichkeit*), the inner experience of social life, supplants history. Both external history and objective "clock-time" are internalized through this concept, which is simultaneously conceived as their ontological foundation. The "ontological difference" manifests itself again. A break occurs between objective reality and its subjective perception.[56] Creating a fissure between clock-time and temporality, however, only hypostatizes experience by detaching it from the historical mediations which concretely shape an individual. Nevertheless, for that very reason, it becomes possible for Heidegger to interpret freedom as the "ground of grounds" (*Grund des Grundes*).[57]

Freedom has no relation to necessity; it rejects any institutional framework capable of securing it or making it concrete. It is enough, for Heidegger, that freedom should enable the individual to wrench himself from the realm of necessity encountered in *das Man*.[58] A constituent category of *Dasein*, by definition, *das Man* stands beyond any class or social stratum. Drained of concrete activity, divorced from determinate social relations, the category embodies the mass, public life, democracy, mediocrity, the world of work, and finally "inauthenticity." The "publicness" (*Öffentlichkeit*) of *das Man* is precisely what subverts the experience of Being as a "Being-unto-death." Its basic structure produces a "leveling down" (*Einebnung*) of all unique possibilities and so a condition in which *Dasein* is "standing off" (*Abständigkeit*) from its particularity. "Averageness" (*Durchschnittlichkeit*) or mediocrity, as opposed to the exceptional or the "authentic," comes to mark what must prove the meaningless "everyday" existence of *das Man*.[59]

Elitist assumptions infect the "autonomous" phenomenology of Heidegger. They reflect the discomfort caused by the spreading equality of bourgeois life and the "decay" of culture. Again, the actual content of Heidegger's concerns are no different than those of numerous other less talented anti-democratic partisans of the Right during the 1920s and 1930s.[60] Again, however, he provides them with a new ontological status. The condemnation of "mass culture" loses its ad hoc quality. "Public" life and everything associated with its *democratic* character is ontologically defined in terms of mediocrity and superficiality. The decayed character of life in *das Man* is confirmed by its modalities: "chatter" (*Gerede*), "curiosity" (*Neugier*) and "ambivalence" (*Zweideutigkeit*). Each is respectively the "inauthentic" form of a modality conducive to creating the encounter with Being as a "Being-unto-death": "speech," "state of mind," and the "intuitive understanding" of what it means to exist.

Das Man makes it possible to deal with, and yet not fully face, existence as a "Being-unto-death." What is truly unique to the individual is "lost" insofar as the attitude towards death becomes "ambivalent." The reason? "In Dasein's public way of interpreting, it is said that 'one dies,' because everyone else and oneself can talk himself into saying that 'in no case is it I myself,' for this 'one' is the 'nobody.' "[61] The "decision" of *Dasein*, with respect to confronting its death, is vitiated. "Chatter" about mortality deprives death of its priority as the "absolute goal" of existence. The "authentic" "state of mind" (*Befindlichkeit*) is kept from surfacing by *das Man* while an "inauthentic" mood of superficial "curiosity" is substituted for it. In short, *das Man* "does not permit us the courage for anxiety in the face of death."[62]

Dasein is inherently "alienated" (*entfremdet*) insofar as its genuine concern "has mostly the character of Being-lost in the publicness of the 'they' (*das Man*)." Heidegger, of course, does not wish to say that this "absorption" into the realm of the "public" (*Öffentlichkeit*) is a form of "not Being." It is rather "Being" of a particular type in which all authentic knowledge is "darkened." Here, however, the use of hypostatized language and categories betrays the fact that no linguistic analysis of the category's roots is offered – and for good reason. The "public," with Heidegger's particular connotation, is a singular product of the modern epoch.[63] Thus, a category which is quintessentially ontic is smuggled into the ontology.

The effects of such a disclosure would, of course, prove disastrous. No longer could Heidegger claim that his ontological inquiry stands above practical concerns or criticisms. Even *das Man* would lose its standing as an *existenzial*. It would become apparent that what is essentially an ontic analysis is taking place in ontological guise. And that is indeed the case. Starting out as an inquiry into "Being as such," whether unintentionally or not, the inquiry turns into what its unacknowledged values always demanded: a critique of the democratic and egalitarian aspects of modern life.

Note: it is the cosmopolitan, egalitarian, and rationalized elements of the public sphere that bear the brunt of the assault. What fosters the particular, the arbitrary, and the provincial is preserved from criticism. It is, in short, the liberal public sphere that comes under attack. There is no concern with protecting the individual from the unwarranted incursions of the state, but from the intrusions of the "public." The issue then is not whether the phenomenology of Heidegger shares the plebian, racist, and biological assumptions of German fascism. It is rather a matter of whether his philosophy manifests the provincial, irrationalist, subject-ivist, and anti-democratic assumptions of the academic aristocrat in Weimar whose sympathies lie with the anachronistic classes.

All this helped crystallize the ideological conditions in which Hitler could rise to power. Heidegger never retracted his commitment to these values or his assault on the enlightenment legacy. It is subsequently in these terms that his association with the Nazis, his *Rectorship Address* and his later retreat into *Begriffsdichtung* makes sense. It was in this speech that he wrote: 'if we wish to combat intellectualism seriously, we must know our adversary, i.e. we must know that intellectualism is only an impoverished modern offshoot of a development long in the making, namely the position of priority gained by thought with the help of Western metaphysics. It is important to curtail the excrescences of present-day intellectualism. But this will not shake or even touch its position. The danger of a relapse into intellectualism persists precisely for those who wish to combat it. A campaign directed solely against present intellectualism lends a semblance of justification to those who advocate a proper use of the traditional intellect. They may not be intellectualists but they come from the same source."[64]

Obviously, while the attack on "intellectualism" is genuine, Heideg-ger is more than a bit ambivalent about the particular brand of anti-intellectualism employed by the Nazis. Often, this type of ambivalence is used by his defenders to qualify Heidegger's political position.[65] "Ambi-valence" of this sort is, of course, "inauthentic" in terms of his own phenomenology. But that is really beside the point. More important is the fact that the break with fascism in power by so many right-wing intellectuals, including Heidegger, actually says very little. These intel-lectuals were never traditional conservatives; they were initially attracted less by the practical aims and traditional elements of fascism than by its revolutionary nihilism. The movement appealed to their radical disgust with liberalism and socialism, mass culture and modern technology, "spiritual decadence" (Heidegger) and "the decline of the west" (Spengler). They prized the assault on mediocrity and equality and believed that the new "stance" of a "hero," a new attitude, an affirmation of "the brotherhood of the trenches" (Jünger), might revitalize a decaying spirit.[66] That was certainly what the Nazis promised.

Following the seizure of power, for most, the idealistic visions crumbled. Having rid themselves of the democratic *das Man*, the "new man" soon showed himself to be something other than what these intellectuals had imagined. They withdrew. An "inner emigration" (Jaspers) defined their "stance." Heidegger was among them. And, with him, he brought his philosophy. It too went into exile. But this doesn't change matters. The fact that the thinking of Heidegger came into conflict with the Nazis, who turned against their revolutionary cadres among the brown-shirts in 1934 during the "night of the long knives," says nothing about how it helped shape the conditions in which the movement could thrive in the first place.

Heidegger's greatness as a philosopher, the architectonic and sweep of his system, does nothing to absolve him of political responsibility. His philosophy reflects less the explicit standpoint of the Nazis than that of the proto-fascist neo-romantic reaction so popular in the years dividing the two world wars. The real political issue thus involves how the phenomenology inherently attacks the most emancipatory elements of the enlightenment legacy. And reference here to its "depth" doesn't help matters. There is too much that is arbitrary, too much that is elitist, too much that is mystical, and too much that is simply self-serving. There is no room here for the rule of law, but enough for the arbitrary exercise of power; there is no room for socialism, but enough for a self-selected elitism; there is no room for cosmopolitanism, but enough for a *Volksgemeinschaft*.

How this philosophy deals with the question of responsibility is also pertinent to its contemporary relevance. The "stance" (*Haltung*) alone, for example, is significant. An aura of mysticism and intensity surrounds it. The stance, after all, "strengthens our resolve to glean the hidden meaning in the technical world: *the openness to the secret*. The serenity towards things and the openness to the secret belong together. They give us the possibility of a wholly different way of maintaining ourselves in the world."[67] We are left with "the secret." As for the content of this "wholly different way," naturally, it remains completely indeterminate since "in the existential analysis we cannot, in principle, discuss what *Dasein factically* resolves in any particular case. Our investigation excludes even the existential projection of the factical possibilities of existence."[68]

The "ontological difference" again comes into play; the ontic result of the ontological analysis is of no real importance. Any ethical differentiation between political, social, or even personal commitments vanishes. What is actually decided loses its significance; essential is only the "wrenching" of oneself from *das Man*. Vitalistic experience, the intensity of the lived moment outside any context or purpose, becomes the primary mode of self-definition. Ethics is sacrificed to ontology and replaced by a pseudo-ethics: a stance lacking in the need for either rational justification or accountability. A statement from a Nazi lieutenant, derisively quoted by Ernst Bloch, leaps to mind: "One does not die for a program that one understands, but for a program that one loves."

The "call" of conscience, just as with Kierkegaard, alone prepares the way for an "authentic" decision.[69] And this has nothing to do with any "reversal." The mystical relation between one's "conscience" and oneself, so central in the later work of Heidegger, already has its roots in *Being and Time*. A conversation begins through this call. Quite along religious lines, insofar as it "holds itself aloof from any way of becoming known," this conversation is carried on in the silence which Heidegger sees as itself a modus of "speech."[70] It is in the silence of "authentic speech," rather than the "inauthentic chatter" of *das Man*, that the final certitude of "Being" is reached; in this silence, "the truth" of "speech" is affirmed, the "decision" is resolved and the "stance" taken.

The "inner" certainty, the stoic acceptance of one's "destiny," and the "heroic stance" taken towards death – all serve to press the individual into conformity with a reactionary image as old as German thought itself. Pathos emanates from the one who contradicts the nameless mass. True enough, in principle, each can wrench himself from the clutches of *das Man*; there is no biological or racial basis for authenticity. But Heidegger knows well enough that "every man" will not. As he said himself: "The true is not for every man, but only for the strong."[71]

Who is the "strong"? Who is the "hero"? Oedipus or Odysseus were ultimately validated by the actions they performed. Heidegger's thought, however, makes it unnecessary to take either the opinion of others or the actual social alternatives available into consideration. *The Letter on Humanism* explicitly stated that moral choices exist "beneath" the essential characteristics of "thinking." But this is merely an elaboration on *Being and Time* wherein, already, authenticity is little more than an arbitrary moment of self-selection disguised as the taking of responsibility for one's life-choices. It cannot be otherwise. Where all alternatives carry the same weight, the world becomes a plaything for the experience of the subject.[72] Stripped of content and normative value, *Dasein* is rendered absolute. But its tyrannical rule is over a nonexistent kingdom. Insofar as the ontological analysis justifies everything, it gives concrete meaning to nothing. And this is precisely where a form of self-mystification is generated. Since the act itself is never of fundamental significance, but only the "decision" which transcends it, the individual is absolved of both his choices as well as their consequences.[73]

The "concrete" philosophy secures the individual from the intrusion of reality. The inner "resolve" of authenticity or the will "not-to-will,"[74] which fits so nicely with the "un-thought" produced by "true" thought and the "silence" generated by "authentic" speech, proves more than convenient. More is at stake than Heidegger's association with the Nazis. It was real and based on more than sheer opportunism. But this does not prove the existence of a "politics of Being" (*Seinspolitik*) any more than the fact that non-fascist artists like Paul Celan and Ingeborg Bachmann were influenced by Heidegger disproves the existence of one.[75] An individual inspired by his philosophy *can* become a liberal or a socialist or anything else; the "ontological difference," after all, divorces a discussion of the particular choice from the ontological decision regarding the character of choosing. The question is whether the choice of a progressive *political* commitment by an individual embracing Heidegger's philosophy *can be* anything other than ad hoc.[76]

Now, in what is similar to many interpretations of Nietzsche, it is possible to claim that Heidegger's philosophy gives rise only to a type of anarchism.[77] Such anarchism, naturally, has nothing in common with the ideology of actual movements like those in Spain during the 1920s and 1930s. It is rather a form of anarchist individualism, which calls all universals and essentialist arguments into question so that, ultimately, solidarity along with any coherent view of politics or society becomes impossible. Such an interpretation ignores the organicist and provincial components of Heidegger's philosophy and the role "destiny" has to play. But, more important, anti-political interpretations of this sort tend to turn against themselves. The attack on all universals necessarily includes the attack on the rule of law and every other ideological underpinning for a democratic order capable of securing the type of individualism the philosophy putatively extols. Heidegger's thinking denies the assumption of reciprocity inherent within any notion of equality or accountability. License becomes the substitute of freedom. And the consequence is an existentially unliveable reality in which the craving for authority is actually intensified. This critique of license extends from Hobbes to Hegel to Erich Fromm.

Two basic alternatives follow from a "stance" predicated on an all-embracing contempt for "public life" coupled with a self-selected form of elitism. The *first* involves an apocalypse in which, upon the debris of Western civilization, a new possibility for experiencing "Being" as a "Being-unto-death" would present itself. The *second* involves a pose of stoic pessimism with an aristocratic tinge. Where the first alternative leads directly to the parlor fascism of the pseudo-revolutionary Nazi sympathizer, the second leads to the postwar hermit of Freiburg transcending previous choices by fiat and "heroically" concentrating on

"Being" in the face of a meaningless public existence. Nor are these two stances mutually exclusive. The one, in fact, complements the other. Thus, while the philosophy can condemn both democracy and fascism, its critique is always launched from within the normative parameters of the latter.

Heidegger's thought offers much to hermeneutics, linguistics, philosophy, religion, and ontological inquiry. But it is no "concrete" philosophy. There is no *practical* answer given to the philosophical questions of the past; there is merely an attempt to define them out of existence. Heidegger provides neither an epistemology, a philosophy of history, a sociology of behavior, an ethic, nor a theory of praxis. His thinking neither overcomes the practical limitations of previous approaches nor forwards a genuinely new standpoint for critique. It cannot analyze historical conditions or the possibilities of solidarity; the phenomenology offers no criteria for distinguishing justice from injustice and it is permeated with a set of reactionary, anti-democratic values. It expels oppression from reality, reduces ethics to a confrontation with one's "own-most possibility," and identifies "responsibility" with a "stance" devoid of content and a "decision" devoid of purpose. There is nothing left. Where life gains its meaning from an inward reverence for its end, where a chasm divides the ontological from the ontic inquiry, the 'concrete' must lose itself in what Heidegger always prized: nothingness.

Notes

1 An earlier version of this piece appeared under the title "Martin Heidegger: The Consequences of Political Mystification" in *Salmagundi* 38–9 (Summer–Fall, 1977), pp. 153–74. An angry defense of the philosopher, built upon a criticism of my translations, was provided by Thomas Sheehan, "Philosophy and Propaganda: Response to Professor Bronner" which I answered in "The Poverty of Scholasticism/A Pedant's Delight: A Response to Thomas Sheehan" in *Salmagundi* 43 (Winter, 1979), pp. 173–84 and 185–99. It occurs to me that, in certain respects, this old debate actually anticipates the more recent controversy in France. Under any circumstances, however, I will take this opportunity to correct earlier mistakes, add some material and revise the contested translations, without making any substantial changes in the original argument. An evaluation of the debate was offered by the editor of the journal in which it took place; cf. Robert Boyers, "Remembering Henry Pachter" in *Salmagundi* 52–3 (Spring–Summer, 1981), pp. 15ff.

2 During the late 1920s and early 1930s, in a number of articles, Marcuse sought to link the phenomenological ontology of his former teacher at the University of Freiburg with the historical materialism of Marx. Cf. "Heidegger's Politics: An Interview with Herbert Marcuse" by Freder-

ick Olafson in the *Graduate Faculty Philosophy Journal* vol. 6, no. 1 (1977).

3　Jürgen Habermas, "Work and Weltanschauung: The Heidegger Controversy from a German Perspective" in *The New Conservatism: Cultural Criticism and the Historians' Debate* ed. and trans. Shierry Weber Nicholson (Cambridge, Mass., 1992).

4　Victor Farias, *Heidegger and Nazism* trans. Paul Barrell et al. (Philadelphia, 1989); Hugo Ott, *Martin Heidegger: Unterwegs zu seiner Biographie* (Frankfurt, 1988); the spadework for the more recent studies was done by Guido Schneeberger, *Nachlese zu Heidegger: Dokumente zu seinem Leben und Denken* (Bern, 1962).

5　Richard Wolin, *The Politics of Being: The Political Thought of Martin Heidegger* (New York, 1990), p. 2.

6　The political issue is dogmatically stated, mystified, and then safely qualified in the claim that "any deduction, even a mediated one, of Heidegger's 'Nazism' from the text of *Sein und Zeit* is impossible, and that in proceeding in this way one succumbs to as sinister an antic as the 'investigations' at the Moscow 'trials'." In the next paragraph, however, the author notes that "Heideggerian 'politics' realizes, 'acts out,' a thought that, as written in *Sein und Zeit, permits* this politics without in any way necessitating it." Jean-François Lyotard, *Heidegger and "The Jews"* trans. Andreas Michel and Mark Roberts (Minneapolis, 1990), pp. 67, 59.

7　It has been suggested that the question of Heidegger's political disgrace ultimately rests less on any connection with Nazism than on his "silence" on the extermination of the Jews; cf. Phillippe Lacoue-Labarthe, *Le Sujet de la philosophie* (Paris, 1979).

8　Habermas, "Work and Weltanschauung," p. 140.

9　ibid., p. 148.

10　Neither the standard translations nor the textual pedants usually catch Heidegger's penchant for Prussian military expressions such as *Entschlossenheit, Entscheidung, Haltung, durchhalten, ausbilden,* and a host of others. The latter two terms were particularly popular during the First World War; cf. Henry Pachter, "Heidegger and Hitler" in *The Boston University Journal* vol. 24, no. 3, 1976. None of this, or even the political connotations of phrases from Heidegger's infamous *Rectorship Address* of 1933 like "earth and blood" (within the context of *erd-und-bluthaften Kräfte als Macht*), or the word *Führer* which "was at that time very common in German" (sic!), is taken into account in the textual analysis by Jacques Derrida, *Of Spirit: Heidegger and the Question* trans. Geoffrey Bennington and Rachel Bowlby (Chicago, 1989), p. 34; on the concept of the "Führer" in Heidegger's thought, also see Lyotard, *Heidegger and "The Jews"*, pp. 71ff. and Wolin, *The Politics of Being*, pp. 75–84.

11　It is simply insufficient, for example, to suspect that "Heidegger could find his way to the temporalized *Ursprungsphilosophie* of the later period only by way of his temporary identification with the National Socialist movement – to whose inner truth and greatness he still attested in 1935." Jürgen Habermas, *The Philosophical Discourse of Modernity: Twelve Lectures* trans. Frederick Lawrence (Cambridge, Mass., 1987), p. 155.

12 Note the discussion with Martin Heidegger translated by William J. Richardson, SJ "Only a God Can Save Us: The *Spiegel* Interview" in *Heidegger, the Man and the Thinker* ed. Thomas Sheehan (Chicago, 1981), pp. 45–67.

13 Ridiculing what is at stake, setting up a straw man, while refusing to justify a set of outlandish assumptions, some view the criticism of Heidegger this way: "The alternative to be decided: if Heideggerian, then Nazi; if not Nazi, then [not] Heideggerian . . . Thus rendered sensational, the Heidegger affair is subject to the urgency of the politics of publishing." Lyotard, *Heidegger and "The Jews"*, p. 51.

14 Generally speaking, and perhaps for self-serving reasons, there is no confrontation whatsoever by Heidegger's postmodern defenders with the possibility that "the words of [his] jargon sound as if they said something higher than what they mean." Theodor Adorno, *The Jargon of Authenticity* trans. Kurt Tarnowski and Frederic Will (Evanston, 1973), p. 8.

15 J. L. Mehta, *The Philosophy of Martin Heidegger* (New York, 1971), p. 6.

16 "As the waves of dissemination progress, they spread in widening circles from authorized interpretations and inspired commentaries to introductory guides and, finally, textbooks; thus, as one slides down the scale of intepretations, and the subtlety of the paraphrases declines, the exoteric discourse increasingly tends to focus on basic truths . . . thus helping to enhance still further the value of the original and originative, discourse." Pierre Bourdieu, *The Political Ontology of Martin Heidegger* trans. Peter Collier (Stanford, 1991), p. 91.

17 Magda King, *Heidegger's Philosophy* (New York, 1964), p. 4.

18 The same sentiments with the same irrationalist and dogmatic implications are expressed by a more sophisticated thinker when he writes: "I shall explain in conclusion why what I am presenting politely as a hypothesis must necessarily turn out to be true. I know that this hypothesis is true, as though in advance. Its verification appears to me to be as paradoxical as it is fated. At stake in it is the truth of truth for Heidegger, a truth the tautology of which does not even have to be discovered or invented. It belongs to the beyond and to the possibility of any question, to the unquestionable itself in any question." Derrida, *Of Spirit*, p. 9.

19 Martin Heidegger, *Phänomenologie und Theologie* (Frankfurt, 1970), p. 17.

20 Martin Heidegger, *Being and Time* trans. John Macquarrie and Edward Robinson (New York, 1962), p. 29.

21 A stone merely "is" while the human being "exists." Cf. Martin Heidegger, *Brief über den Humanismus* (Tübingen, 1949), p. 15.

22   "Phenomenology is our way of access to what is to be the theme of
      ontology, and it is our way of giving it demonstrative precision. *Only as
      phenomenology is ontology possible.*" Heidegger, *Being and Time*, p. 60.
23   Ibid., p. 27.
24   Cf. Karl-Otto Apel, *Transformation der Philosophie* 2 vols, (Frankfurt,
      1973) vol. 1, p. 238.
25   An excellent example of the abstract nature of Heidegger's method
      occurs in the analysis of *das Man*. Arising within speech, a particular
      ontological status is simply bestowed on the term. Where in English we
      say 'one does this or that,' or 'they' do this or that, in German the phrase
      would read '*Man* tut . . . ' etc. This 'one' or 'they,' "*das Man*), is
      simultaneously *everyone* and *no one*. The term inherently retains a
      deprecatory connotation. The emptiness of *das Man* is its defining
      characteristic and marks out social existence for the individual. Its very
      "neutrality" (*das Neutrum*) tends to undercut any culling of "meaning"
      from existence. Consequently, the individual must at a minimum
      attempt to exist "alongside" *das Man* in order to *de-neutralize* or vitalize
      an "authentic" existence. Note the discussion by Heidegger, *Being and
      Time*, pp. 167–89.
26   Heidegger is quite explicit on this point. There is a "science (*Wissens-
      chaft*) of existences, ontic science – and a science of Being, ontological
      science, Philosophy." Heidegger, *Phänomenlogie und Theologie*, p. 14.
27   "When, moreover, we use the term 'ontology,' we are not talking about
      some definite philosophical discipline standing in interconnection with
      the others. Here one does not have to measure up to the tasks of some
      discipline that has been presented beforehand; on the contrary, only in
      terms of the objective necessities of definite questions and the kind of
      treatment which the 'things themselves' require, can one develop such a
      discipline." Heidegger, *Being and Time*, p. 49.
28   Martin Heidegger, *Gelassenheit* (Tübingen, 1959), p. 22.
29   It is, of course, possible to produce what Thomas Sheehan called "verbal
      analogies" between the thought of Heidegger and Georg Lukács or
      other sophisticated exponents of the dialectical method. But, in fact, this
      results in little more than an abstract way of linking fundamentally
      opposed theorists. Such abstract similarities *might* stem from Heideg-
      ger's reification of various concepts developed by Lukács. That, in any
      event, is the argument made by Lucien Goldmann, *Lukács et Heidegger*
      (Paris, 1973).
30   Apel, *Transformation der Philosophie* vol. 1, p. 226.
31   "Through the elimination of the vocabulary deriving from Greek and
      Latin," particularly in the later work, "Heidegger is able to use a
      purified language rooted in the native dialect, free from the philosophi-
      cal suggestions clinging around that vocabulary and thus capable of
      uttering the truth of Being in ways that were barred to it." Mehta, *The
      Philosophy of Martin Heidegger*, p. 76; also, note the discussion over
      whether Western speech is inherently metaphysical or whether other

possibilities for expression exist within it in Martin Heidegger, *Identität und Differenz* (Pfüllingen, 1957), p. 72.

32 Habermas, "Work and Weltanschauung," p. 164.

33 With the reversal, Heidegger will emphasize that "it is not we, as philosophers, who should discuss the question of Being with Dasein; rather the whole mode of reflection should be, so to speak, 'reversed' and Being should be made responsible for bringing itself to expression in Dasein. The result is a quasi-mythical form of 'reminiscence' of Being which Heidegger's later philosophy makes intelligible in such an ambiguous and difficult style." Rüdiger Bubner, *Modern German Philosophy* trans. Eric Matthews (New York, 1981), p. 25; also, cf. Mehta, *The Philosophy of Martin Heidegger*, pp. 34ff.

34 Even though examples are abundant, this point is totally missed by Lyotard, *Heidegger and "The Jews"*, pp. 72ff., 91ff. and Derrida, *Of Spirit*, 73ff., *passim*. It is enough to consider the following paragraph from 1936 in which, with the censor's pen in mind, Heidegger can arbitrarily shift the earlier understanding of time and Being when he writes: "We say: 'I am!' Each man can assert the being here intended only for himself: my being. Wherein does it consist, and where does it reside? Seemingly this is what should be easiest for us to bring to light . . . And yet the truth is that everyone is remotest from himself, as remote as the I from the you in 'you are.' But today it is the we that counts. Now is the 'time of the we,' not of the I." Martin Heidegger, *Introduction to Metaphysics* trans. Ralph Mannheim (New York, 1961), pp. 57–8.

35 For differing interpretations in this regard, see Peter Fürstenau, *Martin Heidegger: Das Gefüge seines Denkens* (Frankfurt, 1958) – who views Heideggerian thought as continuous – and Karl Löwith, *Heidegger, Denker in der dürftiger Zeit* (Frankfurt, 1953), for the opposite point of view.

36 The belief that thinking and discourse require an object, in Heidegger's opinion, makes it impossible for traditional philosophy – and in particular that of Max Scheler and Edmund Husserl – to adequately address the question of "Being." Heidegger, *Being and Time*, pp. 71–3.

37 Heidegger, *Über den Humanismus* (Frankfurt, 1959), p. 42.

38 In spite of Heidegger's claims to philosophical originality, he "does not care to admit that his specific structuring of the question [of "Being" – trans.] is in no way original, but rather stands in the context of every thinker who goes back over Schelling, Hölderlin and Hegel to Böhme; furthermore, he would like to deny his theological origins, that the historical existence of *Being and Time* borders off an area of specifically Christian experience." Jürgen Habermas, *Philosophische und politische Profile* (Frankfurt, 1971), p. 73.

39 At issue is neither a religious revelation of God nor a belief in the dogma of any established church. Heidegger's "Being" is the "Being" of existence; there is no concern here with an after-life, a question which he leaves open. It is important to note, however, that Heidegger has often

attacked interpretations which perceive his thought as fundamentally atheistic. Cf. Herbert Spiegelberg, *The Phenomenological Movement: A Historical Introduction* 2 vols, (The Hague, 1971), vol. 1, p. 292.

40   Martin Heidegger, *Aus der Erfahrung des Denkens* (Stuttgart, 1968), p. 15.

41   "What is unthought in a thinker's thought is not a lack inherent in his thought. What is *un*-thought is there in each case only as the un-*thought*." Martin Heidegger, *What is Called Thinking* trans. Fred D. Wieck and J. Glenn Gray (New York, 1968), p. 76.

42   These are not diametrically opposed concepts; indeed, the ontological spheres defined by them are fluid. "Solicitude," after all, "can, as it were, take away 'care' from the other and put itself in his position in concern." Heidegger, *Being and Time*, p. 158.

43   Karl Löwith, *From Hegel to Nietzsche* trans. David E. Green (New York, 1962), p. 369.

44   Cf. Theodor W. Adorno, *Negative Dialectics* trans. E. B. Ashton (New York, 1973), pp. 97ff.

45   Heidegger, *Being and Time*, pp. 25–6, 90.

46   Ibid., p. 78.

47   Ibid., p. 219.

48   Heidegger takes pains to emphasize that this "fall" is an *existential* category of existence. Though he is not speaking about a fall from paradise, however, the religious influence is still clear. The pejorative judgment embedded in the concept is, furthermore, readily apparent since *verfallen* means not only to fall, but to rot or decay. Ibid., pp. 220ff.

49   "Authenticity" first emerges in the thought of Angelus Silesius and obviously retains a certain quasi-religious connotation. The roots of the concept of "inner freedom," preserved from external oppression, are in stoicism. With Martin Luther, however, it became a mainstay of religious thought and took modern form. Cf. Herbert Marcuse, *Negations* (Boston, 1969), pp. 43–159; and *Studies in Critical Philosophy* (Boston, 1972), pp. 49–79.

50   When the first version of this article appeared in 1977, Daniel Bell sent me a letter generously praising it while quite correctly suggesting that I had overlooked how Heidegger's thought reflected the values of a reactionary academia as well as the anachronistic classes. The point was made ten years later, through emphasizing the influence of Heidegger's academic *habitus* on his philosophy, by Bourdieu, *The Political Ontology of Martin Heidegger*, pp. 43–51.

51   Heidegger, *Being and Time*, p. 307.

52   Ibid., p. 284.

53   "[O]nly being free *for* death, gives *Dasein* its goal outright and pushes existence into its finitude." Ibid., p. 435.

54   "It is not only when he comes to die, but always and essentially that man is without issue in the face of death. Insofar as a person *is*, he stands in

the issuelessness of death. Thus his being-there is the happening of strangeness (*Unheimlichkeit*)." Heidegger, *Introduction to Metaphysics*, p. 133.

55 Heidegger, *Being and Time*, p. 438.

56 This notion assumes clarity if one considers experiencing a boring movie. One sits inside the theater and the movie seems "endless" – though in fact it only runs an hour and a half. If the experience is theoretically isolated, abstracted from the continuum of time, then the Heideggerian notion takes on validity. But, if it is turned back into the continuum of experience, it is easy to see that there are other factors simultaneously at work. If I *know* that I have an appointment in two hours, I *can* sit through this "endless" experience. In fact, if I am looking forward to this appointment with great expectation, it may well be the hour and a half – "clock-time" – which is making this particular experience "endless." Another example from the cinema is appropriate. Often a director will *add* five minutes of celluloid in order to *shorten* a movie. This, however, presupposes a basis for knowing what the particular subjective effect of such an objective action upon the *experience of time* would be. In any case, the internal experience of the subject will necessarily take its bearing – even as it differentiates itself – from clock-time. The experience is always mediated by the activity in which the subject is engaged. But that is precisely what Heidegger fails to take into account. Thus, he remains blind to how even the "inner" experience of time is open to manipulation.

57 Martin Heidegger, *Vom Wesen des Grundes* (Frankfurt, 1973), p. 5.

58 Authenticity, to put the matter crudely, is impossible while haggling with a street vendor. Using the language of Husserl, although in a somewhat non-technical way, it becomes necessary to "bracket" the concerns of "everyday life" in order to create the authentic "state of mind" in which the perception by *Dasein* of itself as a "Being-unto-death" becomes possible. Given this "Being-unto-death" is considered the "essence" of *Dasein*, Heidegger makes use of the intuitive comprehension marking the *Wesenschau* even though it retains a very different philosophical function than with Husserl whose thought is developed from within the Cartesian tradition. It is subsequently mistaken to view Husserl and Heidegger within the tradition of *Lebensphilosophie* or lump them together within the "irrationalist" tradition as does Georg Lukács, *Die Zerstörung der Vernunft*, 3 vols, (Darmstadt, 1962) vol. 2, pp. 153ff.

59 Heidegger, *Being and Time*, pp. 164–5.

60 Cf. Wolin, *The Politics of Being*, pp. 28ff; Bourdieu, *The Political Ontology of Martin Heidegger*, pp. 7–39.

61 Heidegger, *Being and Time*, p. 297.

62 Ibid., p. 298.

63 "In German, the noun was first formed from the older adjective "public" (*öffentlich*) – analogous to '*publicité*' and 'publicity' – during the eighteenth century . . . If *Öffentlichkeit* acquired its nominal expression

only during this period, we can assume that it first assumed its function then. This sphere belongs specifically to that of 'civil society' (*bürgerlichen Gesellschaft*) which, at the same time according to its own laws, had established itself as the domain of the exchange of goods and social labor." Jürgen Habermas, *Strukturwandel der Öffentlichkeit* (Berlin, 1962), p. 15.

64   Heidegger, *Introduction to Metaphysics*, p. 103.

65   Analyzing the *Rectorship Address*, Derrida can note that Heidegger tended to "spiritualize" National Socialism and that he cannot "exempt himself from any responsibility." But then, with a naive willingness to ignore how the same pseudo-defense was employed by numerous fascist supporters from less philosophical walks of life, he can go on to say that "by taking the risk of spiritualizing Nazism, (Heidegger) might have been trying to absolve or save it." Derrida, *Of Spirit*, p. 39.

66   The strategy of Heidegger is "typical of the 'conservative revolutionaries' (and particularly of Jünger); the strategy which consists in jumping into the fire to avoid being burnt, to change everything without changing anything, through one of those *heroic extremes* which, in the drive to situate oneself always beyond the beyond, unite and reconcile opposites *verbally*, in paradoxical, and magical propositions." Bourdieu, *The Political Ontology of Martin Heidegger*, pp. 61–2.

67   Heidegger, *Gelassenheit*, p. 24.

68   Heidegger, *Being and Time*, p. 434.

69   Ibid., p. 335.

70   Ibid., pp. 316–20.

71   Heidegger, *Introduction to Metaphysics*, p. 112.

72   Carl Schmitt, *Political Romanticism* trans. Guy Oakes (Cambridge, 1986), pp. 17ff.

73   Nor will it do to claim that spiritualizing Nazism and the opposition to it is infected by the same "metaphysics of subjectivity . . . The only choice is the choice between the terrifying contaminations [such spiritualizing] assigns. Even if all forms of complicity are not equivalent, they are *irreducible*." Derrida, *Of Spirit*, p. 40. It sounds good. But what this means "concretely" is unclear. If the "spirit" of democracy is *qualitatively different* from that of fascism then whether they are "irreducible" – a strange term used in a strange manner – becomes a matter of purely abstract concern. If they are not *qualitatively different*, however, then it remains to be shown why they cannot be treated as "equivalent."

74   "We must first of all respond to the nature of technology and only afterward ask whether and how man might become its master. And that question may turn out to be nonsensical, because the essence of technology stems from the presence of what is present, that is, from the Being of beings – something of which man never is the master, of which he can at best be the servant." Heidegger, *What is Called Thinking?*, p. 235.

75   Wolin, *The Politics of Being*, pp. 12, 99, and *passim*.

76   This point is often missed by those who would engage in a "humanistic" defense of Heidegger. Cf. Fred Dallmayr, "Rethinking the Political: Some Heideggerian Contributions" in *The Review of Politics* vol. 52, no. 4 (Fall, 1990), pp. 524–52.

77   Reiner Schurmann, *Heidegger on Being and Acting: From Principles to Anarchy* (Bloomington, 1987).

7

Reclaiming the Fragments: On the Messianic Materialism of Walter Benjamin

He wished, in 1930, "to be considered as the premier critic of German literature."[1] His output was already impressive. The translator of Baudelaire and Proust, he had authored *The Origin of German Tragic Drama*,[2] some unique autobiograpical writings for what would become *Berlin Childhood Around 1900*, a compilation of aphorisms entitled *One-Way Street*, a few scholarly books, a remarkable set of literary studies, and numerous articles for major newspapers. But his greatest work, the thousand-page compilation of notes and citations for *The Arcades Project*, was never completed.[3] Similarly, while his acquaintances ranged from Bertolt Brecht and Hugo von Hoffmansthal to André Gide and Paul Valéry, he was always on the verge of poverty and died fleeing the Nazis in 1940 at the age of 48, virtually unknown. Only due to the efforts of friends like Theodor W. Adorno, Hannah Arendt, and Gershom Scholem – who themselves only rose to genuine fame after the war – was his work rediscovered.[4] They published his correspondence, individual works, and volumes of his selected writings in the 1950s. They wrote reminiscences and spread his name around academic networks. Nevertheless, it was only with the popularity gained by the Frankfurt School during the student movement of the 1960s that Walter Benjamin's wish for recognition was truly fulfilled.

His intellectual standing has now reached almost mythical proportions, and it is not Marxists alone who quote him like "holy writ."[5] Quite the contrary. Benjamin has become a pillar of the literary establishment. He is embraced by everyone from linguistic formalists to fashionable Marxists and postmodernists. Excellent work on his legacy has, in fact, been done by a host of scholars. Ironically, however, his extraordinary fame does not simply derive from that. Other factors are at work: his spirituality, his personal idiocyncracies, his preoccupation with the most varied esoteric interests, his Marxism, his submersion in everyday life, his life as an outcast. And then there is a prevailing intellectual cultural climate which not only prizes these values, but renders suspect the very attempt to formulate an internally consistent argument. Indeed, beyond the intrinsic worth of his works, external factors of this sort have helped turn Walter Benjamin into an intellectual cult figure.[6]

All this would be well and good if the reception did not subvert the critical quality in his thinking. It has. Too many admirers avoid dealing with the gaps in his thought as well as the specific nature of his contribution or the contradictions in his peculiar form of messianic materialism. Simply enjoying his diverse insights into the seemingly insignificant details of everyday existence, suggesting that he is engaged in a postmodern form of "playing with language," dishonors his achievements. Ignoring the epistemological character and political intent of Benjamin's approach, in fact, undercuts any determination of how his enterprise furthers or hinders the critical enterprise. Superficially viewing Benjamin's work as a "tapestry," while forgetting about his inability to weave together the diverse strands of his thought, thus becomes only a backhanded compliment. Nor is it enough to note that his political naiveté and epistemological weaknesses created the interpretive space for appreciating the singular and the unique. Praising the fragmentary and idiocyncratic qualities of his work has only tended to liquidate his most essential concerns.

Exploring these epistemological and political concerns is the purpose of this undertaking. It is a thankless, perhaps even a hopeless, task. Hopeless because no article can possibly assimilate his extraordinary range of interests; thankless because, even on the epistemological level, a multitude of intellectual forces were at play in which the appropriate expertise of the critic is weak with respect to one or the other. That, however, is precisely the allure of dealing with Benjamin. His thinking does not follow a "one-way street." It shifts gears and often stops short. Then it starts and again and takes on speed through each encounter with a new viewpoint or discipline. Benjamin makes good on the promise of the Frankfurt School for an interdisciplinary approach in perhaps the most radical possible manner. His method truly calls into question the strategems and abstractions of "traditional" theory and, whether it succeeds or not, seeks to inform the quest for emancipation.

Reflection takes on new objects of concern; it turns upon itself. Materialism seeks a hermeneutic underpinning while the messianic encounters history. Benjamin's thinking exposes the problems associated with simultaneously seeking to follow paths which, even while they occasionally intersect, still ultimately separate as they recede from view. It was a perilous intellectual undertaking. Nevertheless, if his "hermeneutics of danger" provided him with an existential way to survive fascism,[7] his intellectual biography does not simply follow a chronological sequence.

Active in the youth movement, Benjamin breathed its air of "romantic" opposition to bourgeois conformity. The experiments of the modernist avant-garde also became known to him early in life through his association with Dadaists like Hugo Ball and expressionists like Kurt Hiller, Ludwig Rubiner, and Franz Pfemfert. Also in his youth, Gershom Scholem, Martin Buber and Hermann Cohen exposed Benjamin to Jewish theology which, in turn, profoundly influenced his later hermeneutics and theory of language. Neo-Kantianism, furthermore, fostered his desire to overcome the tension between reflexivity and experience, the metaphysical and the material, abstraction and the particular. As for Marxism, Benjamin's interest was awakened after Scholem left for Palestine in 1923.[8] Around that time he also met Asja Lacis, a communist and innovator of children's theater, with whom he would fall deeply in love.[9] Already influenced by the messianic radicalism of Gustav Landauer and Ernst Bloch, Benjamin was introduced by her to Brecht and Korsch. Indeed, while the new worldview did not affect his dissertation or habilitation,[10] its impact on his thinking was profound.

Utopian speculation played a role in all these traditions and Benjamin never surrendered the insights and perspectives of earlier days.[11] The concerns of his dissertation entitled *The Concept of Artistic Criticism in German Romanticism*, for example, stayed with him. Immanent criticism, utopian longing, spiritual crisis, historical rupture, the importance of tradition and the dangers of its manipulation, as well as the self-renewing set of intepretive possibilities within the work of art, would prove crucial for every aspect of his future work.[12] Perhaps, in the future, he gave up on the attempt to develop a standpoint "on the ground of the Kantian system."[13] But he preserved the theological terminology and symbolism no less than the preoccupation with experience beyond the rational.[14] This interest, in fact, led Brecht to criticize his friend for retaining elements of "mysticism in spite of an anti-mystical attitude." The concern with experience, however, enabled Benjamin to maintain his commitment to subjectivity in a world increasingly dominated by totalitarian terror and the commodity form. Thus, his attempt to "refunction" dialectical materialism and messianism while fusing the facticity of historical with the experience of myth.[15]

An emphasis on "experience," the limitations of traditional "systems," and "concrete" philosophy defined the intellectual climate of his youth.[16] The similarities with the exponents of existentialism and phenomenology, who were gaining popularity in the 1920s, is striking. In fact, whatever their protestations to the contrary, that is the case for many within the camp of critical theory. With Benjamin's thinking in particular, however, "the philosophical faculty is extended to non-philosophical objects, to seemingly blind, unintentional materia."[17] And this interest in bringing the objects of everyday life into the purview of philosophy stayed with him even after his conversion to Marxism. Thus, Ernst Bloch could note that: "Benjamin had the quality which was so extraordinarily lacking in Lukács. He had a unique eye precisely for the important detail, for that which lies by the wayside, for the fresh element, which breaks open in thinking and in the world, for an unusual and unschematic disconnected singularity which doesn't fit any preconceived purpose, and which therefore earns a completely private attention that turns one inward."[18]

Walter Benjamin called upon dialectical thinking to confront the particular and the exception to the rule. It was the "rubbish" of history that a radical messianism should reclaim. A boulevard, postage stamps, children's books, unpacking one's library, eating, and untold other elements of everyday life became the objects of critical scrutiny and manifold associations; each takes on an allegorical, mythical, significance. A view of this sort obviously set him in opposition to the vagaries of official Marxism and placed him squarely within a certain current of critical theory best exemplified in the writings of Siegfried Kracauer and Theodor Adorno. Their unique form of analysis wished to show how the macrocosm is mirrored in the microcosm. Unique to Benjamin, however, is that he always let the object speak for itself; its singularity was never lost.[19] Nevertheless, therein lay the danger.

No less than his friends, Benjamin was never tempted by empiricism; indeed, he wished to perserve the dialectic. But, while he might have had that sense of the singular and the exceptional lacking in Lukács, he also lacked what Lukács had. Rejecting the structured and mediated concept of "totality" in favor of a constantly shifting "constellation, wherein the relation between objects and the perspective of the viewer is always in a state of flux,[20] Benjamin neither situated his objects of concern within what Marx termed the "ensemble of social relations" nor invoked abstract categories to structure it. Even worse, while his method was thus rendered "non-systematic" in form and inherently experimental in content, this "essential corrective to a narrowly totalizing ideology at the same time (risked) hardening, like certain contemporary theories, into no more than that ideology's inverted mirror-image, replacing a theoretical myopia with a corresponding astigmatism."[21]

Allegory and the commodity form alone remained to shoulder the analysis.[22] And these two constructs tore at one another. Benjamin never produced the internally consistent worldview of Lukács, or Bloch either for that matter. Which is not to say that he didn't want one. Rejecting fixed systems is not the same thing as denying the need for coherence. Centering on the experience of the object immanently calls for uniting history with the conditions which make such experience possible and comprehensible.[23] Such an undertaking, central to neo-Kantianism, is actually part of a tradition extending from Fichte to Lukács. It implies overcoming the tension between immanence and transcendence or the metaphysical and the historical. And this attempt was already made in what is perhaps his greatest essay: the study of Goethe's *Elective Affinities*.

Gershom Scholem was correct in noting the importance of this work for Benjamin's career insofar as "his speculative talent was aimed no longer at devising something new, but at penetrating something existent, interpreting and transforming it."[24] Prior inquiries into language and the form philosophy should take in the coming period give way to a standpoint dependent upon the existence of an empirical object. His essay thus notes that "critique" is intrinsically related to unearthing the transcendent "truth content" (*Wahrheitsgehalt*) of the work while "commentary" is concerned with its immanent "subject matter" (*Sachgehalt*). Originally, in the production of a completed work, the two are bound together; they divide, however, once it enters the public realm. How to reconnect them was never made clear. Nevertheless, Benjamin claimed that the more compelling the "truth content" the more intimately is it bound up with the "subject matter" of the work.

Truth resides within language.[25] And the "true," in this sense, is the "whole." Unfortunately, however, it is precisely this wholeness which history has rent asunder. This "totality," not the infinitely mediated category of Hegel and Lukács, is the one Benjamin initially wishes to restore. It is a wholeness associated in the works of various of Benjamin's contemporaries like Martin Buber and Karl Jaspers with the mystical and the God-head. In contrast to these thinkers, however, Benjamin never assumes its existence "behind" reality. In fact, according to him, it is the very loss of this wholeness which necessitates language. Only in language can the comprehension take place of an experience which "makes uniform the continuous multiplicity of knowledge."[26]

Allegory is to language what ruins are to things.[27] It gives power to memory and creates the "horizon" wherein transcendence becomes possible.[28] Allegory, or so it is argued in *The Origin of German Tragic Drama*, provides a structure for conceptualizing the past no less than the mutability of all significations; it allows the shapelessness of materia to take an eternally mutable shape within an immutable context. Allegory makes a continual substitution of disparate particulars possible precisely because "things and occurances do not meaninglessly stand next to one another, but rather refer to one another."[29] The concept, after all, has scholastic roots and it was traditionally used to explain the manner in which secular reality is linked to the beyond and, epistemologically, how a conception of the beyond can arise.[30] Indeed, through the ability of allegory to provide every particular with symbolic properties, language presents both the possibility of giving and transforming the meanings of things.

Neither "political" nor "formal" analysis can then exhaust the meaning of an artwork. That belief would separate Benjamin from many contemporaries and followers; it would also inform *The Arcades Project* which, in its attempt to provide an "*ur*-history of modernity" entirely through the use of quotations, necessarily presupposes the existence of transcendent possibilities within works of the past as well as a sociological standard with which to judge their relevance for the emergence of the "modern." Benjamin was no relativist. More open than others in the Frankfurt School to film and popular culture, he nevertheless told Scholem of his need for "texts of canonical importance in order to develop his philosophical ideas adequately to comment on them."[31] Nor was he afraid to thematize reality; *The Arcades Project* is an attempt to offer a "grand narrative," albeit built on fragmentary foundations, which also evidences his desire to connect transcendence with immanence. Indeed, the belief in the existence of such a connection created the basis for his famous claim that there is no cultural artifact of civilization which is not at the same time an expression of barbarism.[32]

Commentary, in short, is unthinkable for Benjamin without critique. His aim was not to engage in word-games, but overcome the academicism of literary criticism and give it a political purpose.[33] This purpose is less negative than positive; it is not deconstructive, but rather reconstructive.[34] The past is a set of "ruins" in need of restoration and the present is more than what first meets the eye. These ruins harbor an untapped content. Works of art no less than philosophy forward a truth in need of judgment. But the evaluation is never final. Judgments and verdicts, as Benjamin said in the prospectus for his proposed journal *Angelus Novus*, always remain open to renewal.

The critical essay, in keeping with the Lukács of *Soul and Form*, transforms itself into an artwork deserving of further commentary. Translation, for example, is understood by Benjamin as a form *sui generis.*[35] It is an attempt to grasp the transcendent potential within a work. An emancipation from the original linguistic assumptions immanent to its creation thus necessarily takes place so that it can speak to a new audience in new conditions. But, in turn, this obviously implies that the viability of the translation will pass and a new one will become necessary.[36] An ongoing process of constitution and reconstitution of the connection between the immanent and transcendent properties of a work takes place. Thus, Benjamin could write that "the critic inquires about the truth whose living flame continues burning over the heavy logs of what was and the simmering ashes of life gone by."[37]

Without some form of prior or contextual justification, however, his claims appear tautologous since the critic seems engaged only in determining the content of concepts arbitrarily imposed on the object in the first place. Which way to turn? Epistemology might define their logical standing, but it is inherently abstract and Benjamin knew that a theory of knowledge can provide neither an ontological nor a material foundation for any particular form of inquiry. Ontology, of course, would ground his project; but, the undertaking of Ernst Bloch notwithstanding, it would do so only in the "systematic" terms against which Benjamin always rebelled. The teleological assumptions of dialectical materialism had proven false. As for a purely heuristic justification, whatever its benefits, he knew it would turn his categories into little more than ahistorical techniques. Not many doors remained open.

Jewish theology provided a way out. And he would employ it in afar more innovative way than either Max Horkheimer or Erich Fromm. This form of thinking, in contrast to popular belief neither presupposes a teleological structure within history nor an abstract epistemology. Theology was not merely an unintegrated component of a fragmentary worldview developed by a philosophical iconoclast.[38] That is reading the story backwards. Theology served a positive function in Benjamin's theory. His aim was to show how aesthetic experience and then historical insights are bound up with theological categories. And for good reason. His method, by relying on the theological moment, would thereby gain a foundation of sorts without recourse to an articulated ontological system. It thus becomes evident from employing what Benjamin himself termed an "epistemologico-critical" approach why the theological component should have remained with him *even after* he had lost his belief in God around 1927 and turned to Marxism.[39]

God, for the young Benjamin, existed as the unattainable center of a system of symbols intended to remove Him from everything concrete and everything symbolic as well;[40] it would only make sense then that, insofar as philosophy participates in such a system, it will reflect an absolute experience symbolically deduced in the allegorical context of language.[41] What remains without God, which explains the superficial allure Benjamin holds for various postmodernists, is thus an allegorical world of symbols capable of endlessly transferring and multiplying the signification not merely of objects, but of categories and philosophical systems as well. The existence of such a world legitimates his fusion of diverse insights from a multitiude of sources and what would originally appear as mutually exclusive systematic claims.

Only montage can, in literary terms, adequately reflect a world dominated by rupture and incoherence. It becomes the theoretical point of entry into the content and the form of *The Arcades Project* as well as his earlier *The Origin of German Tragic Drama*. Both demonstrate a pre-occupation with spiritual rupture and the possibilities of montage for explicitly socio-philosophical purposes. The boundaries between disciplines fades in both. The blending of the historical, the theological, and the epistemological also results in a constantly shifting foundation for the critical inquiry. Justified by the existence of a metaphorical world, however, the fusion of Marxian materialism and messianic Judaism offers a standpoint for Benjamin with which to overcome relativism. Indeed, for all the emphasis on the fragmentary and the singular, both tendencies seek a harmony lost to the modern world.

Utopia remains. Only, with Benjamin, it is a reflexively comprehensible yet materially unattainable condition ripped from any interconnection with unilinear progress. And that is because progress does not simply extend into the future, but depends upon the manner in which the past is appropriated.[42] The affirmative notion of unlinear progress, subverted in any event by the experience of World War I and the rise of fascism, is contested in the name of history. Its unrealized possibilities give content to utopia which, in turn, provides a positive foundation for critique. Every element of the past becomes open to redemption on the messianic Day of Judgment.[43] Giving the apocalypse secular shape thus permits reintroducing an emancipatory point of reference just as the possibility of instituting a genuinely classless society was becoming ever more remote. A theological notion of remembrance, which finds its way into the thinking of Marcuse and Adorno as well, contests the perversion of history by totalitarianism. It becomes the only way to deal with that "single catastrophe" on which one gulag after another "keeps piling wreckage upon wreckage."[44]

Such a view places new responsibility on the critic; Walter Benjamin was aware that "the task of history is not only to give the oppressed access to tradition, but also to create it." The past stands in need of "reawakening," which is precisely where the theological moment enters and converges with the modernist emphasis on montage and the unconscious. A critical intervention is necessary to shake the audience from its complacency. The "mémoire voluntaire" of Proust was thus considered insufficient for turning history into "the object of a construction whose foundation is not that of homogeneous and empty time, but rather that of a time filled and informed by the present time (*Jetztzeit*).[45] A reflexive and experiential "tiger's leap" into the past had become necessary to crack open what is usually considered dead within the continuum of time and reaffirm it for a contingent future.[46] And so, for Benjamin, "to interpret phenomena materialistically meant not so much to elucidate them as products of the social whole but rather to relate them directly, in their isolated singularity, to material tendencies and social struggles."[47] Whether he ever made good on this intention, however, is a highly debatable proposition.

Walter Benjamin wished to retrieve what Hegel had thrown into the historical dustbin. He sought to discover an unrealized emancipatory potential from the facts considered useless and irrelevant by the dominant classes. The question involved how to make that potential recognizable. And, in this respect, Benjamin never had a clue. Revolution, for him, was always a messianic projection or a romantic longing; reform and organization were tedious and boring. "Never in politics," he could write in January of 1913, "does the Idea appear, always the party." And so, in his youth, Benjamin became interested in Sorel and reached the preposterous conclusion that "law" – in contrast to "justice" – is an order capable of being established only in a world of myth.[48] His naiveté regarding the world of politics was simply extraordinary. His analysis of fascism was blind to conflicts between political parties, economic imperatives, and institutional interests. Indeed, Benjamin never understood anything of institutional constraints or the concrete options facing the working class.

His response to the petrification of theory and practice under Stalin was to argue that each moment held a revolutionary potential and that it was time to reconsider the legacy of Blanqui.[49] There is barely a word in his *Moscow Diary* on the momentous struggle between Stalin and Trotsky nor did his sojourn in France show any insight whatsoever into the Popular Front which he basically opposed in favor of the spontaneous strike wave of 1936. He seemed completely unaware that the strikes were purely economic in character, that France stood on the brink of civil war, that the parties of the working class neither constituted a majority nor were prepared for military conflict, or that the overwhelming majority of workers embraced Leon Blum's call for a "reform of the structure." His position was sectarian from the start and evidenced a bohemian romanticism common to others of his circle like Brecht and Bloch.[50]

Given his immersion in the history of nineteenth-century France and his admiration of Blanqui, always a favorite of Lenin and Marx to a lesser extent, his thinking reflects a tentative left-Leninist critique of Stalin; his discovery of "the eternal prisoner," in conjunction with his messianism, thus led him to argue that an immanent revolutionary possibility presented itself with each moment in time.[51] Attacks on "contemplation" abound in Benjamin's work. But his thought yields no insight into the relation between theory and practice. Mistakenly, in the "Theses on the Philosophy of History," he even identified Marx's idea of revolution with "a leap into the open skies of history."

It was a strange form of Marxism embraced by Benjamin.[52] His interpretation involved the puzzling combination of a rather orthodox technological reductionism with a completely exaggerated conception of the method's utopian capacities. The point of Marxism for Benjamin was less to inform the creation of a "socialist" society than to provide the foundation for a utopia ultimately brought in from the outside. And to speak of a "materialist theology," in this sense, is merely playing with words. Neither the proletariat nor any other earthly agent could help in realizing what Benjamin wished to achieve. Marxism is gutted of its content and purpose; its usefulness is relegated to certain key concepts like the commodity form and perhaps the manner in which it can function as a "myth" (Sorel).[53] The romantic conception of "violence," the exaggeration of revolutionary possibilities, becomes a temptation for all who don't have to deal with power, and it was prevalent in the thinking of Bloch and certain members of the Frankfurt School as well. Benjamin, however, gave it a particularly radical stamp and was unafraid to expose the theological foundations for a Marxism of this sort. Indeed, Scholem was surely correct when he called his friend "a theologian marooned in the realm of the profane."[54]

Benjamin's attempt to fuse theology with historical materialism, for all its grandeur, was questionable from the beginning.[55] The "secular" (*Diesseitigkeit*) is only metaphorically compatible with the "beyond" (*Jenseitigkeit*).[56] The proletariat may have had "no goals of its own to actualize" which, originally, was meant as a call to realize the unrealized democratic goals of the bourgeoisie.[57] Whatever Marx meant by the phrase, however, he surely did not wish to suggest that everything in the past – including the dead – is capable of resurrection through some apocalyptic moment of redemption.[58] Benjamin, of course, wished to confront the unilinear and teleological view of history inherited by Marxism from the Enlightenment. His undertaking was marked by compassion for what had been irretrievably lost and a new view of the past as open and capable of constant reconstruction.[59]

A messianic hermeneutic renders whole or gives cohesion to what has become fragmentary and redeems the suffering of the past. Utopia, previously conceived by Marx as immanent within history, is now transformed into an external standpoint with which to judge progress.[60] It becomes, in keeping with Georges Sorel, a form of myth. History now becomes, in keeping with Nietzsche, a product of the subjective will. Arbitrary, without derivative categories for coherent interpretive judgment, its employment is an experimental exercise without any coherent relation to economic development, actual movements, or even cultural traditions. The historical standpoint thus retains assumptions that provide an insight into the sympathy so often expressed by Benjamin for the revolutionary voluntarism of Blanqui.

Just as voluntarism confronts history, apocalypse confronts revolution; the end of time is not equivalent, except metaphorically, with the substitution of one class for another and one order for another. Nor is qualitative change the same as rupture, especially since, from a dialectical perspective, the counter-concept of continuity alone gives it meaning. Rendering a judgment about quality, no less than defining the empirical content of such change, becomes impossible since everything outside utopia is necessarily painted with the same shade of grey. For that very reason, however, Benjamin must envision a new messianic form of appropriating of the past. The problem is that a determination of the conditions under which such an appropriation can occur is liquidated in the same instant that the wish materializes.

Remembrance is introduced into the science of orthodoxy. But its actual relation to critical interpretive work remains unclear since the criteria for employing it are never brought into play. Nor is it sufficient to remain content with the truism that all attempts at liberating the past must remain fragmentary. The plea to forget nothing turns into its opposite. Coherent attempts to appropriate the past presuppose a systematic view of history, which Benjamin's "Theses" render impossible. Materialism has subverted everything except the messianic will to redemption. Theology, for Benjamin, thus offers the last desperate expression of human freedom under actual conditions which, with the onset of the war and the failure of the radical uprisings in France and Spain, rendered hope impossible. Thus, the connection between these last jottings of Benjamin and the essay on Goethe's *Elective Affinities* which ends with the beautiful and oft-quoted line: "only for the sake of the hopeless is hope given us."[61]

Walter Benjamin wrote much about the social condition of the writer. For him, however, he always "remains the figure on the fringe who refuses to take part."[62] Benjamin was aware of the danger Western concepts of consumerism and egoism posed for the ideology of a newly emerging workers' state, but unaware of how the strategy of modernization would introduce precisely these values. Along with Bloch, he recognized the role of utopian motivation in revolutionary commitment and, following Lukács, anticipated the manner in which the commodity form would produce a "poverty of the interior."[63] But, while his call to reinvigorate revolution with the surrealist spirit of revolt may have later endeared him to the *enragés* of 1968, it was little more than a metaphysical gesture from the very beginning. His desire to offer an alternative mode of praxis remained at the intellectual level of challenging the dominant notion of progress, reaffirming "the radical concept of freedom," obliquely criticizing the Communist Party apparatus, and demanding revolution for its own sake. And when it was finally too late, anticipating works like *The Dialectic of Enlightenment*, Benjamin extrapolated one terrible moment of horror into the future.[64]

Most assume that, unlike Adorno, Benjamin sought to find the potential for transcending the given order immanently or from within its contradictions.[65] Actually, however, this was more a wish than a reality. The "dialectical image," through which the past offers itself to immediate experience in the present, is insufficient for such a task. Not only does it presuppose a revelatory "shock" of recognition on the part of the audience, whose unity and ability to appropriate the object depends upon a vaguely defined notion of collective unconsciousnessness, but it does nothing to help define the criteria for constructing a new history which "brushes against the grain." More is subsequently involved than Adorno's criticism that metaphysical essences do not become immediately manifest in facts. The real question is whether such essences exist at all or whether a prior worldview, external to the derivation of any potential within the image, is necessary to set the *political* context for appropriating the unrealized emancipatory potential within the object.

Marxism provided an "epistemologico-critical" context of this sort. Only from within such a normatively inspired and concrete context would the audience gain an "interest" in the work and a "reason to think" (Brecht); only with such a set of presuppositions could "crude" dialectical images begin to speak for themselves.[66] The problem was, however, that Benjamin could not uncritically embrace the necessary assumptions. He may have used Marxism to illuminate the commodity form, but he doubted its teleological claims. He may have stood in solidarity with the proletariat, but he was skeptical with respect to the party; he may have publicly embraced materialism, in his own unique way, but it was always qualified with theological messianism. His life and work were undoubtedly marked by empathy with suffering and the exploited.[57] But he never articulated even the beginnings of an ethic or a theory of socialist democracy. There are only the ongoing references to freedom and the power of fantasy.

Dialectics may have been Benjamin's preferred mode for reconstructing the lost possibilities within the phenomenon. But, in his theory, the particular is neither open to manipulation through transcendent categories nor situated within contradictions projecting determinate emancipatory possiblities. The transcendent potential of the material object, in messianic fashion, is simply presupposed; making that potential manifest is, in keeping with Blanqui, turned into a matter of arbitrary decision. The two perspectives complement one another. Existing in a metaphoric universe, wherein each element of the past is recoverable in messianic terms, the signification of an object appears directly in relation to that of other objects. There is no place for genuine "mediation." Thus, in keeping with Benjamin's refusal to accept ideas which did not somehow take an immediately outward shape,[68] it makes sense that he should have sought to relate elements of the superstructure directly to one another and sometimes even to the economic base.

The Arcades Project was, of course, an attempt to create an objective context of signification wherein the subject might orient his or her choices.[69] Benjamin may well have sought to explode the immediacy of the present and any sense of linear development by creating "constellations" of dialectical images; he knew that recovering the past is a political act. But the approach was incapable of providing a determination of specific contradictions or any positive way of resolving them. Any connection between the physical and the metaphysical, the historical and the speculative, the historically concrete and the allegorical, falls asunder. Each cancels the other, so to speak, and what remains in the chasm are fragments, objects within an experiential "horizon," seemingly unviolated by the imposition of external categories and open to a relentless continuum of transformation disguised as historical appropriation by the oppressed.[70] Indeed, much more clearly than Adorno, Benjamin had a presentiment of the problem when he spoke of "dialectics at a standstill."

His theory, in any event, divides against itself by mirroring the object under consideration from two irreconcilable positions simultaneously. Allegory provides the object with signification and the endless possibility of transformation even as it subverts the concern of historical materialism with determinacy and mediation. By the same token, however, dealing with such concerns will rob the object of its allegorical transcendence. And so, while the need for a concrete appropriation makes an allegorical interpretation impossible, the emphasis on allegorical transcendence undercuts the ability to offer a concrete mode of appropriating the object. Nevertheless, Benjamin's undertaking shifts the focus of traditional cultural inquiry and raises concerns crucial for the development of any emancipatory aesthetic.

Benjamin maintains that the cultural inquiry must evidence a commitment to freedom. This places him squarely within the tradition of critical theory. His recognition of the need for oppressed groups to reappropriate the past, however, suggests that critique rest upon a positive sense of purpose. Benjamin was content to "show," not to tell; the objects were to speak for themselves.[71] But the problem is precisely that they don't or, even if they do, the language will change with each appropriation by any particular group; this will either relativize the import of the phenomenon in question or, even worse, turn it into little more than an object of contemplation.

"Interest," as Horkheimer knew, cannot serve as the criterion of "truth" since truth will then always remain in the service of the strong.[72] The choice, however, is not restricted to either imposing abstract categories or letting the object speak for itself. Perhaps aesthetic inquiry, whatever its unique practices and claims, is always informed by a broader social theory whose empirical and ethical justification are external to it. The inadequacies of his approach make clear how the valid use of a genuinely interdisciplinary standpoint will depend upon the ability to differentiate between disciplines and the areas of their relevance. Benjamin, however, did not see that. He was thus condemned to leave his materialist aesthetic hanging in the abstract and skirt any coherent encounter with the problem raised by his own analysis: How is a critical appropriation of the past possible without teleological assumptions?

Surely the inability to deal with this question systematically derived from Benjamin's opposition to the totalizing impulse. But, interestingly enough, his most important contribution emerges from its embrace: his willingness to offer a material explanation for the aesthetic experience. Rereading his early essay on "Experience" in 1929, Benjamin noted: "In an early essay I mobilized all the rebellious forces of youth against the word 'experience.' And now that word has been carried over into much of my work. I none the less remained true to myself since my attack cut through the word without destroying it. It forced itself into the center of concern."[73] And he was right. His aesthetic ultimately highlighted the metaphysical experience of the commodity form, the interplay between technological development and fantasy, and his original preoccupation with transcendence.

An emphasis on specificity and mediation does, in a way, make itself felt. Benjamin may have been pessimistic with regard to progress, but his perception of technology is another matter entirely. There is, admittedly, something objectionable about simply divorcing the two. Progress, from such a standpoint, becomes a matter of the spirit without a material referent while technology loses its normative justification.[74] Benjamin, however, does not mechanically pit the two against one another; the sense of historical decay and the openness to the possibilities of technology exist in a state of tension. He subsequently never reifies the concept of technology like others within the Institute's "inner circle." Nowhere does this become more evident than in the famous analysis of the "aura."

The concept is difficult and it underwent a series of permutations before receiving its final elaboration in Benjamin's study of Baudelaire and his essay "The Work of Art in the Age of Mechanical Reproduction."[75] Especially the latter, for all the criticism it has undergone, is a landmark in the history of aesthetics. Never before did the moment of aesthetic recognition become open to scrutiny in material terms. And, just as the experience of an artwork becomes interwoven with the conditions of its production and reception, so do the most basic alternatives of the commodity form emerge. In any event, however, the basic idea is that

> . . . experience of the aura rests on the transposition of a response common in human relationships between the inanimate or natural object and man. The person we look at, or who feels he is being looked at, looks at us in turn. To perceive the aura of an object we look at means to invest it with the ability to look at us in return.[76]

André Malraux told the story of how medieval peasants fell to their knees before religious masterpieces when they were paraded through the streets, thinking that these were not simply objectifications of holy figures, but rather their living embodiments. Benjamin understood how the singular experience of the work, in an inherently premodern and religious context, provides it with a nimbus, a glow, as well as an anthropomorphic quality. The primacy placed on revelation, on faith, on noninstrumental forms of thought, and the embeddedness of the work within a tradition and an organic community, make this possible. Mediation vanishes and determination as well. The work of art is the intermediary between communicating subjects even as it is non-reflexively imbued with their experiences.

Technology liquidates the singularity of the work and even renders aesthetic forms obsolete;[77] the experience of the work no less than the work itself is ripped from the socio-historical context and the preconditions for an organic community are destroyed.[78] Photography and then film, for the historical creation of the one "dreamed" the other, made the reproduction of the original work possible. The consequences of this situation are extraordinary. Art now becomes an object for the masses; the conditions for its production no less than for its distribution are made more democratic. A scientific worldview and the application of technology create a secular attitude which impinges upon the interaction of the individual with the work; the religious quality of awe is lost and the aura is conquered. The immediacy of experience and the aura give way before something new.

Artistic experience is no longer singular. Fashion substitutes itself for the myths of old and the movie-stars replace the demi-gods. But this does not mean that the mythical element is liquidated. Quite the contrary. Technology enables it to take new forms. Immediacy defines the changed historical situation. The technological ability to detach the object from tradition seemingly obliterates all mediations and creates new possibilities for propaganda. This becomes particularly evident with film wherein the alternatives of the new situation present themselves most starkly.

Of course, in the beginning, new methods of production are still interwoven with the old and "dialectical images" still arise from which it is possible to deduce various collective ideas of wish-fulfillment. The past still retains its utopian residue. But, especially with the increasingly pronounced effect of technology upon art, the existence of old forms will become ever more precarious;[79] the ability to fasten upon the utopian residue of painting, for example, could then become ever weaker. It all depends upon a commitment by the audience and the artist that is at once philosophical, political, and aesthetic. With the loss of aura, after all, it only follows that the traditional notion of the masterpiece should make way before the work of "intervention." An "organizing function" thus defines the artist in the new era since art is now a mass phenomenon. A choice between conformism and individuality, irrationalism and reflection, also presents itself to the audience. Indeed just as technology makes possible new forms of mass manipulation, the loss of aura opens the way for political analysis and what Benjamin termed a "heightened presence of mind."

This is why he showed such respect for Brecht and his notion of "epic theater." Not merely did the author of *The Threepenny Opera* emphasize the need for "crude thinking," which might make the determination of "dialectical images" somewhat easier, but his "estrangement-effect" also prized reflection, concentration, and sobriety in coming to grips with reality. Making the audience aware of how it is being fooled creates an interest in knowledge; keeping it simple enables it to comprehend the complex; forging a sense of distance from the play increases the outrage over oppression; politics mixes with fun; indeed, commenting on Brecht's technique, Benjamin put it nicely when he wrote that "there is no better starting point for thought than laughter; speaking more precisely, spasms of the diaphragm generally offer better chances for thought than spasms of the soul."[80]

Reflection and social reality are not simply juxtaposed against experience and fantasy. If Benjamin illuminated the manner in which a structural transformation takes place between experience and the productive forces of society, he also recognized that commodities hide a desire which takes new shape with each change in fashion; the commodity is always "bathed in a profane glow."[81] An analysis of commodity fetishism therefore cannot rest at the economic level of production, but must also include the experience of consumerism. Consequently, the experience of commodity fetishism will appear only in the analysis of the particular phenomenon.

Critique, for Benjamin, always demands an empirical object. And here, in contrast to so much contemporary literary discussion, Benjamin stood with Schlegel when he wrote that "in what is called philosophy of art usually one of two elements are missing – either the philosophy or the art." The experience demands its material or constituitive referrent. Perhaps this often led Benjamin to make reductivistic claims regarding the relation between a poem or an image with the existing productive forces.[82] While he may have exaggerated the relation, however, his approach made it possible to show how artistic innovation no less than its experience is anchored in those forces. Indeed, for this very reason, it makes no sense to condemn the entire realm of mass culture in the manner of Horkheimer, Adorno, and Marcuse.

"The separation of the true from the false," Benjamin could write, "is not the starting point, but rather the goal of the critical method."[83] It is with the particular object rather than with a judgment of the general form that an inquiry must begin. The culture industry engages in manipulation, but produces works incarnating forgotten dreams. Reconstructing those dreams seemingly crushed beneath the boot of fashion is the only way to rub history "against the grain." There is nothing too small, too insignificant, from which to draw pictures of unfulfilled wishes. That is the injunction behind the aphorism from *The Arcades Project* which runs: "Those who are alive at any given time see themselves in the midday of history. They are obliged to prepare a banquet for the past. The historian is the herald who invites those who are departed to the table."

But the banquet is composed of leftovers. It is not meant for those who "sit at the golden tables" (Brecht). An undertaking of this sort will thus employ an allegorical frame of reference to interpret the commodity form. Only then will the inquiry into the commodity illuminate a repressed desire that confronts the course of history. There is no theoretical mesh between these two constructs and it is true that, incompletely integrated into either perspective, the object ends up suspended between them. That was why, whatever his anti-systemic tendencies,[84] Benjamin wished to fuse the messianic with his own brand of materialism. Only in that way would it become possible "to rescue the metaphysical experience of the objective world."[85]

This hermeneutical undertaking, according to Benjamin, is justified insofar as the loss of aura is a symptom of what Max Weber termed the "disenchantment" of the world. Did Benjamin then wish to "re-enchant" it? That depends. An affirmation of experience deadened through the reification process is an obvious derivation of his position. He was fascinated by the thought processes of children; hashish fostered visions; the occult held an allure. Experience, however, still retains a material referent. Innovation, new experience, will thus make it incumbent upon artists to exploit new technical innovations. Just as photography forced painting in the directions of cubism and expressionism, and film transformed the meaning and experience of the photograph, so will holographs provide a new impetus for film.

Fashionable claims about the "end of art" appear foolish from such a perspective. Artistic innovation, now interwoven with the development of technology, will survive so long as technology survives. Nor should there be any mistake. Benjamin's materialist insight is not some paen to technology; he does not claim that every artistic innovation is positive because it employs new technological forms. He is aware that innovations can be introduced from any political perspective. A definition of the relation between literary and political judgments thus becomes necessary. Indeed, this is of crucial importance precisely because the new mass media tends to blur the distinction between art and politics.[86]

Disentangling the one from the other, rather than engaging in some form of postmodern resignation, becomes the task of the critic whom he termed, "the strategist of the literary struggle."[87] Without a framework with which to evaluate the existing political situation, or determine the normative conditions for appropriating the emancipatory potential within an object, judgments will become arbitrary. And the fact is that Benjamin the critic was not exempt from such arbitrariness; thus, he could appreciate Leskov and Gide, but summarily dismiss Bulgakov by claiming that "the tendency is completely counter-revolutionary."[88]

The need for criteria to render judgments thus, once again, asserts itself. Benjamin knew that neither epistemological categories nor aesthetic standards can arise from literary criticism "commenting" on itself or trying to appear as philosophy in a new guise. Nor was he content to accept criteria derived *a priori*. Especially in his early writings, but also from a certain view of *The Arcades Project*, they emerge only from an analysis of the particular text. Benjamin's emphasis upon the object in its uniqueness, the particular text and the practices capable of being inferred from it, is the strength – the genuinely materialist aspect – of his method. But his work offers neither the necessarily transcendental coordinates with which to make sense of the particular nor an insight into the sociological dynamics of its constitution. How then to secure the conditions for a "rescue"?

The answer could emerge only by analyzing the conditions for mechanical reproduction defining the new age. Given the new connection between technology and art, he believed, a "political tendency which is correct [will] comprise a literary tendency which is correct."[89] Benjamin did not wish to argue that the positive judgment of literary works depends upon the manner in which they provide a "correct" depiction of political concerns. Quite the contrary. In keeping with his emphasis on technical innovation, and the "organizing function" of the writer, he emphasized that:

> Commitment is a necessary, but never a sufficient condition for a writer's work acquiring an organizing function. For this to happen it is also necessary for the writer to have a teacher's attitude. And today this is more than ever an essential demand. *A writer who does not teach other writers teaches nobody.* The crucial point, therefore is that a writer's production must have the character of a model: it must be able to instruct other writers in their production and, secondly, it must be able to place an improved apparatus at their disposal.[90]

The implications of this statement confront both the fashionable notion that form alone counts, as well as the belief that the content of the work is the criterion upon which a judgment rests. Bob Dylan is a case in point. Judging the singer on his various religious conversions or the manner in which he does, or does not, offer a pathway to revolution is to employ criteria outside the practice in which he is engaged. The extent to which he articulates utopian wishes and dialectical images, the degree to which he makes other artists aware of new technical innovations and the ways in which his songs evidence transcendence by changing their function, become the criteria with which critics can judge his work and that of others as well.

Progressive use of literary technique and the identification with a progressive political position, however, are not intrinsically connected with one another; T. S. Eliot or Ezra Pound employed progressive literary techniques and believed in reactionary politics at the same time; Anatole France or Romain Rolland, on the other hand, employed less sophisticated techniques even as they associated themselves with more progressive political positions. Transforming the political judgment into one of utopian possibility is merely an evasion. Nor is Benjamin's theory of the dialectical image sufficient; indeed, if reference to the struggle is insufficient for evaluating the techniques employed in the work, the use of those same techniques will not depend upon a particular political insight into social reality.

For all that, however, Benjamin saw the work as "a living center of reflection."[91] He may have been wrong. Perhaps, using a phrase from Leo Lowenthal, its sparks illuminate only what once was possible.[92] No matter. Even the irrecoverable possibility can become relevant in different ways in changing circumstances. What made Benjamin a great critic was his knowledge that the work is always new and fresh. Endless paths may lead back into the past. But there are others, unnoticed for now, which project new challenges for people with clear eyes and a free imagination. Walter Benjamin did not shut his eyes or close his mind. Indeed, such was the nature of his genius.

Notes

1 Benjamin, *Briefe* 2 vols. ed. Gershom Scholem and Theodor W. Adorno (Frankfurt, 1966) vol. 2, p. 505.

2 Note the evaluations regarding its incomprehensibility by Hans Cornelius and Franz Schütz in *Walter Benjamin 1892–1940: Eine Austellung* ed. Rolf Tiedemann et al. for *Marbacher Magazin* 55, 1990, pp. 72–3; also note the similar reception by Karl Kraus of Benjamin's laudatory essay on his work, pp. 120ff.

3 On its proposed structure, cf. Susan Buck-Morss, *The Dialectics of Seeing: Walter Benjamin and the Arcades Project* (Cambridge, 1991), pp. 47ff.

4 Decisive for the reception of Benjamin in America was the article, which originally appeared in *The New Yorker* by Hannah Arendt and then served as the introduction to her edition of Benjamin's *Illuminations* trans. Harry Zohn (New York, 1969); it was also included in her own essay collection *Men in Dark Times* (New York, 1973).

5 Gershom Scholem, "Walter Benjamin and His Angel" in *On Jews and Judaism in Crisis* ed. Werner J. Dannhauser (New York, 1976), p. 198.

6 This has now produced a response from the Right. In a superficial piece of intellectual biography, which actually confronts none of Benjamin's important works other than a single essay, an insulting and unscholarly attempt to debunk his influence and achievements was undertaken by Richard Vine, "The Beatification of Walter Benjamin" in *The New Criterion* (June, 1990), pp. 37ff.

7 Ottmar John, "Fortschrittskritik und Erinnerung: Walter Benjamin, ein Zeuge der Gefahr" in Edmund Arens et al. *Erinnerung, Befreiung, Solidarität: Benjamin, Marcuse, Habermas und die politische Theologie* (Düsseldorf, 1991), pp. 13ff.

8 Note the discussion by Eugene Lunn, *Marxism and Modernism: An Historical Study of Lukács, Brecht, Benjamin, and Adorno* (Berkeley, 1982), pp. 188ff; Gershom Scholem, *Walter Benjamin: The Story of a Friendship* trans. Harry Zohn (New York, 1981), pp. 121ff, 227ff.

9 It was primarily in order to visit Lacis, who had fallen ill, that Benjamin made his only trip to the Soviet Union. His stark description of life in

the increasingly authoritarian workers' state, along with the difficulties of following the official line in his work, led him to decide against joining the German Communist Party. Cf. Walter Benjamin, "Moscow Diary" trans. Richard Sieburth in *October* 35 (Winter, 1985), pp. 9–121.

10 It is interesting, however, that Benjamin should already have published a somewhat stilted review of the Lenin–Gorky correspondence in 1924. Cf. Walter Benjamin, *Gesammelte Schriften* eds. Rolf Tiedemann and Hermann Schweppenhäuser (Frankfurt, 1972), vol. 3, pp. 51ff.

11 That there is no simple break between the early and the mature Benjamin is emphasized by Sándor Radnóti, "The Early Aesthetics of Walter Benjamin," *International Journal of Sociology* (vol. 7, no. 1, Spring, 1977), p. 76 as well as in Rolf Tiedemann's "Nachwort" to Walter Benjamin *Charles Baudelaire: Ein Lyriker im Zeitalter des Hochkapitalismus* (Frankfurt, 1969).

12 Note the letter to Scholem of June, 1917 where Benjamin describes romanticism, which reproduced the inner unity between the religious and the historical in thinking and life experience, as the last movement seeking to explore the transcendent element of tradition. Walter Benjamin, *Briefe* vol. 1, pp. 137ff.

13 Benjamin, "Über das Programm der kommenden Philosophie," p. 27.

14 He could thus approvingly note that when children think about a story they become "directors" and do not bother about what makes sense in conventional terms. The element of play and the attempt to free objects from "use" are utopian themes which recur throughout Benjamin's writings. Cf. "Aussicht ins Kinderbuch," in *Angelus Novus: Ausgewählte Schriften* (Frankfurt, 1966), pp. 151ff.

15 Somewhat simplifying the issue and exaggerating the similarity, one important critic could claim that: "Benjamin's intellectual dilemma was essentially the same as Adorno's: how could he reconcile his Marxist commitment with his Kantian effort in philosophy, especially when, furthermore, he considered religio-mystical and philosophical experience as one?" Susan Buck-Morss, *The Origin of Negative Dialectics. Theodor W. Adorno, Walter Benjamin, and the Frankfurt Institute* (New York, 1977), pp. 21ff.

16 Note, in this regard, the beautiful essays which link memory to the experience of eating, or that of smoking hashish. Cf. "Essen," in *Angelus Novus*, pp. 161–9; cf. also, Walter Benjamin, "Hashish in Marseilles," in *Reflections* ed. Peter Demetz and trans. Edmund Jephcott (New York, 1979), pp. 131ff.

17 Theodor W. Adorno, in *Über Walter Benjamin* (Frankfurt, 1968), p. 11.

18 Ernst Bloch, "Erinnerung" in *Über Walter Benjamin*, p. 17.

19 "The thing," according to Benjamin, "must not be grasped as a mere instantiation of some universal essence, instead, thought must deploy a whole cluster of stubbornly specific concepts which in Cubist style refract the object in myriad directions or penetrate it from a range of diffuse angles. In this way, the phenomenal sphere is itself persuaded to

yield up a kind of noumenal truth, as the microscopic gaze estranges the everyday into the remarkable." Terry Eagleton, *The Ideology of the Aesthetic* (London, 1990), p. 328.

20 "Ideas are to objects as constellations are to stars. This means, in the first place, that they are neither their concepts nor their laws . . . It is the function of concepts to group phenomena together, and the division which is brought about within them thanks to the distinguishing power of the intellect is all the more significant in that it brings about two things at a single stroke: the salvation of the phenomena and the representation of ideas." Walter Benjamin, *The Origin of German Tragic Drama* trans. J. Osborne (London, 1977), p. 34; also cf. Buck-Morss, *The Origins of Negative Dialectics*, pp. 96ff.

21 Eagleton, *The Ideology of the Aesthetic*, p. 334.

22 "Metaphors are the means by which the oneness of the world is poetically brought about. What is so hard to understand about Benjamin is that without being a poet he *thought poetically* and therefore was bound to regard the metaphor as the greatest gift of language." Hannah Arendt, "Walter Benjamin", in *Men in Dark Times* (Harmondsworth, 1955) p. 164.

23 It thus makes sense that history should have been viewed by him as early as 1915 as "the objective element in time, something *perceptibly* objective." Scholem, *Walter Benjamin: The Story of a Friendship*, p. 13.

24 Ibid, p. 113.

25 ". . . the expression that is linguistically most existent (i.e. most fixed) is linguistically the most rounded and definitive; in a word, the most expressed is at the same time the purely mental. Exactly this, however, is meant by the concept of revelation, if it takes the inviolability of the word as the only and sufficient condition and characteristic of the divinity of the mental being that is expressed in it." Walter Benjamin, "On Language as Such and on the Language of Man," in *Reflections*, p. 321.

26 Benjamin, "Über das Programm der kommenden Philosophie," *Angelus Novus*, p. 321.

27 Benjamin, *The Origin of German Tragic Drama* (London, 1977), pp. 178ff.

28 "Allegory is always a symptom that, in a certain respect the Subject–object distance has been sublated (*aufgehoben*), that the object-world has been transformed in its signification, that it has been worked through by the subject . . . Thus we approach the essence of allegory only then when we recognize it as a possibility which lies in the depths of the essence of language" in Hans Heinz Holz, "Prismatisches Denken", *Über Walter Benjamin*, p. 77.

29 Ibid., p. 76.

30 Georg Lukács, *Aesthetik* 4 vols, (Darmstadt, 1972) vol. 4, p. 164.

31 Scholem, "Walter Benjamin and His Angel," p. 203; Scholem, *Walter Benjamin*, p. 135.

32 Cf. Walter Benjamin, "Eduard Fuchs, der Sammler und der Historiker," *Angelus Novus*, pp. 302ff.

33 Thus, "the art of the critic in nuce: offer slogans without betraying ideas." Walter Benjamin, "The Technique of the Critic in Thirteen Theses" in *Marbacher Magazin*, p. 112.

34 Restoration as the function of commentary is made evident in the Talmud; note the superb essay by Jürgen Habermas, "Gershom Scholem: The Torah in Disguise" in *Philosophical-Political Profiles* trans. Frederick G. Lawrence (Cambridge, Mass., 1985), pp. 201ff.

35 Again, in Talmudic terms, the redemptive power of language comes into play. See the intelligent discussion by Susan A. Handelman, *Fragments of Redemption: Jewish Thought and Literary Theory in Benjamin, Scholem, and Levinas* (Bloomington, 1991), pp. 25ff.

36 Walter Benjamin, "The Task of the Translator" in *Illuminations* trans. Harry Zohn (New York, 1969), pp. 69ff.

37 Walter Benjamin, "Goethes Wahlverwandtschaften" in *Schriften* 2 vols, (Frankfurt, 1955) vol. 1, p. 56.

38 Cf. Michael Löwy, *Rédemption et Utopie: Judaisme libératrice en Europe Central* (Paris, 1988).

39 His ties were to a "mystical tradition and to a mystical experience which nevertheless was a far cry from the experience of God, proclaimed by so many oversimplifying minds as the only experience deserving to be called mystical. Benjamin knew that mystical experience is many-layered and it was precisely this many-layeredness that played so great a role in his thinking." Scholem, "Walter Benjamin and His Angel," p. 201; also note the discussion by Irving Wolfarth, "On Some Jewish Motifs in Benjamin" in *The Problems of Modernity: Adorno and Benjamin* ed. Andrew Benjamin (London, 1989), pp. 157ff. and Michael Löwy, "Religion, Utopia, and Counter-modernity: The Allegory of the Angel of History in Walter Benjamin" in *On Changing the World: Essays in Political Philosophy, From Karl Marx to Walter Benjamin* (Atlantic Highlands, NJ., 1992), pp. 164ff.

40 Cf. Handelman, *Fragments of Redemption*, pp. 137ff.

41 Scholem, *Walter Benjamin*, p. 56; also Benjamin, "Programm der kommenden Philosophie," p. 41.

42 Thus, the famous image of Klee's painting entitled *Angelus Novus*, which "shows an angel looking as though he is about to move away from something he is fixedly contemplating . . . His face is turned toward the past. Where we perceive a chain of events, he sees one single catastrophe which keeps piling wreckage upon wreckage and hurls it in front of his feet. The angel would like to stay, awaken the dead, and make whole what has been smashed. But a storm is blowing from Paradise; it has got caught in his wings with such violence that the angel can no longer close them. This storm irresistibly propels him into the future to which his back is turned, while the pile of debris before him

grows skyward. This storm is what we call progress." Walter Benjamin, "Theses on the Philosophy of History," in *Illuminations*, p. 258.

43   "Nothing that has ever happened should be regarded as lost for history. To be sure, only a redeemed mankind receives the fullness of its past – which is to say only for a redeemed mankind has its past become citable in all its moments. Each moment it has lived becomes a *citation à l'ordre du jour* – and that day is Judgment Day." Ibid., p. 254.

44   Ibid., p. 257.

45   Ibid., p. 261.

46   "Only the historian is firmly convinced that *even the dead* will not be safe from the enemy if he wins. And this enemy has not ceased to be victorious." Ibid., p. 255.

47   Theodor Adorno, "Charakteristik Walter Benjamins," in *Prismen: Kulturkritik und Gesellschaft* (Frankfurt, 1955), p. 294.

48   Walter Benjamin, "Zur Kritik der Gewalt" in *Angelus Novus*, pp. 42ff.

49   Rolf Tiedemann, "An Interpretation of the 'Theses On the Concept of History' " in *The Philosophical Forum* vol. 2, nos. 1–2 (Fall–Winter, 1983–4), pp. 91ff.

50   Benjamin's actual political commitments are rarely discussed and when they are, even in the otherwise superb study by Susan Buck-Morss, an uncritical stance incapable of relating them to his metaphysics is generally the norm. Cf. Buck-Morss, *Dialectics of Seeing*, pp. 317ff; also, for my own interpretation of the strike wave, see the chapter entitled "Leon Blum and the Legacy of the Popular Front" in Stephen Eric Bronner *Moments of Decision: Political History and the Crises of Radicalism* (New York, 1991), pp. 57ff.

51   "We know that the Jews were prohibited from investigating the future. The Torah and the prayers instruct them in remembrance, however. This stripped the future of its magic, to which all those succumb who turn to the soothsayers for enlightenment. This does not imply, however, that for the Jews the future turned into homogeneous, empty time. For every second of time was the strait gate through which the Messiah might enter." Benjamin, "Theses on the Philosophy of History," in *Illuminations* p. 264.

52   Note the discussion by Richard Wolin, *Walter Benjamin: An Aesthetic of Redemption* (New York, 1982), pp. 213ff; also, Arendt, "Walter Benjamin," p. 164.

53   It is logical, in a way, that Carl Schmitt – the legal thinker and fascist collaborator – should have expressed his admiration for Benjamin's essay on Sorel. Cf. Jürgen Habermas, "The Horrors of Autonomy: Carl Schmitt in English" in *The New Conservatism: Cultural Criticism and the Historians' Debate* ed. and trans. Shierry Weber Nicholson (Cambridge, Mass., 1992), p. 137.

54   Scholem, "Walter Benjamin," p. 187.

55   The theologizing terminology of the theses "attempts to preserve the content of the proletarian revolution within the concept of the Messiah,

the classless society within the messianic age and class struggle within messianic power. At the same time the revolution which does not come is supposed to be standing at the gate at any moment, like the Messiah. There, in some historical beyond, it can quickly put together a classless society, even if it is nowhere to be seen around here. The retranslation of materialism into theology cannot avoid the risk of losing both: the secularized content may dissolve while the theological idea evaporates." Rolf Tiedemann, "Historical Materialism or Political Messianism? in *The Philosophical Forum* vol. 15, nos. 1–2 (Fall–Winter 1983–4) p. 96.

56 Note the discussion by Karl Korsch, *Karl Marx* (New York, 1938), p. 84; also note Karl Marx, "Theses on Feuerbach" in Karl Marx and Friederich Engels, *Selected Works* 3 vols. (Moscow, 1969) vol. 1, p. 13; also, Handelman, *Fragments of Redemption*, pp. 163ff.

57 The belief that it is impossible to confront the proletariat with preconceived utopian tasks is a constant in the work of Marx; the remark about the proletariat not having goals of its own to realize must be set in the context of the young Marx's concern with extending democracy from the realm of the state into civil society in works like *On the Jewish Question* and *The Holy Family*. Note my discussion on the political development of Marx's thought in *Socialism Unbound* (New York, 1990), pp. 1–30.

58 Indeed, alluding to this point, Horkheimer stated the obvious when he chastized his friend in a letter: "The injustice, the terror, the pains of the past are irreparable;" cited in Buck-Morss, *The Origins of Negative Dialectics*, p. 57.

59 Cf. Christian Lenhardt, "Anamnestic Solidarity: The Proletariat and its Manes" in *Telos* 25 (Fall, 1975), pp. 136ff, 141ff.

60 Löwy, "Revolution against 'Progress': Walter Benjamin's Romantic Anarchism" in *On Changing the World*, pp. 143ff.

61 Walter Benjamin, "Goethe's Wahlverwandtschaften," p. 131.

62 Leo Lowenthal, *An Unmastered Past* ed. Martin Jay (Berkeley, 1987), p. 227.

63 "How misery, and not just social misery but rather architectonic misery as well, the misery of the interior turns enslaved and enslaving things into revolutionary nihilism, of that no one before these seers and astrologers has been aware . . . " Benjamin, "Der Surrealismus: Die letzte Momentaufnahme der europaischen Intelligenz," *Angelus Novus*, p. 204.

64 "Whereas earlier interpreters have seen his pessimism regarding the course of history as a late characteristic of his thinking, coming as a response to the Nazi–Soviet Non-Aggression Pact or the impending war, the *Passagen-Werk* makes it clear that it was his long-standing (if intensifying) concern." Buck-Morss, *The Dialectics of Seeing*, p. 79.

65 Eugene Lunn, *Marxism and Modernism*, p. 166.

66 Walter Benjamin, "What is Epic Theatre?" in *Understanding Brecht* trans. Anna Bostock (London, 1973), pp. 2,4,8.

67 Lowenthal, *An Unmastered Past*, p. 224.

68 "The construction of life at the moment lies far more in the power of facts than in convictions." Walter Benjamin, *Einbahnstrasse* in *Schriften* vol. 2, p. 515.

69 But, if this much is clear, obvious problems arise if it is true that Benjamin "charts philosophical ideas visually within an unreconciled and transitory field of oppositions that can perhaps best be pictured in terms of coordinates of contradictory terms, the 'synthesis' of which is not a movement toward resolution, but the point at which their axes intersect." Buck-Morss, *The Dialectics of Seeing*, p. 210.

70 In discussing allegory's scholastic and formal nature, Lukács notes that: "after all, in such actions interchangeable things and details are only sublated (*aufgehoben*) in their being-as-they-are (*Geradesosein*). The act of sublation directs itself only to their character at that particular time and substitutes something which is exactly the same from within their inner structure. Thus, insofar as it is only a particular which is being replaced by something just as particular, this sublation is nothing more than the restless reproduction of their particularity." Lukács, *Aesthetik* vol. 4, p. 169.

71 If this desire along with the importance attributed to montage appears in the collection of letters by historical personalities, which appeared individually in the *Frankfurter Zeitung* in 1931/2 and were then published by Benjamin under the pseudonym Detlef Holz in 1936, the need for introductions to them – no less than their importance – evidences the difficulty of the having aesthetic or historical objects speak for themselves. Walter Benjamin, *Deutsche Menschen: Eine Folge von Briefen* (Frankfurt, 1984).

72 Max Horkheimer, "Notes on the Crisis" in *Critical Theory and Society: A Reader* eds Stephen Eric Bronner and Douglas Kellner (New York, 1989), p. 52.

73 Cited in *Marbacher Magazin* p. 45.

74 Cf. Löwy, "Fire Alarm: Walter Benjamin's Critique of Technology" in *On Changing the World*, pp. 175ff.

75 It apppears in an earlier essay entitled the "Short History of Photography," for example, where Benjamin notes that early photographs by Eugene Atget retain elements of the aura which they would later lose owing to commercial exploitation. Note the critique of Benjamin's mechanical juxtaposition of the auratic against the mass-produced in T. W. Adorno, *Aesthetic Theory* eds Gretl Adorno and Rolf Tiedemann and trans. C. Lenhart (London, 1984), pp. 82–3.

76 Walter Benjamin, *Charles Baudelaire: A Lyric Poet in the Era of High Capitalism* trans. Harry Zohn (London, 1973), p. 148.

77 Adorno is correct when, concerning Benjamin's compilation of historical letters, he observes that "a historical judgment over the letter as form [has been rendered]. It is anarchronistic; who is still able to write them highlights capacities grown archaic; actually, letters can no longer

be written. Benjamin provided them with a monument." Theodor Adorno, "Nachwort" to *Deutsche Menschen*, p. 95.

78 "One might subsume the eliminated element in the term 'aura' and go on to say: that which withers in the age of mechanical reproduction is the aura of the work of art. This is a symptomatic process whose significance points beyond the realm of art. One might generalize by saying: the technique of reproduction detaches the reproduced object from the domain of tradition. By making reproductions it substitutes a plurality of copies for a unique existence. And in permitting the reproduction to meet the beholder or listener in his own particular situation, it reactivates the object reproduced. These two processes lead to a tremendous shattering of tradition which is the obverse of the contemporary crisis and renewal of mankind." Walter Benjamin, "The Work of Art in the Age of Mechanical Reproduction" in *Illuminations*, p. 221.

79 "Novels did not always exist in the past, nor must they necessarily always exist in the future; nor, always, tragedies; nor great epics; literary forms such as the commentary . . . we are in the midst of a vast process in which literary forms are being melted down, a process in which many of the contrasts in terms of which we have been accustomed to think may lose their relevance." Walter Benjamin, "The Author as Producer" in *Understanding Brecht*, p. 89.

80 Ibid., p. 101.

81 Benjamin, *Charles Baudelaire*, p. 105.

82 This is why Adorno could attack the notion of "dialectical images," and further claim that Benjamin's Baudelaire manuscript "lacks one thing: mediation" in "Letters to Walter Benjamin," *New Left Review* 81 (September–October, 1973), p. 70; also note the evaluation of the dispute by Wolin, *Walter Benjamin*, pp. 163ff.

83 Benjamin, *Charles Baudelaire*, p. 103.

84 It is subsequently legitimate to claim that "for all his renunciation of system, his thought, presented as that of a fragmentarian, yet retains a systematic tendency. He used to say that each great work needs its own epistemology just as it had its own metaphysics." Gershom Scholem, "Walter Benjamin," in *On Jews and Judaism in Crisis*, p. 182.

85 Buck-Morss, *The Dialectics of Seeing*, p. 221.

86 Ibid., p. 142.

87 Benjamin, "The Technique of the Critic in Thirteen Theses" in *Marbacher Magazin*, p. 112.

88 Walter Benjamin, "Die politische Gruppierung der russichen Schrift-steller" in *Angelus Novus*, p. 193.

89 Benjamin, "The Author as Producer," p. 86.

90 Ibid., p. 98.

91 Walter Benjamin, *Der Begriff der Kunstkritik in der deutschen Romantik* (Frankfurt, 1973), p. 67.

92 Lowenthal, *An Unmastered Past*, p. 110.

8

Political Aesthetics in Retrospect: Reflections on the Expressionism Debate and its Contemporary Relevance[1]

In Memory of Christopher Johnson

Political aesthetics in the 1930s was always undertaken with an eye on the Soviet Union. Expressionism, for example, became the subject of sharp political controversy precisely because of the cultural attempt to unite the masses behind the industrialization of the USSR. This began with Stalin's "left turn" of 1929, which was no step toward liberation. The Five Year Plan and the slogan of "socialism in one country" were not signals of revolution, but testaments to the seeming stabilization of capitalism. They reflected the fact that communism had turned inward and the onset of what Korsch termed the "counter-revolution."

Quickly enough, intraparty democracy was destroyed, cultural innovation ceased, and Marxism became transformed into the dogma of dialectical materialism or "diamat." Divorce and abortion now became difficult to obtain in the new police state. Emphasis was placed upon the family and, with the introduction of Stakhanovism, cultural puritanism was extended to the artistic arena. Tolerance for radical modernist experiments, like those undertaken by the constructivists and suprematists, vanished. Art would now directly relate to the immediate needs of the party. Thus, "socialist realism" came to define its official line.[2]

The political character of this cultural change, however, only becomes clear if the Popular Front is taken into account. The 1920s had witnessed an increasing sectarianism on the part of the communist movement. The triumphs of Hitler, combined with fears of the growing fascist threat in France, forced a change in the position previously taken by the Communist International. A new preoccupation with "bourgeois" realism became the aesthetic extension of a political policy which called upon communists to align themselves with all anti-fascist forces. No longer was their purpose the destruction of bourgeois culture. The communists were now to inherit its most "progressive" aspects and employ them against the more "decadent" elements that had led to fascism.

An "International Writers' Conference for the Defense of Culture" took place at the Paris *Mutualité* in 1935. This meeting of anti-fascist, but not necessarily communist, writers occurred in the wake of the Comintern directive to build a Popular Front, which was issued at its Seventh World Congress under the leadership of Georgii Dimitrov. Its most visible member was Heinrich Mann. But a host of other luminaries took part: André Malraux, André Gide, Theodor Plivier, Aldous Huxley, Ilya Ehrenburg, Julien Benda, Alfred Döblin, Lion Feuchtwanger, Ernst Bloch, Madalaine Paz, Bertott Brecht, Anna Seghers, Waldo Frank, and others. While the congress expressed the unity among anti-fascists, however, many participants were left with the bitter feeling that dogmatism was running rampant and that those who had not accepted the new line, or who believed that no line should be imposed, were unwelcome. It was in this political atmosphere that the "expressionism debate" took place.[3] It could just as easily have been labeled the "realism" debate, however, since its content derived from the first attempt to stamp a uniform orientation on socialist art and culture.

Most of the debate was carried on in *Das Wort* (The Word). The journal grew out of this anti-fascist conference and appeared for the first time in 1936 with an editorial board composed of Willi Bredel, Brecht, and Feuchtwanger. The debate achieved an almost legendary status among intellectuals of the European Left especially during the 1960s and 1970s.

Anything connected with the Weimar Republic and the Nazis seemed to hold a certain fascination. And, given the emphasis placed on culture by the emerging social movements of the 1960s, questions concerning the relation between the expressionist avant-garde and fascism were of some interest. There was also the fact that the major disputants in the expressionism debate were dominant intellectual figures. Even the secondary contributors, however, were of importance. Alfred Kurella, for example, was one of the most influential communist critics of the age. Johannes R. Becher had been a famous expressionist poet and later became one of the leading cultural commissars of East Germany. Anna Seghers, author of *The Seventh Cross*, had also become a major figure in communist cultural politics. It was the stature of the participants, the quality of argumentation, and the context, which contributed to the aura surrounding the expressionism controversy.

Linking expressionism with fascism ostensibly seems somewhat forced. Modern art is usually associated with the Left. But the fact remains that certain segments of the intellectual avant-garde initially supported fascism. They identified with its irrationalist, violent, and apocalyptic tendencies; they believed it would bring a "new man" into existence and make an end of bourgeois society. Once in power, of course, the fascists retreated from much of the rhetoric they had used while their movement was on the rise. As the *SA* gave way to the *Wehrmacht* and the *SS*, as order came to rule, the fascists' tolerance for these bohemians waned. The artists either became servants of the new regime or engaged in an "inner emigration," which ultimately led to their inclusion in the infamous "Degenerate Art Exhibition" of 1938.

None of this, of course, says much about the extent to which expressionism shaped the climate in which the Nazis came to power. If ideology is lived then culture must have at least an indirect impact upon society. Expressionism, furthermore, had been the dominant avant-garde tendency in Germany just before and after World War I. These were the years of *Die Brücke* and *Der Blaue Reiter* of the transformation of theater by figures like Ernst Toller, Walter Hasenclever, and Georg Kaiser, and of the revolution in music by Schönberg. Expressionists, whatever the stylistic and political differences between them, basically harbored similar feelings. They felt alienated from established society and they yearned for a better world. They protested against what they considered a sterile rationalism and a vapid materialism with heightened emotion and metaphysical despair over the "death of God."

The modernist assault on bourgeois society had started much earlier. The beginnings occur in romanticism with its emphasis on the autonomy of experience and the purity of nature. It gained momentum through symbolism, fauvism, cubism, futurism, and expressionism and generated ever more vehement statements of secession from the constraints of convention in ever accelerating cycles. The modernist movement fought hard for its triumphs, withstanding ridicule and staunch opposition during those periods in which its most radical aesthetic innovations were developed. And, in aesthetic terms, it was successful. Modernism had called everything associated with artistic tradition into question: its subject matter, its modes of representation, its public and even its boundaries.

Arguably, however, the years of aesthetic vitality are not necessarily the most important for a movement. Its effects and definition generally come about only when the owl of Minerva has spread its wings. The

1920s were the time in which expressionism came into its own. The German movement had initially been confined to a small group of bohemian artists and intellectuals. The 1920s, however, saw its assimilation by the same bourgeoisie it had originally held up to ridicule. Economic dislocation, ideological disillusionment, a pervasive sense of decay, and a new republican order with liberal convictions helped create a somewhat broader public for artists like Frank Wedekind and Yvan Goll, Georg Heym and Gottfried Benn, Emil Nolde and Wassily Kandinsky. Oskar Kokoschka, who was called the "Austrian terror" in the years preceding World War I, received a professional chair while Alban Berg's *Wozzeck* was performed amid great fanfare.

Expressionism was incorporated into the cultural constellation of bourgeois taste. Among that thin strata of the "modern" bourgeoisie who voted for the German Democratic Party, snorted cocaine, and underwent psychoanalysis, expressionism was in vogue. Bankers paid thousands of dollars to have their portraits done by expressionist painters while the National Gallery and the Neue Pinakothek greedily bought paintings by Ernst Barlach, Paul Cézanne, Ernst Ludwig Kirchner, Franz Marc, Max Pechstein and others. The satirical papers had great fun with this symbiosis of wealth and self-laceration.

The sad truth is, however, that expressionism had few political defenders. The Nazis denounced it as "cultural bolshevism" and part of a deliberate design by the Elders of Zion to demoralize the German people. Their own populist protest against the machine age had found expression in popular (*völkisch*) kitsch, "heroic realism" and sentimental lyricism. Nor did the organized labor movement, even prior to the birth of Stalinism, have much sympathy for modernism in general or expressionism in particular. It pointed proudly to Gustav Courbet and Honoré Daumier, Anatole France and Maxim Gorky, Käthe Kollwitz and Heinrich Zille. Cézanne or Matisse, however, were alien to both the socialist and communist press. It was by accident of personality, rather than ideology, that a few intellectuals like Paul Levi appreciated modern art. Thus the major expressionist journals *Der Sturm* and *Die Aktion* found their audience among ultra-left bohemians and intellectuals rather than in the working class.

Expressionism seemed to hang suspended between the major classes and the existing political formations. This is what made its political message and social impact so difficult to decipher. Expressionism had not yet become classical, Marxism played a very different role, and the fascist threat was far more real than today. Many of the issues bitterly contested in the expressionism debate may thus seem somehow anachronistic. Questions concerning the nature of a "revolutionary" or "progressive" art, however, retain their relevance. Nor have issues concerning the

social impact of cultural products lost their importance. The enlightenment heritage no less than the appropriation of modernism continue to
define current debate. Other historical and philosophical matters concerning the struggles being waged to revivify the liberating possibilities
of Marxism also have a certain currency. Thus, while various unwarranted political and epistemological assumptions become evident in the
debate, even the errors of the participants can help in orienting future
forms of critical aesthetic inquiry.

Georg Lukács: Expressionism and Critical Realism

The stage for the expressionism debate was set in 1934 with the
publication of *"Grosse und Verfall' des Expressionismus"* which Georg
Lukács originally published in *Internationale Literatur*. His earlier pre-
Marxist works, like *Soul and Form* and *Theory of the Novel* had themselves
been reflections of the modernist sensibility. Following his retraction of
History and Class Consciousness in 1924, however, he had engaged in an
ever more critical re-evaluation of his development.[4] His philosophical
shift away from vitalism and idealism, in fact, mirrored his growing
attachment to bourgeois or "critical" realism. Thus, especially given the
new Popular Front line of the Communist Party, it only makes sense that
he should have defended this tendency against its decadent counterpart:
expressionism.

Grounding himself within the tradition beginning with Walter Scott,
which found its greatest twentieth-century proponent in Thomas Mann,
Lukács claimed that a work of art grows out of a given society and
"mirrors" that society. This "mirroring," however, is not simply based
on the artistic accumulation of facts, impressions and experiences. It
occurs insofar as the realist work presents the dialectical "totality" of
mediations, contradictions and interconnections defining a given society.
A work of "realism" subsequently exposes the "objective" social context
so often ignored in the subjective experience. Ideological veils are
stripped away as the difference emerges between the way society "really"
functions and the way it merely "appears."

Lukács draws the distinction between essence and appearance and, in
doing so, defines himself in the tradition of the most progressive
representatives of the rising bourgeoisie on which Marx himself relied.
Kant first gave the essence-appearance relation its modern epistemological expression. Appearance, or the "phenomenon," took on a dual
meaning. It was simultaneously an "object of empirical intuition" and
the product of an essence, or a "noumenal" thing-in-itself, which
remains closed to rational investigation. Kant's cleavage between essence

and appearance, however, was overcome by Hegel who maintained that the essence of an object will become manifest in the series of its appearances. History will evidence the "essence," or "idea," underlying all purposive human activity: freedom. Marx, however, strips away the idealist trappings. A historically specific system of production is seen as giving rise to objective class contradictions, which constrain the exercise of freedom and subjectivity. The essence of society is thus the "totality" mediating given "moments" of action. No less than Kant and Hegel, however, Marx maintains that discovering the essence of reality involves a rational form of critical inquiry: only through a concrete analysis of the totality is it possible to comprehend the particular in the mediations constituting it. Thus, for Lukács, the prime purpose of literature presents itself.

> If literature is indeed a special mode of mirroring objective reality, then it is of the utmost importance that it comprehend this reality as it is actually constituted and that it not limit itself to a rendering of that which immediately [*unmittelbar*] appears.[5]

An articulation of the mediated totality is precisely what Lukács finds in the work of the great realists. In Tolstoy, for example, the characters and their interactions, the changes which they undergo and the opinions which they form, are seen as emerging from within a changing context. Especially expressionism, in contrast, seems to favor an unmediated rendering of experience. An emotive, unreflective, irrational and subject-ivistic mode of apprehending reality confronts the progressive legacy of the bourgeoisie no less than the method of Marx. This is why, from the first, Lukács championed objective and realistic aesthetic forms against the subjectivism of expressionist art.

Lukács is not blind to the importance of the inspirational element in artistic creation. But he maintains that the inspirational and emotive factor cannot be considered by itself or in a reified fashion. Inspiration, from his perspective, thus becomes artistically viable when it becomes a "moment" within the cognitive process as a whole. Consequently, the categories seeking to make sense of the creative process in art must stand in coherent relation to those employed in understanding the world of production.[6]

The ability to comprehend society as a totality ultimately separates the realist from the expressionist. Without an explicit dialectical relation between the particular and the totality of which it is a part, for Lukács, the work cannot offer a cogent and rational worldview.[7] The inability, or better the refusal, to develop such a worldview is precisely what is seen as defining the "decadence" of the expressionists in relation to the realists who preceded them. The inherent relation between "essence" and "appearance" breaks down along with the way the world is experienced and the way subjectivity is itself constituted within a context.

And this was seen as having political consequences. Where the expressionists might subjectively have considered themselves free from bourgeois influences, as the avant-garde initiating the "regeneration of man" (*die Erneuerung des Menschen*), objectively they appear to Lukács in a different light. Though preoccupied with attacking conservative social mores, militarism, and the bourgeoisie itself, these issues were never framed concretely. They instead were ripped from their historical context. So, for example, the expressionists tended to label their characters "The Son," "The Friend," "The Father," in order to cloak them in universality. The expressionist critique, according to Lukács, remained a purely abstract form of humanism embodied in the cry: "*O Mensch.*" Subjectivism and moralism infected the expressionist worldview. So, whether consciously or unconsciously, they proved unable to confront the reality which they sought to expose and judge. Their criticisms only reproduced the very problems they sought to confront. Thus, no matter how "radical" the expressionists may have thought themselves, their opposition to bourgeois life was merely "romantic" and "petit bourgeois."

Life, from the expressionist perspective, becomes a conglomeration of experiential fragments. Insofar as they are preserved from "interconnection" with the social totality, and closed to dialectical reason, reality becomes a "chaos" or a "riddle" to which an answer becomes impossible *a priori*. The world is robbed of values and meaning even though, from the perspective of Lukács, it is possible for the subject to situate himself or herself and analyze any given concerns through a rational examination of his socio-historical conditions. The avant-garde, however, rejects that alternative and thus turns its back on the progressive heritage of the bourgeoisie. Consequently, for Lukács, it is no accident that various avant-gardists like Barlach or Kandinsky should have embraced a vague spiritualism or even that the more politically inclined like George Grosz and John Heartfield should ultimately have turned from expressionism to the "new objectivity" (*Neue Sachlichkeit*).

Apocalyptic visions play an important role in expressionist art. For Lukács, however, this is just another example of the way in which the "concrete potential" for qualitative change was ignored by the avant-garde. Abstracting itself from the existing society prevented expressionist art from "mirroring" it which, in turn, assured the irrational response towards it. Social reality could appear only as an indecipherable "chaos." And, for this very reason, it was no longer capitalist society to be overcome, but rather the "chaos" as such. Revolution gave way to the apocalypse and, according to Lukács, it is precisely in this expressionist syndrome, "often unrecognized by its victim," that the danger appears. For, in the mysticism and the abstract use of categories, the left-wing attack on the status quo could easily veer to its opposite extreme. It could turn into "a critique of bourgeois values from the Right, into that same demagogic critique of capitalism to which fascism subsequently became indebted for its mass base."[8]

Expressionism, in this vein, helped create the cultural climate in which fascism could thrive.[9] Irrationalism turned the avant-garde into a symptom of the crisis rather than a cure.[10] The issue is not merely the "abstract" quality of their work. The realists, after all, also employed abstraction. But their usage opposed the expressionist abstraction away from reality (*Wegabstrahierung*). A twofold creative as well as ideological (*weltanschauliche*) effort takes place: "namely, first the intellectual discovery and creative formation of the inter-relations [of reality – trans.] and second, yet inseparable from the first, the artistic concealment of these abstractly worked-through inter-relations – the sublation [*Aufhebung*] of the abstraction."[11]

Lukács is aware that the realist will "abstract" from everyday individuals in order to create a character. The special emphasis placed upon him or her will render the character "atypical." Insofar as the character is brought back into a milieu, however, he or she will regain an element of "typicality" even while remaining "atypical." A character like Hans Castorp in *The Magic Mountain* or Pierre in *War and Peace* is then "atypically-typical" with the sublation (*Aufhebung*) of the initial abstraction.[12] A character in an expressionist play by Ernst Toller, by contrast, *can* never appear in this light since the context in which experiences occur is never fully defined. Expressionist works *can* therefore never distinguish the "appearance" from the "essence" of reality and, precisely to this extent, they reproduce the ideology they claim to criticize.

Contextualizing the particular, according to Lukács, is what validates the initial abstraction and the use of fiction to expose truth. And so, where the abstraction of the expressionist can produce only illusion, the abolition of the initial abstraction by the realist employs illusion to reveal the objective reality veiled by ideology. The strength of realism subsequently derives from its ability to destroy the illusions of its characters by confronting them with the social processes in which they are formed. Tensions emerge within an organic whole, or a "closed" totality, which enables the audience to contemplate "objectively" the actions taking place. The intrinsic clarity of realism makes the work accessible to the masses in a way expressionist works cannot with their subjectivism, formal difficulty, and often purposeful obscurantism. Realism thus projects a certain relation to the life of the masses (*Volkstümlichkeit*) even as it retains a pedagogic function.

Lukács surely stressed the *Volkstümlichkeit* of realism in order to salvage the concept from the Nazis who employed it merely as an ideological tool to justify their own "heroic" forms of pseudo-classical kitsch. By the same token, however, he probably also sought to accomodate the new cultural policy of Stalin. Lukács spoke positively of certain "socialist realist" works.[13] But, in emphasizing the legacy of "critical" realism, he clearly sought to preserve the enlightenment legacy for Marxism. Thus, it is possible to suggest that he was engaging in a type of literary "guerilla war" against the unbending dogmatists.[14]

Realism, according to Lukács, is "critical" precisely insofar as it objectively explicates the specific conditions of capitalist social relations and the manner in which they impinge on individual experience. But there is no reason to think that this "critical" quality cannot extend to what was called "actually existing socialism"; indeed, there is nothing ironic about the fact that Lukács should have praised the early work of Alexander Solzhenitsyn. His basic point is simply that any work seeking to perform a critical or pedagogic function must situate itself within the historical and artistic traditions of a particular society. Nor need such a stance result in an "evolutionary" conception of either history or art. Indeed, following Hegel, Lukács claimed that only in relation to the most progressive innovations of the past can the emancipatory possibilities of the present become concrete.

It is not realism that is aligned with "evolutionary" conceptions of change, according to Lukács, but modernism insofar as it un-dialectically opposes all traditions and proclaims with Antonin Artaud: *"A finir avec les chefs-d'oeuvres!."* It sees in history only ruptures and catastrophes so that, instead of serving as a genuine negation, it becomes merely the anarchistic opposition of evolutionary reformism.[15] For Lukács, again following Hegel and Marx, history is the "living dialectical unity" between continuity and discontinuity. Insofar as the avant-garde is incapable of grasping the social totality, however, it must logically remain blind to this "unity." Expressionism cannot help but mystify reality and distort the historical crisis of bourgeois society. Thus, for Lukács, there remains little the oppressed can learn from an irrationalist and elitist avant-garde which, in fact, constituted a "subordinate" (*untergeordnetes*) moment of the fascist victory.

Lukács, in articulating these views, initiated the "expressionism" debate. Both Ernst Bloch and Bertolt Brecht took exception to his unqualified defense of realism, the reductivism of his approach, and the often mechanistic nature of his analysis. In this context, their response becomes as much the attempt to preserve the need for a novel and experimental art as to justify expressionism itself.

Ernst Bloch: Expressionism and Liberation

Ernst Bloch was also critical of irrationalism and liked to call mysticism the "ignorant caricature of profundity."[16] But he still believed there was much to be gained from an "anticipatory movement" like expressionism insofar as it projects emancipation beyond the constraints of the existing discourse. And this suggests that, insofar as it is still a viable category, the totality cannot remain confined to the sphere of "objectively" discernible interactions; if the totality is in fact really total then it must come to terms with the fantasy and the imaginative components of subjective experience.[17] According to Bloch, in fact, analyzing expressionism sociologically results in an "academic" standpoint incapable of appreciating what is most important: the anticipation of emancipation, the experimentation with new forms, and the experience of "artistic joy" (*Kunstfreude*).

Transcendence confronts immanence. And this becomes particularly apparent in poetry, music, and painting. The omission of these forms of expression skews Lukács's analysis in favor of literature. It is, in fact, "all the more surprising since, not only were the relations between painting and literature of the closest kind at the time, but the expressionist paintings are far more indicative of the movement than the literature."[18]

The chord which Bloch had already struck with the publication of his *Spirit of Utopia*, a work which he later termed a "testament to the original expressionist impulse," is carried over into the debates. There he wrote: "We are starting from scratch. We are poor and have forgotten how to play."[19] This was the time when an an extremely close personal as well as working friendship still existed between Bloch and Lukács, which ended around the time of Lukács's self-criticism for *History and Class Consciousness*. Bloch never retracted his association with the avant-garde and, ironically, his position in the debates was clearly influenced by the early work of Lukács. Nevertheless, while Lukács emphasized the role of naturalism in the emergence of the avant-garde,[20] Bloch saw the power of expressionism in its liquidation of the "real."

Against those content with equating the empirical with the real, according to Bloch, it is necessary to confront reality in its dynamic movement.[21] This, however, demands an ability to portray the "exact fantasy." The "true," in the sense of the non-alienated and non-reified, exists outside the calculating logic of capitalist reality. "Mirroring" existing forms of social relations does not exhaust the criteria for evaluating an artwork. It is thus less important that expressionism should have reflected what "is" than that it should have provided a sense of "what is not" by indicating a new set of unrealized emancipatory hopes and fantasies. Here, in the "dream content" of expressionism, lies its radical indictment of the status quo and its connection with the revolutionary inheritance of the past.

The revolution must move beyond the economic and the social realms. It must also speak to the cultural and the psychological. Expressionism makes that move by exploding the possibility of objective contemplation on the part of the audience. It distorts objects, juxtaposes unrelated fragments of reality, subverts syntax, and transvalues time. All this tends to force the onlooker to see reality in a new way and draw his own conclusions.

Nowhere is this more apparent than in the use of montage, which necessarily involves the spectator in a mode of comprehension which effects changes in his perception of reality; a qualitatively different idea of reality emerges as montage reveals a richness within existence which cannot be discovered in the usual ways in which it is perceived. Expressionism sought to free the unconscious and give voice to fantasy. It fostered a return of the repressed and generated new forms of empathy through attempts to "transfer" oneself into what resists "progress." There is, of course, a naive and romantic quality to all this. A naive idea, however, can have very sophisticated consequences. Just such emotions fostered a new cosmopolitan concern with African art and inspired the wonderful animal paintings of Franz Marc. Social concerns can thus become connected with the revulsion against the suffering inflicted by capitalist industrialization even while the content of aesthetic tradition no less than the very definition of art were broadened.

Expressionist artists often offered confused theories to justify their experiments in montage and non-representational painting. But their philosophical weakness is irrelevant if writings, like *Point and Line* by Kandinsky, helped clarify certain problems of artistic production. Perhaps it is even in such disjunctures that the works of the avant-garde resist rigid categorization and are able to constantly recommence an interaction with a changing audience. Bloch is aware of this, in fact, when he writes that a "picture is never painted to completion, a book is never written to the end." Non-representational works in particular may generate the need for constant reinterpretation in light of the self-renewing emancipatory fantasy they throw in the face of repression.

Abstraction, in this sense, receives a justification in its own right. Liberation from the constraints of the given opens a space for fantasy and the experience of "artistic joy." And all this presupposes a willingness to "experiment" with the content of reality. Expressionists could not have created anything, according to Bloch, had they simply relied on the forms handed down to them by bourgeois realists like Goethe, Balzac, and Tolstoy. They chose different masters like Matthias Grünewald, El Greco, and Georg Büchner. In so doing, furthermore, they refused to consider "tradition" as some type of organic or "objective" phenomenon; indeed, it was expressionists and other modernists who first recognized that tradition is always "invented."

Nor did the break with representation occur by chance at that particular point in time. The crisis of capitalism had its effects; the totality changed its face. Traditional values and customs were confronted by the experience of World War I.[22] They lost their relevance and, from this perspective, the attempt to retain them becomes reactionary from the start. Maintaining the classical totality thus becomes a prejudice, according to Bloch, which perhaps explains why Lukács should have turned

> against every artistic attempt to bring about the dissolution of a worldview (even when this worldview itself was capitalistic) . . . He sees nothing except subjectivistic ruptures in an art which interprets the actual ruptures of the surface interrelations of the existent, and which attempts to discover the new that already exists in reality's crevices. Thus, he equates the experiment of dissolution with the state of decadence.[23]

Realism, from the standpoint of Bloch, is not treated historically. It is not the unalterable aesthetic norm by which decadence should be judged. Nor is it legitimate to judge art through externally imposed categories or in in terms of its implications for practice. The very priority given by Lukács to the totality, in fact, condemns art to follow precedent even as it undermines the anticipation of new conditions. It is interesting to note, in this regard, how Brecht once said that Kafka was a writer who saw what was coming without seeing what was there. The insight also applies to Marc's *Fate of the Animals* or a host of other avant-gardists who anticipated World War I. Bloch admits that expressionism evidenced an abstract pacifism and neglected real class contradictions. But he considers it illegitimate to judge the activities of the past by the results of the present especially when so many expressionists opposed the war.[24] It was just this kind of thinking, in fact, which enabled Lukács to relegate any non-communist resistance to the ranks of the bourgeoisie or petit bourgeoisie. Indeed, for Bloch, the pacifism of the expressionists and even their moralism constituted a valid political response.

But, in a way, he overstates the case. Support for the communist cause was not a basic criterion of aesthetic judgment; Thomas Mann, for example, publicly supported World War I in a particularly vile manner and Lukács never wavered in his admiration for him. By the same token, enough expressionists aligned themselves with the reaction. Gottfried Benn, Hanns Johst, Emil Nolde, Wyndham Lewis, D. H. Lawrence, the Pound–Eliot clique and the futurists all expressed support for the dictatorships at one time or another.

The real sociological question is not *who* was a fascist, of course, but which literary form tends to promote what kind of values. And here Bloch made it easy for himself. He could thus praise the futurists for their "passion for frenzy, dynamism, and all-pervading sense of immediacy," while neglecting to mention the other proto-fascistic ideological concerns with which these qualities were intertwined.[25] None of this, however, really concerns him. The defense of expressionism is a defense of experimenting in the name of the "concrete utopia." Its "horizon" is what art projects and where the "prospective horizon is left out, there reality appears only as what it has already become, as the dead, and here it will be the dead – namely the naturalists and empiricists – who will bury their dead."[26]

Art is an experiment, for Bloch, and he wants to highlight its reliance on fantasy. Lukács is correct, however, in claiming that he confuses the fantastic with the real and the concrete with the abstract. In asserting that non-objective painting retains an object – namely the color itself (*Farbigkeit*) – Bloch falls into precisely this mistake. It is, in this vein, obviously impossible to provide a negation for the real without a perception of its mediated historical content. Emphasizing the importance of fantasy does not necessarily call for denigrating the value of naturalism; indeed, these different artistic forms project very different possibilities for criticism and liberation. Fantasy can illuminate reality from the perspective of what it could or should become. But fantasy cannot substitute for an explanation of reality. Its projection of utopia creates a gap with reality, which cannot be bridged at will.

Emancipation was the goal of expressionism and, for this reason, it only made sense to Bloch that the Nazis should have decried modernist art. Experimental artforms, with their emphasis on the imagination and fantasy, always spell danger for repressive regimes cloaking themselves in cultural provincialism. No wonder, from the standpoint of Bloch, that even the artists who had originally expressed support for fascism should soon enough have been vilified. Expressionism contested the banality and provincialism of the *Spiessbürger* and the *Bildungsphillister*. Those were the cultural values on which the Nazis relied and they had little to do with the complex technical innovations of the avant-garde.

Expressionism was appalled by the existing society. Its cries of despair projected the need for a new sensibility, a different world, and a utopian mode of experience. It too was informed by bourgeois humanism. All this separated expressionism from fascism. Bloch was ultimately correct in *Erbschaft dieser Zeit* when he defined expressionism as a movement "which the philistine spat upon, an art wherein human stars – however inadequate, however singular – burned or wished to burn."

Bertolt Brecht and the Laboratory of Art

Bertolt Brecht approached the debate in a very different way than either Lukács or Bloch. He detested irrationalism, prided himself on his "realism," conceived of his work as part of the attempt to transform the existing order, and was always concerned with keeping close ties to the Communist Party; indeed, for precisely this reason, Brecht never published his contributions to the debate. In contrast to the idealist heritage embraced by Lukács, however, the philosophical inspiration for Brecht's art derived from enlightenment materialism. Nor was he ever enthusiastic about the Popular Front or the aesthetic line of the party. Nevertheless, whatever his differences with Lukács, it is mistaken to suggest that Brecht's views were the same as those of Bloch.

Brecht was far less concerned with utopian theory than the need to change traditional aesthetic assumptions in order to meet the contemporary needs of artistic production.[27] Nor was he ever a great friend of either the modernist avant-garde in general or expressionism in particular. *Baal*, his very first play, was quite openly directed against Hanns Johst's *Der Einsame* (The Lonely One). The unleashing of emotion (*Eindrucksauslösung*), the pathetic scream of "*O Mensch*," the plaintive appeals in the name of "poor little humanity," and the excessive emotional baggage of expressionism were all repulsive to Brecht. Nor did emotional attempts to involve the audience have much in common with what became his famous "estrangement-effect" (*Verfremdungseffekt*). Surprise, shock, playfulness and distortion all occur in the plays of Brecht. But, in his own way, Brecht was an aesthetic puritan.[28] He always felt that the impact of an art relying principally on exciting and manipulating the emotions would prove fleeting. Thus, "the most extreme effect of a work of art occurs but once. The same tricks won't, on any account, go over a second time. To a second invasion of new ideas which make use of familiar, more or less proven devices, the spectator is already immune.[29]

He wrote this in the context of criticizing dadaist happenings and futurist *soirées*. But the statement also has consequences for the discussion of realism. Any fetishism of technique, for Brecht, was anathema due to the constraints it could impose on artistic production and the experience of an audience. He, no less than Bloch, sees the work as "open." Its aim is to begin and then recommence a dialogue with a changing public. In contrast to Bloch and the expressionists, however, Brecht is unconcerned with fostering empathy or articulating some abstract utopian potential.[30] It is rather a matter of forcing the public to confront political and moral choices, which stem from the contradiction between the way social forces appear and the way they actually function. Brecht's notion of the relation between "essence" and "appearance" thus takes a unique form. It is no longer derived from the objective presentation of the "totality," or from an exclusive concern with the utopian *novum*, but from an immanent critique of existing ideology and the speculative elaboration of its effects upon the possibilities for radical practice.

Realism is less a matter of form than an ability to render historical class contradictions concrete for a particular public in a particular society.[31] Forms are merely products of changing social and aesthetic needs. It is thus misguided to speak of "decadence" in art since this already reduces cultural production to the historical development of the bourgeoisie. Nor is it possible, even if such a reduction is undertaken, to demarcate the "vigorous" art of the nineteenth century from the "decadent" art of the twentieth. The periods marking the high points of expressionist popularity were, for Brecht, transitional. They required new modes of experimentation precisely because the prewar no less than the immediate postwar periods harbored a genuine revolutionary potential; indeed he clearly has a point if the the mass strike actions and controversies of 1905–12 along with the international workers' revolts of 1918–21 are taken as the defining moments in time.

Brecht, of course, realized that this potential was never fully realized. But, according to him, condemning artists like Picasso or Döblin in the name of realism simply binds art to the past and constricts its ability to illuminate new contradictions in new ways in the future. The real is itself historically malleable. Chaining the concept of realism to a nineteenth-century mode of depicting objective conditions thus turns the concept and the totality into a trans-historical formulae, which only contributes to the reification of Marxism.

The relation to tradition, for Brecht, is determined by the needs of cultural production in the present. He implicitly comprehended the subjective factor in the choice of the aesthetic form which crystallizes, or translates, possibilities for transforming the existing order. Tradition is no rigid set of precedents or rules. Consequently, even though he was never an expressionist, Brecht made use of certain formal devices initiated by the movement. Why not?

> We cannot allow ourselves to be held up too long by the problem of form or, at least, we must be exact as to what we mean and speak concretely. Otherwise, as critics, we will become formalists, no matter what vocabulary we use. It disconcerts our contemporary writers when they have to hear, all too often, "that's not the way grandmother used to tell it." Okay, say that the old woman was a realist. Assuming that we are also realists, would we then have to recount something in exactly the same way grandmother did? There must be some misunderstanding here.[32]

"Form" and "content" are not, for Brecht, realities unto themselves.

They are merely heuristic categories useful in analyzing a work, which is itself an organic unity. A separation of the the two can occur only abstractly. Calling for the retention of old forms at any cost thus inherently leads to a blindness to the content enlarged by new discoveries and new forms of practice. Art must keep pace with history. The comprehensibility of a work is not assured by taking on the style of Balzac or Tolstoy. Brecht was always skeptical of highly abstract art and sought to keep his own language simple and concrete. But, in his opinion, a viable art "should bring forth the thing-in-itself, the incomprehensible. Yet, art should neither depict things as self-evident (seeking an emotional response) nor simply as incomprehensible. Rather it should depict them as comprehensible, but not yet comprehended."[33]

The audience, for Brecht, should never feel too comfortable. Art must train the intellect. Marxists always maintained that consciousness does not change with the same speed as the infrastructure. As a Leninist, however, Brecht could consider it legitimate for art to remain a step – "but only a step" – ahead of existing cultural forms reinforcing the ideology of the status quo. This might make for a certain difficulty regarding the comprehensibility of the work and its accessibility to the masses (*Volkstümlichkeit*). Brecht, however, never saw this as a problem. Rather than accept what has already been made comprehensible as the only authentically "popular" form, in his opinion, the future socialist culture must experiment with new forms. Indeed, this is the sense in which Brecht views art as a "laboratory."

A truly socialist art must also develop new *forms* of hearing, seeing and understanding the world along with a new content. One of his primary aesthetic concerns as a playwright involved undermining old forms of experience and showing how they hampered the class consciousness of the masses. The point is not simply to copy bourgeois realism from a socialist perspective. It is a matter of bringing a "new art" into existence. That is only possible, however, by learning from the past rather than seeking to dismiss it or break with it in the manner of most expressionists.

> The new exists, but it arises out of the struggle with the old, not without it, not out of thin air. Many forget about learning or treat it disdainfully as a formality, and some even take the critical moment for granted, treating that as a formality as well.[34]

Unlike Bloch, in this vein, Brecht is concerned with the relativizing of "realism" and he attempted to counter this from a class standpoint. But his "standard" is different from the one employed by Lukács. Referring to the past is inadequate. The critique of ideology provides a point of departure; the realistic work must expose how "the reigning views are the views of those who reign."[35] It must also, however, bring into focus the concerns of those who do not reign. This twofold undertaking is what, according to Brecht, marks a realistic art. It is in this way, without rules or precedents determined *a priori*, that art can serve as a moment of political practice.

Sketch for an Emancipatory Aesthetics

An emancipatory aesthetic cannot begin by choosing between realism and expressionism. This can result only in reifying the social immanence or the utopian transcendence of art. The particularity of the work, whatever the choice, is subsumed within the judgment of a style. Nor is it legitimate to equate a style with a worldview, identify the worldview with a particular class standpoint, and then use that standpoint to evaluate a work without the least concern for genre. The original concept of totality, in fact, was developed to overcome reductionism of this sort. Employing philosophical and political categories for cultural analysis thus belies its purpose.

There is no reason why, in contrast to social theory, art must presuppose answers within its formal ways of framing questions. Ignoring this even impairs the ability to make political judgments; it is simply inadequate, for example, to maintain that an essentially internationalist and pacifist movement like expressionism is defined by the same petit bourgeois class standpoint as a self-consiously proto-fascist movement like the futurists. Determination and a sense of historical "specificity" (Korsch) disappears. The "dialectic" becomes a tool for political sophistry.

A practical aesthetic must derive its categories from the changing practice of artistic production. Imposing categories, or turning the form of one period into a standard for judging art in a new period, simply reifies the interpretive enterprise. Forming new interpretations becomes increasingly difficult; the artwork is readied for the museum. The ability to perceive contradictions in an irreconciled state no less than to intimate the possibility of new experiences is dismissed. No longer is it possible to *de-ideologize the ideology* within a work and extract the insight buried beneath the mystifying worldview of a particular artist.

Kandinsky is a case in point. His non-objective paintings shatter the empirical world of appearances supposedly in order to determine what lies beneath it. The essence which he finds is the movement of an inexplicable "spirit" whose presentation demands a radical break with artistic traditions of the past. The affirmation of "objective" reality is impossible, from the perspective of Kandinsky, without its denial.

Whatever his subjective intentions, however, objectively he validates the subjectivity lost within the reified world of industrial society. Perhaps, in his own way, he even "mirrors" the indeterminate labor power lost in the object. Interpretation informed by the concerns of Horkheimer and Benjamin can thus employ Kandinsky to inspire a memory of the lived moment.

It is mistaken, however, to believe that emancipatory insights of this sort simply present themselves in a work. Kant recognized the problem when it came to the philosophy of history. To find manifestations of emancipation the critic must, in the first place, make the commitment to look for them; indeed, this is precisely what calls into question the drive toward a purely formalist notion of aesthetic inquiry. The semiotic isolation of elements or codes, in this vein, is merely the flip side of a stance condemning interpretation as such. Criticism without an "emancipatory interest" (Habermas) will either engage in a sterile reflection upon itself or consign art to the realm of immediate experience. Neither framework is willing to confront the interests in interpretation or the prevailing relativism perpetuated by a culture industry concerned with appealing to the lowest common denominator in order to generate the greatest possible profits.

Aesthetics can neither justify nor generate a coherent set of political values just as political theory can neither justify nor generate viable categories for aesthetic inquiry. An emancipatory aesthetic must logically take its social values from theories dealing with the social realm of action and institutions. But, for its part, emancipatory aesthetic criticism must provide the tools for confronting an expanding range of cultural phenomena in which the potential for liberation is defined very differently.

No longer can radical cultural criticism violate the integrity of the work by simply imposing political or philosophical criteria external to it. A typology of categories is necessary to help define the internal dynamics (*Eigendynamik*) of a given work and open it to genuine mediation or appropriation as a moment within the totality. Not every artwork will fit squarely into one or another category and, of course, their employment and relevance will differ with differing genres. More than one category can even apply to a given work and the broader aesthetic must assume that the "anticipatory" interpretation speaks less to private experience than to a public sphere in which its critical claims can become open to discourse. There are other provisos. A framework remains necessary, however, for overcoming reified antinomies and maintaining the connection between the work and its contribution. Thus, in keeping with the spirit of Hegel, the following is an attempt to sketch the most basic interpretive categories of an emancipatory aesthetic.

Immediacy

Even the products of "mass culture" can evidence the desire for gratification. But, as in the case of television sit-coms or certain rock songs that harp on sex or love, the presentation of such desires will prove neither self-reflexive with regard to prior forms of expression nor with regard to the constraints inhibiting their fulfillment. A judgment of the desire itself is, in fact, usually precluded and, for this very reason, this unreflexive and indeterminate mode of utopian anticipation is the most easily manipulated by commercial advertising and the "culture industry." The critic's role in dealing with works fitting this category would first involve subjecting the need (or plurality of needs for which it is the condensed expression) evidenced by them to critical evaluation and then show the gap existing between the need and the structural conditions denying its satisfaction.

Indeterminate reflexivity

A second form of anticipatory consciousness occurs in the critical confrontation with the prevalent forms of the genre in which the given work is situated. Artworks of this sort reflect a preoccupation with new experience and the limitations on expression of earlier styles even if they don't evidence any comprehension of the contextual sources for their own content or concerns. They are indeterminate even while they often evidence a profound reflexivity. Expressionist works, for example, tend to ignore questions of immanence, historical genesis, and social context in favor of issues pertaining to formal innovations. A major task of the critic therefore involves specifying the value of the technical contribution while placing the work within a meaningful context of interests.

Unreflexive determinancy

The "realist" or "naturalist" works of Balzac and Zola provide a useful counterpoint. These might very well comprehend a given socio-historical complex, and perhaps even "mirror" a mediated totality, but they don't necessarily question traditional forms of aesthetic experience or illuminate what Benjamin termed "the poverty of the interior." They provide a sense of historical determination without confronting the aesthetic forms with which history is perceived in a critical or reflexive fashion. Employing the logic of representation, while examining the structures of the existing order, the vision of an emancipated alternative sensibility and a new ordering of social relations tends to vanish. The role of the critic thus becomes particularly difficult. It becomes necessary to question the work's epistemological assumptions and simultaneously subject it to a criticism capable of defining what remains unexpressed.

Reflexive determinacy

There are, of course, also artworks capable of confronting formal traditions of presentation while illuminating a given social complex. The plays of Shakespeare or even Brecht for that matter provide an example. Reflexive in their ability to transvalue the formal inheritance of the past in an emancipatory fashion, they also render determinate the material conditions making necessary such an undertaking. The principal function of the critic in dealing with such works thus involves elaborating the manner in which the given vision of social and aesthetic self-comprehension can radicalize existing cultural, social and political forms in different ways.

A work of art, once finished, separates itself from the author. It becomes an "objectification" (*Vergegenständlichung*) or autonomous entity in which original intentions become moments of the organic whole. The work can, in this way, turn against the prejudices of the author; Engels could thus respond to an inquiry concerning his admiration for Balzac, an ardent supporter of the minor nobility, with "his irony is never sharper than when he employs it against the class he loves." Even the work of a political reactionary can retain critical or emancipatory elements. But no work ever fully escapes its genesis. History remains; there is always a *contextual residue*. The critic must, for this reason, confront both the emancipatory potential within the work and the repressive society out of which it arose.

The choices posed in the expressionism debate have become anachronistic. It is no longer a matter of deciding on a style consonant with a correct political stance. The issue is rather one of choosing a conceptual framework capable of clarifying the diverse contributions different works can make to an inherently unfinished vision of "the best life." The anticipation of liberation is what calls forth the "invention" of tradition. Nor does a work of art ever exert even its indirect effects in an autonomous manner. They are always mediated by the effects of co-existing works and styles no less than the institutions structuring the existing public sphere. Neither the expressionist nor the realist work exists in a vacuum; where there is Kafka there is also Thomas Mann and where there is Klee there is already Daumier. A willingness to recognize the differing contributions of diverse works in different styles thus only reflects the actual conditions in which criticism must currently operate.

Radical cultural criticism, in this same vein, has no choice other than to view art as an experiment. This means balancing the awareness that every technique can be employed in the most regressive way with the knowledge that only the innovative use of form prevents art from becoming repetitive. Montage, for example, is constantly used in the worst television commercials. By the same token, however, it is surely more than a "subjectivist" disortion of reality. New meanings can become manifest, as objects take on new relations to one another. Nor need montage involve an arbitrary throwing together of "fragments." The bond between objects is often purposively withheld to foster reflexivity concerning the "ratio of the irratio" (Bloch). Montage can even generate a narrative and, while engaging the audience in the construction of the work, also create an awareness of what is assumed in the restructuring of reality; indeed, this is precisely what occurs in the photo-montages of John Heartfield.

Expressionism not only engenders subjectivity and the autonomy of art from reality. Tendencies within it also foster individual responsibility insofar as the audience is made to take part in the active construction of something new. This is as true in the plays of Toller as in those of Brecht; it occurs as surely with Döblin as with Feuchtwanger. Expressionism helped proclaim in a new way that freedom is only freedom for the subject. Lukács, however, was not simply "academic" in noting how such concerns can engender formalism and aestheticism. It is realism which generates a concern with redressing the repressive institutional and material conditions in which the actual exercise of freedom might universally take place. A space for the "exact fantasy" only appears through the interpretive interplay of these styles.

An emancipatory aesthetic must, in this vein, rest on a revolutionary tolerance. Such a mode of thinking seeks to grasp the emancipatory "horizon" of a work; it recognizes that the exposure of repression and the illumination of utopia may not occur in the same work or even in the same style. It militates against closure and constantly generates reinterpretation of the works whose meanings are considered fixed and finished. Above all, however, revolutionary tolerance contests the dogmatism of a critic who criticizes an artist for not writing the book he or she would like to read.

But there is also no doubt about it: art in class society is still practically restricted to those with the time, education, and socially motivated desire to appreciate it. The very relativism generated by the culture industry is what an emancipatory aesthetic must seek to contest. It needs to derive criteria for making judgment between works and differentiating their quality. There is, for example, no sense in comparing Louis Armstrong with Mozart. It is, however, extremely useful to compare either with any number of less innovative composers working within his own tradition and the artists dominating the cultural context of his time.

Transcendent concerns have their place. The formal elements of a work can anticipate the interpretive assumptions of a future public. Because modernist movements were separated from the struggles of the masses does not alone invalidate their progressive qualities nor does it deny the possibility that the masses might ultimately become a public for their works; not a single prewar critic would ever have imagined that a million people would come to see an exhibition of Picasso or Matisse. And these are only particularly blatant examples. Nor is it legitimate to maintain that their renewed popularity somehow nullifies their possible emancipatory contributions.

The culture industry may well turn works into commodities, and critical theory was correct in emphasizing its more debilitating effects. But the extent to which works become commodities is not necessarily the extent to which they lose their artistic quality. Charlie Chaplin's films provide a case in point. The particular work, once again, gets lost in the all embracing character of the formal claim. Contesting the power of the culture industry, however, is not a matter of the work internally generating tensions capable of maintaining what Adorno considered the "non-identity" of subject and object. It is rather a matter of recognizing that pockets of cultural resistance can emerge on the periphery, which became evident in the events of 1968 in France, and that critical education in unions and universities – and perhaps even through the culture industry – can mitigate the dulling of reflexive capacities and what Russell Jacoby once called the "falling rate of intelligence."

Cultural relativism provides no critical perspective when the bulk of artistic stimulation for the great bulk of the populace is overwhelmingly supplied by the culture industry. Believing seriously that the working class and the poor either already read Kafka and Thomas Mann, or alternatively that they have no need of them, results only in idealism or elitism. The point is no longer one of creating an art for the masses; the culture industry has already realized that goal. An emancipatory aesthetic must, in the contemporary era, seek to provide the broader public with exposure to what the culture industry ignores and a framework for judging the quality of different works within an increasing number of traditions and genres.

Cultural criticism must become more aware of the various publics with which different works register what Max Weber termed an "elective affinity." The public for a given work can, of course, change over time and Brecht was correct in maintaining that "difficulty" in the present does not preclude a sense of fascination in the future. It is, furthermore, a serious mistake to neglect the intelligentsia in the name of "reaching" the masses or constantly preach the need for "simplicity" when the "popularity" of even Sartre or Camus pales before that of Harold Robbins or Jackie Collins. Nor is it sensible to believe that the impact of a work is always commensurate with the degree of its popularity. Multiple publics exist beneath the smooth surface of advanced industrial society. Their boundaries are fuzzy and, while their values often conflict, they sometimes overlap. Analyzing the complex of values in the differing publics, such as the concern over pornography particularly in the feminist or religious communities, is a matter of exceptional importance for cultural criticism. But this should not detract from the guiding principle.

The mere fact that multiple publics exist suggests that a new and radical form of tolerance – not relativism, but tolerance – is necessary for those works seeking to undermine the hegemony of dominant ideas in different social spheres and arenas. Building an emancipated culture is a manifold act. An emancipatory aesthetic must thus begin with the assumption that there are manifold and indirect ways of effecting what Marx called "the material level of culture." Articulating new categories for appropriating the differing contributions of differing works is, for this reason, a pragmatic necessity. Indeed, such is the principle task of any new critical form of aesthetics with practical aims.

Notes

1 This is a revised version of an article originally entitled "Expression and Marxism: Towards an Aesthetics of Emancipation" in *Passion and Rebellion: The Expressionist Heritage* edited by Stephen Eric Bronner and Douglas Kellner (New York, 1988, 2nd edition).

2 An excellent collection on socialist realism has been edited by Hans-Jürgen Schmidt and Gödehard Schramm, *Sozialistische Realismuskonzeption: Dokumente zum 1. Allunionskongress der Sowjetschriftsteller* (Frankfurt, 1974).

3 The articles comprising the debate have been collected by Hans-Jürgen Schmidt, *Die Expressionismusdebatte: Materialen zu einer marxistischen Realismuskonzeption* (Frankfurt, 1973). Sections of the debate also have been collected by Frederic Jameson, *Aesthetics and Politics* (London, 1978), while many of Brecht's contributions have appeared in "Brecht on Social Realism" in *New Left Review* 84 and in John Willet (ed.) *Brecht on Theatre* (New York, 1975).

4 Note the 1967 introduction to Georg Lukács, *History and Class Consciousness: Studies in Marxist Dialectics* (Cambridge, Mass., 1971), p. ix.

5 George Lukács, "Es geht um den Realismus" in *Marxismus und Literatur* ed. Fritz Raddatz (Hamburg, 1969), vol. 2, p. 64.

6 "The formative depth (*Gestaltung*), the breadth and durability of a

realistic writer's effectiveness depends largely on the extent of his formal (*gestalterisch*) awareness of what the manifestations described by him actually represent. This conception of the relation of a significant writer to reality does not in any way exclude, as Bloch believes, the realization that the surface of reality manifests ruptures (*Zersetzungen*) and accordingly reflects itself in the consciousness of men." Ibid.

7   The aesthetic position developed in the expressionism debate prefigures the philosophical assault on irrationalism launched in 1954 by Lukács in *Die Zerstörung der Vernunft* 3 vols (Darmstadt, 1974 edition).

8   Georg Lukács, " 'Grosse und Verfall' des Expressionismus" in *Marxismus und Literatur* vol. 2, p. 17.

9   Perhaps the real instigator of the entire debate, Alfred Kurella, argued that expressionism led directly to fascism. Lukács was never in accord with this far more crude interpretation. Note the discussion by Kurella in "nun ist dies Erbe zuende . . ." in *Marxismus und Literatur*, vol. 2, pp. 43ff.

10   Lukács, "Grosse und Verfall," p. 13.

11   Lukács, "Es geht um den Realismus," p. 70.

12   Cf. Georg Lukács, *Realism in Our Time* trans. John and Necke Mander (New York, 1964).

13   Note the evaluations of Fadeyev, Makarenko, and Sholokov in Georg Lukács, *Russische Revolution, Russische Literatur* (Berlin, 1969), pp. 166ff; also cf. Georg Lukács, "Briefwechsel mit Anna Seghers," in *Marxismus und Literatur* vol. 2, p. 118.

14   Cf. Henry Pachter, "Orthodox Heretic, Romantic Stalinist: On the Ninetieth Birthday of George Lukács" in *Socialism in History: Political Essays of Henry Pachter* ed. Stephen Eric Bronner (New York, 1984), pp. 295ff.

15   Lukács, "Es geht um den Realismus," p. 83.

16   Ernst Bloch, *Erbschaft dieser Zeit* (Frankfurt, 1973), p. 149.

17   Ibid., p. 270.

18   Ibid., p. 266.

19   Ernst Bloch, *Geist der Utopie* (Frankfurt, 1974 edition), p. 20.

20   Cf. Georg Lukács, "Narrate or Describe?" in *Writer and Critic and Other Essays* (New York, 1971).

21   Ernst Bloch, *Die Kunst, Schiller zu Sprechen* (Frankfurt, 1974 edition), p. 65.

22   Bloch, *Erbschaft dieser Zeit*, p. 258.

23   Ibid., p. 270.

24   Ibid., p. 267.

25   Bloch, *Geist der Utopie*, p. 43.

26   Ernst Bloch, *Das Prinzip Hoffnung* (Frankfurt, 3rd edition), vol. 1, p. 257.

27   The diary notation of Walter Benjamin speaks to this concern. "The publication of Lukács, Kurella et al. are giving Brecht a good deal of trouble. He thinks, however, that one ought not to oppose them at the

theoretical level." Walter Benjamin, *Understanding Brecht* trans. Anna Bostock (London, 1973), p. 116.

28 Henry Pachter, "Brecht's Personal Politics" in *Weimar Etudes* (New York, 1982), pp. 225ff.

29 Bertolt Brecht, "Über den Dadaismus" in *Gesammelte Werke* (Frankfurt, 1967), vol. 18, p. 6.

30 Cf. Jost Hermand "Brecht on Utopia" in *The Minnesota Review* 6 (Spring, 1976), pp. 96ff.

31 Bertolt Brecht, "Förderungen an eine neue Kritik" in *Gesammelte Werke*, vol. 18, p. 113.

32 Bertolt Brecht, "Praktischen zur Expressionismusdebatte" in *Gesammelte Werke*, vol. 19, p. 327.

33 Bertolt Brecht, "Über alte und neue Kunst" in *Gesammelte Werke*, vol. 19, p. 314.

34 Bertolt Brecht, "Bemerkungen zum Formalismus" in *Gesammelte Werke*, vol. 18, p. 314.

35 Bertolt Brecht, "Volkstümlichkeit und Realismus" in *Gesammelte Werke* vol. 19, p. 326.

9

Dialectics at a Standstill: A Methodological Inquiry into the Philosophy of Theodor W. Adorno

He was perhaps the most dazzling of them all. His dialectical style, his command of the dialectical aphorism, and his uncompromising assault on banality and repression turned Theodor Wiesengrund Adorno into perhaps the most alluring and surely the most complex representative of critical theory when he died in 1969 at the age of 66. His range seemingly knew no bounds. He was a musicologist who had studied with the great Alban Berg, a composer in his own right, a philosopher with expertise in the intricacies of phenomenology, a social theorist steeped in the tradition of Western Marxism, a sociologist engaged in complicated empirical studies, a connoisseur of literature and poetry, an anthropological thinker, and an aesthetician committed to the new and the technically innovative. He incarnated the interdisciplinary perspective of the "Frankfurt School," and made contributions in all his fields of endeavor. He, above all, played a decisive role in shifting the interest of Horkheimer and the Institute away from its political and economic preoccupations of the 1930s. Adorno, in his own way, transformed the meaning of critical theory. It was Adorno, after all, who asked whether writing poetry was still possible after Auschwitz. It was Adorno who railed against the "liquidation of the subject." It was Adorno who claimed that the whole is false.

His thinking stands and falls on his confrontation with the "ontology of false conditions" in the name of an endangered subjectivity. Reacting against this ontology led him, "in opposition to Hegel's practice and yet in accordance with his thought,"[1] to explode the moment of positivity in favor of an uncompromising emphasis on negation. Affirming the "non-identity" between the subject and his world was the logical consequence. Conceptualizing this threatened subjectivity involved leaving nothing unscathed: not phenomenology with its ontological flattening of the very experience it claimed to valorize; not empiricism with its blindness to the context of oppression; not positivism for its expulsion of normative values; not instrumentalism for sanctioning of what exists; and not even Hegel or Marx with their teleological commitment, their affirmation of progress, their emphasis on positivity, and their vagaries concerning revolutionary change.

No reductionism would infect the mature theory of Adorno, no theological remnants of the Other, no soft humanism,[2] no retreat into "play." This time there would be no illusions. Or better: illusion, the semblance of reality, would serve both a critical and a utopian purpose. Embedded within art, created by technique, illusion confronts the impoverishment of experience generated by the "inverted world" of the commodity form. Adorno stands up against the "ontology of false conditions" with the emancipatory truth demanded by negative dialectics and retained in works of art. He knew that this truth is politically impotent, that its ability to contradict the unfreedom of the social whole exists only in the fleeting glimpse and the momentary experience. That is why Adorno simultaneously rejected the category of totality, elicited the evanescent and the fragmentary, and still called for a systematic reading of his own work and a contextual understanding of all social phenomena.[3] He would, for better or worse, define freedom by the ontology it denies. The dialectic would grind to a halt and, in this way, remain true to the reality it sought to comprehend. Adorno could not draw the practical conclusions. Nevertheless, through exposing the inverted "truth" of an "inverted world," illusion provided his "negative dialectics" with its uncompromisingly critical thrust.

Reification and its Inversion

Negative dialectics was, from the start, a confrontation with the "false condition" of things. It thus always presupposed the commitment to a vision of truth critical of the ways in which they were presented. History is that presentation. It develops through the rational domination of nature, which presupposes the expulsion of subjectivity and value-laden concerns from the process. Instrumental rationality, for example, transforms capital from the object of production into its subject and the actual producers of wealth into objects for the creation of profit.[4] Even with its eradication of "use value" by "exchange value," however, capitalism is merely the highest expression of an anthropological development dedicated to dominating "inner" and "outer" nature while transforming qualitative distinctions into quantitative ones. Externalization of what is internal to the subject impoverishes the subject; that is the key.[5] Rationalization is thus rendered equivalent to reification;[6] the objectifying "form" of productive activity produces it.

Reification becomes the fundamental fact of human existence, which is then read back into each historical epoch and every facet of human experience. Such a stance contests the claim that objectification is an anthropologically neutral phenomenon and that contingent historical conditions, rather than interaction with nature per se, creates alienation. An anthropological standpoint, albeit of a "negative" sort,[7] thus begins to take shape. No wonder that, in contrast to Erich Fromm, Adorno should have called upon the Institute to place less emphasis on attempts to "sociologize" psychology and more on an independent appropriation of the instinct theory and metapsychological inheritance of Freud.[8] The domination of nature through history would now receive grounding in the repressive forms of sublimation offered by civilization. Maintaining any genuine commitment to happiness would then involve contesting the ways in which instinctual gratification is offered, delayed and distorted. The metapsychological and anthropological standpoint would make the need for a "total" break with reality evident.

Adorno won Max Horkheimer over to his new metacritical position thereby supplanting Fromm's important role in the Institute. It would directly influence the "dialectical logic" of *Dialectics of Enlightenment* and, in a way, the metapsychological utopianism of Marcuse no less than the later work of Horkheimer. If ontology exists it will define the "false condition" in which freedom has no place. That false condition is history. No reform is capable of altering its structure any more than the effects of a reification process identified with objectification; liberation must subsequently involve an apocalyptic transformation in which a new order will emerge capable of preventing the conflation between subject and object while introducing a new harmony between humanity and nature.

The emancipatory inversion starts to take shape. The response to reification occurs in terms of "what lies beyond" it. The impossibility of bringing about such a change, making "present" what inherently lies beyond, complements the ethical need to confront the encompassing reality of repression. Not simply an identification with suffering,[9] but guilt at the inability to eradicate its pervasiveness is what produces the commitment to negative dialectics. Practical pessimism will subsequently stand in "dialectical" tension with a certain variant of philosophical utopianism in the thinking of Adorno no less than the others whom his thinking influenced. Critical theory, in his opinion, cannot deny this tension.

Contesting the hegemonic claims of mainstream sociology, for that very reason, becomes imperative; its objectivistic prejudices become inverted as the point of departure becomes a repressed subjectivity. Empiricist and positivist forms of sociology not only ignore how subjectivity remains unexhausted by the processes supposedly constituting it, they also remain blind to the manner in which society is itself constituted by subjects. Remaining stuck within the realm of "social facts" necessarily produces a form of thinking in which the subject or individual is collapsed into the object or society. Mainstream sociology, by stripping the social outcome from the value-laden conditions of its constitution, thus contributes to the reification of the very subject it seeks to study.

A new "critical" approach to sociology is introduced by Adorno. Such an approach will prove as useful for empirical studies of authoritarianism as for criticisms of astrology. But these do not fulfill its methodological purpose. The point of a new "critical" sociology, from the standpoint of Adorno, is to highlight the "intrinsic tension" between the need for the structures of society, which are open to reflection, and the ways they inhibit subjectivity and its desire for freedom.[10] It is in order to explore this tension that Adorno has recourse to the categories of idealism, like totality and mediation, which were ignored by the mainstream. Nevertheless, these categories undergo a fundamental change of purpose and quality from the way they were employed by Hegel, Marx, Weber, and Lukács.

"Mediation," for example, becomes a way of preserving experience by undercutting any sense of "false immediacy". The "totality" loses its validity as a "comprehensive principle of explanation;"[11] grasping it is no longer possible from the standpoint of the proletariat.[12] Adorno turns both "mediation" and "totality" into conceptual tools with which to indicate the subjectivity that escapes social and historical objectification. The indeterminate metaphysical character these concepts assume is precisely what justifies their determinate sociological employment. This is the sense in which inversion as an oppositional strategy comes to underpin the entire enterprise.

Inverting the "inverted world" of the commodity form, without reference to the proletariat as the revolutionary agent of history, will demand that critique presuppose a realm external to the object of analysis. Only in that way is dialectical tension maintained. Potentiality, for this reason, contests actuality while the subject confronts the object. Critique must confront all forms of identity thinking, which Adorno once called the "*Urform*" of ideology, even those of Hegel and Marx. Indeed, this must occur in the name of that "non-identity" between subject and object wherein freedom becomes manifest.

History, with its implicit involvement in the increasing subordination of nature through technology, militates against this non-identical relation between subject and object. That is why Adorno must break the identification of history with categories such as progress. And this is also undertaken from the perspective of a radical inversion. Progress is turned against itself, freedom is expelled from history, and the individual is pitted against a reality itself of human making. Adorno thus employs an "inverted historicism" to confront various enlightenment versions of the philosophy of history with their teleological assumptions.[13]

> Universal history must be construed and denied. After the catastrophes
> that have happened, and in view of the catastrophes to come, it would be
> cynical to say that a plan for a better world is manifested in history and
> unites it. Not to be denied for that reason, however, is the unity that
> cements the discontinuous, chaotically splintered moments and phases of
> history – the unity of the control of nature, progressing to rule over men,
> and finally to that over men's inner nature. No universal history leads from
> savagery to humanitarianism, but there is one leading from the slingshot to
> the megaton bomb."[14]

Heilsgeschichte, or history as providing salvation, is transformed by Adorno into a history of damnation.[15] This reflects the claim made in *Dialectics of Enlightenment* that, just as myth served as a premodern form of enlightenment, enlightenment retreats into "myth."[16] In principle, either philosophically or historically, no "reform" is possible; the negation of the negation cannot produce anything "positive."[17] History is a boot in the face. Nor does this derive merely from class contradictions. It is rather a result of the the constraints imposed by instrumental reason from the very beginnings of human history.[18] Reality is a constant assault on freedom. Only as an illusion is it possible to reassert the freedom lost in the reification process. And this demands a different language capable of asserting its "sensuous" quality for a subject; it must remain irreducible to either philosophical categories or any set of objective conditions. No wonder then that, for Adorno, the "mimetic" language of artworks should most directly express what is, in the terms of a reified reality, the illusion of freedom.

Illusion projects emancipation. Its truth content (*Wahrheitsinhalt*) subsequently provides illusion with an element of truth, which propels it beyond magic and make-believe. This truth, however, has nothing in common with the assumptions of logic or instrumental reason. That, in fact, is precisely what separates aesthetic illusion from ideology and preserves its critical character. Adorno, following the dialectical thinking of the Western Marxists, sought to preserve potentiality from actuality. He knew that "it is not ideology in itself which is untrue, but rather its pretension to correspond to reality."[19] Nevertheless, he gave the original historicist criticism with a political intent a very different twist.

Adorno refashioned the confrontation with reality. Freedom, for him, was no longer grounded; its concrete and secular quality (*Diesseitigkeit*) is lost since aesthetic illusion, wherein the repressed potential of subjective experience is preserved, can only exist outside reality in the "beyond" (*Jenseitigkeit*).[20] Inversion provides the standpoint of Adorno's "immanent criticism." Only from outside reification is it possible to engage in a defetishizing of reality. Artworks incorporate the subjectivity expelled from history and thus the quality of transcendence. They are, of course, created from the elements of the real. Adorno, for this very reason, can claim that artistic innovation is a "counterpart to the expanding reproduction of capital in society."[21] Nevertheless, it is the emancipatory inversion of that process.

Emancipation conceived in this way can never receive any concrete determination. Negative dialectic sunders the wish from the deed. And it does so in a very particular way. The "determinate negation" emanating from within the contradictions of a given historical epoch must, in terms of aesthetic critique, appear one-sided and insufficient.[22] The seemingly indeterminate critique of reality projected by aesthetic illusion subsequently becomes determinate precisely because it realizes that "the whole is false."[23] Rationality, the technical fetish, stands open to critique only from what it denies. The negation, for this reason, can become manifest only through the inversion of reality.

Illusion is that inversion. Its existence in reality was precisely what Adorno always sought to confront; its manifestation in art offered precisely that palpable indictment of history that he always sought to embrace. Philosophy makes sense of that indictment; it is illusory because emancipation is preserved from history. The "totality" is real only in its negation by aesthetic illusion. Totality must cease in its attempt to encompass the subject and, instead, become its creation. The concrete does not precede the subject. Truth will not appear within history, as its intentional product, but in its "intentionless" manifestations.[24] The point is to assemble the whole, in a form of "parataxis," from a series of partial complexes whose relations are not hierarchically defined.[25]

Generating the idea from these propositions and partial complexes of elements, making connections without creating a system, is the "higher praxis" of which Adorno's supporters tend to speak.[26] It is not a matter of rejecting concepts in the manner of irrationalism, but of using them to comprehend a freedom beyond concepts.[27] Subjectivity is preserved as the "constellation" becomes the category with which to expose the dynamic character of reality. Naively, Adorno can assume that "out of the construction of a configuration of reality the demand for its real change always follows promptly."[28]

His aesthetics shows how artworks become "constellations" and "unintentionally," or in a "purposefully purposeless" manner, evidence their "truth." History has, in any event, thrown philosophy on the defensive; it continues to exist only because the historical moment for realizing its emancipatory truth – presumably during the workers' revolts of 1917–23 – was missed.[29] The legitimation of metaphysics, not the creation of a "materialist metaphysic of modernity,"[30] is what takes historical form. Adorno wished to render metaphysics "negative," anti-systemic and capable of discerning the threat to subjectivity, through its metacritical inversion.

The undertaking proceeds directly from his friendship with Walter Benjamin and Siegfried Kracauer, no less than his encounter with Husserl wherein – whatever his criticisms of phenomenology – he defended him for seeking to "destroy idealism from within," for maintaining a commitment to philosophical truth against relativism, and preserving the subjective experience from the "concrete" ontology of Heidegger.[31] Adorno had originally given his study on Husserl, which can be literally translated as *Towards a Metacritique of Epistemology*, the working title "Dialectical Epistemology."[32] He always insisted on the *logic* behind his immanent subversion of concepts.[33] He was as little engaged in formulating an "anti-epistemology," the official English translation of this work, as in denying the truths embodied in the "untruth" of idealism.

The issue for him involved recognizing the impossibility of identifying particular objects with concepts even while thinking always crytallizes in particulars.[34] A concern with the unregimented and the spontaneous, which manifests itself in art as well as "nonidentical thinking," is the basis for Adorno's assault on idealism. Critical reflexivity, however, remains the only way to uncover the "untruth" of identity and the manner in which subjectivity is repressed. Adorno maintained his commitment to immanent criticism.[35] Indeed, he did so in the name of what always served as both the foundation and goal of idealism: freedom.

His own "metacritique of practical reason," furthermore, followed certain currents of Husserl's work.[36] It would, admittedly, emphasize the ignored antinomies of traditional phenomenology. But it too would seek to preserve philosophy from the incursions of social theory and histor-icism, reject ontology, radicalize idealism by exploding its formalism, and subject its positive assumptions to critical scrutiny. None of this has anything to do with materialism unless that concept is configured in the most abstract terms. Habermas is subsequently correct when he writes that "the Marxist theory of society is recast into pure philosophy through the form of Adorno's negative dialectic."[37]

A severing of the relation between "theory and practice" occurs as well.[38] Adorno feared the subordination of theory to the exigencies of practice. To a certain extent, furthermore, this is understandable given his experiences in the interwar period.[39] Arguably, Adorno's later works build on Horkheimer's materialist writings of the 1930s and the anthropological stance they elaborated in the 1940s. In sealing the divorce between theory and practice, however, his works from the postwar era constitute a break with the earlier attempts of the Institute to inform the struggles of the oppressed. They tend to legitimate what Leo Lowenthal considered Adorno's motto: "don't participate."[40]

Philosophical reflection continues to project emancipation even if only, given the argument of *Minima Moralia*. by asking how things might look from the perspective of their redemption. The importance of understanding freedom in terms of unqualified autonomy remains. "Freedom," writes Adorno, "is really delimited by society, not only from outside, but in itself. We no sooner put it to use than we increase our unfreedom; the deputy of better things is always also an accomplice of worse ones."[41] The historical process, in Adorno's view, has expelled freedom while the hegemony of instrumental reason threatens subjectivity. The goal of critical thinking thus becomes clear. It is necessary for reason to project freedom in the *form* of new images so that "in the age of the individual's liquidation, the question of individuality [can] be raised anew."[42]

Adorno is closer to Kierkegaard in this respect than he would probably care to admit.[43] The universal does not vanish; it is merely inverted regarding its relation to the particular. Both philosophers understand that "the principle of individuation, while encapsulating the demand for aesthetic particularization, is of course, itself a universal. What is more, it inheres in the subject that seeks to free itself. In short, it has a universal – spirit – which is not beyond the particulars, but in them."[44] The singular becomes the universal. And the need for such an inversion is the same in the realm of culture. Consequently, even in the sphere of music, "the collective powers are liquidating individuality, which is irrecoverable – but against them only individuals are capable of consciously representing the aims of collectivity."[45]

A crucial difference, however, does assert itself. Adorno believes that the tradition of existential phenomenology stemming from Kierkegaard obliterates real subjectivity by subsuming it within an ontological framework. Individuation substitutes itself for subjectivity, under these circumstances, in the same way that prefabricated and standardized forms of entertainment supplant the immanent elaboration of genuine artistic concerns.[46] A philosophical critique of subjectivist ontology, if not the ontological character of external reality, complements Adorno's aesthetic critique of the culture industry. Both have as their goal the reassertion of subjectivity. Thus, contesting Kierkegaard's notion of inwardness, Adorno will assume that "the constitution of the domain of art resembles the constitution of an inner space of ideas in the individual."[47]

His position, however, is defined less by an attempt to develop a "materialist reincarnation of the Kierkegaardian subject"[48] than a traditional emphasis on immanent critique and an unwillingness to identify subjectivity with anything external to it. This makes it possible for Adorno to suggest that a dour irrationalism, predicated on the experience of "dread" (*Angst*),[49] is merely the flip side of the "happy consciousness" (Marcuse) generated by advanced industrial society. Again, it becomes apparent that freedom demands transcendence. Theory must "rise above the individuality that exists as well as above the society that exists."[50]

Art embodies that transcendence; it rejects the "pure immanence" of positivism. The artwork, whose various moments exist in constant struggle with one another,[51] becomes the most obvious way of contesting the given petrified arrangement of reality. Every genuine artwork, according to Adorno, "exposes something which is lacking." Art makes the individuated person aware of a repressed subjectivity. It follows from his modernist convictions, in fact, that a genuine artwork always produces a "tremor."[52]

The aesthetic inquiry must begin with the object and its critique of the world in which the subject is enmeshed. For this very reason, art must "hurt." Pleasure and entertainment, even when transvalued within the artwork, lose their validity; "entertainment and art are antithetical to each other."[53] The specter of false immediacy presents itself and, insofar as pleasure and entertainment are rationalized, severed from the critique of repression,[54] they become the enemies of aesthetic appreciation. "The value of a thought is," thus, "measured by its distance from the continuity of the familiar. It is objectively devalued as this distance is reduced."[55]

Alienation from the alienated social relations of the whole, the "ontology of actuality," is the aim of art. And that is only possible by emphasizing the formal, rather than the substantive, character of the work. Adorno's first cultural essay, "Expressionism and Artistic Truth," already emphasized that the form employed by this movement rather than its rebellion against the "father" or its political ambitions projected its emancipatory character.[56] Nevertheless, by highlighting the question of form, Adorno necessarily places particular weight on the specialized knowledge of artistic technique.

The division of labor, a fundamental source of alienation in the realm of social interaction, subsequently becomes essential to an aesthetic practice committed to abolishing alienation. Initially, of course, the critical theory of society initiated by the Institute for Social Research was "supra-disciplinary" in character; it was meant to serve as a propaedeutic with which to inform the specialized empirical sciences and maintain the commitment to the unrecognized concerns of humanity as a universal. In the later writings of Adorno, however, "art can realize its universal humanity only working within the framework of specialization. All else is false consciousness."[57] What occurred in response to the traditional philosophy of history with its teleological assumptions, now takes place with respect to specialization. Adorno engages in another inversion. Specialization is changed, when employed by critical aesthetic inquiry, from a servant of alienation into a rebel seeking to contest its power.

Obscured by the increasing division of labor, without a subject to thematize its transformation, and thus incomprehensible from the standpoint of social theory, the totality becomes the focal point of an aesthetic built upon specialized knowledge. What sociologically appears as emphasis on subjectivity, from the standpoint of the aesthetic, gives "primacy to the object." The artwork offers a critique of the whole precisely because its rejection of direct political commitment prevents it from leveling a critique of anything in particular. Its illusionary quality confronts the real, its indeterminacy supplants meager determinations of freedom, so that "praxis is not the impact works have; it is the hidden potential of their truth content."[58] Freedom covers its face. Adorno, like Max Horkheimer, rejects any attempt to provide the most radical illusion with a content. He, too, will embrace the *Bilderverbot* – or the Jewish injunction against seeking to depict God – and extend it to utopia.

Aesthetic Inversion and Illusion

Adorno never surrenders the concept of freedom. So, for the hopeless, he holds out a moment of hope. But, in his view, utopia rests upon a "compact with failure." His is a *telos* without teleology. Emancipation thus becomes a floating opposition to a reality ontologically structured by reification. The truth of illusion contests the untruth of repression. It was for this reason he could write that "truth is inseparable from the illusory belief that from the pictures of the unreal one day, in spite of all, real deliverance will come."[59] The unreal and the non-discursive confront the reification of the real and the rational. This deliverance is neither articulated with respect to its meaning nor justified in terms of its "concrete possibility" (Lukács). It is really, for want of a better term, a myth, and thus the inversion of what the Enlightenment sought to dispel.

Such is the manner in which art evidences what Stendhal termed its *promesse de bonheur*. Philosophy once proclaimed a similar promise. History, however, remained deaf to it. Philosophy, for this reason, lack foundations and even negative dialectics recognizes that its status has become indeterminate.[60] Contradiction is now redefined as that which opposes reality per se.[61] Illusion alone, generated in the form of art, can thus contest the real; it alone can secure the moment of transcendence by remembering the past.[62] Indeed, with the unceasing assault on philosophical reflection by technological rationality and reification, "art may be the only remaining medium of truth in an age of incomprehensible terror and suffering."[63]

The aesthetic inversion of reality now serves as its negation. Art redeems truth by illuminating its sensuous quality. It does not, like philosophy, assume that "the authentic question will somehow almost always include its answer."[64] Emancipation lies in fantasy and the language of experience irreducible to linguistic rules: mimesis. Freedom is sensed beyond the conditions defining it while experience is preserved from closure in fixed philosophical categories and formulae.[65] Philosophy loses the unassailable primacy given it by Hegel; it now complements or "overlaps" with art in the idea of truth content.[66] It receives a new task. It must now discursively shape the non-discursive and "mimetic" elements of art.[67]

The fusion between art and philosophy is, however, impossible to achieve.[68] Their identity is actually little more than a utopian longing predicated on the "non-identity" between them. It is the same with the "logical essence," the internal coherence of an artwork,[69] which underpins the ongoing conflicts between the elements composing it. Tension of this sort is always felt. It is precisely what disrupts the sleek and smooth unfolding of technological rationality and secures the unrealized potential of freedom. The internal volatility of art is what resists the world and fosters the "non-identity" between subject and object.[70]

An inversion of the relation between universal and particular thus takes place within it; the object must highlight the subject in the realm of the aesthetic, if not in reality per se, which is why Adorno can claim that "art speaks in universals only when it moves away from universals to specific impulses."[71] This, in turn, renders art incapable of being defined ontologically or by any determinate set of logical, philosophical propositions.[72] The artwork stands apart. it has no external referent; its autonomy testifies to its freedom; it is always *sui generis*.

Adorno is no traditionalist. The innovative and the new, inverted in the aesthetic realm, confront the tricks and the fads of the culture industry. Judging the innovative character of a work, however, presupposes a knowledge of artistic technique. Artworks may not be reducible to technique, which may threaten the non-conceptual "language" of art.[73] But only technical knowledge of the work provides an objective referent for criticism and a corrective to interpretations based on experiential or historicist criteria.[74] Technique, whose origins derive from the external world the artwork contests, becomes internal to its effect. The manifestation of reification turns into the criticism of it. Thus, with its inversion, technique "alone guides the reflective person into the inner core of art works, provided of course he also speaks their language . . . It is rational but nonconceptual, permitting judgment in the area of the non-judgmental."

Aesthetic form, precisely insofar as it transfigures empirical being, "represents freedom whereas empirical life represents repression.[76] A work's truth content is thus necessarily transcendent.[77] The illusion generated by technique projects a promise beyond the suffering caused by the triumph of technical reason. That is the sense in which works of art "want us to become aware of what is true and what is false in them."[78] Technique, in this way, helps elicit the "meaning" of the work:[79] the hidden moment of reconciliation demanded by the unreconcilable opposition to reality. Aesthetic negation thus suggests positivity which, within the terms of a reified reality, remains always negative. This is the sense in which Adorno's later work fulfills the earlier desire to provide a "positive concept of enlightenment."[80]

The work is that positive concept. It is the central concept of the aesthetic; "art," Adorno can write, "is as inimical to 'art' as are artists."[81] For this reason, in contrast to Benjamin or Marcuse, he seeks to introduce categories of aesthetic judgment. Intensity, accomplishment, depth, and articulation become the conceptual tools with which to divine quality.[82] Categories such as these are meant to rescue the work from submersion within the experience of the subject. Indeed, given these categories, it becomes apparent what he meant by his claim that "aesthetic experience must pass over into philosophy or else it will not be genuine."[83]

Aesthetics becomes metaphysical.[84] So it must, if experience is to resist reality and remain immune to relativism.[85] Adorno, unwilling to surrender the concept of reflection,[86] maintains its intrinsic connection with a thematized object. He is not intent merely on deconstructing reality, denying the need for categories of differentiation, obliterating universals, or promulgating subjectivism. Quite the contrary. Adorno may have opposed the neo-classicism of Stravinsky and Hindemith along with "new objectivity" (*Neue Sachlichkeit*) and its belief that the composer is a "musical engineer." Nevertheless, the problems with his own aesthetic derive precisely from an objectivism of a different sort."

"Dialectics is not some rule on how to handle art, but something that inheres in it."[87] The artwork, so to speak, takes on a life of its own. It retains a set of dynamics from which possibilities arise for reconciling internal tensions while contradicting the external reality from which it arose.[88] While interpretation, commentary and criticism are necessary to elicit the "truth content" (*Wahrheitsinhalt*) of the work, in fact, they are little more than midwives. They only articulate what is already extant, the elements of quality, within the work as a whole. It is rather a matter, for Adorno, of employing reflexivity to "retrace" the dynamic of a work by examining its particular aspects and how they are "wanting."

The autonomy Adorno seeks implies that "works of art are their own standard of judgment. They themselves stipulate the rules they then follow."[89] The influence of Benjamin is apparent in his refusal to divorce categories from the empirical objects they describe.[90] Universality will make itself felt in the particularity generated by the aesthetic monad. The artwork lives, assumes its most critical character when it first appears, and then dies in the museum; indeed, "neutralization is the social price art pays for its autonomy. Once art works are buried in the pantheon of cultural exhibits, their truth content deteriorates.[91]

Amor fati: the authentic work of art, no less than Nietzsche's authentic individual, loves its fate because it determines that fate. Art does not progress for Adorno, it pulsates. The work of art, with its appropriated materials and dynamic capacity for engendering reflection, produces its own temporality. Adorno knows, of course, that art participates in the history of society. It is a product of social materials; there is also no way in which a genuine work of art will not put those materials to critical use. No matter how art is mediated, then, art will constitute itself as autonomous beyond its existence as a social fact.[92]

The participation of an artwork in history thus occurs only partially by its appropriation of technology from the external world.[93] Progress in art, which it is legitimate to discuss only because "there is no progress in the real world,"[94] is comprehensible only in terms of an inherently contingent form of such appropriation. It is neither linear nor apparent in the arbitrary comparison of particular works; indeed, fashion makes sense of Adorno's claim that artworks die.[95] The discontinuous progress of art, which actually subverts the concept, differs qualitatively from that of social development. The only point of continuity within art history is the constant rejection of that domination inherent in the social conditions making for its own genesis. Thus, the work of art must internally set its technologically appropriated devices in motion so that they transcend the merely functional.

The moment of art within the artwork accomplishes that in the name of freedom.[96] Adorno never rejects the concept of "essence" even if only as the "irreducible" differentiating subject from object.[97] He does, however, back away from the irrationalist implications of what initially appears as an inverted form of aesthetic *Lebensphilosophie*. Metaphysics provides the corrective in a world dominated by instrumental reason on the one hand and irrationalism on the other. Adorno's point is to assert precisely what has been lost. The question of whether metaphysical experience is still possible, which animates *Negative Dialectic*,[98] receives its answer in *Aesthetic Theory* where experience is preserved in the work of art. Thus, in order to explicate works of art, Adorno can claim that "they have to be honed to the point where they become philosophical. It is in the dynamic of the internal constitution of works and of the relation that particular works have to the concept of art in general that we obtain proof of the fact that art, its monadic essence notwithstanding, is an aspect of the movement of spirit and social reality."[99]

Philosophy prevents art, with its ability to generate an irreducible experience or a "somatic moment" of cognition, from slipping into "the abyss of relativity."[100] Metaphysical reflection preserves the work from historicism and makes it possible to perceive the moment of universality projected by the monadic "essence" of the work. It is possible to argue that, just as philosophy makes the truth of art comprehensible, art makes the truth of philosophy concrete.[101] The moment of reflection, however, is itself interwoven with experience. Adorno does not ignore the excitement of art or its elemental attraction. Thus, while praising the manifold possibilities for new experience offered by the circus, he can eloquently describe fireworks as the "prototype of art."

This is, in fact, the key to understanding his commitment to art and the manner in which it embodies freedom. "The work of art," he can write, "is both a process and an instant."[102] Fireworks evidence the evanescent, the fleeting moment, which prods memory; indeed, Adorno can write that "the tendency to objectify what is evanescent rather than what is permanent may well be one that runs through art history as a whole."[103] Subjectivity experiences itself in that moment.[104] But, even this does not simply belong to the subject. Adorno maintains his rejection of "false" immediacy, of enjoyment,[105] in the name of a structured experience capable of grasping the utopian. Aesthetic feeling, even in the case of fireworks, retains its critical and reflexive edge. Thus, he can write

Aesthetic feeling is not what is being aroused in us. It is more like a sense of wonderment in the presence of what we behold; a sense of being overwhelmed in the presence of a phenomenon that is non-conceptual while at the same time being determinate. The arousal of subjective effect by art is the last thing we should want to dignify with the name aesthetic feeling. True aesthetic feeling is oriented to the object; it is the feeling of the object, not some reflex in the viewer."[106]

Fireworks demonstrate the idea of art as a *tour de force*. The display is defined by antinomies. Its particular elements rebel against unification even as they form a unity without a fixed center. Colors clash, mosaics form, the work lives and then it dies. Fireworks are not reducible to the interpretive description and the meaning of the event occurs only in the attempt to "retrace" it. The work retains its own internal discipline, [107] forms its own "mimetic" language, and binds people together while leaving the singularity of their experience intact. The prototype of art secures the non-identity of subject and object in the experience of a non-objectifiable freedom, which begins to vanish as soon as it appears, like utopia. Reality can never measure up to the illusion. Nevertheless, for that very reason, reality can take its revenge.

Exploding the Inversion

"The gentleman does not find the world to his liking? Then let him go and look for a better one."[108] Adorno hated this kind of talk. But he protested too much. For, while such a view might well shackle artistic experimentation and limit the range of experience, its relevance for politics is obvious. Adorno, however, could not – or would not – make the distinction. And this has profound implications. The question is whether the cult embracing Adorno, identifying his ideas with those of critical theory per se, are willing to draw them.

It is irrefutable that Adorno made seminal contributions to aesthetics by reaffirming the centrality of the work. Exploring its inner dynamics, and opposing its reduction to psychology and historicism were surely also noteworthy. Early in his career, however, he argued that transcendental philosophy must give way before a standpoint predicated on the "critique of ideology" (*Ideologiekritik*). He had maintained then that the function rather than the manifest content of philosophy demands analysis. Nor did he ever really retract that claim. It would inform his negative dialectics, his defense of an idealist tradition betrayed by history, and his decision to emphasize the primacy of the artwork. Consequently, it is only fair that Adorno's own standpoint be confronted with the same standard of criticism he embraced.

Clearly, from his early commitment to the "critique of ideology,"

Adorno's thinking became increasingly marked by a retreat from the concrete and an affirmation of the status quo he always putatively rejected. The critique of ontology becomes defined by what it opposes. The "truth" of illusion is pitted against the "untruth" of reality, the determinate confronts the indeterminate, metaphysics rejects history, and aesthetics opposes anthropology. A divide results. The theoretical architechtonic and the concrete reality are separated in terms of an *ontological chasm*. Nor does it help to claim that Adorno is turning dialectics against itself, whatever that means. The result is not dialectics, but stasis wearing the costume of radical change. The result neither provides a method of concrete analysis nor a theory of practice. This is, indeed, what Walter Benjamin termed "dialectics at a standstill."

Adorno's theory, whatever its contributions, does not constitute an extension of the Marxian method capable of dealing with either the collapse of its teleology or the world of "late" capitalism.[109] The character and aims of his thought, even while predicated on the reinversion of a world inverted by the commodity form, are different. There is no objective referent for solidarity,[110] and no immanent analysis of the production process. Adorno may occasionally have spoken about his commitment to a "genuine liberalism." But there is no institutional analysis of the divergent political systems representing advanced industrial society. The philosophical importance of his work, in fact, derives from its greatest sociological weakness: an exaggeration of the integrative power of advanced industrial society and the impossibility of practical resistance.[111]

Its extraordinary integrative power is precisely what makes aesthetics alone capable of testing reality in the name of freedom. In the process, however, freedom is robbed of its content and subjectivity becomes just as nebulous as in the most reactionary of phenomenological approaches. Adorno's unwillingness to engage in discussions of "grounding" is no excuse. Neither is his fear of "systems." His refusal to justify the status of either aesthetics or philosophy was, in fact, what left him in this unenviable theoretical situation. And its implications become manifest in a variety of ways. Adorno claims, for example, that a progressive work of art provides an immanent critique of the formal limitations of existing artworks and, simultaneously, a rejection of repression. His justification, however, is based on little more than a previous definition of form as embodying freedom and an identification of empirical reality with repression.[112] The argument thus becomes tautological.

Tautology legitimates the supposedly radical use of inversion. Intervention is, for this very reason, equated with the inversion of reality. The formal moment of aesthetic freedom, indeterminate from the perspective of social interaction, is equated with a determinate response to repression by Adorno;[113] any concrete response to oppression is, by the same token, criticized from the utopian stance for its indeterminate and partial character; indeed, this equation explains the link between his aesthetic radicalism and his fear of concrete political change.[114] Other inversions follow from this one. Aesthetic objectification insures subjectivity while work in the social realm demeans it. Concrete praxis, or a theoretically informed political intervention into the status quo, loses its standing as such in favor of a "higher praxis" lacking in any material effect whatsoever. Thus, Adorno can write:

> Concrete and positive suggestions for change merely strengthen [the power of the status quo], either as ways of administrating the unadministratable, or by calling down repression from the monstrous totality itself. The concept and the theory of society are legitimate only when they do not allow themselves to be attracted by either of these solutions, when they merely hold in negative fashion to the basic possibility inherent in them: that of expressing the fact that such possibility is threatened with suffocation. Such awareness, without any preconceptions as to where it might lead, would be the first condition for an ultimate break in society's omnipotence.[115]

No concrete practice is ever radical enough. Theory simply turns its back on the reality it is to transform and detaches utopia from history. Art can metaphysically put "an advance on a praxis which has not yet begun."[116] But it can do so legitimately only insofar as the work does not project any concrete alternatives. Adorno never provides even the hint of an institutional alternative like the workers' councils, which informed the sectarian thinking of Korsch, from which to launch his critique. He is content to affirm that "a free society would situate itself beyond both the irrationality of its false costs and the means–ends rationality of utility. This ideal is encoded in art and is responsible for art's social explosiveness."[117]

Whether such an encoding actually exists in a painting by Mondrian, for example, is debatable. Whether such an ideal is relevant to an emancipated order, especially given any serious commitment to non-repressive interaction with nature, is not. Such a standpoint, whatever Adorno's intentions, has less to do with freedom than license. No wonder then that his theory of freedom should lack a notion of the public good or derivative categories like reciprocity and responsibility. If Adorno is correct in maintaining that materialism eliminates epistemology by fiat, his aesthetics does the same with politics. It is simply insufficient to speak of the "unfulfilled promise" of the Enlightenment without direct reference to the emancipated political institutions its theorists envisioned.

It is true, of course, that the old teleological unity between theory and practice had broken down; it was no longer a matter of the "future appearing as present." But, in principle, theory was still capable of speculating about the new conditions necessary for realizing its emancipatory promises. Adorno, however, never tried to reformulate the relation between theory and practice. Weimar, the experience of being a Jew in a failed republic, would always remain with him and so would the failure of the Russian Revolution. In looking back on these historical experiences, he came to believe that:

> The call for unity of theory and practice has irresistibly degraded theory to a servant's role, removing the very traits it should have brought to that unity. The visa stamp of practice which we demand of all theory became a censor's placet. Yet whereas theory succumbed in the vaunted mixture, practice became nonconceptual, a piece of the politics it was supposed to lead out of it; it became the prey of power.[118]

Power is inherently evil; it is always reifying insofar as it speaks to the realm of "necessity." This result of identifying reification with objectification, however, is not only naive; it also obscures the fact that power is a relationship in which contingency always plays a role. Power is identified with the "system" rather than the struggles between people and institutions within it. A reified notion of domination substitutes itself for power and, as dialectics becomes little more than running in place or an engine idling, metaphysics supplants social theory.

Breaking the relation between theory and practice, while identifying autonomy with the one and repression with the other, defines the new brand of critical theory associated with Adorno. But the problem with Adorno's thinking is not simply one of "metacritique." It derives instead from the way metacritique is initially elaborated in *Dialectics of Enlightenment*. In that work, after all, freedom is expelled from history. It loses both its form and its content. Freedom becomes anchored in the subject. Nevertheless, what this means remains open to question.

Construing freedom as the Other necessarily renders irrelevant any concern with expanding, reciprocally and universally, the range of choices in the present. Thus, in contrast to either Hegel or Marx, Adorno identifies freedom with subjectivity rather than a socio-political arrangement capable of making reciprocal claims upon its members under a liberal interpretation of the rule of law. Freedom is now content to contest power and thus forgets that power is necessary to constrain its arbitrary exercise.[119] The ethical and practical function of freedom is lost. It becomes transcendent and loses its immanent connection with human affairs. Freedom, from the standpoint of social reality, must appear as an illusion.

Politics is liquidated in the name of a methodological critique incapable of either specifying the conditions needing transformation or positing an alternative form of institutional organization. It only makes sense then that, with the sundering of theory from practice, a divorce between form and content should follow. A sacrifice of the concrete and the particular occurs when Adorno is analyzing the formal and the universal and vice versa. He would contend, of course, that balancing the antinomies and fostering the tension between them is necessary to preserve the 'non-identity' between subject and object. But, especially given his oft-stated desire to explode the distance between category and object, this is actually nothing more than yet another manifestation of the chasm dividing his thought.

Sociologically, the problem becomes apparent in the famous study of *The Authoritarian Personality*. There, in collaboration with a team of researchers, Adorno developed an "f-scale" for testing the degree to which authoritarian values had taken hold in an individual. It becomes evident, in contrast to *Dialectics of Enlightenment*, that fascism is not the necessary outcome of liberal society and that mass culture can play a positive role. Enlightenment and education become tools to mitigate the worst forms of racism and intolerance. The study was a major contribution and, with its quantitative techniques caused a great deal of controversy. Adorno, however, never integrated the results into his general theory. And for good reason. Extending its sociological insight would have involved subverting the broader experience. *The Authoritarian Personality* calls into question, after all, the *formal* identification between alienation and objectification as surely as the claim that attempts to engender "mass enlightenment" will only result in "mass deception."

Now, of course, defenders of Adorno might argue that the general formal claim can never fully encompass the particular. That is, in fact, precisely the point of Adorno's "negative dialectics." It resists the distorting power lurking in concepts as surely as in institutions. But the real issue is whether the particular and the empirical contradicts the general and the formal. Mediating categories are necessary to show the connection if it doesn't. These, however, are never supplied. There is subsequently only one conclusion to draw: the empirical analysis in *The Authoritarian Personality* excludes the formal analysis forwarded in Adorno's philosophical studies.

The situation is the same in the famous analysis of the "culture industry" first articulated in *Dialectics of Enlightenment*. The purpose of Horkheimer and Adorno was undoubtedly a noble one. They wished to examine the effects of the commodity form on culture. They had seen how the state could employ the new media in advanced industrial society; they recognized its potentially negative effects on political consciousness no less than on what Marx had termed "the material level of culture." The issue was its form; the increasing power of the culture industry was a direct reflection of the expanding power of the commodity form and instrumental reason. And, from the perspective of the general theory, the commitment to a criticism of the culture industry must prove uncompromising. That is why Adorno could write that, no less than dissonance, "black as an ideal" – the color devoid of colors – would alone enable art "to stand its ground."[120]

This argument makes it logical to assume that a particular type of reflexive discernment is necessary with respect to art.[121] The proper experience of a work as a *tour de force*,[122] in contrast to the false immediacy propagated by the culture industry, is interconnected with a technical knowledge of its form. There is no place here for condescension. Guernica by Picasso is, from this standpoint, meaningless to a person who knows nothing of the context it embodies or the techniques it employs. Adorno might have concerned himself with questions dealing with how to improve the "material level of culture." Even so, however, there is something profoundly legitimate about his criticisms of those whose cultural politics stem from guilt or who glorify the "underdogs" by embracing anti-intellectualism.[123]

Aesthetic form of the most innovative and complex variety preserves subjectivity, indeed, even when emptied of its most expressive content, the form recalls – without redeeming – the horrors spawned by progress along with those aspects of individuality weakened by a pervasive culture industry. The subject experiences his subjectivity then in response to the "slaughterbench of history" and his freedom in the rejection of prefabricated forms of "entertainment." This only makes sense given that "the emancipation of the subject by art was co-extensive with the shift towards autonomy in art itself."[124] Nevertheless, if subjectivity is freed to the extent that art becomes autonomous, then the extent to which art can fulfill its purpose is the extent to which it contests and breaks free of its subservience to the commodity form.

What then of the positive comments Adorno makes about the circus, fireworks, or even the Marx Brothers? He is, after all, willing to consign *all* sports to the realm of "unfreedom" and maintain that jazz is simply a "commodity in the strict sense."[125] The contradiction is obvious and there is only one way to resolve it. Adorno will sacrifice the empirical and experiential reality of these works for their formal and symbolic value. A bizarre situation results in which even the "prototype of art," fireworks, must be embraced as a formal principle and then rejected when employed – in what is actually its most flamboyant form – by the "systems" on occasions ranging from Independence Day to Chinese New Year. It is the idea of "fireworks" not the reality which Adorno enjoys. Nor is the cooptation of fireworks by Walt Disney Productions to introduce its programs, ever mentioned. The idea of fireworks is lifted above its real manifestations just as freedom is defined outside its immanent exercise.

Nor is the situation any different with the Marx Brothers. Sensitive literary critics can note that Adorno praises the simple and the outrageous quality of their skits.[126] Radical differences of quality, however, define their films no less than the rapid-fire delivery and relentless routines within them; Adorno does not have even the most general categories to make such distinctions, judge them against imitators like the Ritz Brothers, or rate them higher than other comic giants of the culture industry like W. C. Fields. Discussion of this sort would obviously contradict his claims about sports and jazz. It would subvert the general theory of the culture industry by suggesting that its products deserve the same analytic treatment as any other work of art. The chasm looms once again. Adorno's aesthetic offers no procedure or categories to justify such judgment; they appear completely arbitrary. Habermas surely overstates the case by claiming that Adorno calls the very commitment to rationality into question.[1] Nevertheless, there is something legitimate in the suggestion that his former teacher followed Nietzsche in turning what should present themselves as discursively justifiable validity-claims into mere preferences.[127]

A new preoccupation with the individual subject marked the change in critical theory initiated by Adorno. It inspired the cultural rebels of the 1960s even if he criticized them for ignoring the dangers of pseudo-uniqueness and "non-conformist conformity."[128] In concrete terms, however, authentic subjectivity remained hanging in the abstract. Adorno was right in suggesting that the system of advanced industrial society had absorbed its revolutionary negation; subjectivity was all that remained when dialectics was at a standstill. Institutional conditions for fostering or inhibiting it, however, are never discussed. He may have insisted: "no emancipation without that of society."[129] But the demand rings hollow. His theory nullifies its promise. All that remains is the long trek inward and a bitter memory of what was left behind.

Notes

1   Theodor W. Adorno, *Minima Moralia: Reflections from Damaged Life* trans. E. F. N. Jephcott (London, 1974), p. 16.
2   "Freedom has contracted to pure negativity . . . The objective end of humanism is only another expression for the same thing. It signifies that the individual as individual, in representing the species of man, has lost the autonomy through which he might realize the species." Ibid., p. 38.

3   Theodor W. Adorno, *Negative Dialectics* trans. E. B. Ashton (New York, 1973), pp. 20ff.

4   Note the discussion in the famous section on "commodity fetishism" in Karl Marx, *Das Kapital* 3 vols, ed. Friedrich Engels and trans. Samuel Moore and Edward Aveling (New York, 1967) vol. 1, pp. 71ff.

5   "The word alienation . . . acknowledges by the very tenacity with which it views the alien external world as institutionally opposed to the subject – in spite of all its protestations of reconciliation – the continuing irreconcilability of subject and object, which constitutes the theme of dialectical criticism." Adorno, *Minima Moralia*, p. 246.

6   Note the excellent discussion by Gillian Rose, *The Melancholy Science: An Introduction to the Thought of Theodor W. Adorno* (New York, 1978), pp. 43ff.

7   Stefan Breuer, "Adorno's Anthropology" in *Telos* 64 (Summer, 1985), pp. 15ff.

8   Cf. Theodor W. Adorno, "Die revidierte Psychoanalyse" and "Zum Verhältnis von Soziologie und Psychologie" in *Soziologische Schriften* (Frankfurt, 1979) vol. 1, pp. 20–85.

9   Cf. Drucilla Cornell, "The Ethical Message of Negative Dialectics" in *Social Concept* (December, 1987), vol. 4, no. 1, pp. 3ff.

10 Cf. Theodor W. Adorno et al., *The Positivist Dispute in German Sociology* trans. Glyn Adey and David Frisby (London, 1976), pp. 35ff.

11 Ibid., pp. 12ff.

12 Cf. George Lukács, *History and Class Consciousness: Studies in Marxist Dialectics* trans. Rodney Livingstone (Cambridge, Mass., 1968), pp. 15ff.

13 Rose, *The Melancholy Science*, p. 146.

14 Adorno, *Negative Dialectics*, p. 320; also cf. Theodor W. Adorno, "Fortschritt" in *Stichworte* (Frankfurt, 1978).

15 Arnold Künzli, "Irrationalism on the Left" in *Foundations of the Frankfurt School of Social Research* eds Judith Marcus and Zoltan Tar (New Brunswick, 1984), pp. 140–1.

16 The critique of ideology, bereft of a practical agent to realize the repressed possibilities of emancipation, can only "*dispute the truth* of a suspicious theory by *exposing its untruthfulness*. It advances the process of enlightenment by showing that a theory presupposing a demythologized understanding of the world is still ensnared by myth, by pointing out a putatively overcome category mistake." Jürgen Habermas, *The Philosophical Discourse of Modernity: Twelve Lectures* trans. Frederick Lawrence (Cambridge, Mass., 1987), p. 116.

17 "Negative philosophy, dissolving everything, dissolves even the dissolvent. But the new form in which it claims to suspend and preserve both, dissolved and dissolvent, can never emerge in a pure state from an antagonistic society. As long as domination reproduces itself, the

old quality reappears unrefined in the dissolving of the dissolvent: in a radical sense no leap is made at all." Adorno, *Minima Moralia.* p. 245.

18 Hartmut Scheible, *Theodor W. Adorno* (Hamburg, 1989), p. 55.

19 Theodor Adorno, in *Prismen: Kulturkritik und Gessellschaft* (Frankfurt, 1955), p. 27.

20 Cf. Karl Marx, "Theses on Feuerbach" in Karl Marx and Friedrich Engels, *Selected Works* 3 vols, (Moscow, 1969) vol. 1, p. 11; Karl Korsch, *Karl Marx* (New York, 1938), p. 84.

21 T. W. Adorno, *Aesthetic Theory* eds Gretl Adorno and Rolf Tiedemann and trans. C. Lenhardt (London, 1972), pp. 30–1.

22 "In the modern administered world the only adequate way to appropriate art works is one where the uncommunicable is communicated and where the hold of reified consciousness is thus broken." Ibid., p. 280.

23 An indication of this becomes apparent in the following: "What is unique about music, however, is the indeterminate conceptual quality; change and articulation by means typical of music alone are highly determinate. Music gains content because it gives itself a totality of defining characteristics." Ibid., p. 282.

24 Cf. Theodor W. Adorno, "The Actuality of Philosophy" in *Telos* 31 (Spring, 1977), p. 128.

25 Rose, *The Melancholy Science.* pp. 13ff. Lambert Zuidervaart, *Adorno's Aesthetic Theory: The Redemption of Illusion* (Cambridge, Mass., 1991), pp. 45ff.

26 Frederic Jameson, *Late Marxism: Adorno, or, The Persistence of the Dialectic* (London, 1990), p. 179.

27 Adorno, *Negative Dialectics*, pp. 24ff.

28 Adorno, "The Actuality of Philosophy," p. 129.

29 Adorno, *Negative Dialectics*, p. 3.

30 Cf. Peter Osborne, "Adorno and the Metaphysics of Modernism: The Problem of a 'Postmodern' Art" in *The Problems of Modernity: Adorno and Benjamin* ed. Andrew Benjamin (London, 1989), pp. 23ff.

31 Cf. Rose, *The Melancholy Science*, pp. 68ff.

32 Schieble, *Theodor W. Adorno*, p. 76.

33 Cf. Christa Hackenesch, "Erfahrung von Nichtidentität" in *Philosophische Rundschau* (1993) vols 1–2, pp. 106ff.

34 Adorno, *Negative Dialectics*, pp. 5, 138.

35 Ibid., pp. 153–4.

36 Ibid., pp. 211ff.

37 Jürgen Habermas, "Der Horizont der Moderne verschiebt sich" in *Nachmetaphysiches Denken: Philosophische Aufsätze* (Frankfurt, 1992), p. 13.

38 Erstwhile defenders of Adorno like Leo Lowenthal tend to dismiss the criticisms of "rebellious youngsters" like the fine scholar Andreas Huyssen and the important activist Hans-Jürgen Krahl with sophistic queries about what disasters would have befallen future culture had

Adorno and his colleagues joined the barricades, or through caricatured references to the radicalism of the 1960s. The mistake made by Huyssen and Krahl is not one of political evaluation. It derives instead from their inability to deal immanently with Adorno's concepts in their own terms. Cf. Leo Lowenthal, "Adorno and His Critics" in *Critical Theory and Frankfurt Theorists: Lectures – Correspondence – Conversations* (New Brunswick, 1989), pp. 54ff; Hans-Jürgen Krahl, "The Political Contradictions in Adorno's Critical Theory" in *Telos* 21 (Fall, 1974), p. 164; Andreas Huyssen, "Introduction to Adorno" in *New German Critique* 6 (Fall, 1975), p. 3.

39 "No theory, not even the true one, is secure from perversion into madness once its spontaneous relation to the object has been externalized." Theodor W. Adorno in *Prismen: Kulturkritik und Gesellschaft* p. 29.

40 "For the intellectual, inviolable isolation is now the only way of showing some measure of solidarity. All collaboration, all the human worth of social mixing and participation, merely masks a tacit acceptance of inhumanity. It is the sufferings of men that should be shared: the smallest step towards their pleasures is one towards the hardening of their pains." Adorno, *Minima Moralia*, p. 26.

41 Adorno, *Negative Dialectics*, p. 297.

42 Adorno, *Minima Moralia*, p. 129.

43 Cf. Theodor W. Adorno, *Kierkegaard: Konstruktion des Aesthetischen* (Frankfurt, 1979). For a summary of the critique developed in this unnecessarily convoluted work, cf. Martin Jay, *Adorno* (Cambridge, 1984), pp. 29ff.

44 Adorno, *Aesthetic Theory*. p. 286; *Negative Dialectics*, pp. 160ff.

45 Theodor W. Adorno, "On the Fetish Character of Modern Music and the Regression of Listening" in *The Essential Frankfurt School Reader* eds Andrew Arato and Eike Gebhardt (New York, 1978), p. 299.

46 "My argument is that precisely because art works are monads they lead to the universal by virtue of their principle of particularization. In other words, the general characteristics of art are more than just responses to the need for conceptual reflection: they also testify to the fact that the principle of individuation has its limits and that neither it nor its opposite should be ontologized. Art works approach this limit by ruthlessly pursuing the principle of individuation, whereas if they pose as universals, they end up being accidental and pseudo-individual like examples of a type or species." Adorno, *Aesthetic Theory*, p. 259.

47 Ibid., p. 11.

48 Irving Wohlfarth, "Dialektischer Spleen. Zur Ortsbestimmung der Adornoschen Aesthetik" in *Materialien zur ästhetischen Theorie Theodor W. Adornos Konstruktion der Moderne* eds Burkhardt Lindner and W. Martin Ludke (Frankfurt, 1980), p. 318.

49 "*Angst*, that supposed 'existential,' is the claustrophobia of a systematized society. Its system character, yesterday still a shibboleth of

academic philosophy, is strenuously denied by initiates of that philosophy; they may, with impunity pose as spokesmen for free, for original, indeed, for unacademic thinking . . . [But] the things philosophy has yet to judge are postulated before it begins. The system, the form of presenting a totality to which nothing remains extraneous, absolutizes the thought against each of its contents and evaporates the content in thoughts. It proceeds idealistically before advancing any arguments for idealism." Adorno, *Negative Dialectics*, p. 24; note also, what was originally to have been included in this major volume by Theodor W. Adorno, *The Jargon of Authenticity* trans. Knut Tarnowski and Frederic Will (London, 1973).

50 Adorno, *Negative Dialectics*, p. 283.
51 "The more the work of art seeks to liberate itself from external determinations, the more it becomes subject to self-positing principles of organization, which mime and internalize the law of an administered society." Terry Eagleton, *The Ideology of the Aesthetic* (London, 1990), p. 351.
52 Adorno, *Aesthetic Theory*, p. 346.
53 Ibid., pp. 20–1.
54 Ibid., pp. 351, and *passim*; also, cf. Max Horkheimer and Theodor W. Adorno, *Dialectic of Enlightenment* trans. John Cumming (New York, 1972), pp. 81ff.
55 Adorno, *Minima Moralia*, p. 80.
56 Scheible, *Theodor W. Adorno*, p. 16.
57 Adorno, *Aesthetic Theory*, p. 334.
58 Ibid., p. 350.
59 Adorno, *Minima Moralia*, p. 122.
60 Habermas, "Motive nachmetaphysichen Denkens" in *Nachmetaphysiches Denken*, p. 45.
61 Ibid., p. 145.
62 "Knowledge as such, even in a form detached from substance, takes part in tradition as unconscious remembrance; there is no question which we might simply ask, without knowing of past things that are preserved in the question and spur it." Ibid., p. 54.
63 Adorno, *Aesthetic Theory*, p. 27.
64 Adorno, *Negative Dialectics*, p. 63.
65 Ibid., p. 151.
66 Adorno, *Aesthetic Theory*, p. 189; also, cf. Eagleton, *The Ideology of the Aesthetic*, p. 361.
67 "Unlike discursive knowledge, art does not rationally understand reality, including its irrational qualities which stem in turn from reality's law of motion. However, rational cognition has one critical limit which is its inability cope with suffering. Reason can subsume suffering under concepts; it can furnish means to alleviate suffering; but it can never express suffering in the medium of experience for to do so would be irrational by reason's own standards." Adorno, ibid., p. 27.

68 Cf. Albrecht Wellmer, *The Persistence of Modernity: Essays on Aesthetics, Ethics, and Postmodernism* trans. David Midgley (Cambridge, Mass., 1991), pp. 5ff.

69 Adorno, *Aesthetic Theory*, p. 197.

70 Ibid., p. 6.

71 Ibid., p. 293.

72 Ibid., p. 3.

73 The tension between them, in fact, casts doubt on Benjamin's belief that "the adjustment of art to extra-aesthetic technique has always automatically spelled intra-aesthetic progress." Ibid., p. 310.

74 "[W]e must look not at the sphere of reception, but at the more basic sphere of production. Concern with the social explication of art has to address the production of art rather than study its impact." Ibid., p. 324.

75 Ibid., p. 304.

76 Ibid., p. 207.

77 Nor does it help to claim that "truth content is that which is not illusory in the artistic illusion. Truth content is that which transcends via that which is transcended." Cf. Zuidervaart, *Adorno's Aesthetic Theory*, pp. 201ff. This is nothing other than playing with words. *What*, concretely, is not illusory in the illusion? *What* mediates transcendence? Technique? The configuration of elements in the artwork? Talk of this sort only turns the products of human activity into human agents. There is, in fact, no mediated transcendence at all since mediating transcendence would involve providing it with a *concrete* and positive historical determination. That, however, is precisely what illusion cannot provide.

78 Ibid., p. 22.

79 "Meaning is responsible for producing illusion and therefore contributes in a major way to the illusory quality of art. Still, the essense of meaning is not synonymous with illusion; it is more. Above all, the meaning of a work of art is also the summoning to appearance of an essence that is otherwise hidden in empirical reality. This is the purpose of organizing the work of art in such a way that the moments are grouped 'meaningfully' in relation ot one another." Ibid., p. 154.

80 Horkheimer and Adorno, *Dialectic of Enlightenment*, p. xvi.

81 Adorno, *Minima Moralia*, p. 214.

82 Adorno, *Aesthetic Theory*, pp. 268ff.

83 Ibid., p. 190.

84 Rüdiger Bubner, "Kann Theorie ästhetisch werden? Zum Hauptmotiv der Philosophie Adornos" in *Materialien zur ästhetischen Theorie Theodor W. Adornos Konstruktion der Moderne*, pp. 108ff.

85 "Relativism, no matter how progressive its bearing, has at all times been linked with moments of reaction, beginning with the sophists' availability to the more powerful interests. To intervene by criticizing

relativism is the paradigm of definite negation." Adorno, *Negative Dialectics*, p. 37.

86 "The less identity can be assumed between subject and object, the more contradictory are the demands made upon the cognitive subject, upon its unfettered strength and candid self-reflection." Ibid., p. 31.

87 Adorno, *Aesthetic Theory*, p. 203.

88 "When we say that works undergo changes we mean something more than changes in reception and appropriation: there are objective changes taking place in the works themselves, which must mean that there is a force bound up in them that lives on." Ibid., p. 276.

89 Ibid., p. 243.

90 "Becoming aware of the constellation in which a thing stands is tantamount to deciphering the constellation which, having come to be, it bears within it." Adorno, *Negative Dialectics*, p. 163.

91 Adorno, *Aesthetic Theory*, p. 325.

92 Peter Bürger, "Das Vermittlungsproblem in der Kunstsoziologie Adornos" in *Materialien zur ästhetischen Theorie Theodor W. Adornos Konstruktion der Moderne*, p. 175.

93 "In art, the criterion of success is twofold: first, works of art must be able to integrate materials and details into their immanent law of form; and second, they must not try to erase the fractures left by the process of integration, preserving instead in the aesthetic whole the traces of those elements which resisted integration." Adorno, *Aesthetic Theory*, p. 10.

94 Ibid., pp. 296–302.

95 Ibid., p. 274.

96 "The development of art works is therefore the posthumous life of this inner dynamic. What an artwork expresses by virtue of the configuration of its moments differs objectively from one epoch to the next, and ultimately this change affects its truth content, namely at the point where it becomes uninterpretable." Ibid., p. 277.

97 "Nietzsche, the irreconcilable adversary of our theological heritage in metaphysics, had ridiculed the difference between essence and appearance. He had relegated the "background world" to the "backwoodsmen," concurring here with all of positivism. Nowhere else, perhaps, is it so palpable how an indefatigable enlightenment will profit the obscurantists. Essence is what must be covered up, according to the mischief-making law of unessentiality; to deny that there is an essence means to side with appearance, with the total ideology which existence has since become. If a man rates all phenomena alike because he knows of no essence that would allow him to discriminate, he will in a fanaticized love of truth make common cause with untruth." Adorno, *Negative Dialectics*, p. 169.

98 Ibid., pp. 362ff.

99 Adorno, *Aesthetic Theory*, p. 278.

100 Ibid., p. 128.

101 Zuidervaart, *Adorno's Aesthetic Theory*, pp. 178ff.
102 Ibid., p. 147.
103 Ibid., p. 312.
104 Ibid., pp. 119-20.
105 "Mistrust is called for in face of all spontaneity, impetuosity, all letting oneself go, for it implies pliancy towards the superior might of the existent." Adorno, *Minima Moralia*, p. 25.
106 Adorno, *Aesthetic Theory*, p. 236.
107 Adorno, *Minima Moralia*, p. 70.
108 Ibid., p. 115.
109 Frederic Jameson, *Late Marxism: Adorno, or, The Persistence of the Dialectic* (London, 1990), pp. 182ff.
110 Adorno, *Minima Moralia*, pp. 51 and *passim*.
111 References to the influence of Adorno on those concerned with developing an immanent critique of the logic of capital does not help matters; indeed, whatever their quality, investigations of this sort were always notoriously lacking in the ability to develop genuine political implications or bridge the gap between the phenomenological and the empirical moments of the analysis. Note the seminal works by Alfred Sohn-Rethel, *Geistige und körperliche Arbeit: Zur Theorie der gesellschaftlichen Synthesis* (Frankfurt, 1970); Roman Rosdolsky, *The Making of Marx's "Capital"* (London, 1977).
112 "By being different from the ungodly reality, art negatively embodies an order of things in which empirical being would have its rightful place." Adorno, *Aesthetic Theory*, p. 322.
113 "The social deviance of art is the determinate negation of a determinate society." Ibid., p. 321
114 Note his conformist stance on the Cold War and his embarrassingly conservative role in the student movement. Cf. Scheible, *Theodor W. Adorno*, p. 131; Rolf Wiggershaus, *Die Frankfurter Schule: Geschichte, Theoretische Entwicklung, Politische Bedeutung* (Munich, 1988), pp. 676ff.
115 Theodor W. Adorno, "Society" in *Critical Theory and Society: A Reader* eds Stephen Eric Bronner and Douglas Kellner (New York, 1989). p. 275; for a critique, see Stephen Eric Bronner, *Socialism Unbound* (New York, 1990), pp. 176ff.
116 Adorno, *Aesthetic Theory*, p. 124.
117 Ibid., p. 323.
118 Adorno, *Negative Dialectics*, p. 143.
119 Cf. Franz Neumann, "The Concept of Political Freedom" in *The Democratic and the Authoritarian State: Essays in Political and Legal Theory* ed. Herbert Marcuse (New York, 1957), pp. 160ff; Henry Pachter, "Freedom, Authority, Participation" in *Socialism in History: Political Essays of Henry Pachter* ed. Stephen Eric Bronner (New York, 1984), pp. 36ff.
120 Adorno, *Aesthetic Theory*, pp. 58-9.
121 "Happiness is an accidental moment of art, less important even than

the happiness that attends the knowledge of art. In short, the very idea
that enjoyment is of the essence of art deserves to be overthrown."
Adorno, *Aesthetic Theory*, p. 22.

122   Ibid., pp. 154ff.
123   Adorno, *Minima Moralia*, pp. 28, 102.
124   Adorno, *Aesthetic Theory*, p. 281.
125   Cf. Theodor W. Adorno, "Zeitlose Mode. Zum Jazz" in *Prismen:
      Kulturkritik und Gesellschaft*, pp. 144ff.
126   Cf. Jameson, *Late Marxism*, p. 137, 145.
127   Habermas, *The Philosophical Discourse of Modernity*, p. 123; also, cf. his
      "Nachwort" to *Dialektik der Aufklärung* (Frankfurt, 1986 edition).
128   "Mass culture in its different branches," Horkheimer could write to
      Leo Lowenthal, "reflects the fact that the human being is cheated out of
      his own entity which Bergson so justly called *durée*." Cited in
      Lowenthal, *Critical Theory and Frankfurt School Theorists*, pp. 203–4;
      also cf. Horkheimer, "Art and Mass Culture," pp. 274–8.
129   Adorno, 'Veblens Angriff auf die Kultur" in *Prismen*, pp. 82ff.
130   Adorno, *Minima Moralia*, p. 173.

10

Fromm in America

America embraced Erich Fromm like few other émigrés. But, ironically, the man who made so many tenets of critical theory part of the American political vocabulary was never really associated with that philosophical tendency in the public mind.[1] Most intellectuals knew him as a social psychologist and one of the founders, along with Karen Horney and Harry Stack Sullivan,[2] of the neo-Freudian "culturalist" school. But no mass public read the wealth of specialized papers he produced or the technical arguments underpinning his "analytic psychology." His fame rested on *Escape from Freedom* and what many intellectuals considered "how to" tracts like *The Art of Loving*, "feel good" books like *The Heart of Man*, or "dilettantish" incursions into the field of politics and social theory like *May Man Prevail*. Perhaps, in the 1950s, important sociologists like his student David Riesman and Paul Lazarsfeld took him very seriously; in fact, sociological journals were rife with citations from the work of Erich Fromm. By the 1960s, however, Fromm had turned into a merely "popular writer." Few considered him an intellect on par with someone like T. W. Adorno and he neither became a titan of academic affairs like Max Horkheimer nor the guru of a movement like Herbert Marcuse. He never prized the aesthetic like Adorno and, in contrast to Horkheimer, employed his organizational talents outside the university; in contrast to Marcuse, furthermore, he was dissatisfied with "the great refusal" or any utopian conception inimically separated from reality.

Aside from Horkheimer, Fromm was the most important theoretician during the early years of the Frankfurt School.[3] Later, however, he was somewhat patronizingly regarded as the "idealist," the "mystic," the "naif," and – above all – the humanist. Perhaps it was because more than any other member of the Frankfurt School, even Marcuse, he touched a nerve in the progressive reading public beyond the university. And that was not, as most commentators maintain, because he "abandoned" critical theory and a "radical" perspective. In fact, certainly more than Horkheimer and Adorno, Fromm consistently and coherently identified himself with the Left during the dark days of the Cold War; he neither denigrated social theory in favor of aesthetics like the one nor used religion to justify political paralysis like the other. The truth is that not even Marcuse identified his aims with a practical political tradition or presented ideas for concrete change as forthrightly as Erich Fromm.

Popularity does not preclude political commitment any more than clarity of style precludes clarity of thought. Fromm's influence did not derive from his betrayal of radicalism or his "integration" by the status quo. It most likely derived from a willingness to reassert the original tenets of the critical enterprise, reformulate them after his own fashion, and present his views in such a way that they might contribute to a broad-based progressive movement that was surfacing in the America of the 1950s and 60s.

It was said of the great Charlie Chaplin that he never discarded a single piece of film; he used everything. Erich Fromm never forgot anything either. That was the case with the Talmudic tradition in which he grew to maturity no less than the critical theory into which he was introduced during the late 1920s. Born in 1900, even as a child he was drawn to the great prophets of the Old Testament like Isaiah, Amos, Hosea less for their warnings of catastrophe than for their utopian visions. Fromm helped establish the legendary *Freie jüdisches Lehrhaus*,[4] and his association with rabbis like Ludwig Krause, Nehemiah Nobel and especially Salman Baruch Rabinkow inspired a commitment to humanism that would last until his own death in 1980.[5] Fromm's earliest works treated religious themes like *The Sabbath* (1927) and, with a Marxian twist, *The Dogma of Christ* (1930) while his dissertation, written for Alfred Weber at the University of Heidelberg, dealt with *The Jewish Law: Toward a Sociology of the Jewish Diaspora* (1922); in fact, the theological strains within his thought would later strike a popular chord in radical works of biblical reinterpretation like *You Shall Be As Gods*.[6] Nevertheless, in America, it was as a social psychologist fusing the thought of Marx and Freud that he first achieved success.

He emigrated early in 1933. Already friendly with a number of important intellectuals, having set up a psychoanalytic practice, he immediately became a guest professor at Columbia University and ultimately would teach at the University of Chicago, Bennington, Yale, and the New School for Social Research. *Escape from Freedom*, originally published in 1941, reached an enormous popular audience. It would most likely not have had such impact in an earlier period. During the depression, in the words of Edgar Friedenberg, the populace "did not take any form of psychoanalytic thought to have serious social implications, but tended to dismiss it as a rich man's toy."[7] The onset of World War II, however, forced the nation to confront the question of totalitarianism and recognize that Nazism was not merely the work of a clique and that it retained a mass base of millions willing to sacrifice themselves for its goals. *Escape from Freedom* inaugurated what would become a spate of studies on the "authoritarian personality" and the "origins of totalitarianism" even as it gave readers a handle with which to confront Hitler's "new man" and the "SS state."[8]

Fromm considered himself engaged, especially during the 1930s, in developing a "materialist psychoanalysis." His social psychology, in this vein, rested on an appropriation of critical theory.[9] It is true that by 1939 he had already broken with his former comrades in the Institute for Social Research.[10] Fromm was angered by what he perceived as a growing discourtesy on the part of Horkheimer, the refusal of the latter to publish *The Working Class in Weimar Germany*, as well as the problems of working together on *Studies on Authority and the Family*.[11] Then, too, there was the growing influence of Theodor Adorno whom Fromm heartily disliked.[12] Most importantly, however, the Frankfurt School changed its view of Freud as well as its political perspective when Fromm left and Adorno became a fully-fledged associate in 1938.

The attempt to expose determinate mediations between the psychological and the sociological in order to overcome economic reductionism, and explore the manner in which revolutionary change was being hindered, now surrendered before Adorno's desire to secure an anthropological foundation for critical theory by employing the instict theory and metapsychology of Freud. The original program of the Institute had called for the development of an interdisciplinary perspective capable of connecting philosophy and empirical analysis; it was believed that social scientific inquiry would thus become imbued with a normative component and overcome the position of those who would separate "fact" from "value." It sought to situate all forms of activity within a totalistic view of social relations, confront the implications of the commodity form, foster a dialectical perspective, and maintain the commitment to an emancipatory alternative.

Fromm's social psychology always highlighted its connection with practice.[13] None of his future work, even his preoccupation with Nietzsche and various "philosophers of life" in seeking a foundation for his psychological arguments, evidences a sharp break with the past. All of it builds on two of his earliest contributions to the *Journal for Social*

Research. These essays, dating from 1929 and 1931, already emphasized that the psychological is neither divorced from the sociological nor its mechanical complement; they already raise questions about the links between the economic and the psychic realm, the manner in which the ego is organized, how the psychic apparatus affects the development of society, and the extent to which psychology can aid the political confrontation with inhuman conditions.[14]

Escape from Freedom (1941) employs this interdisciplinary perspective in order to analyze a specific historical occurrence: Nazism. Much to the chagrin of his former comrades in the Institute,[15] most of whom were still virtually unknown, the book created a sensation with its depiction of the sadomasochistic character as the specific historical response to the loneliness and alienation caused by capitalism and the political institutions it engendered in Weimar Germany.[16] Identifying neurosis as a social product, whose mitigation or intensification depends upon the transformation of living conditions,[17] it culled insights from work undertaken with Horkheimer during the thirties in which the family was seen as a primary agent of repressive socialization. Inaugurating what would become a virtual obsession with the "authoritarian personality" among American intellectuals, this study provided a concrete example of the manner in which socio-economic conditions are translated into a particular "social character."

And, with this, Fromm begins his "revision" of Freud.[18] The influence of Karen Horney and Harry Stack Sullivan, whose emphasis on the role of interpersonal interaction in producing anxiety never resonated with other members of the Frankfurt School, was surely evident in Fromm's elaboration of the concept. Still, it served as an important contribution to critical theory. That philosophical tendency, after all, had emerged in response to the failure of the proletarian uprisings following the First World War and the inability of that class to make good on the "objective conditions" for revolutionary transformation provided by the economic collapse of 1929. The concern with various aspects of what had previously been considered the "superstructure" by the Institute must be understood in this light. That is also the case with the increasing emphasis placed on the debilitating role of "the culture industry" by Adorno, Horkheimer, and Marcuse.

Fromm often criticized the mass media. But his criticisms lacked the dogmatic and arrogant tone so common with his former colleagues at the Institute for Social Research. This, in turn, made it possible for him to engage American public life in a way that they could not. He never really developed a general theory of the culture industry. Fromm was wary of claims suggesting that it inherently appealed to the lowest common denominator or suggestions that all emancipatory impulses become absorbed or invalidated once they become popular.[19] His approach was different; it built upon a different category and set of assumptions. Thus, his most sustained critique of alienated consumption was built upon the category of "social character."[20]

This concept derives from the original desire of the Institute, in keeping with the thought of Korsch and Lukács, to situate all phenomena within the context of the totality, and reaffirms his commitment to the original critical enterprise. It militates against viewing consciousness from the standpoint of simple institutional manipulation from the top down and reaffirms its sociological connection with practice

> The concept of *social character,* refers to the matrix of the character structure common to a group. It assumes that the fundamental factor in the formation of the "social character" is *the practice of life as it is constituted by the mode of production and the resulting social stratification. The "social character" is that particular structure of psychic energy which is molded by any given society so as to be useful for the functioning of that particular society.* The average person must *want* to do what he *has* to do in order to function in a way that permits society to use his energies for its purposes.[21]

Too many misconceptions, however, surround the intellectual relationship between Freud and Fromm.[22] It was not that Fromm simply denied the validity of categories like the Oedipus complex, the unconscious, or the existence of a certain instinctual energy. His concern was rather that Freud's instinct theory, his partriarchal bias and focus on sexuality led to interpretive distortions of the Oedipal myth. Fromm rejected all claims regarding the universality of the Oedipal complex and believed that each society retains a certain libidinal structure which has an impact on the lives of its inhabitants.[23] He was also willing to speak of human nature – though one that is neither fixed nor infinitely malleable. Were it static, change would prove impossible a *priori*; were human beings totally malleable, the need to resist oppression could be sociologically extinguished.[24] Fromm's approach maintains that a "dynamic adaptation" of human nature to the contradictions of a given social complex will occur;[25] the result can prove beneficial under stable circumstances and explosive when the economic infrastructure is in a state of rapid change. Under any circumstances, while modifying the somewhat functional or mechanical view of the relation between the psychological and the sociological apparent in his earliest essays, Fromm rejected Freud's emphasis on a fixed, libidinally centered, ahistorical theory of the instincts in favor of the historically unique "social character."

Of crucial importance, however, is the generally overlooked fact that Fromm's revision of instinct theory made possible an interpretation which most nearly renders Freud, Marx, and even Nietzsche for that matter, theoretically compatible. This had been one of the central concerns of the Frankfurt School almost from the beginning. But the ahistorical character of Freud's instinct theory and Nietzsche's vitalistic subjectivism created a logical stumbling block for those seeking to integrate their thinking with that of historical materialism. No accident then that the attempts by Wilhelm Reich should have floundered on the reef of vitalism even as freeing the subject for Adorno and Horkheimer would ultimately involve breaking not only with history, but society as well.

According to Fromm, society remains at the center. Rejecting Freud's ahistorical characterization of individuals through distinct structural categories like the id, ego, and superego, he chose to view the individual from the perspective of an integrated being grounded within society.[26] And so, if the existence of psychic energy is recognized, it is no longer identified as biological or with sexual libido; this energy, which Nietzsche also emphasized, becomes manifest in the living of life as a social being. A logical connection emerges with the anthropological perspective of the young Marx wherein "the eye becomes the human eye, the ear the human ear."[27] It is the complex of existing institutions which, according to Fromm, subsequently either inhibits or facilitates the expression of subjective potentialities which Nietzsche understood in the reified form of a "will to power." The existential need to overcome loneliness and find meaning can thus occur in a "productive" or "destructive" fashion.[28]

Opposing the metapsychology of Freud, especially with respect to the power accorded the trans-historical "death instinct," seeking to employ categories like the oedipus complex to explain forms of social action,[29] Fromm's approach stands in accord with the critique of metaphysics developed by Korsch, Lukács, and in the writings of Horkheimer prior to World War II. Repression, from such a perspective, retains an intrinsically historical dimension and can take a manifold set of social forms. In fact, unless the death instinct and repression are seen historically, the existence of the one can always be used to justify the maintenance of the other. The "ruthless critique of everything existing" demanded by the young Marx thus becomes necessary in order to confront authority and actualize the full potentiality of each individual. Thus, it only makes sense that Fromm could maintain "understanding the unconscious of the individual, presupposes and necessitates the critical analysis of his society."[30]

His attempt to establish a unified social psychology placed him at the center of postwar debate in his discipline and opposed to the desire of his former comrades at the Institute to preserve an arena of autonomous psychological subjectivity from society.[31] Marcuse, for example, argued that individuality must be understood "either" in terms of a repressive social order "or" in transcendent utopian terms. According to Fromm, however, such a standpoint is reified from the start; freedom for the subject, from a dialectical perspective, cannot appear as some state of pure otherness beyond any positive determinations or as predicated on the existence *ex novo* of a new biological infrastructure for humanity.[32] Indeed, since subjective freedom is a social phenomenon, maintaining sanity depends upon the ability of the individual to fill a social role and affirm his or her fullest potential.[33]

Fromm's belief in the need for some objective referent in the discussion of subjectivity is the principal reason why his "revisionism" was condemned and seen by his former associates as a betrayal of the radical impulse within Freud's thought. [34] Adorno, in particular, believed that the libido theory provided a substratum for subjective experience and a way of attesting to the "non-identical" character of the individual in relation to society. Only in a society where all contradictions are abolished is a methodological integration of subject and object legitimate.[35] But this would necessarily sever any connection between theory and empirical research as well as the freedom of the individual and the determinate conditions in which he lives.[36] Fromm thus will have little use for a "negative dialectic" which views the freedom of the subject from "outside" the existing order, an avant-gardist notion of "the great refusal" (Marcuse), or some quasi-religious commitment to what Horkheimer termed "the totally other."

According to Fromm, in keeping with Aristotle, only when freedom is identified with the potentialities of the subject *within* society can it inform political struggles. The attack on Marcuse's utopian interpretation of Freud's metapsychology, in this vein, surely distanced him from the radical minority. But his critique certainly does not subvert the need for an alternative; "social character" was, after all, intended to offer criteria to distinguish between the social interactions of the existent and those of an emancipated order. Nor is it legitimate to claim that Fromm engaged in some capitulation to the forces of exploitation and conformism. Against various exponents of ego psychology, in fact, Fromm never stressed adaptation by a "rational" ego to the repressive values of the status quo and, in the name of the "social defect," he explicitly opposed the idea that a "consensual validation" of norms by the members of society attests to their truth or emancipatory value.[37] The rejection of cultural and political conformism was precisely what made possible his appropriation by so broad an audience on the left.

"Conscience," he would write, "by its very nature is nonconforming . . . to the degree to which a person conforms he cannot hear the voice of his conscience, much less act upon it."[38] By the same token, no less than Freud, he retained a willingness to examine collective neurosis and social pathologies.[39] Indeed, Fromm's belief that a profound alienation existed beneath the affluence of America in the 1950s and 1960s made for his popularity and animated his controversial contention that "destructiveness is the outcome of the unlived life."[40]

Erich Fromm's work did not achieve such enduring popularity among progressives only because it provided a psychological analysis of a totalitarian regime. *Escape from Freedom* was not just a book about what the United States was fighting against, but also raised the existential question of the what it was fighting for. The defeat of the fascist enemy left a world dominated by two superpowers and what would soon become a type of spiritual malaise. The onset of the nuclear arms race poised humanity at the edge of the abyss and seemed to render the life of the individual meaningless. The experience of Hitler coupled with the revelations about Stalin's concentration camp universe, and his policies in Eastern Europe, simultaneously produced a politics of Cold-War partisanship and a left culture in which Kafka, the existentialists, and the "Beats" claimed center stage. The growing British movement to abolish nuclear weapons would admittedly become an important influence on the new social movements of the sixties and many were thrilled by the great struggles for national self-determination in the Third World. Beyond the burgeoning civil rights movement in the United States and the anti-communist hysteria inspired by Senator Joseph McCarthy, however, a new intellectual absorption with the self, coupled with an uncritical belief in the promise of science and technology gripped the United States.

Fromm's popularity in this period, no less than the one that followed, is directly attributable to the manner in which he confronted these concerns. While Horkheimer began his retreat from any kind of radical political involvement, warning against political activism or turning philosophy into "propaganda,"[41] Fromm was playing an important role on the political Left. A co-founder in 1957 of the National Committee for a Sane Nuclear Policy, he helped develop a critique of both West and East that would further the commitment to a "socialist humanism;" indeed, his international symposium on that topic brought together the thinking of more than thirty of the world's leading socialist scholars in a quite influential volume entitled *Socialist Humanism* that appeared in 1965.

Erich Fromm was a "public intellectual" par excellence. He was involved with various progressive organizations like Amnesty International, the Socialist Party of America, and a number of small journals on the left. But it was not as if Fromm suddenly became a "party man." His association for example with the Socialist Party, which he joined in 1960, was tumultuous. His political activity was as an intellectual and when he offered his well known platform for the movement it was harshly criticized. American social democracy, far more than on the continent, was animated by an uncritical economism. And so, when "Let Man Prevail: A Socialist Manifesto and Program," was published during 1960 in *Socialist Call*, its insistence that the movement "aim at a goal which transcends the given reality" was perceived as a slap at the traditional wisdom.

Whether it *actually* was or not is an open question. His comrades like Irving Howe, Lewis Coster, H. Stuart Hughes, Sidney Lens, Norman Mailer, and A. J. Muste on the editorial board of *Dissent*, the leading social democratic journal in the United States, had in 1953 basically reached the conclusion that the socialist movement could not effectively intervene in American political life and that a new educational project to instill critical ideas should be on the agenda.[42] It was not so much that they abandoned trade union economism as that they saw the need to provide a new intellectual justification for it in a particularly reactionary climate. Staunchly anti-communist, essentially conservative on cultural matters and always wary of spontaneous activism from below, *Dissent* was not particularly enamored of Fromm's existential psychological concerns any more than his critique of technology. There were real and bitter differences between him and other editors on Israel and a host of other issues. He was subsequently always on the outside. But, in countless articles and numerous books, Fromm presented a set of forward-looking positions with a clarity and rationality that is enviable. Thus, even while no expert in political science or foreign policy, he stood in the forefront of those committed to nuclear disarmament and willing to distinguish between ideology and reality in the foreign policy of the Soviet Union.

Under conditions wherein the Soviet Union has dissolved, and historical revision has uncritically recast the Cold War in terms favorable to the victor, it is important to consider what Erich Fromm had to say. That is particularly the case with respect to his contention, underpinning his entire position, that the Soviet Union was neither "revolutionary" nor "expansionist," but rather cautious in terms of its foreign policy and concerned with maintaining the status quo.[43] Without in any way excusing the repressive policies pursued by that nation,[44] particularly when it came to the lack of independent trade unions,[45] this implied the need to distinguish between ideology and reality when dealing with the Soviet Union. And it is in this way that the attack on the legacy of Joseph McCarthy becomes most pronounced. The ability to make such a distinction is impeded by "paranoid thinking," "projection," and "fanaticism."[46] Indeed, these characteristics did not merely define a certain perspective on foreign matters in the United States, but also the type of domestic anti-communism undertaken by the far Right.

By now, such terms have entered the mainstream political discourse on international relations. Fromm gave them a relatively precise meaning, however, which is often forgotten. Paranoid thinking, in his view is not simply a form of irrational fear; it is the willingness to substitute an abstractly deduced logical *possibility* for the *probability* that a particular form of action will occur. Developing a realistic and sensible foreign policy is difficult when that occurs. And the difficulty is only increased when the intentions of one party are unconsciously identified with those of its enemy. This kind of projection, no less than the ability to hold two contradictory beliefs at the same time, is justified by fanaticism in the form of some particular idolatry. And Fromm knew that such prejudices can taint technocratic thinking which is presumably value-free. It is subsequently no accident that he should have criticized the notion of "tactical nuclear war" developed by Henry Kissinger, which would thrust the future Secretary of State into the limelight and turn him into an object of satire in Stanley Kubrick's *Dr Strangelove*, as well as the truly insane attempts by Herman Kahn to calculate the effects of thermonuclear war in terms of cost/benefit analysis.

As always, however, Fromm's critique was informed by the vision of a positive alternative directed to a broad progressive public. He believed that foreign policy is a strategic rather than a tactical enterprise which, holding in abeyance whether it should be or not, is highly debatable.[47] Henry Pachter, a socialist political theorist and friend of Fromm's, was probably more on target in suggesting that even the aims of foreign policy are inherently specific to a particular moment in time. And that moment passes. Judging Fromm's views thus becomes difficult under circumstances when the assumptions underpinning the Cold War are no longer valid.

Even when viewing the past from the perspective of the present, however, he was clearly correct in opposing any monolithic view of communism and maintaining that the split between the USSR and China was real.[48] Recognizing that splits did exist in the communist world prevented Fromm from falling for the "domino theory" and, without romanticizing Mao or national liberation movements like those in Vietnam, made it possible for him to take seriously the groundswell of support for them no less than the way in which backing right-wing dictatorships throughout the Third World undermined the credibility of American foreign policy. Fromm, anticipating thinkers like Paul Kennedy, suggested that a "multi-polar" world loomed on the horizon. Still, he knew that a certain threat from the USSR existed. And so, he did not simply embrace the calls by a minority for total unilateral disarmament by the West; his commitment to arms control, however, anticipated the "nuclear freeze" movement of the early eighties while his criticism regarding the economic stake of the given system in a high defense budget obviously retains a certain relevance in the present period.

Fromm probably did not see how the cynical exaggeration of the expansionist threat posed by the USSR served to create an arms race that would economically weaken it; nor did he extend his critique of the United States to the foolish military priorities created by the Soviet establishment. Arguably, in this respect, he was a man of his times. But no less so than those committed to the "totalitarianism" thesis who maintained that no change had occurred from the time of Stalin, that the possibility of internal reform was non–existent, and that the Soviet Union would forever ruthlessly hang on to its empire. Finally, Fromm's belief in the need for a *modus vivendi* between East and West was justified insofar as internal pressues were actually creating conditions for reform in the Soviet Union and Eastern Europe as well.[49]

Fromm's general stance on foreign policy, no less than his interventions on specific issues like Cuba and Vietnam,[50] fit nicely with what would become the basic worldview of the New Left. But more is at stake here than his support of the presidential candidacy of Senator Eugene McCarthy or the apocryphal story that *The Sane Society* was one of the four or five books that inspired Tom Hayden in working on the founding document of Students for a Democratic Society: *The Port Huron Statement*. Fromm was able to emphasize certain fundamental strands which, whatever the crucial differences, tied the political theory of the Old to the New Left.

Interestingly enough, he accomplished this by drawing on the origins of critical theory. And here perhaps it is important to mention that, prior to the publication of *One-Dimensional Man* by Herbert Marcuse in 1964, most intellectuals were totally unaware of the Institute for Social Research.[51] Camus, Hesse, Sartre, were Europeans who exerted a real influence on America in those years. But not the Frankfurt School. The notion that "critical theory" was somehow of importance to the formation of the New Left is actually a myth.[52] *History and Class Consciousness* by Georg Lukács only appeared in 1971, Korsch's *Marxism and Philosophy* was first published in 1970, and a severely edited version of Benjamin's *Illuminations* only in 1969; Horkheimer's collection entitled *Critical Theory* along with *Dialectic of Enlightenment* were published in 1972, *Negative Dialectics* in 1973, while Ernst Bloch *Principle of Hope* appeared in 1986. None of these works became known when the movement was on the rise, or even when the future of Martin Luther

King's "Poor People's Movement" was actually on the agenda, but rather only when the original flame began to flicker.

Long before 1968, however, Fromm was already a figure. *Escape from Freedom*, *The Sane Society*, and *The Art of Loving* were acknowledged bestsellers when *The Revolution of Hope* appeared. All these works were animated by the concept of alienation and a humanism which, whatever its roots in pre-capitalist thought, was fundamentally inspired by the writings of the young Marx. In fact, it is probably fair to say that Erich Fromm's *Marx's Concept of Man* introduced the young Marx to America and provided the dominant interpretation of this thinker for the students of the New Left.

Marx had been a casualty of the Cold War. Identified in America with vulgar materialism and economic determinism, the laws of *Das Kapital* and the dogma of Lenin, Fromm popularized his *Economic and Philosophic Manuscripts of 1844*. He offered a critique of Marx very different from the claims of the mainstream that his thought intrinsically led to totalitarianism. The problems for Fromm were that Marx did not fully acknowledge the moral factor in social relations, that he underestimated the resilience of capitalism, and that he considered the socialization of the means of production a sufficient condition for the transformation of the capitalist into the socialist society.[53] But, ultimately, Fromm gave the humanitarian, idealist, and romantic proponents of the New Left a Marx they could love. His interpretation emphasized Marx's contribution to establishing a philosophical anthropology and a "critique of political economy," which presupposed that people are not driven merely by pursuit of narrowly "rational" or material interests.[54] Indeed, from this perspective, it is precisely the dependence on such interests which the socialist project must confront insofar as it distorts and alienates all social interactions.[55]

Was it the real Marx that came to life? That is framing the question poorly. Revolution and economic contradictions, class struggle and the unaccountability of political institutions, vanished from Fromm's analysis.[56] But no less than in the time of the First International, or the Second or the Third, Marx was interpreted to fit the needs of the time. The roots of Fromm's Marx lay in a liberal tradition whose promises had been betrayed by the USSR even more than by capitalism. This Marx gave primacy to the creative fulfillment of individual potential and the creation of a "free association of producers" predicated on social equality and participatory democracy. Indeed, the Marx of Erich Fromm provided a critical perspective with which to confront the "military-industrial" complex and the affluence bought through a deadening standardization of production and consumption, work and leisure.[57]

Tradition, organization, style, and some basic values separated the

New from the Old Left. Unique about Fromm was that he bridged the gap. Along with most partisans of the New Left, he no longer believed that the working class constituted a revolutionary subject. He also assumed that the business cycle had run its course and that American economic supremacy would remain as it had been since the close of the Second World War. Many social democrats, however, tacitly held similar views. Admittedly many progressives from the Old Left were skeptical about the New Left's critique of consumerism.[58] Then too, they saw that he had no use for the type of mysticism and irrationalism propagated by elements within the New Left or the burgeoning commitment to cultural relativism;[59] Fromm's commitment to the Enlightenment never wavered.[60] He was outspoken in his conviction that democratic regimes like those in the United States demand basic support even should they not live up to their promises.[61]

Nor did Fromm ever abandon his commitment to basic socialist demands. He was completely committed to the need for vigorous independent trade unions and programs which would provide national health insurance and a guaranteed income; above all, he maintained a critique of capitalism as a system of suprapersonal market forces wherein individuals must treat others as potential competitors and so become estranged from themselves and their own possibilities.[62] Where he differed from other social democrats like Daniel Bell, a thinker equally concerned with the effects of inequality and even alienation, was in his skepticism about the priority accorded a technocratic resolution of grievances.[63] This did not make Fromm a Luddite; he recognized the need for large-scale enterprise in certain institutions and businesses as well as organizational planning. Nevertheless, in keeping with the New Left, he feared that a mechanized society with a centralized bureaucratic apparatus might turn its members into automatons despite the multiplicity of interest groups and formal democratic guarantees.[64]

Lacking in the vision of the Old Left was a perception of how the technocratic consumer society debilitated the internal lives of individuals and a program that stood for something beyond piecemeal reform from above. Where he wondered was the "whole human being" of whom Marx and host of visionaries before him had spoken? Where was the concern with a new emancipated relation between man and nature? Socialism, for Fromm, was not reducible to an economic enterprise. It was rather a quintessentially moral project capable of providing a system of orientation and devotion so that every person might deal with what the meaning and aim of his life might prove to be.[65] Indeed, according to him, the validity of socialist thought for the modern age would depend upon its ability to answer the question: what kind of society is fit for unmutilated human beings?

An answer to that question could only emerge through an attack on "alienation." No concept gripped the white student radicals of the 1960s like that one. The score of academic books and articles dealing with the concept pale before the degree to which it became manifest in popular movies like *The Graduate*, which turned Dustin Hoffman into a star, or the music industry and the first great hit by the Rolling Stones: "Satisfaction". In the process, of course, alienation tended to become a pose. Still, the search for personal meaning and the creation of an emancipated social order were an intrinsic part of the movement; Fromm, in fact, was surely correct in claiming that such concerns play a role in every genuine movement.

Of course, in a way, Fromm had already tackled the problem in *Escape from Freedom*. There, in keeping with Max Weber and the Frankfurt School, he noted how technological society had "disenchanted the world" and eradicated both religious faith and the humanistic values bound up with it. Freed from feudal bonds, the individual now stood isolated on the market without roots in the world. Fromm's interpretation of Marx, however, resulted in a broadening and deepening of the concept. Alienation is no longer confined to the objective effects of the division of labor or any particular class.[66] Fromm made the concept live by analyzing how it affected personal life. The issue for him was not merely the mechanized society over which humanity has lost control, but the internal passivity and mental dullness that it fostered.[67] His works spoke to the young people sick of the men in gray flannel suits and fearful that a mechanized society had put them "out of touch" with their own feelings and those of others as well. Public administration, which simply reduced social concerns to calculable issues, thus could not possibly provide an adequate response. A new emphasis on civic participation and social interaction alone seemed capable of confronting the crisis. And, that is precisely what Fromm provided in his notion of "communitarian socialism."

His vision of a decentralized and egalitarian order anticipated and then converged with the type of Jeffersonian populism associated with the New Left.[68] It gave Fromm something in common with Paul Goodman, the great anarchist educator who was nevertheless also a long-standing member of the *Dissent* editorial board until his tragic death, as surely as with the thinking of Martin Buber to whom he is so often compared.[69] Critical of hierarchy, contemptuous of the ideology behind an all-pervasive consumerism, Fromm sought a new spirit to actuate human relations. He was concerned neither with the introduction *ex nihilo* of a "new man," in the manner of Herbert Marcuse or Frantz Fanon, nor with finding some way in which to "escape from authority."

Just as he distinguished authoritarian ethics from humanistic ethics, insofar as the former assumes the inability of the mass to know what is good or bad and so answers the question in terms of what benefits authority itself,[70] so does he differentiate "rational" from "irrational" authority. Such a distinction is deeply lacking in the main proponents of "critical theory." Of course, Fromm's view on rational authority lacked an adequate analysis of the relation between law and ethics. Nor did his theory have an institutional referent or a coherent view of the constraints on freedom produced by the existing logic of accumulation.[71] But this only makes sense given that the most important influence for his social theory derived from the tradition of anarcho-socialism exemplified by figures like Buber, Gustav Landauer, and Augustin Souchy.

None of these anarchists was "revolutionary" in the sense that they believed in imposing their will through violence and the centralization of authority like Lenin, or by insisting on an explosive moment of transformation like Bakunin; indeed, the point was rather to extend socialism "from the center to the periphery" precisely because "the freedom of all can only be achieved when realized in the self-consciousness of each."[72] How that would occur always remained open to question. These communitarians were thus utopian insofar as they stressed the responsibility and goodness of individuals without really discussing how contemporary conditions and values affected the populace, the transformation of society without engaging in the existing political arena, the creation of a new order without reference to the institutions by which its emancipatory character could be maintained, and the introduction of new values without reference to any mass movement.

But indebted as Fromm was to the anarcho-socialists, he shifted the focus. Arguably, he was just as abstract. Unwilling to accept the notion of a radical rupture between present and future,[73] ready to question whether the mere existence of a subjective need is a sufficiently valid reason for its fulfillment, his ill-fated call to project the "Voice of the American Conscience" through public councils was an attempt to build consciousness in the present without constructing an overarching organization.[74] His formulation was assuredly naive. But, for all the sarcasm it spawned, the idea nonetheless fit nicely with a burgeoning populist set of attitudes in America. It was an attempt at reform, but not from above. His suggestion was not viewed as elitist. He was trusted. Recognized as a spokesperson for the importance of community, and the need for every individual to assert himself through it, everyone knew that the learning process Fromm had in mind was directed to the heart as well as the mind. He liked to speak of "being" rather than "having;" a person, according to Fromm, was more than what he accumulated, just as education was more than the minimum knowledge necessary to function properly at work.[75] Then too, in keeping with the original thrust of critical theory, Fromm believed in happiness and always maintained that "every increase in joy a culture can provide will do more for the ethical education of its members than all the warnings of punishment or preachings of virture could do."[76]

All this endeared him to the counter-culture. And, surely, he had a good influence on its proponents. His interest in the Third World was serious rather than fashionable; helping found the Mexican Pyscho-analytic Association in 1962, beyond his activities in opposition to the Vietnam War and numerous organizations, he would become one of the most influential figures in the development of Latin American psycho-analysis.[77] His openness to Eastern philosophy was also carried on with seriousness and dignity; his philosophical emphasis on faith and hope was, in fact, never dogmatic or somehow opposed to rational inquiry any more than his search for the good life was ever reducible to the mystical quest for "the totally other" (Horkheimer). No less than Martin Buber, the Baal She'em Tov, or the great exponents of the Talmudic tradition, he treated religious experience as a type of "wisdom" capable of being employed in the world no less than as a mystical experience by which an individual can transcend his selfishness and separateness;[78] Fromm's "religiosity" was never at the expense of the world and, thus, his concern with exploring the possibilities of subjective experience was never self-indulgent.

The Art of Loving, perhaps his most popular book, also evidences this quality. There is, in this vein, something snide about viewing it merely as some "how to" manual. Lapses into the type of vacuous pseudo-philosophical language that anticipate the worst excesses of the counter-culture admittedly occur.[79] But, in the consumer society of the fifties with its stultifying conformism and basic belief that happiness can simply be bought, his book served an important and legitimate purpose.[80] Not only did it attempt to help individuals confront the emptiness of their lives by bringing out the best in themselves, it also finally overcame the vacillation between subjectivity and solidarity which had plagued the thinking of the Frankfurt School from its inception.[81]

The Art of Loving established an existential relation between autonomy and dependence. Fromm's view of love, after all, is not based on narcissism or social conformity, sentimentality or sexual attraction. Quite the contrary.[82] His concern, no less than that of the early Horkheimer, involved developing an ethical perspective that was not confined by formal rationalism. But, where Horkheimer sought to employ Schopenhauer's concept of "compassion," Fromm emphasized a notion of love that has much in common with the concept developed by

Feuerbach. The love between two people thus ultimately rests on a generalized notion itself predicated on a sense of individual self worth, or what Rousseau called *amour propre*, along with a moral willingness to care for humanity;[83] Fromm liked to quote the great Rabbi Hillel: "If I do not stand up for myself, who will; but if I stand up only for myself, what am I then?"

It only makes sense, from such a perspective, that violence should have been anathema to him; he opposed guerilla tactics not only for their practice, but also on principle.[84] Similarly he sought a "sane society" rather than a utopian one which might solve every basic existential dilemma.[85] The unqualified claim that "Fromm, in short, is a revolutionary and a utopian" is thus misleading.[86] Rejecting any stance that would view the individual as something other than an end unto himself, maintaining the original pacifism of the social democratic movement, and never showing the least contempt for the masses, it is obvious why his humanist philosophy should have dovetailed so nicely with the concerns fostered through the grass-roots organizing of the civil rights and anti-war movements of the 1950s and 1960s. Nor is it any wonder that Fromm should have had so little influence on the abstract utopian thinking of that "revolutionary" minority existing on the political fringes of left-wing politics which, around 1968, was able to steal the limelight precisely because the truly radical potential of the older movement had already begun to wither.[87]

The passing of Fromm's influence can be understood in the same terms. With the fragmentation of the New Left, and the rise of a relativist and non-essentialist postmodernism, his work now appears almost quaint. The old concern with inner development or the emancipatory content of new social relations is no longer what it once was. What John Kenneth Galbraith termed "the affluent society" has changed. America has become poorer following the triumph of conservatism in the 1980s; its cities are rotting, a rollback of the welfare state has taken place, a new militarism has become manifest, and an ideological counter-offensive has taken hold. "Issues" have supplanted the concern with alienation and the like. Too often, however, they appear only as the demands of "special interests;" the moral spirit that enabled activists to believe that they stood with history and justice is conspicuously absent in the new pragmatism. Erich Fromm has a role to play in rekindling such convictions. The critics were wrong; his socialist humanism defies what has become the dominant logic of both the Left and the Right. As for that "logic, [it] is doubtless unshakeable." No less than Kafka, however, Fromm always believed that "it cannot withstand a man who wants to go on living." Such is the hope that keeps the spirit of progressive politics alive.

Notes

1 It is regrettable that the only full-length study of Fromm's work to appear in English for many years abstracted his arguments from their social and philosophical context and, through a deadening textual critique, often trivialized them. It is noteworthy that the influence of neither his religious background in Talmudic studies and critical theory, nor the broader intellectual and political milieu of the Weimar Republic was made clear. Cf. John Schaar, *Escape from Authority: The Perspectives of Erich Fromm* (New York, 1961). Notable improvements were made in the succeeding full-length studies by Don Hausdorff, *Erich Fromm* (New York, 1972); Rainer Funk, *Erich Fromm: The Courage to be Human* (New York, 1982); Helmut Wehr, *Erich Fromm zur Einführung* (Hamburg, 1990); and Daniel Bursten, *The Legacy of Erich Fromm* (Cambridge, Mass., 1991). Note also the forthcoming work by Neil McLaughlin, *Escape from Orthodoxy: The Rise and Fall of Erich Fromm* (City University of New York: Ph.D Dissertation).

2 On his friendship and conflicts within this circle, see Rainer Funk, *Erich Fromm: Selbstzeugnissen und Bilddokumenten* (Hamburg, 1983), pp. 54ff. and *passim* and the excellent discussion of the various controversies by Bursten, *The Legacy of Erich Fromm, passim*.

3 Rolf Wiggershaus, *Die Frankfurter Schule: Geschichte, Theoretische Entwicklung, Politische Bedeutung* (Munich, 1988), p. 14; also, cf. Erich Klein-Landskron, "Max Horkheimer und Erich Fromm" in *Erich Fromm und die Frankfurter Schule* eds Michael Kessler and Rainer Funk (Tübingen, 1992), pp. 161ff.

4 Cf. Erich Fromm, *Beyond the Chains of Illusion. My Encounter with Marx and Freud* (New York, 1963), pp. 5ff. Funk, *Erich Fromm: Bildnisse und Zeugnisse*, pp. 28–45; also Wiggershaus, *Die Frankfurter Schule*, pp. 67ff; Zoltan Tar and Judith Marcus, "Erich Fromm und das Judentum" in *Erich Fromm und die Frankfurter Schule*, pp. 217ff.

5 Rainer Funk, "Der Humanismus in Leben und Werk von Erich Fromm: Laudatio zum 90. Geburtstag" in *Jahrbuch der Internationalen Erich-Fromm Gesellschaft* vol. 3 (1992), pp. 133ff.

6 Cf. Michael Kessler, "Das Versprechen der Schlange: Religion und Religionskritik bei Erich Fromm und die Frankfurtern" in *Erich Fromm und die Frankfurter Schule*, pp. 131ff.

7 Edgar Z. Friedenberg, "Neo-Freudianism and Erich Fromm in *Commentary* (October, 1962), p. 307.

8 See also Fromm's penetrating psychological profile of Hitler in *The Anatomy of Human Destructiveness* (New York, 1973), pp. 411ff.

9 Arguably, in fact, Fromm was among those who developed the tools of social theory necessary to actualize the formulated intentions of members who later became more closely associated with Horkheimer's "inner circle." Axel Honneth, "Kritische Theorie: Vom Zentrum zur Peripherie einer Denktradition" in *Kölner Zeitschrift für Soziologie und Sozialpsychologie* vol. 41, no. 1 (March, 1989), pp. 2ff.

10 Wiggershaus, *Die Frankfurter Schule*, pp. 298ff.

11 Note the excellent introduction by Wolfgang Bonss to Erich Fromm, *Arbeiter und Angestellte am Vorabend des Dritten Reiches. Eine sozialpsychologische Untersuchung* (Stuttgart, 1980).

12 The personal relation of Fromm to Marcuse was different than the one he had with Horkheimer and Adorno. There was never a friendly relationship with Adorno. Horkheimer certainly made a strong impression on Fromm in the 1930s. But Fromm began to feel in Horkheimer the effects of Adorno's attempt to 'rephilosophize' the later 'critical theory' or what was called the Marxist theory of society. Fromm later interpreted this development on the part of Horkheimer as a retreat into the bourgeoisie and bourgeois society which received its most consequent expression in Horkheimer's rediscovery of established religion ('the longing for the totally other') and in his acceptance of honorary citizenship by the city of Frankfurt." Funk, *Erich Fromm: Selbstzeugnisse und Bildokumenten*, p. 98.

13 Wolfgang Bonss, "Analytische Sozialpsychologie: Anmerkungen zu einem theoretischen Konzept und seiner empirischen Praxis" in *Erich Fromm und die Frankfurter Schule*, pp. 23ff.

14 Erich Fromm, "Psychoanalysis and Sociology" along with "Politics and Psychoanalysis" in *Critical Theory and Society: A Reader* eds Stephen Eric Bronner and Douglas Kellner (New York, 1989), pp. 37–9, 213–18.

15 See the letter of September 13, 1941, from Leo Lowenthal to Max Horkheimer where he writes: "Mr. Fromm's book . . . is a work of inexpressible boredom. Despite our requests, we didn't receive a review copy, probably due to the author's own wish. Fromm, incidentally, has now landed where he belongs. The courses he is giving at the secessionist psychoanalytic union have been incorporated in the New School's lecture program. Since you enjoy an outstanding memory, you no doubt recall that a few years ago none of us were capable of besting Mr. Fromm in characterizing that institution negatively." Leo Lowenthal, *Critical Theory and Frankfurt Theorists: Lectures, Correspondence, Conversations* (New Brunswick, 1989), p. 186.

16 American interpretors have often mistakenly argued that Fromm identified the formation of the authoritarian personality with the degree to which capitalist individualism flourished in order then to criticize him for forgetting that fascism was not successful in the United States or Great Britain. Cf. Bruce Mazlish, "American Narcissism" in *The Psychohistory Review* vol. 10, no. 3/4 (Spring-Summer, 1982) pp. 192–3.

17 Every neurosis is an example of dynamic adaptation; it is essentially an adaptation to such external conditions as are in themselves irrational and, generally speaking, unfavorable to the growth of the child." Erich Fromm, *Escape from Freedom* (New York, 1965 edition.), p. 30; also note the 1944 essay by Fromm, "Individual and Social Origins of Neurosis" in *Jahrbuch der Internationalen Erich Fromm Gesellschaft* (Münster, 1993),

vol. 4 pp. 231ff; and the critique of anthropologial instinctivism in Fromm, *The Anatomy of Human Destructiveness*.

18 Note the critique of this revisionism by Theodor W. Adorno "Die revidierte Psychoanalyse" in Bernhard Görlich, Alfred Lorenzer, Alfred Schmidt *Der Stachel Freud: Beitrage und Documente zur Kulturismus-Kritik* (Frankfurt, 1980), pp. 119ff; also, Herbert Marcuse, *Eros and Civilization: A Philosophical Inquiry into Freud* (New York, 1962 edition), pp. 217ff.

19 Moving public opinion to effect institutional decision-making was, whatever the "obstacle" posed by the mass media, always considered a "real possibility." Erich Fromm, *The Revolution of Hope: Toward a Humanized Technology* (New York, 1968), p. 143.

20 Erich Fromm, *The Sane Society* (New York, 1955), pp. 131ff.

21 Erich Fromm, "The Application of Humanist Psychoanalysis to Marx's Theory" in *Socialist Humanism: An International Symposium* (New York, 1966), p. 231.

22 Note the summary of his views in Erich Fromm, *Greatness and Limitations of Freud's Thought* (New York, 1980).

23 A critical psychoanalytic view of this position is offered by Otto Fenichel, "Psychoanalytische Bemerkungen zu Fromms Buch *Die Furcht vor der Freiheit*" in *Der Stachel Freud*, pp. 93ff; also, cf. Bernard Görlich, " 'Trieb' und/oder 'Gesellschaftscharakter'? Anmerkungen zu Fromms Versuch einer 'Neubestimmung der Psychoanalyse' " in *Erich Fromm und die Frankfurter Schule*, pp. 75ff.

24 Erich Fromm, *Man for Himself: An Inquiry into the Psychology of Ethics* (New York, 1947), pp. 21ff.

25 Thus he "emphatically disagrees with [Freud's] interpretation of history as the result of psychological forces that in themselves are not socially conditioned [and] as emphatically with those theories which neglect the role of the human factor as one of the dynamic elements in the social process." Fromm, *Escape from Freedom*, pp. 28–9.

26 Note the excellent discussion by R. B. O'Neill, "Character, Society, and the Politics of Hope: A Comparative Look at the Theories of Wilhelm Reich, Erich Fromm, and Herbert Marcuse" in *The Humboldt Journal of Social Relations* vol. 2, no. 2 (Spring/Summer, 1975), pp. 39ff.

27 Erich Fromm, *Marx's Concept of Man* (New York, 1961), p. 133.

28 At stake is "the dialectic character of the process of growing freedom. Our aim will be to show that the structure of modern society affects man in two ways simultaneously: he becomes more independent, self-reliant, and critical, and he becomes more isolated, alone, and afraid. The understanding of the whole problem of freedom depends on the very ability to see both sides of the process and not to lose track of one side while following the other." Fromm, *Escape from Freedom*, p. 124.

29 Fromm, *The Sane Society*, pp. 40ff.

30 Erich Fromm, *Sigmund Freud's Mission* (New York, 1959), pp. 109–11.

31 Note the intelligent discussion by Honneth, "Kritische Theorie," p. 22; also, Martin Jay, *The Dialectical Imagination: A History of the Frankfurt School and the Institute of Social Research, 1923–1950* (Boston, 1973), pp. 229ff.

32 Erich Fromm, *The Crisis of Psychoanalysis: Essays on Freud, Marx, and Social Psychology* (New York, 1970), pp. 1–30; also, Erich Fromm, *The Revision of Psychoanalysis* (Boulder, 1992), pp. 1ff; on the debate with Marcuse, cf. Daniel Burston, "Auf den Spuren Freuds: Fromm und Marcuse" in *Erich Fromm und die Frankfurter Schule*, pp. 61ff.

33 Fromm, *Escape from Freedom*, p. 159.

34 Note the discussion by Russell Jacoby, *Social Amnesia: A Critique of Conformist Psychology from Adler to Laing* (Boston, 1975), pp. 13–15, 33ff; also, Bernhard Görlich, "Die Kulturismus–Revisionismus–Debatte: Anmerkungen zur Problemgeschichte der Kontroverse um Freud," in *Der Stachel Freud*, pp. 13ff.

35 Cf. Martin Jay, "The Frankfurt School in Exile" in *Perspectives in American History* vol. 6 (1972), p. 351.

36 Fromm, "The Application of Humanist Psychoanalysis to Marx's Theory," p. 233.

37 Fromm, *The Revolution of Hope*, pp. 32–4.

38 Fromm, *The Sane Society*, p. 173.

39 Ibid., pp. 12ff, 40ff, 237ff. and *passim*.

40 Fromm, *Escape from Freedom*, p. 207.

41 Max Horkheimer, *Eclipse of Reason* (New York, 1947), pp. 184.

42 Leland M. Griffin, "The Rhetorical Structure of the New Left Movement" in *The Quarterly Journal of Speech* vol. 1, no. 2 (April, 1964), p. 114.

43 Erich Fromm, *May Man Prevail? An Inquiry into the Facts and Fictions of Foreign Policy* (New York, 1961), pp. 67ff; also note the articles collected in *Ethik und Politik: Antworten auf aktuelle politische Fragen* ed. Rainer Funk (Basle, 1990) pp. 53–86. On the character of Soviet foreign policy, see Henry Pachter, *Weltmacht Russland: Aussenpolitische Strategie in Drei Jahrhunderten* (Oldenburg, 1968). For my own views on the transformation of the Soviet Union from a "revolutionary" state to a partisan of the status quo, see *Socialism Unbound* (New York, 1990), pp. 91ff.

44 His critique of Soviet repression with respect to its eradication of an independent ethical realm no less than its puritanism and authoritarian attempts to insure conformism and production, interestingly enough, rely heavily, on the important study by his principal antagonist in the debate over Freud: Herbert Marcuse, *Soviet Marxism* (New York, 1958)

45 Fromm, *May Man Prevail?*, p. 57.

46 Ibid., pp. 17ff.

47 Fromm, *Ethik und Politik*, pp. 135ff.

48 Fromm, *May Man Prevail?*, pp. 154ff.

49 Note the debate over Fromm's claim that non-intervention was a

necessary Cold War policy even if it meant maintaining the status quo in *New Politics* vol. 1, no. 3 (Spring, 1962) and vol. 1, no. 4 (Fall, 1962).
50 Fromm, *Ethik und Politik*, pp. 94ff; 132ff; 204ff.
51 Even in Europe, "only with the student movement, which was led back to the writings of the Institute for Social Research while engaged in its own search for an orientation, did [critical theory] enter into the public consciousness as a unified theoretical project." Honneth, "Kritische Theorie," p. 1.
52 It did, however, have a marked influence on the intellectuals who comprised what has been called "the generation of '68." Martin Jay, *Marxism and Totality: The Adventures of a Concept from Lukács to Habermas* (Berkeley,1984), p. 19.
53 Fromm, *The Sane Society*, pp. 263ff.
54 "Marx's concern was man, and his aim was man's liberation from the predomination of material interests, from the prison his own arrangements and deeds had built around him." Fromm, "The Application of Humanist Psychoanalysis to Marx's Theory," pp. 228–9; also, cf. Fromm, "Freedom and the Work Situation" in *Jahrbuch* vol. 4, pp. 238ff.
55 "Man's drives, inasmuch as they are transutilitarian, are an expression of a fundamental and specifically human need: the need to be related to man and nature and to confirm himself in this relatedness." Fromm, *The Revolution of Hope*, p. 69.
56 Leszek Kolakowski, *Main Currents of Marxism* trans. P. S. Falla (New York, 1978), vol. 3, pp. 386ff.
57 "The majority of the population in America is well fed, well housed, and well amused, and the sector of 'underdeveloped' Americans who still live under substandard conditions will probably join the majority in the foreseeable future. We continue to profess individualism, freedom, and faith in God, but our professions are wearing thin when compared with the reality of the organization man's obsessional conformity guided by the principle of hedonistic materialism." Erich Fromm, *The Revolution of Hope*, p. 27.
58 In fairness, however, it is important to note that Fromm did not believe "production as such should be restricted; but that once the optimal needs of individual consumption are fulfilled, it should be channeled into more production of the means for social consumption such as schools, libraries, theaters, parks, hospitals, etc." Fromm,"The Application of Humanist Psychoanalysis to Marx's Theory," p. 238.
59 "The growing doubt of human autonomy and reason has created a state of moral confusion where man is left without the guidance of either revelation or reason. The result is the acceptance of a relativistic position which proposes that value judgments and ethical norms are exclusively matters of taste or arbitrary preference and that no objectively valid statement can be made in this realm. But since man cannot live without values and norms, this relativism makes him an easy prey for irrational value systems . . . Irrationalism, whether veiled in psychological,

philosophical, racial, or political terms, is not progress but reaction. The failure of eighteenth- and nineteenth-century rationalism was not due to its belief in reason but to the narrowness of its concepts. Not less but more reason and an unabating search for the truth can correct errors of a one-sided rationalism – not a pseudo-religious obscurantism." Fromm, *Man for Himself*, pp. 4–5, ix.

60   "The contemporary human crisis has led to a retreat from the hopes and ideas of the Enlightenment under the auspices of which our political and economic progress had begun . . . The ideas of the Enlightenment taught man that he could trust his own reason as a guide to establishing valid ethical norms and that he could rely on himself, needing neither revelation nor the authority of the church in order to know good and evil." Ibid., p. 5.

61   Fromm, *The Revolution of Hope*, p. 143.

62   Fromm, *Escape from Freedom*, p. 80.

63   "Planning itself is one of the most progressive steps the human race has taken. But it can be a curse if it is 'blind' planning, in which man abdicates his own decision, value judgment, and responsibility. If it is alive, responsive, 'open,' planning, in which the human ends are in full awareness and guiding the planning process, it will be a blessing." Fromm, *The Revolution of Hope*, p. 55.

64   Ibid., pp. 32–5.

65   Erich Fromm, *To Have or To Be?* (1976), pp. 155–60.

66   "The managerial elite are also different from those of old in another respect: they are just as much appendages of the machine as those whom they command. They are just as alienated or perhaps more so, just as anxious, or perhaps more so, as the worker in one of their factories. They are bored, like everyone else, and use the same antidotes against boredom." Fromm, *The Revolution of Hope*, p. 32.

67   Cf. Fromm, *The Forgotten Language* (New York, 1951), pp. 7ff.

68   Fromm, *The Sane Society*, pp. 183ff.

69   Note in particular Buber's *Paths in Utopia* trans. R. F. C. Hull (Boston, 1958).

70   Fromm, *Man for Himself*, pp. 9–10.

71   Schaar is correct in noting that Fromm's use of alienation lacks the "precision" of Marx's original formulation. Unfortunately, however, he doesn't carry through this insight and focuses his criticism on an exaggerated rendering of Fromm's *Lebensphilosophie* rather than any problems caused by the lack of emphasis on class, institutions, and production. Schaar, *Escape from Authority*, pp. 193ff.

72   Augustin, Souchy, *'Vorsicht: Anarchist!' Ein Leben für die Freiheit: Politische Erinnerungen* (Darmstadt, 1977), p. 11.

73   "For if one is not concerned with steps between the present and the future, one does not deal with politics, radical or otherwise." Fromm, *The Revolution of Hope*, pp. 8–9.

74   Ibid., pp. 154–6.
75   Fromm, *To Have or To Be?*, pp. 40–1.
76   Fromm, *Man for Himself*, p. 230.
77   Cf. Jorge Silva Garcia, "Erich Fromm in Mexiko: 1950–1973" in *Jahrbuch der Internationalen Erich-Fromm Gesellschaft* vol. 3, pp. 11ff; Alfonso Millan, "Die Entwicklung der Mexikanischen Psychoanalytischen Gesellschaft und des Mexikanischen Instituts für Psychoanalyse" in *Jahrbuch der Internationalen Erich-Fromm Gesellschaft* vol. 3, pp. 27ff; also, Funk, *Erich Fromm*, pp. 116ff.
78   Even the attempt to view this as a "negative theology" places an unwarranted philosophic and systematic character on this perspective; cf. Rudolf J. Siebert, "Fromm's Theory of Religion" *Telos* 34 (Winter, 1977–8), pp. 111ff. Fromm's view of God, his emphasis on spirituality without idols, is beautifully articulated by Ramon Xirau, "Erich Fromm: What is Man's Struggle" in eds Bernard Landis and Edward S. Tauber, *In the Name of Life: Essays in Honor of Erich Fromm* (New York, 1971), pp. 150ff.
79   "Even whether there is harmony or conflict, joy or sadness, is secondary to the fundamental fact that two people experience themselves from the essence of their existence, that they are one with each other by being one with themselves, rather than by fleeing from themselves. There is only one proof for the presence of love: the depth of the relationship, and the aliveness and strength in each person concerned; this is the fruit by which love is recognized." Erich Fromm, *The Art of Loving* (New York, 1956), p. 103.
80   "Success, prestige, money, power – almost all our energy is used for the learning of how to achieve these aims, and almost none to learn the art of loving . . . Could it be that only those things are considered worthy of being learned with which one can earn money or prestige and that love, which 'only' profits the soul, but is profitless in the modern sense, is a luxury we have no right to spend much energy on?" Ibid., p. 6.
81   Jay, "The Frankfurt School in Exile," pp. 343ff.
82   "I want the loved person to grow and unfold for his own sake, and in his own ways, and not for the purpose of serving me. If I love the other person, I feel one with him or her, but with him as he is, not as I need him to be as an object for my use." Fromm, *The Art of Loving*, p. 28.
83   "The point I want to make is to uphold the principle that a person has an inalienable right to live – a right to which no conditions are attached and which implies the right to receive the basic commodities necessary for life, the right to an education and to medical care; he has a right to be treated at least as well as the owner of a dog or a cat treats his pet, which does not have to 'prove' anything in order to be fed." Fromm, *The Revolution of Hope*, p. 125.
84   Ibid., p. 142.
85   "The assumption that the problems, conflicts, and tragedies between

man and man will disappear if there are no materially unfulfilled needs is a childish daydream." Ibid., p. 107.
86 Schaar, *Escape from Authority*, p. 22.
87 Note my discussion in "Reconstructing the Experiment: Politics, Ideology, and the New Left in America" in *Moments of Decision: Political History and the Crises of Radicalism* (New York, 1992).

11

Remembering Marcuse*

Herbert Marcuse was 81 when he died in July of 1979. I never met him.
But I heard him lecture often enough, and I was among those who were
profoundly affected by his thought. Even now, roughly two decades
after the events of 1968, it is difficult to describe his influence. His
background was so different from what was familiar to American
radicals. Even his critics recognized the erudition of this man, so steeped
in classical European culture, who seemed to possess the key to the
dialectic. The most tumultuous events of the century seemed etched on
his face: World War I, the Russian Revolution, the German Revolution
of 1918, Weimar, Nazism, Stalinism, World War II. Marcuse had
participated in the Berlin Workers Council of 1919, he had studied with
Martin Heidegger, and became part of the "inner circle" in what we only
vaguely knew as "the Frankfurt School." He was a product of what
Stefan Zweig termed "the world of yesterday."

Marcuse, in contrast to what the popular media maintained, was never
a "guru" of the New Left. His thought was too radical for a movement
whose worldview depended upon a vague conglomeration of welfare
liberalism, populism, romanticism, and anarchism. Few of us knew
anything about philosophical idealism or Marxism let alone phenomenology and the modernist avant-garde. Most of us, even in spirit, were far
closer to Paul Goodman. Nevertheless, Marcuse struck a chord in a way
no one else ever did.

He offered an intellectual challenge. He called upon people to think
beyond what they had been taught. He gave "alienation" a palpable
meaning and made young people confront the "system" in which they
were reaching maturity. Above all, perhaps, he gave us an image. *One-
Dimensional Man*: he was the central character in a hundred rock songs
and a thousand poems which articulated the cultural strain of the

* Text of a speech given at the CUNY Graduate Center in 1989.

movement. Marcuse's most famous work seemed to expose the mechan-isms of integration and constraint that cloaked the objective contradic-tions operating within advanced industrial society. No matter that others had already shown how the revolutionary consciousness of the working class had been defused, or demonstrated the pervasive power of the "culture industry." It was Marcuse who, whatever the difficulty of his prose, gave the young an image they could grasp.

The rebellion sought to counter this one-dimensional being with what Marcuse, following André Breton, termed "the great refusal." Revolu-tion would now seek to transform the everyday life of the "establish-ment." Our generation on the left was composed of people who hated the stultifying sexual relations, the vapid music, and the style of success extolled during the 1950s. Marcuse seemed to expand our horizon in an age championing "the end of ideology." Marcuse taught us otherwise by employing *Ideologiekritik* to attack the "operationalist" mentality and suggest that political repression existed within the supposedly value-free rationality of scientific discourse.

He fostered the belief that current modes of production were historic-ally mutable. He demanded that we envision a "new technology" and a "new science;" indeed, no matter how naive this may have been, his thinking provided us with a new respect for nature and helped generate what would become a new environmental consciousness. But, even more than that, his thinking inflamed our hopes. *Eros and Civilization* taught us about utopia and, whatever the problems with this work, he almost single-handedly gave a new dignity to a complex concept alien to American pragmatism.

Marcuse made us consider what Stendhal called *"la promesse de bonheur."* He turned aesthetics into an issue for social theory. And again, whatever the problems with his theory, that was an intellectual achieve-ment. It spawned discussion and gave a new cultural connotation to the notion of revolution. It was rarified. Perhaps too much so. His thinking had no place for sexual promiscuity, drugs, or the extension of pornography. In fact, it is almost laughable to re-read the charges of Marcuse's numerous mainstream critics who claimed that, like Socrates, he was undermining the morals of the young.

Nothing could have been further from the truth. Marcuse, no less than Adorno or Brecht, was a moralist *par excellence*. He envisioned a new way of individuals treating one another, loving one another. He envisioned new emancipated forms of social and personal interaction; indeed, he would accept nothing less. His heroes were not Herman Hesse, Carlos Castaneda, or others who were fashionable at the time; they were Schiller, Hegel, Marx, and Freud. Marcuse was as disgusted with the anti-intellectual, mystical, and irrationalist strands of the movement as any of the New Left's more conservative critics.

But, in making his criticism, there was one difference everyone except the worst dogmatists recognized: Marcuse always spoke as a friend. Whatever the parallels that existed between Marcuse's ideas and those of his former comrades at the Institute for Social Research, his criticisms were always seen as those of a partisan. They were understood as coming from a revolutionary of the past to a movement half-conscious of its goals, groping with new organizational possibilities in the midst of bitter sectarian squabbles.

His thinking gave a new place of importance to the seemingly unintegrated "marginal groups" of advanced industrial society: bohemians, students, minorities, and women. He provided an impetus for a host of thinkers who would concern themselves with the "new social movements." But if the students served as catalysts for the French working class, which is what was suggested in *An Essay on Liberation*, Marcuse none-the-less overestimated their revolutionary character. He simply did not anticipate that they would give rise to interest groups seeking to extend the unfulfilled ideals of the bourgeois state to their own constituencies. Institutional analysis was never Marcuse's strong suit. Indeed, if he exposed how hegemony is practiced under the guise of free speech in "Repressive Tolerance," his conclusion concerning the need to repress the proponents of repression was vague and bureaucratically ill-conceived.

Marcuse had a certain neo-Leninist streak. Still, the partisans of orthodoxy despised him. His *Soviet Marxism* was a devastating critique from the left of the petrification which the "fatherland of the revolution" had undergone. He showed how the revolution had turned against itself and the terrible effects of authoritarian control on the life and culture of the soviet citizenry. Marcuse earned the unmitigated hatred of the Old Left long before the rise of the student movement. Few philosophers, in fact, received such abuse. Marcuse even went into hiding for time after threats were made against his life. It was disgusting by any standard. Marcuse was called an "intellectual termite," a "cretin," and worse.

Most of his critics, of course, probably never read his remarkable essays from the 1930s or knew that his *Reason and Revolution: Hegel and the Rise of Social Theory* had become one of the seminal interpretations on the great idealist philosopher. It is still easy to forget how Marcuse held up a mirror to advanced industrial society, challenged its notion of progress, brought the quest for happiness back into the political vocabulary. His work is an enduring commitment to the most radical and concrete impulses of critical theory. A pacified existence defined his utopia, but his dialectic never came to a halt. That is why, wherever the revolt against oppression surfaces, someone will remember the legacy of Herbert Marcuse.

12

The Anthropological Break: Herbert Marcuse and the Radical Imagination

Resistance has many sources. It can result from the friction created by economic contradictions; it can emerge in response to the arbitrary exercise of political power. Ideas can inspire it; the aesthetic imagination can inflame it. Its sources might even lie deeper within the psychological infrastructure of the individual or the species. Herbert Marcuse made a stubborn commitment to resist the alienation and repression of advanced industrial society even as he feared that affluence and the integrative power of advanced industrial society was rendering it irrelevant. Here, in this contradiction, lies the foundation for his undertaking. It is the reason for his abiding concern with rendering critical theory capable of building solidarity and informing radical practice.[1] It is what generates a break with the logic of progress and the most radical utopian vision ever generated by the dialectical tradition.

Progress for Hegel and his followers always implied an ability to shape the world in terms of its unrealized potentiality for freedom.[2] It inherently retained a moral connotation. According to Marcuse the ethical element was ever more surely in danger of being eradicated by an advanced industrial society seeking to render progress commensurate with the commodity form and the alienating logic of instrumental rationality.[3] But it was not merely advanced industrial society, which threatened subjectivity and reflection or the possibilities for the "good life." Horkheimer and Adorno's *Dialectic of Enlightenment* had already suggested an anthropological basis for reification. Their analysis, however, produced the practical pessimism and flight from political engagement so obvious in their later work.

Marcuse proceeded differently; it only makes sense then that his politics should have taken a different turn. He sought to counter the anthropological basis of alienation and the repressive character of progress in a positive fashion.[4] He never surrendered the totality to some notion of the constellation, or the speculative vision to the theological comprehension of the "totally Other." He rather attempted to fuse the speculative, the aesthetic, and the political moments of the critical enterprise. How well he succeeded is open to question. Nevertheless, in the process, he made good on the most radical implications of critical theory from its origins in the 1930s and provided it with a new relevance.

Nowhere else in the postwar works of the Frankfurt School is either the aesthetic question discussed in such directly social terms or the need for a break with "the dialectic of necessity" (Adorno) argued from a perspective outside that of the individual subject. Theory, according to Marcuse, was to again inform practice. He knew, of course, that the proletariat was no longer the "revolutionary subject" of history and that the old motivations for political action did not suffice for the new era. He believed, in fact, that advanced industrial society was increasingly projecting a "closure of the political universe."[5] Nevertheless, for that very reason, Marcuse called upon the dialectical method to "risk defining freedom in such a way that people become conscious of and recognize it as something that is nowhere already in existence."[6]

An anthropological break becomes the goal of a speculative theory which seemed to have reached a crossroads. In fact, with progress having expelled freedom from social reality, it appeared that only two ways remained of preserving the quest for liberation. Theology, which never held quite the same allure for Marcuse as for Horkheimer,[7] was one possibility. Aesthetics, which intrigued Marcuse from the beginning of his career, was the other.[8] He was not content, however, to emphasize the artwork in the manner of Adorno. Nor did he wish to treat liberation as a moment of experience withdrawn from an advanced industrial society intent on turning art into

> part of the technical equipment of the household and of the daily work world. In this process, [artistic works] undergo a decisive transformation; they are losing the qualitative difference, namely the essential dissociation from the established reality principle which was the ground of their liberating function. Now the images and ideas, by virtue of which art, literature, and philosophy once indicted and transcended the given reality are integrated into the society, and the power of the reality principle is greatly extended.[9]

The reality principle becomes the barrier to an anthropological break. It underpins the existing technological notion of progress no less than the ability of the culture industry to nullify all emancipatory alternatives. The culture industry performs this task in a particular way. Its concern is not merely with portraying social conditions and individual life posit- ively in the manner of traditional propaganda and so strengthening the "happy consciousness." The culture industry is more insidious. Conservative fashion may prevail at one time and radical fashion at another; the sole concern of the culture industry is to turn every cultural object into a commodity for sale. Relativism is its philosophy and the creation of a fad or a scandal just another way to maximize profits. The culture industry is a business and, in keeping with the prerequisites of the accumulation process, matters of quality become secondary. Such developments undermine the power of reflection and the commitment to emancipatory concerns. Negative thinking, the only viable source of creativity in Marcuse's view, is thus constantly threatened with elimina- tion as even the most radical and bohemian works are condemned by the culture industry to

> suffer the fate of being absorbed by what they refute. As modern classics, the avant-garde and the beatniks share the function of entertaining without endangering the conscience of the men of good will. This absorption is justified by technical progress; the refusal is refuted by the alleviation of misery in the advanced industrial society. The liquidation of high culture [thus becomes] a by-product of the conquest of scarcity.[10]

Progress renders the aim of artworks irrelevant. The experience of them – following the logic of Walter Benjamin – becomes increasingly prefabricated; indeed, the endless production of one fad after another robs art of its ability to highlight the memory of past suffering.[11] The autonomy of the artwork has thus been rendered illusory. Necessity, however, can be turned into a virtue. Insofar as art still projects the illusion of freedom, it confronts the reality of unfreedom; insofar as it embodies the wish for beauty, it confronts the reality of ugliness and repression. Nor does this illusion derive from the "content" or materia with which art concerns itself; the beautiful illusion (*schöner Schein*) appears rather in the shaping of that content; it appears in the "form" of art which, in turn, affirms the resistance of the subject against becoming integrated by objective reality.

A break with the logic of progress can then only take place through a renewed commitment to aesthetic form. This form, according to Marcuse, projects both the potentialities for a genuine experience of subjectivity and what Stendhal called a utopian *"promesse de bonheur."* It retains the normative component of progress increasingly subverted through its appropriation by advanced industrial society and subsequently manifests the "truth of the human condition [which] is hidden, repressed – not by a conspiracy of some sort, but by the actual course of history."[12] Echoing Schiller, in contrast to Adorno, Marcuse thus could write that "the realm of freedom lies beyond mimesis."[13]

Utopia, from the perspective of an anthropological break with the reality principle, thus becomes a legitimate object of inquiry. The repressed wish for its realization lies at the anthropological core of art. Its projection in aesthetic form assures the transcendence of art and affirms the fact that a "rational transgression [of the existent becomes] an essential quality of even the most affirmative art."[14] An ongoing commitment to formal experimentation becomes the logical consequence of Marcuse's position and, in keeping with Adorno and Bloch, ties him to the tradition of the modernist avant-garde. Experimental use of aesthetic form, keeps "words, sounds, shapes, and colors insulated against their familiar ordinary use and functions: thus they [are] freed for a new dimension of existence."[15] Even in the case of representational works, however, the same dynamic is involved. With Flaubert or Balzac, for example, the possibility of any resolution between existential demands and a repressive external reality "can only be illusory. And the possibility of a solution rests precisely on the character of artistic beauty as illusion."[16]

Utopia resides in that illusion. Beauty, or the manner in which this illusion is formed, inherently becomes "the negation" of the commodity world along with the values and attitudes required by it. That negation, insofar as it involves an anthropological break with what exists, is necessarily "indeterminate." Still, for Marcuse, the "beautiful illusion" (*schöner Schein*) is precisely what helps "render incorrect even one's own assertion that one is happy."[17] Existing outside reality, aesthetic *experience* retains a "truth content" beyond philosophical demands of falsifiability or verification. It is a truth, in keeping with Adorno, which unifies what are usually seen as the mutually exclusive demands of sensuality and reason. Such is the real character of a freedom now comprehensible only in the realm of the imagination.[18] Art is thus the most radical way of presenting "a negation of the principle that governs civilization . . . [Art] is attained and sustained fulfillment, the transparent unity of subject and object; of the universal and the individual."[19]

But the encounter with art is grounded neither in a knowledge of technique nor in subjective experience. Solidarity and the wish for a "pacification of existence" are built into the aesthetic which, in turn, suggests the existence of a "second nature" (Lukács) beneath the conflict and exploitation on which civilization has been constructed. Justifying it, however, is impossible in empirical terms or even from the historical perspective of Hegel or Marx; their teleological belief in progress subverts the legitimacy of their claims. Utopia now stands in need of a different justification; Marcuse believed this could occur only in the form of a "negative anthropology." It was for this very reason, following the concern generated by Adorno and opposed by Erich Fromm during the late 1930s,[20] that Marcuse entered into a critical encounter with the metapsychology of Freud.

Civilization, according to Freud, is "first of all progress in work – that is work for the procurement and augmentation of life."[21] Work, however, is predicated on a denial of "Eros" and the life instinct's desire for immediate gratification. Or, putting the matter another way, the "pleasure principle" is constrained when humanity first confronts economic scarcity and the "reality principle" which, in capitalist society, soon becomes consonant with the "performance principle" so that "under its rule society is stratified according to the competitive economic performance of its members."[22]

Socialization will subsequently emphasize competition as progress becomes identified with instrumental rationality and the domination of nature. Emancipatory alternatives concerning the "pacification of nature" will thus fall by the wayside, fantasy will ever more surely become circumscribed within the aesthetic dreams of the individual subject, and a blunting of speculative reason will take place. Additional limits on gratification, well beyond the minimum level of repression indispensable for human interaction, will also take institutional form in the patriarchal-monogamic family, the church, the hierarchical division of labor, the bureaucratic state, and a mass media inherently desirous of subverting a genuinely private sphere of life.[23] Institutions such as these will become the instruments through which "surplus repression" is extracted and maintained for the benefit of the given order.[24]

Derived from Marx's notion of "surplus value," "surplus repression" seemingly has its objective basis in the "false needs" that are endemic to the production process of advanced industrial society. "Planned obsolescence" provides an example of how specific commodities are created so that they will not last and enforce the need for work to buy new ones. But this is just a quantitative instance of what is at stake. The point, for Marcuse, is that the system is structured by the creation and satisfaction of "false needs" even as new ones are produced. Bereft of alternatives, lacking in reflexivity, individuals caught within what Heidegger might have termed the "whirl" of such an existence will find the repressive values of the production process "reproduced" in their own consciousness.[25] Surplus repression, whatever its objective character when understood from the perspective of institutions, is thus also qualitative insofar as its effects are introjected into the subjective, psychological "infrastructure" of society's members. Thus, the transformation of objective conditions becomes all the more difficult as social controls enforce guilt when a transgression of the existing order is attempted.

Metapsychology provides an understanding of this condition and situates the experience of guilt under capitalism within an anthropological framework.[26] Marcuse, engaging in a critical interpretation of Freud, starts with the claim that human history does not begin with the revolt of the sons and brothers against the primal father. It begins instead with the original ascension of the father who, in monopolizing the mother(s), limits enjoyment to himself alone as he imposes labor on the sons. Exploitation and domination result from the unequal distribution of work and satisfaction which ultimately drive the sons to revolt.[27] That revolt, however, results in guilt. And so, following their victory, the sons imitate the father and develop their own forms of punishment to relieve their guilt. Institutions such as religion fulfill that function. In the process, however, they also perpetuate guilt insofar as they manifest an organizational and material interest in the continuation of repression even under conditions in which it is no longer necessary.

Coming to terms with this anthropological situation is rendered more difficult insofar as the past is shrouded in mist. Too terrible to recall, its effects remain since "the essence of repression lies simply in the function of rejecting and keeping something out of consciousness."[28] Humanity thus loses control of its history since such repression fosters unconscious and undirected activity. This activity will result less in a demand for emancipatory transformation than destruction, the intensification of guilt, and a desire for punishment. Thus, in keeping with the prewar concerns of Horkheimer and Adorno, Marcuse offers an articulated metapsychological grounding for what they considered a dialectic defined by necessity and repression rather than freedom.

Non-directed libidinal activity of the sort normally identified with progress stands in sharp contrast to the "sublimated" practice engendered by art. Sublimation is, after all, based on a previously desexualized libido which is directed towards a specific object. In contrast to the acts which are spurred by repression, sublimation is thus necessarily creative since it will always "retain the main purpose of Eros – that of uniting and binding insofar as it helps towards establishing the unity or tendency to unity which is particularly characteristic of the ego."[29] The emphasis on creation, however, is not juxtaposed to happiness. Quite the contrary. Indeed, just as surely as he breaks with the teleological notion of progress forwarded by German idealism, Marcuse contests its emphasis on duty by introducing happiness as the goal of politics.[30]

Marcuse does not believe that the crucial psychological problem of advanced industrial society involves the primacy of the ego. Quite the contrary. His claim, in fact, is that advanced industrial society weakens the ego and that it does so through the "culture industry" and attendant institutions.[31] With its pursuit of profit and the widest possible audience, its commitment to commercial simplification and the lowest common denominator, its unending concern with the new and the fad, a conformism is instituted which deforms the ego among the broad masses. The strength of the culture industry enables it to supplant the "father" as the super-ego against which the ego of the child tests and strengthens itself. Pliant, unconcerned with quality or purpose, equally tolerant of all positions, the child becomes incapable of contesting the existing "reality principle." Myths give way to concrete achievements while stars and sports figures achieve the status of heroes with whom the consumers of mass industrial society compare themselves.[32] Ceaseless competition, anxiety, and an increasingly weakened ego subsequently drive historical progress and become the pillars of advanced industrial society.

The performance principle, with which the reality principle is now identified, is also strengthened insofar as all creative attempts to vent libidinal energy result in its absorption once the object is made popular by the culture industry. In keeping with Adorno's critique of jazz,[33] for example, it becomes possible to suggest that, whatever its nonconformist intention, the repetition of the basic rhythm and the noise level of rock music serve "to break down the ego to permit the diffuse release of sexual and aggressive energy, thus substituting annihilation and explosion – escape from the self – for discovery and integration."[34]

Opposition in this way becomes integrated. The aesthetic "truth" of the object is turned against itself as sublimated activity is channeled into socially acceptable and ultimately repressive forms. This is what Marcuse calls "repressive desublimation,"[35] which is another way of speaking about the manipulation of the ego through a perversion of the aesthetic.[36] His position, however, has nothing in common with the deconstructionist assault on representation and aesthetic "truth;" indeed, he notes the vacuity of a stance in which "the oeuvre drops out of the dimension of alienation, of *formed* negation and contradiction, and turns into a sound game, a language game – harmless without commitment [while employing a] shock which no longer shocks."[37] Still, he was mistaken in suggesting that "the passing of anti-art [will result in] the re-emergence of form. And with it, we find a new expression of the inherently subversive qualities of the aesthetic dimension, especially beauty as the sensuous appearance of the idea of freedom."[38]

Marcuse follows Kant in suggesting that the aesthetic form subordinates "reality to another order, subjects it to the 'laws of beauty.'"[39] But, in defining that form, he will also radically reinterpret Kant's *Critique of Judgment* by making the claim that:

[The] aesthetic form in art has the aesthetic form in nature (*das Naturschöne*) as its correlate, or rather desideratum. If the idea of beauty pertains to nature as well as to art, this is not merely an analogy, or a human idea imposed on nature – it is the insight that the aesthetic form, as a token of freedom is a mode of existence of the human as well as the natural universe [and so retains] an objective quality.[40]

The transformation of a purely subjective experience into a utopian reordering of existence, according to Marcuse, is predicated on an anthropologically repressed form of solidarity. This, in fact, is what provides emancipation with its inherently social character. He will, in this vein, appropriate the insights developed by Schiller in his *Letters on the Aesthetic Education of Man*.[41] Fueled by fantasy, according to Schiller, the aesthetic form is estranged from an inherently repressive reality. But it also embodies humanity's "inner truth."[42] The "play impulse" within fantasy mediates between an ethereal passive "sensuous impulse" and a "form impulse," which seeks to exert mastery over nature. What Kant originally considered the "purposeful purposelessness" of the artwork now projects a new emancipated order committed to actualizing "all aesthetic qualities of phenomena and – in a word – what we call *Beauty* in the widest sense of the term."[43] Aesthetic experience, beyond the "performance principle," thus calls for its transfiguration into a "living shape."

A transformation of life, from this utopian perspective, becomes the objective aim of the artwork. Segregating art from the real, contesting instrumental notions of work and progress, results not merely in the preservation of subjectivity. It also involves the projection of what Schiller originally saw as the essential quality of play: "lightness" (*Leichtheit*). "Blackness," in the sense of Adorno, no longer serves as the "ideal." Every genuine artwork, according to Marcuse, provides the audience with the hint of a repressed happiness "common to art and reality." And, if it is true that abundance no less than an equal distribution of wealth would underpin such a world, it is also true that in the reproduction of that world

> Techniques would then tend to become art, and art would tend to form reality: the opposition between imagination and reason, higher and lower faculties, poetic and scientific thought, would be invalidated. Emergence of a new Reality Principle: under which a new sensibility and a desublimated scientific intelligence would combine in the creation of an aesthetic ethos.[44]

Progress takes on a new face; its character is described in a new way. A world defined by the aesthetic form and the "play principle" is seen as engendering a new science with a new logos. Technology will no longer produce products for the sake of producing them and humanity will finally become the true master of the machine. The operationalist rationality under which contemporary society functions, along with the division between technology and art, will disappear with the creation of a new "sensibility." An anthropological break would take place. Such a sensibility, biologically averse to cruelty and domination, would inform a new rationality in which art's "ability to project existence, to define yet unrealized possibilities would be envisaged as validated by and functioning in the scientific transformation of the world."[45] Indeed, within such a world, humanity would then finally recognize nature as a subject in its own right and initiate new modes of interaction to foster the "pacification of existence."

Aesthetic purpose would invade the logos and harmonize reason with sensuality. History would assume a new meaning and, in this utopian future, realizing the unrealized emancipatory possibilities from the past would become the aim of activity in the present. Marcuse's vision reaches into the darkest recesses of human experience and seeks the transformation of time. No longer conceived in unilinear terms, but rather as an internal circular process, an emancipatory "eternal recurrence" (Nietzsche) would truly enable humanity to recapture its repressed past. The utopia of Marcuse thus confronts death itself by seeking to abolish the angst, which is ontologically anchored in an "existence" whose being is by definition a "being unto death" (Heidegger).[46] Only by transvaluing the fear of death, according to Marcuse, will reality genuinely manifest the "attained and sustained fulfillment" of the aesthetic form. Thus, the experience of reality itself would change by breaking the "tyranny of becoming over being."[47]

The break with progress presupposes the break with time. Marcuse's utopia thus speaks to the existential transformation of reality and rejects Marx's view of the human being as *homo faber*. Perhaps the need for a "limited" mastery over nature will remain. But, ultimately, a merging of labor and "play" will take place to the point where "in this utopian hypothesis, labor would be so different from labor as we know it or normally conceive of it that the idea of the convergence of labor and play" would become a possibility.[48] This would result in a "new science" and a "new technology." But it is unclear whether Marcuse was actually calling for the type of apocalyptic transformation capable of bringing about this anthropological change. Part of the problem is that he never delineated what a new science or technology might look like. Other problems arise form various statements suggesting that, interested in the liberating possibilities of automation, his break with scientific rationality was actually predicated on maintaining the existing technological infrastructure.[49] In any event, however, his most radical arguments tended to conflate the critique of "science" with the uses to which it is put.

This way of framing the matter initiated a major debate over whether work itself has ontological constituents, which militate against its utopian transformation into play.[50] In the same vein, even if his analysis of surplus repression lacked any objective referent, it engendered a controversy over the character of progress and happiness no less than the aims of psychology.[51] Opposing the reduction of social repression to questions of private psychology, seeking to anchor social transformation in the transformation of the instincts,[52] Marcuse brought to public awareness the fact that the human character is not fixed and that a transformation of the relation between nature and humanity is fundamental to the formation of an emancipated order.

Divorcing Freud's metapsychology from any practical or clinical referent, admittedly, results in serious problems. There is no way to differentiate between suppression and psychological repression, for example, so that it becomes impossible to deal with the consideration that certain elements of the unconscious and a historically conditioned human experience may deserve to be suppressed. Then too, in seeking the harmonious reconciliation between "subject" and "object," the individual with his world, Marcuse ignores what Geza Roheim – just as surely building upon Freud – called the "dual unity situation."[53]

As society becomes the mother who will equally distribute her bounties to a universe of brothers freed from the repression and guilt of their relation to the father, any truly private realm obviously becomes a threat to that very communality which has been achieved. Even the desire to create an individual personality would then reimpose that guilt originally stemming from the primordial attempt to overthrow the father. The consequence of pacifying existence might therefore lead less to making the tension between subject and object "non-aggressive" and "non-destructive" than to lowering ego boundaries, which both Freud and Roheim view as "a characteristic feature of schizophrenia."[54] The ultimate result might even produce that state of "psychological misery" (Freud) in which the identification between members of a society is so close that there can be no ego reward for any activity at all.[55]

All this is necessary, however, in order to recapture the repressed erotic character of existence and a host of unactualized utopian possibilities. Humanity would then become "playful" and "beautiful." It would no longer be ashamed of sensuousness or continue to punish itself for the atrocities committed in the past. The guilt of the primal crime would be expiated through the newly found and liberating potential of memory. In this utopia, people would be "biologically" incapable of committing violence.[56] Evil would be banished and Thanatos, the death instinct, would be conquered. Sexuality would turn into sensuality as the erogenous zones began to spread over the whole body, abolishing genital sexuality in favor of a new "polymorphous perversity."[57] Thus, quoting Baudelaire, Marcuse envisioned a truly new world where *"tout n'est qu'ordre et beauté: Luxe, calme, et volupté."*

A newly freed Eros would manifest itself politically in a desire to destroy repressive institutions and make people conscious of their "irrationality." But the transcendent moment of art inherently becomes a self-criticism of the revolution and its historical limitations. The political issue revolves around freeing the erotic content of art so that it can guide new revolutionaries, imbued with a "new sensibility,"[58] in combating surplus repression. Marcuse never clarified the organizational forms through which this might occur any more than the manner in which "false" needs could be distinguished from "true" ones. Caught within the utopian paradox, which essentially maintains that a revolution of this sort will already require the existence of a "new man" in the old society, it becomes impossible to develop a theory or practice for the revolutionary transition.

There can be no transition. The anthropological rupture with progress must prove complete. But, for that very reason, it subverts the political character of the radical enterprise. Revolution is expelled into the realm of art, which inherently resists its concrete manifestation. There is no connection of the radical theory with institutions or an articulated set of interpretive categories capable of making it concrete. Revolution becomes abstract, and resistance too. What makes a need "false" is never defined. Thus, no differently than with Adorno, an arbitrary quality constantly sneaks into Marcuse's analysis of particular works.

Nor can it be otherwise. Content to delineate the utopian truth of the "aesthetic dimension," rather than formulate an aesthetic, the work is stripped of its technical particularity, its specific emancipatory content, and becomes subsumed within what a general philosophical category claims it must project. There is, in short, no "determinate" way of either investigating the work or defining the relation between art and political revolt. The interpretation of art vacillates between the belief that art *must* manifest what André Breton called the "great refusal" of all reality and that the dream it projects "must become a force of changing rather than dreaming the human condition: it must become a political force."[59]

Demanding a "negation" of the status quo, while continuing to insist that the aesthetic form remain "opposed" to reality, Marcuse seeks to achieve a Hegelian purpose with a Kantian form of presentation. An internal contradiction within the theory combines with what Hegel might have termed an "abstract," or one-sided, characterization of art's utopian potential. Art may provide a sensuous experience of freedom. According to Hegel, however, this form is always bound to an empirical content and stands in need of external mediation for freedom to become reflexively appreciated by individuals. Thus, in contrast to Marcuse, Hegel is unwilling to speak of an inherently abstract aesthetic form and capable of arguing that art is able to supply "out of the real world what is lacking to the notion."

Extracting an emancipatory content from an artwork presupposes a link between the interpretive apparatus and a social theory capable of making its commitment to freedom determinate with respect to institutions and the possibilities of practice. Neither an interpretive apparatus nor a social theory of that sort is ever provided by Marcuse. And the reason is that, insofar as art is opposed to reality, both are rendered irrelevant. Marcuse claims that the aesthetic experience thrusts a work beyond the reality principle and objective judgment. Fantasy provides art, from such a perspective, with its autonomy and perhaps even its oppositional character. But, it is a mistake to believe that an artwork inherently calls forth a critical indictment of the status quo or some political imperative. Kant knew better.

Simply positing the emancipatory potential or "erotic truth" within art, which justifies the anthropological break with progress, blurs the distinction between utopia as "the wholly other" and utopia as a regulative idea. Speculations about the transcendence of art, without any determinate reference to society, can result only in the depiction of an aesthetic "life–world." But what this concept has to do with any particular works of art, or the ability to interpret them, remains open to question. For, even if a work does arise *from the urgings of* the repressed life instinct, it is one thing to say that Eros provides a psychological moment in the creative process and quite another to identify that urging with the object created; this may become evident in specific works like *Tristan und Isolde* while in others, like those of Georges Bataille or the Marquis de Sade, it need not become evident at all.

Qualitative differences between works exist and interpretive categories are necessary to extract their diverse contributions. Transcendence is not an immanent characteristic of "art," Marcuse's claims notwithstanding, but a complex material phenomenon based upon the interaction between given artworks and a changing set of audiences. By divorcing "art" from popular culture and ignoring the need for evaluative criteria, however, the concrete works are left hanging in the abstract. Indeed, this becomes readily apparent in Marcuse's ideas on censorship.

He was willing to argue that censorship of certain ideas is imperative where "the pacification of existence, where freedom and happiness are at stake."[60] It is true, of course, that there are certain extreme situations imaginable in which censorship becomes politically necessary. There is a danger, however, in turning necessity into a virtue. Marcuse, in his choice of language and insofar as he ignores the institutional dynamics of censorship, comes dangerously close to doing that.

His point is that the culture industry, with its inherent desire to reduce all phenomena to the lowest common denominator and eradicate qualitative differences between ideas and works, was actually turning the original emancipatory intent of tolerance against itself. Tolerance has become "repressive" insofar as it hinders the ability of individuals to develop their critical faculties and contributes to a climate of thoroughgoing relativism.[61] His awareness of danger seems circumscribed. Thus, he can emphasize that:

> [C]ensorship of art and literature is regressive under all circumstances. There are cases where an authentic oeuvre carries a regressive political message – Dostoevsky is a case in point. But then the message is canceled by the oeuvre itself: the regressive political content is absorbed (*aufgehoben*) in the artistic form: in the work as literature.[62]

Art rejects merely instrumental notions of progress, but it somehow becomes inherently aligned with speculative components within what always was an ethical concept. That is why Marcuse can claim that the regressive political message is "canceled" by the artistic form. But this is simply an assertion. Whether the reactionary content is absorbed or not, obviously, depends upon who is judging the work and the conditions under which such a judgment is taking place. Aesthetic mastery, when considering Louis-Ferdinand Celine or Ernst Jünger, need not cancel a reactionary political content: the two can happily co-exist. Even more important, however, is Marcuse's lack of any institutional understanding of censorship or the mechanisms by which it works. Real censors have never discriminated between art and politics precisely because the lack of democratic accountability, inherent in the very enterprise, makes it unnecessary to do so.

Censorship functions through a bureaucracy which, following Max Weber, always seeks to expand itself and its domain. Arbitrariness is, furthermore, endemic to censorship. Only in the most general terms is it possible to determine whether works which carry an explicit political appeal should be regarded as propaganda or as works of art. Thus, if Marcuse is willing to accept the authoritarian logic of censorship in the realm of philosophy and politics, it is illogical for him to ignore a similar threat to freedom and the "pacification of existence" when it is leveled from the artistic realm.

All this suggests that claims regarding the autonomy of aesthetic form are inherently abstract. Hegel already knew that form is always the form of a content and that the limitations of a given content will not disappear even if, as an objectification, the work can contest the original intentions and prejudices of the artist who produced it. Nor is there anything intrinsically progressive in the choice of one form or style over another; the radical utopian images projected by the assault on representation, or reality per se, are no more "emancipatory" than the concrete historical indictments of realism. From such a perspective, in fact, emancipation loses its concreteness. And that is also true of transcendence. Art is not transcendent; some *works* become transcendent and others do not for a variety of reasons. But Marcuse refuses to offer an explanatory apparatus for investigating the phenomenon. Transcendence is not considered a social act. And for good reason. Viewing the concept in this way would necessarily involve recognizing some connection between transcendence and *the historical order which is transcended.*

Different works express different needs, different hopes, and different possibilities. The emancipatory potential of each, however, becomes concrete only when it is grasped by what Marx termed an "audience of art lovers." Transcendence is not simply an intrinsic quality of the aesthetic form, and it is impossible to simply presuppose the perception of an artwork's utopian potential. An act of conscious appropriation is necessary which might well set audiences of different socio-political persuasions against one another. Progressive critics will subsequently find themselves engaged in a continuous battle to elucidate, preserve, and potentially redefine, that *promesse de bonheur* which the work may harbor. Censorship will only inhibit an undertaking of this sort. And the reason is clear. Aesthetic interpretation is inherently linked to a social theory capable of justifying its normative values and views of political transformation in a free discourse.

Utopia, aesthetics, and revolution: Herbert Marcuse fused them in an almost seamless manner. His thinking evidenced every influence deriving from "critical theory" in its most radical phase. His social theory is predicated on the notion of reification developed by the young Marx and Lukács; his negative anthropology is powered by the metapsychology of Freud; and his commitment to utopia, both practically and existentially, makes good on Schiller as well as the radical implications of Hegel's speculative historicism. None of his comrades in the Frankfurt School ever so fully expressed the revolutionary intent of the dialectical method or so radically contested the predominant understanding of progress.[63]

Horkheimer and Adorno had, of course, already analyzed advanced industrial society as part of an anthropological development defined by instrumental rationality and the domination of nature. According to them, however, the point of reference and the culmination of this development was totalitarianism and the concentration camps. They viewed the future in terms of what Benjamin called that single catastrophe which keeps piling up debris. Without forgetting the past, however, Marcuse gave the argument a new and far more radical twist. He brought critical theory in from the cold by highlighting the devil's bargain wherein a "pacification of existence" is exchanged for affluence and genuine autonomy for the sham freedom offered by the culture industry.

And this transformed the political stakes. It was one thing for Adorno to assert the subjectivity of the subject against a totalitarian or bureaucratic world of grey, and for Horkheimer to indulge in a "yearning for the wholly other."[64] It was quite another for Marcuse to articulate a positive utopian conception and call for revolutionary solidarity under conditions of previously unimaginable affluence and democratic rule in which the "happy consciousness" seemed dominant.[65] He never sacrificed solidarity to subjectivity and always remembered that freedom is always connected with an enterprise engineered by the masses in motion. Similarly, in the most radical expressions of his thought, culture is more than a set of emancipatory resources for preserving subjectivity in the face of reification. It also projects the explosion of everyday life by a movement with a "new sensibility."

Cultural transformation was the goal. And Marcuse inherited that concern less from Freud or Marx than from Schiller. Just as the *Letters on the Aesthetic Education of Man* from 1793 were an attempt to preserve the spirit of emancipation from the political thermidor of the French Revolution in 1793, similarly, the utopian speculation of *Eros and Civilization* and *One-Dimensional Man* constituted an attempt to maintain the hope for an alternative in response to the increasing dominance of technological rationality and the failure of the working class to realize a new emancipated political order. The chief writings of Marcuse, however, did not constitute a rearguard action. Published in 1955 and 1964 respectively, they anticipated the concerns of 1968. The adherents of the new movement identified themselves with new forms of expression, free sexuality, and cultural politics. They too believed, with Marcuse, that "the fight for Eros is a political fight."

Western ideals became the popular subject of radical criticism. Marcuse spoke to the victims of progress as surely as those who retained an "unhappy consciousness" or what Hegel viewed as the ability to recognize new possibilities for emancipation without any clear idea of how to realize them. Both were among those considered marginal to the functioning of advanced industrial society: the minorities in the ghettos, women, the students bristling under the conformity of university life in the early 1960s, the colonized suffering under the yoke of imperialism.[66] They would serve as "catalysts" for a working class increasingly seduced by the new affluence and the growing integrative power of the culture industry. Indeed, considering the remarkable French strike wave of 1968 inspired by uprisings at Nanterre and elsewhere, Marcuse's analysis was not far off the mark.

Romanticism, of course, influenced his view of these marginal groups.[67] He ignored their lack of revolutionary tradition, their political inexperience, the lack of institutions uniting them, and the dynamics of what would become identity politics.[68] But the commitment to liberation and resistance remained firm. Marcuse even argued that immediate economic interests could not serve as the primary motivation for a radical political undertaking in the modern era. And that was precisely the reason for his influence. Given the degree of material affluence during the 1960s, after all, this standpoint was anything but illogical in advanced industrial society. Affluence, mass democracy and a new "nonconformist conformity" (Adorno), had called into question the old motivations for social transformation.

Revolution lost its identification with the seizure of power and the creation of new institutions. It took on a new, more peaceful, and more existential definition. But whatever the idealism of the new position it becomes impossible to maintain – with Lukács – that Marcuse like other members of the Frankfurt School was content to watch the decay of civilization from the "grand hotel abyss." Marcuse knew that the revolutionary negation of repression would demand new modes of cultural expression. The important part of his legacy deals not with political naivete, or mistaken attempts to realize the aesthetic,[69] but the real way in which his thinking anticipated attempts to contest the culture of capitalist society. Indeed, within certain boundaries, these were successful.

"Legitimation" became an issue in the 1960s. A new empathy with the victims of imperialism was forged. What had previously been private problems like spouse abuse and incest did become open to public scrutiny and legislation. Mores concerning relations between the races and sexes did change. The "quality of life" and nature emerged as new matters of fundamental concern. And there is little doubt that aesthetic perceptions changed as well. These were the practical results of the ways in which the aesthetic theory of Herbert Marcuse tended to converge with the spirit of a student movement intent on transforming not merely a set of policies, but the everyday life of advanced capitalism.

Of course, in basic ways, the marriage of the abstract and the concrete was never really happy even during the honeymoon. Marcuse distrusted the populism of the movement, its irrationalist tendencies, and he had little use for rock music and popular culture. He was also highly critical of "sexual liberation" and rejected those who believed in the possibility of merging art with reality as it exists. That, he believed would result only in "barbarism at the height of civilization." In contrast to many of his old colleagues from the Institute, however, he never withdrew his support from the movement.[70]

Even in his last effort, which more directly allied him with the aesthetics of Adorno, Marcuse argued that even if art "cannot change the world . . . it can contribute to changing the consciousness and drives of the men and women who could change the world."[71] Still, especially in *The Aesthetic Dimension*, his desire was not to subordinate art to politics. Quite the contrary. "Socialist realism" never played a role in his aesthetic, which only makes sense given his critical analysis of soviet ideology and the manner in which the transcendent character of art is undermined by government-sponsored styles of this sort.[72] He always maintained the impossibility of drawing the consequences from a genuine artwork and then mechanically seeking to actualize them in political practice. Nevertheless, the analysis of aesthetic questions was less political than in any of his previous works.[73]

The Aesthetic Dimension appeared when the movement was over and advanced industrial society had – seemingly – absorbed the gains. Progress had triumphed once again. The critical individual stood isolated and perhaps in more danger than before, while the spirit of the "new sensibility" vanished. Probably as a consequence, Marcuse emphasized even more strongly the need for a total break of the aesthetic from the real. An abstract aesthetic "life–world" became a substitute for the rich utopia elaborated in *Eros and Civilization*, while the moment of solidarity implicit within *la promesse de bonheur* was surrendered in favor of subjective redemption through aesthetic experience. *The Aesthetic Dimension* is a work of defeat that portrays the impotence of art when confronted with the victory of reaction. Thus, in a way, it serves as a corrective for the power which Marcuse originally vested in art and which the aesthetic does not – and arguably should not – possess.

Despite everything, however, Herbert Marcuse was the philosopher of the "cultural revolution" of the 1960s. And his achievements were real. He was the pivotal figure in introducing the Frankfurt School to the United States and it is no exaggeration to say that the young intellectuals used footnotes from *One-Dimensional Man* to learn more about Theodor Adorno, Walter Benjamin, Max Horkheimer and the rest. Marcuse's friends were still untranslated and a world apart. Initiating the debates over consumerism, the environment, the malleability of science, the content of progress, the value of work, the role of ideology, the impact of mass media, and the character of revolutionary agency fell to him. Philosophical idealism, which he transmitted through a host of classic essays and works like *Reason and Revolution*, received a new intellectual legitimacy and became an antidote to the stultifying dominance of behaviorism in the social sciences and "new criticism" in literary theory. And he never forgot the moment of practice; indeed, his "marginal groups" theory provided a foundation for the analysis of the "new social movements" by thinkers like Lucien Goldmann, Jürgen Habermas, Claude Lefort, and Alain Touraine. His utopian conception and call for an anthropological break, furthermore, gave intellectual work a needed sense of emancipatory purpose and motivated people to once again think of happiness and beauty as social concerns.

For all the economic differences, with the fall of communism and the perceived hegemony of capitalist values, his concept of "one-dimensional man" is arguably more applicable today than when it was first articulated.[74] But the fortunes of the Left have changed radically. Marcuse's influence has waned and his writings are now read only by specialists. No longer is there much sympathy for his attempt to articulate a utopian alternative. Between the international triumph of conservatism during the 1980s, the failure of the communist experiment, and the economic recession of the 1990s, cultural radicalism itself has given way before a new concern with the welfare state and the principles underpinning it. With this shift, indeed, Marcuse's speculative concerns of the 1960s have essentially vanished from the public discourse.

Marcuse, of course, also helped dig his own intellectual grave. He undervalued the liberal and social democratic traditions. His meta-psychological and anthropological critique of advanced industrial society obscured the qualitative differences between the various forms it could take. His assumptions about affluence and, by implication, the end of the business cycle were simply incorrect. He woefully neglected institutional and organizational questions of power even as he exaggerated the emancipatory alternative any revolution could possibly provide. His works were never able to generate categories for making logical distinctions between needs, systems or artworks. For all that, however, the pragmatism of the present is hollow and, with the conservative upsurge, a deadening of the spirit has taken place. Consequently, if the theory of Herbert Marcuse does not offer a fully coherent alternative, it certainly sparks the imagination and begins to elicit reflection about what has been forgotten.

Notes

1   "The final culmination of philosophy is thus at the same time its abdication. Released from its preoccupation with the ideal, philosophy is also released from its opposition to reality. This means that it ceases to be philosophy. It does not follow, however, that thought must then

comply with the existing order. Critical thinking does not cease, but assumes a new form. The efforts of reason devolve upon social theory and social practice." Herbert Marcuse, *Reason and Revolution: Hegel and the Rise of Social Theory* (Boston, 1969), p. 28.

2   Ibid., p. 9.

3   Herbert Marcuse, *One-Dimensional Man: Studies in the Ideology of Advanced Industrial Society* (Boston, 1964), p. 144.

4   An unpublished, three-part, sociological analysis entitled "The Theory of Social Change," which Marcuse undertook in collaboration with Franz Neumann, was discovered in the Marcuse archives in Frankfurt. Note the discussion by Douglas Kellner, "The Marcuse Archives: Material for a Renaissance of Marcusean Thought" in the forthcoming volume *Marcuse Revisited* eds John Bokina and Timothy J. Lukes, University of Kansas Press.

5   Ibid., pp. 19ff.

6   Herbert Marcuse, "The End of Utopia" in *Five Lectures*, (Boston, 1970), pp. 68–9.

7   For a provocative argument, which claims that his social theory implicitly projects a theological discourse, cf. Peter Rottlander, "Philosophie, Gesellschaftstheorie, und die Permanenz der Kunst; Theologische Reflexionen zur Herbert Marcuse" in Edmund Arens et al., *Erinnerung, Befreiung, Solidarität: Benjamin, Marcuse, Habermas, und die politische Theologie* (Düsseldorf, 1991), pp. 81ff.

8   Herbert Marcuse, "Der deustsche Kunstlerroman" in *Schriften* (Frankfurt, 1978) vol. 1, pp. 7ff. In this vein, however, the radical interpretation of what remains the best general biography on Marcuse can suggest that his work is basically a critical meditation on Marx and an experiment with the utopian implications of his thought; cf. Douglas Kellner, *Herbert Marcuse and the Crisis of Marxism* (Berkeley, 1984).

9   Marcuse, "The Obsolescence of the Freudian Concept of Man" in *Five Lectures*, p. 58.

10   Marcuse, *One-Dimensional Man*, p. 70.

11   "The authentic utopia is grounded in recollection . . . Forgetting past suffering and past joy alleviates life under a repressive reality principle. In contrast, remembrance spurs the drive for the conquest of suffering and the permanence of joy. But the force of remembrance is frustrated; joy itself is overshadowed by pain . . . If the remembrance of things past would become a motive power in the struggle for changing the world, the struggle would be waged for a revolution hitherto suppressed in the previous historical revolutions." Herbert Marcuse, *The Aesthetic Dimension: Toward a Critique of Marxist Aesthetics* (Boston, 1978), p. 73. Note also the excellent discussion by Martin Jay, *Marxism and Totality: The Adventures of a Concept from Lukács to Habermas* (Berkeley, 1984), pp. 224ff.

12   Herbert Marcuse, "The Affirmative Character of Culture" in *Negations*, trans. Jeremy J. Shapiro (Boston, 1969), p. 230.

13   Marcuse, *The Aesthetic Dimension*, p. 47.
14   Marcuse, *One-Dimensional Man*, p. 63.
15   Herbert Marcuse, *Counterrevolution and Revolt* (Boston, 1972), p. 98.
16   Marcuse, "The Affirmative Character of Culture," pp. 118–19.
17   Ibid., p. 122.
18   "The truth value of the imagination relates not only to the past, but also to the future: the forms of freedom and happiness which it invokes claim to deliver the historical *reality*. In its refusal to accept as final the limitations imposed upon freedom and happiness by the reality principle, in its refusal to forget what can *be*, lies the critical function of fantasy." Herbert Marcuse, *Eros and Civilization: A Philosophical Inquiry into Freud* (New York, 1962), p. 135.
19   Ibid., p. 105.
20   Cf. Rolf Wiggershaus, *Die Frankfurter Schule: Geschichte, Theoretische Entwicklung, Politische Bedeutung* (Munich, 1988), pp. 398ff.
21   Ibid., p. 74.
22   Ibid., p. 41.
23   The attempt to reintroduce a sense of harmony and what has been excluded or repressed from consciousness results, for some, in Marcuse contributing along with Carl Jung to a "feminization" of political thought by his employment of utopian aesthetics as a form of therapeutic practice. That the concrete character of such a therapy is never disclosed, that Marcuse is explicitly engaging in a *meta*psychological discourse, that the aesthetic is not a substitute but rather the goal of politics, and that – in contrast to Jung – his politics is predicated on progressive and rationalist assumptions is not entertained by Gertrude A. Steuernagel, *Political Philosophy as Therapy: Marcuse Reconsidered* (Westport, Conn., 1979), pp. 117ff. Also, since the author does not seem clear about why Marcuse never embraced Jung, it is useful to consider the excellent critique of Freud's former disciple from a critical utopian standpoint by Ernst Bloch, *Erbschaft dieser Zeit* (Frankfurt, 1973), pp. 344ff; *Das Prinzip Hoffnung* (Frankfurt, 1973) vol. 1, pp. 181ff. For an overview of the psychological dimension of Marcuse's thought, see Edward Hyman, "Eros and Freedom: The Critical Psychology of Herbert Marcuse" in *Marcuse: Critical Theory and the Promise of Utopia* eds Richard Pippen et al., (London, 1988), pp. 143ff.
24   *Eros and Civilization*, p. 34.
25   Marcuse, *Counterrevolution and Revolt*, pp. 29ff.
26   Paul A. Robinson, *The Freudian Left: Wilhelm Reich, Geza Roheim, Herbert Marcuse*, (New York, 1969), p. 208; note also Daniel Burston, *The Legacy of Erich Fromm* (Cambridge, Mass., 1991).
27   Marcuse, "Progress and Freud's Theory of Instincts" in *Five Lectures*, p. 37.
28   Sigmund Freud, "Repression" in *General Psychological Theory* ed. Philip Rieff (New York, 1962), p. 105.

29 Sigmund Freud, *The Ego and the Id*, trans. Joan Riviere (New York, 1960), p. 35.

30 This becomes apparent in the evaluation of hedonism which, whatever its subjectivism and inability to distinguish between prefabricated and autonomously chosen forms of enjoyment, emphasized that happiness is a moment of truth. Cf. Herbert Marcuse, "On Hedonism" in *Negations*, pp. 159ff.

31 Marcuse, "The Obsolescence of the Freudian Concept of Man," p. 47.

32 "The stars, the consorts of royalty, the kings and champion sportsmen have the function which demigods had in mythology; they are human to a superlative degree and therefore to be imitated, their behavior has a normative character. But as they are not of this world one can only imitate them in a small way, on one's own level, and not presume to match oneself with them in reality." Reimut Reiche, *Sexuality and Class Struggle* trans. Susan Bennett (New York, 1971), p. 71.

33 Cf. Theodor W. Adorno, "Zeitlose Mode. Zum Jazz" in *Prismen: Kulturkritik und Gesellschaft* (Frankfurt, 1955), pp. 144ff.

34 Marcuse, "The Obsolescence of the Freudian Concept of Man," p. 55.

35 Marcuse, *One-Dimensional Man*, pp. 73ff; *Eros and Civilization*, pp. 75ff.

36 "The perversion of the aesthetic: whereas the aesthetic is a totality formed by sublimation of the instincts, the spectacle releases instinctual energies but does not bind them into forms. On the other hand, the spectacle as aesthetic and as consumption prevents the individual from experiencing action and process; he is an actor only as an object and a subject only as a spectator; he consumes rather than makes." Shierry M. Weber, "Individuation as Praxis" in *Critical Interruptions: New Left Perspectives on Herbert Marcuse* ed. Paul Breines (New York, 1970), p. 37.

37 Marcuse, "Art and Revolution," *Partisan Review* (Spring, 1972), p. 178.

38 Ibid., p. 179.

39 Marcuse, *Counterrevolution and Revolt*, p. 99.

40 Ibid., p. 67.

41 His interest in this extraordinary artist and intellectual already occurred early in life; thus, the research which resulted in Herbert Marcuse, *Schiller-Bibliographie* (Berlin, 1925).

42 This fits with Freud's view of fantasy as the only thought activity still preserved from reality testing and subordinate to the pleasure principle; it inherently wishes "to satsify those wishes which reality does not satsify." Sigmund Freud, "The Theme of the Three Caskets" in *Character and Culture* (New York, 1963), p. 76.

43 Friedrich Schiller, *On the Aesthetic Education of Man* (New York, 1965), p. 76.

44 Herbert Marcuse, *An Essay on Liberation* (Boston, 1969), p. 24.

45 Marcuse, *One-Dimensional Man*, p. 239.

46 Cf. Alfred Schmidt, "Existential Ontology and Historical Materialism in the Work of Herbert Marcuse" in *Marcuse: Critical Theory and the Promise of Utopia*, pp. 47ff.

47   Marcuse, *Eros and Civilization*, p. 110.

48   Marcuse, "The End of Utopia,", p. 78.

49   Still, Marcuse was less clear on the subject than many may believe. Varied statements suggest that his desire to break with the formal principle of progress was predicated on a commitment to maintain its substantive foundations. This, of course, would produce a fundamental contradiction. Note the discussion by Andrew Feenberg, *The Critical Theory of Technology* (New York, 1991), pp. 76ff; Kellner, *Herbert Marcuse*, pp. 227ff, 326ff.

50   Cf. Jürgen Habermas, "Technology and Science as Ideology: For Herbert Marcuse on His 70th Birthday" in *Toward a Rational Society: Student Protest, Science, and Politics* trans. Jeremy J. Shapiro (Boston, 1970), pp. 81ff.

51   Cf. Erich Fromm, *The Crisis of Psychoanalysis: Essays on Freud, Marx, and Social Psychology* (New York, 1970), pp. 1ff; also Erich Fromm, *The Revision of Psychoanalysis* ed. Rainer Funk (Boulder, 1992), pp. 111ff.

52   Herbert Marcuse, "Gesellschaftliche und psychologische Repression. Die politische Aktualität Freuds" in Bernard Görlich, Alfred Lorenzer, Alfred Schmidt, *Der Stachel Freud: Beitrage und Dokumente zur Kulturismus-Kritik* (Frankfurt, 1980), pp. 186ff.

53   Géza Roheim, *Magic and Schizophrenia* (Bloomington, 1970), p. 4.

54   Ibid., p. 111.

55   Sigmund Freud, *Civilization and its Discontents* trans. and ed. James Strachey (New York, 1961), pp. 62–3.

56   Marcuse, *An Essay on Liberation*, pp. 21–8.

57   Vincent Geoghegan, *Reason and Eros: The Social Theory of Herbert Marcuse* (London, 1981), pp. 1–5.

58   "The new sensibility . . . emerges when the struggle is waged for essentially new ways and forms of life," negation of the entire Establishment, its morality, culture, affirmation of the right to build a society in which the abolition of poverty and toil terminates in a universe where the sensuous, the playful, the calm, and the beautiful become forms of existence and thereby the form of society itself." Marcuse, *An Essay on Liberation*, p. 25.

59   Marcuse, *Counterrevolution and Revolt*, p. 102.

60   Marcuse, "Repressive Tolerance," in Robert Paul Wolff, Barrington Moore, Jr., and Herbert Marcuse, *A Critique of Pure Tolerance*, p. 88.

61   Cf. Richard Lichtman, "Repressive Tolerance" in *Marcuse: Critical Theory and the Promise of Utopia*, pp. 189ff.

62   Marcuse, "Repressive Tolerance," p. 89.

63   Cf. Marcuse, "Progress and Freud's Theory of the Instincts" in *Five Lectures*, p. 28.

64   Marcuse was indeed aware that the crucial problem is that advanced industrial society throws the subject "back upon himself, [so that he or she] learn[s] to bear, and in a certain sense, to love his isolation." Herbert Marcuse, "The Affirmative Character of Culture," p. 122.

65   Marcuse, *One-Dimensional Man*, pp. 56ff.

66   Ibid., pp. 46ff, 256ff.

67   It is interesting, in this vein, that Marcuse was no political neophyte. As Chief of the Central European Branch, Divison of Research, of the Department of State, "he exerted an enormous influence in discussion and theory formation" with respect to questions dealing with denazification and organizations like the social democrats and the trade unions capable of contributing to the democratic reconstruction of Germany. Indeed, especially during the postwar years, "this picture of Marcuse as the proponent of Anglo-Saxon democratic constitutionalism or Social-Democratic reform seems to clash with every familiar image of him and his politics – the radical thinker of Weimar, the intellectual precursor of the student movement, the vehement critic of social democratic quietism who grasped the repressive tolerance inherent in American liberalism and its paralyzing of every radical opposition." Alfons Sollner, "Marcuse's Political Theory in the 1940s and 1950s" in *Telos* 74 (Winter, 1988), pp. 69, 73; also cf. Barry Katz, "The Frankfurt School Goes to War" in *Journal of Modern History* 59 (September, 1987), pp. 439ff.

68   Cf. Stephen Eric Bronner, "Reconstructing the Experiment: Political Culture and the American New Left" in *Moments of Decision: Political History and the Crises of Radicalism* (New York, 1992), pp. 101ff.

69   To this extent, even while the general theoretical point is correct, the historical reality is not taken into account when the critic of Marcuse simply claims that politics "must remain until those who continue to profit from an adversary relationship with nature are deposed; for they are the 'serious ones' who could easily take advantage of individuals committed to aesthetic transcendence. The aesthetic perspective may be crucial to the liberated society; however, it cannot be expected in any way to be responsible for the creation of such a society." Timothy J. Lukes, *The Flight into Inwardness: An Exposition and Critique of Herbert Marcuse's Theory of Liberative Aesthetics* (Cranbury, NJ., 1985), p. 162.

70   Cf. Paul Breines, "Marcuse and the New Left in America" in *Antworten auf Herbert Marcuse* ed. Jürgen Habermas (Frankfurt, 1968), pp. 134ff.

71   Marcuse, *The Aesthetic Dimension*, p. 32.

72   Herbert Marcuse, *Soviet Marxism* (New York, 1961), pp. 113ff.

73   Marcuse, *Counterrevolution and Revolt*, p. 101.

74   Brad Rose, "The Triumph of Social Control? A Look at Herbert Marcuse's *One-Dimensional Man*, 25 Years Later" in *Berkeley Journal of Sociology* vol. 35 (1990), pp. 55ff.

13

Left Instrumentalism: A Critique of Analytic and Rational Choice Marxism*

A cynic [is] a man who knows the price of everything and the value of nothing.

Oscar Wilde

Orthodox Marxism derived much of its theoretical power from an explicit commitment to "scientific materialism." This scientific quality of Marxism was seen as differentiating it from bourgeois metaphysics as well as various forms of ethical and utopian socialism. No wonder, then, that the inability of the theory to make good on its promises and predictions should have caused enormous disorientation and a profound crisis of purpose for so many concerned with the interests of working people.

New interpretations and theoretical tendencies arose to confront the theoretical and practical inadequacies of the Marxian heritage. Among the most vibrant, however, is the tendency known under the rubric of either "analytic" or "rational choice" Marxism whose most important representatives include Jon Elster, Gerald Cohen, Adam Przeworski, Erik Olin Wright and John Roemer among others. All seek to restore the scientific character of the Marxian enterprise and accept positivist criteria of truth. "Analytic" and "rational choice" Marxism are not exactly reducible to one another since adherents of the former need not embrace all the particular categories and assumptions regarding modeling normally identified with rational choice.[1] But the two terms have essentially been used interchangeably, and for good reason. Analytic and rational choice Marxism both assume a utilitarian theory of action and a set of beliefs, which actually derive from neo-classical economics, centering

---

* Revised version of "Politics and Judgement: A Critique of Rational Choice Marxism" first published in *The Review of Politics* (Spring, 1990).

around the idea that subjects pursue only those strategies which best optimize profit or utility. Both, furthermore, see the need for providing a "micro" foundation for "macro" analysis or phenomena and for this reason, whatever the hesitations of some, analytic assumptions concerning individual and group behavior can thus easily become defined and determined according to the rules of mathematical modeling and game theory.

Many proponents of the new scientific approaches claim that it was precisely the inability to provide such a "micro" foundation for "macro" phenomena, and so link the general with the particular, which made traditional forms of Marxism too abstract for viable scientific inquiry. In a similar vein, they have criticized the inability of orthodox views to confront the fact that socially beneficial behavior is not necessarily worthwhile for particular individuals. Paying attention to the cognitive and situational moments of action, they have also attacked interpretations of Marx that inadequately explain fragmentation among workers or only indirectly base collective behavior on individual action. It was in attempting to overcome these deficiencies that the new analytic tendency first sought to infuse Marxism with the insights of "rational choice" and then develop a "ground" or epistemological basis for the sociological argument through what has been termed "methodological individualism."

The desire of analytic Marxists to connect the general with the particular need not involve the acceptance of the more rigorous demands of "methodological individualism" developed by those committed to rational choice Marxism. Other differences within and between these two positions, exist as well. Some partisans of the new scientistic position have reduced Marx's contribution to a series of distinct philosophical claims or sought to define his categories with the precision of analytic philosophy. Others have emphasized the connection between Marxism and the logic of collective action in order to analyze class interaction solely from the perspective of instrumental rationality. Certain thinkers have emphasized the need for game theoretical formulations while still others have taken a different path to supplant Marx's "collectivist" assumptions. Clearly, not every theorist will accept all the claims or even concerns of the others. Nevertheless, the real issue revolves around the *political* status of the new "scientific" enterprise as a whole rather than this or that thinker.

Of course, from such a perspective, there is the danger of tarring all with the same brush. This is mitigated, however, by the fact that a distinct set of epistemological premises unify the adherents to the new approach. Virtually all the proponents of analytic and rational choice Marxism basically agree that Marxism must justify itself as a (social) science; that its principal importance derives from the empirical power of its explanatory apparatus; and that rationality is defined by instrumentally strategic concerns particularly those emanating from the confrontation with scarcity. Given its desire to scientifically update Marxism, and philosophically ground collective behavior in the individual, many would even maintain that this new tendency represents a "continuation of the concerns of Western Marxism and a critical return to the classical agenda."[2]

Much has been made of the *critical* character of this new scientistic tendency. A misunderstanding, however, too often presents itself. For, even while many thinkers committed to it have reworked their own insights in light of discussion with colleagues, an uncritical acceptance of the existing framework of production along with its reifying assumptions is made. Neither analytic nor rational choice Marxism is reflexive, which only makes sense insofar as both have chosen simply to ignore the contribution of Kant, Hegel, and the tradition of speculative idealism to the socialist project.[3] The new scientific standpoint is built on the same empiricist and positivist claims, which critical theory always sought to contest; the implications of the old dualism between fact and value reassert themselves. Thus, whatever the extravagant claims made by some of its partisans, analytic and rational choice Marxism is actually little more than a set of techniques or a middle range theory whose explanatory power applies only under limited circumstances.[4]

Unfortunately, however, those seeking to evaluate rational choice and analytic Marxism have themselves too often uncritically accepted its basic presuppositions. This, in turn, has blunted attempts to provide an immanent criticism even as it has narrowed the contemporary socialist discourse over methods and aims.[5] Usually, the wrong targets have been chosen. It is no longer a matter, as it was for Max Horkheimer, of condemning instrumental reason per se. Instrumental theories have their uses, especially when dealing with problems standing outside an ideological context, and the issue is not whether science must make "realist" assumptions.[6] The question is rather whether the attempts to fashion analytic or rational choice Marxism into a general theory is legitimate and whether instrumental forms of analysis need any form of grounding at all. Nor is it a matter of whether the proponents of this new tendency have conformed to some abstract notion of what Marx "really" said. The real question is whether the new perspective can deal with the most important practical and ethical problems deriving from the breakdown of Marxian teleology.

The Context: Marxism and Rational Choice

History is not irrelevant to epistemology. As far as "rational choice Marxism" is concerned, an immanent critique presupposes an understanding of how the tendency actually stands in relation to the tradition which it has claimed to confront and appropriate. Under the circumstances, then, a brief overview of Marxism as the theory that "gripped the masses" becomes necessary in order to evaluate the contributions and limits of this new approach.

"Orthodox Marxism" emerged during the last quarter of the nineteenth century and, no less than any great theory, it served to "comprehend its epoch in thought" (Hegel). The Kantian separation between fact and value fell before a reality which, in the years between the Franco-Prussian War and World War I, was roughly conforming to the predictions of Marx as interpreted by Karl Kautsky, Paul Lafargue, Georgi Plekhanov, and others. It seemed that the proletariat, along with its organizational embodiment in the first great mass parties of social democracy, was expanding everywhere. "Objective" conditions were thus producing a revolutionary subject, which appeared to require nothing more than political unity and a reflexive comprehension of its "mission" to transform the existing order of capitalism.

This apparent empirical verification of Marx's predictions did not create passivity or a belief in some "automatic" historical development, but rather inspired the growth of political organization, class consciousness, and a commitment to democratic values.[7] Marxist "science" thus served as a type of impetus to praxis which, while *verifiable*, actually intensified the desire of workers to bring about the socialist transformation that much sooner. This very connection between the empirical and the normative provided Marxism with an ability to comprehend actual developments as well as inspire a unique political posture.

Building on Hegel, Marx embraced a stage theory of history wherein feudalism gave way to a capitalist order whose own development would produce a steadily growing proletariat. Intrinsically connected to the expansion of the very system which enslaved it, the proletariat would subsequently become the "gravedigger" of the old and the "inevitable" harbinger of a new socialist society. According to the stage theory of Hegel and Marx, humanity builds on itself as the future produces a "sublation" (*Aufhebung*) of the past.[8] Both thinkers, furthermore, believed that this development was not merely confined to scientific knowledge or technology, but also referred to the world of culture and the most radical egalitarian and democratic achievements of the past. The future incarnated within the proletarian mission would provide these values with an even more radical articulation.

No less than reality as a whole, the creation of a new socialist order was thus seen from the start as a value-laden enterprise – which is what necessarily renders any rigid "objectivistic" appropriation of Marx "one sided" or, in Hegelian terms, "abstract."[9] Of course, it is true that "production" served as the peculiar foundation for Marx's worldview. Nevertheless, the concept was predicated on an essentially *inter-subjective* standpoint committed to toppling the towering figure of Robinson Crusoe and the atomistic individualism of bourgeois political economy.

Marx's notion of inter-subjectivity was defined in terms of a continuously evolving interaction, what he called a "metabolic exchange," between humanity and nature.[10] It follows, then, that individuals always find themselves within historically determinate modes of work which structure the ways specific groups produce a social surplus and fight over its appropriation. Culture and historically determinate values are also explicitly recognized as moments of this production process. Consequently, whatever the often fascinating philosophical attempts to define history as a mere instrumental confrontation with scarcity,[11] Marx's attempt to understand the change from one "ensemble of social social relations" to another first made it possible to truly speak of humanity as creating its own *mutable* history while endowing it with a *mutable* meaning.[12]

The "materialist" character of Marx's theory, in this sense, never depended upon a flat and trans-historical instrumentalism or its ability to "operationalize" concepts.[13] Whatever the importance mathematical models may have in dealing with such concerns, from Marx's perspective, a normative purpose logically informs the investigative enterprise. And for good reason: only a normative stance can illuminate the "unnecessary" character of existing socio-political constraints and call for the resolution of contradictions with an eye to extending both formal and substantive freedom.

It was the call to extend and deepen the democratic values of 1789 and 1793, which the bourgeoisie would betray in 1848, that linked socialism to the revolutionary philosophy of its class enemy and defined the "mission" of the proletariat. Gradually becoming aware of its existence in the "inverted world" (*verkehrte Welt*) of the "commodity form," wherein capital is the "subject" of the production process and the worker merely the "object" for its use, Marx believed that the proletariat would ultimately confront this reality as a self-conscious and internationalist "subject" ready to subordinate capital – as the "object" of production – to the democratic control of society as a whole. On the basis of such an interpretation, the telological standpoint Marx inherited from Hegel was normative in character and predicated on the fusion of ontology, epistemology, and historical development.[14]

That unity was shattered by the failure of the proletariat to fulfill its revolutionary role as the subject–object of history. As a consequence, the connection between fact and value collapsed. An erosion subsequently began with respect to that original sense of certainty which had simply rendered irrelevant questions about how to "ground" the theory, justify its scientific character, or articulate its ethical purpose. Critical theory in its various manifestations placed primacy on the role of the subject and "consciousness" in order to resurrect the sense of emancipatory purpose that the "dialectical" method presupposed. Its thinkers thus became interested in questions of alienation, cultural critique, psychological repression, and forms of state coercion. Interdisciplinary in approach, concerned with exploring how the mediated "totality" of advanced industrial society threatened the integrity of the individual, as well as the character of resistance, their explicit commitment to dialectical thought generally placed them outside the social scientific mainstream both in their particular concerns and in their self-conscious rejection of empiricism and positivism.[15]

The claim that the proponents of analytic or rational choice Marxism somehow continue this critical tradition is simply wrong. The normative moment vanishes from this thoroughly anti-idealist and anti-Hegelian standpoint. These thinkers do not place primacy on psychological repression, alienation, or cultural questions. What's more, in their attempt to confront the loss of teleological certainty through a commitment to (social) "science," like Louis Althusser, they actually expel the subject from the discourse even though, unlike him, they refuse to admit it or call the overarching criteria of science into question.[16] Preoccupying themselves with the "object," they generally choose to justify their inquiries in terms of mathematical or game theoretical criteria. As a consequence, they liquidate – more charitably, perhaps, simply presuppose – the normative purpose of the entire theoretical and practical enterprise.[17]

A strange situation results. If analytic and rational choice Marxism directly oppose the problematic of critical theory, they are still unable to confront the political implications of orthodoxy's teleological collapse. This is of particular importance since the very primacy placed upon the "object" as well as the conventional truth criteria of the social sciences, which have themselves been profoundly shaped by positivism and its offshoots, seem to create certain basic epistemological links with classical Marxism. Thus, in what would become an important article for the development of the new tendency, Adam Przeworski examined the theoretical implications within the work of Karl Kautsky.[18]

Though the actual influence of positivism on Marx is highly questionable,[19] its impact on his "orthodox" followers like Karl Kautsky is not. The "pope of Marxism" subsequently becomes crucial for determining the concerns of this new standpoint. Kautsky was probably the first to construct a Marxist anthropology which, in anticipation of Gerald Cohen, maintained that a confrontation with nature from the standpoint of scarcity lies at the root of social antagonism.[20] Though he clung to a basic economism, and certainly never anticipated the new developments in decision or game theory, Kautsky was also fundamentally preoccupied with establishing a discernible "objective" truth with respect to class interests that could essentially dispense with irrational or ideological concerns. Anticipating important figures of the new movement, Kautsky furthermore sought to provide *criteria* for judging an investigation's "scientific" character by emphasizing the need for determinations that might fit the prerequisites of instrumental rationality. No less than certain rational choice theorists, and in a manner totally inimical to the concerns of Western Marxism and critical theory, Kautsky and his contemporaries also began with the assumption that the "labor theory of value" is predicated on establishing the quantity of labor embodied in the commodities workers consume and produce even though he – in contrast to Cohen, Elster, and Roemer – did not see either the problems or contradictions which such a standpoint would engender.[21]

Of course, the differences between the new scientific tendency and the orthodox tradition are telling. There have been real contributions made by thinkers like Cohen, in clarifying the problems with Marx's discussion of forces and relations of production, Przeworski in analyzing the obstacles toward a socialist transition, Roemer in establishing a theory of exploitation that speaks to conditions where private property has putatively been abolished, or Elster on the question of democratic and trade union solidarity. At the same time, virtually all proponents of the new tendency reject teleology as well as the processive and determinate conception of class contradictions.[22] Most also seek to undercut the role "functionalist" tautologies play in Marxian analysis,[23] and eliminate the "privileged position" of the working class which endowed every traditional investigation with its unique normative standpoint and distinct political meaning. Nevertheless, the partisans of analytic or rational choice Marxism provide no point of reference to inform either a new political or cultural worldview.[24]

The "objectivist" and "scientistic" concerns of the past remain. But they are given a new twist. All political phenomena in general, and movements in particular, now become equalized through the mathematical or game theoretical laws in which they gain their definition as social actors. At best, the question of qualitative change is circumvented by claiming that various forms of exploitation are subsets of a general theory predicated on the refusal to acknowledge a "conditionally feasible alternative" under which the oppressed could lead more satisfactory lives.[25] Usually, however, all classes and political movements are identified with specific units of analysis which are treated in the same way. Their unique character, as well as the constitutive role of the

qualitatively different ideologies informing them, is subsequently eradicated. Uncritically accepting the "facts" as they are presented, as well as
the "values" of capitalist society that allow for their interpretative
formulation, the laws of the existing order become the immutable
foundation for "science" and what constitutes "rational" behavior.[26]

Interestingly enough, just like the metaphysicians it putatively seeks to
oppose, this new "Marxist" approach leaves the "object" of reality
untouched and closed to qualitative transformation. Marxism is thus
made palatable by eliminating the critical moment that makes it radical.
No development of the critical method takes place. Quite the contrary.
A far stronger connection emerges between analytic or rational choice
Marxism and American political science which, virtually from its
inception, took stability as the norm and found itself unable to explain
qualitative change.

Epistemology: Rational Choice and Methodological Individualism

Rejecting the idealist inheritance, modern scientific Marxists have clearly
decided to interpret Marx and socialist thought as a simple extension of
that materialism whose "bourgeois" roots lie in René Descartes, Thomas
Hobbes, John Locke, David Hume, and Jeremy Bentham. Though the
justification for such an interpretation has not been coherently argued, it
is enough that the influence of these thinkers has been channeled into the
various forms of thought which dominate contemporary social science.
Indeed, the ability of rational choice Marxism to enter the dominant
discourse is predicated on the willingness of its proponents to accept
these epistemological assumptions and so agree to adjudicate all theoretical claims by the standards of a "neutral" and "objective" (social)
science.

This standpoint is reflected in the attempt to fracture the Hegelian
concept of "totality." No longer is it seen as a dynamic "ensemble of
social relations" (Marx) whose particular interconnected "moments" are
qualitatively differentiated. Seeking to reaffirm the status of Marxism as
a science, in contrast to thinkers like Benjamin and Adorno, the
proponents of the new tendency interpret it as a system and render its
object mechanical. It only follows then that they should define Marx's
thought in terms of its contributions to distinct branches of knowledge
such as anthropology, economics, the philosophy of history, and
speculative theories concerning the future of society.[27] Given a certain
level of tolerance, in this way, Marxism emerges as a current within each

of the major disciplines and open to academic discussion. The whole is fractured and reifying assumptions are built into the procedure. No wonder that, from such a stance,[28] it becomes impossible to either thematize capitalist society with respect to its latent contradictions or inform an ongoing political practice.

Rejection of the Hegelian inheritance forces the proponents of rational choice Marxism to structure group interaction in ways which elict interests susceptible to purely instrumental formulation. This explains the emphasis on a fundamental "logic" of collective action wherein it can no longer be assumed that similarity breeds solidarity. This has led to the investigation of the "free-rider" problem and the differential costs of information as well as other game theoretical concerns. These fruits of rational choice have also been useful in exposing the various structural difficulties working class organizations *may* face in seeking to transform the given order.[29] In fact, *when viewed as a set of techniques,* rational choice can illuminate the barriers to class consciousness, the material interests of crucial actors, and the "objective" context of constraints in which particular decisions are made.[30] Analytic and rational choice Marxism thus help counteract a variety of mystifying theories, which tend to view movements in purely subjective terms or, on a more sophisticated plane, according to the more voluntarist interpretations advanced by social historians of the working class like E. P. Thompson or David Montgomery.

But, problems arise with the attempt to turn this middle-range set of techniques into a general theory. Particular facts only become such within a systemic framework of interpretation. According to certain important proponents of this new tendency, however, the framework is defined by ahistorical decisionist or game theoretical axioms. It thus becomes necessary to claim that all socio-political and economic actors are open to similar treatment within an environment "where its laws can be inspected without outside interference" (Lukács). Since such laws putatively apply to individuals just as easily as to groups, the comprehension of behavior by a collective can take place in exactly the same terms as that of its constituent elements. The "macro" is thus "grounded" within the "micro" analysis.

A commitment to "methodological individualism" is the logical next step.[31] All social phenomena are, from this standpoint, explicable from the standpoint of the "individuals" who engage in them so that any potential disparity between the general and the particular is resolved. Arguably then, along with the attack on all generalistic theories, methodological individualism will reinstate that very subject which collectivist theories have expelled.[32] Nevertheless, there is some serious confusion over what is meant by an "individual."

This initially becomes apparent in the formal claim – which does not move a step beyond Brentano and Husserl – that an individual is really nothing more than an "intentional person confronting causal forces within himself."[33] Such a predefined abstract entity is easily open to manipulation. Any actor exhibits intentions and, to this extent, the "subject" actually becomes nothing more than the irreducible element within a neo-classical equilibrium or game theory. Thus, the "subject" becomes open to redefinition in the form of a firm, a family, a state, and so on.[34]

This sleight of hand stems from the epistemological assumptions on which the method rests. These are intent on subordinating the "mediated totality" to the determination of causal relations between isolated particularities which, in turn, are then rendered equivalent. As a consequence, the rather elementary philosophical mistake is made of identifying the formally discrete entity with the subject and *individuation* with the *individuality* that actually defines the uniqueness and experience of a given actor or person.[35] Consequently, just like the older theories, these newer ones cannot deal with the constitutive role of ideology and or the qualitative differences between disparate actors in the putatively neutral framework they employ.

Since intentionality is never defined with any referance to the distinction between instrumental and speculative reason, it only follows that the motivations of such "individuals" should prove reducible to those "rational" interests which a given analytic or game theoretical framework deems acceptable. "Irrational" factors are either invalidated, presupposed, or – perhaps even worse – transvalued into instrumental ones. Analytic Marxism can naturally choose to ignore the dualism and, by conventionally defining itself as a science, reject all concerns with grounding the connection between micro and macro forms of analysis. But this would mean sacrificing the superiority of its claims and the criticism of other more ideological forms of Marxism.

Some analytic Marxists, of course, admit that the historical constitution of subjectivity is a concern worthy of attention.[36] But that only creates a new set of problems. The analysis of actions within an already constituted framework is after all, divorced from the analysis of how that framework was constituted.[37] Overcoming this problem is not easy. The new science can introduce the category of inter-subjectivity, but this would undermine every assumption involved in providing micro foundations for macro phenomena. Alternatively, of course, its definitions can receive ontological status in order to justify a game theoretic approach. But this will necessarily involve obliterating all qualitative distinctions between particulars and the unique character of their intentions. Analytical or rational choice Marxism, for all these reasons, is inherently unable to challenge the stuctural imbalance of power or invest the examination of social reality with a normative standpoint that might guide the formation of a radical politics.

Politics, in fact, becomes the forgotten word in this analytic discourse. Connecting general with particular forms of analysis is nothing new. Kant, Hegel, and Marx also subordinated the particular individual subject to an abstract epistemological or historical "subject." But they did not make the same mistake. The type of ethical indeterminacy plaguing analytic and rational choice Marxism was never a problem for them because the individual was seen as capable of normatively interacting with others in a changing objective reality. In the same vein, even the formal or abstract reconciliation of the "subject" with "objective" reality was conceived in terms of realizing those generalizable principles that would further enhance the possibilities of subjectivity and choice for each person. Thus, where Kant sought to link the choices of individuals to the progress of humanity and Hegel viewed the "rule of law" incarnated in the *Rechtsstaat* as defining the freedom of individual citizens, Marx formulated the speculative principle behind his new order of the future in such a way that "the free development of each is the condition for the free development of all."

But that is not the case with those thinkers who anticipated the epistemological assumptions of analytic and rational choice Marxism. These include Hobbes, whose "science" of politics rested on an epistemological egoism that placed primacy on survival; Hume, whose skepticism left only causality as the useful artificial construct for determining any possible truth; and Bentham, whose attempt to determine a "calculus of happiness" projects the concern of those rational choice theorists seeking to develop an ethical dimension for their enterprise by extending instrumental reason into the speculative realm.

Bound to their age, whatever the transcendent aspects of their thought, none of these philosophers concerned themselves with questions regarding the inter-subjective constitution of historical reality. Unconcerned with the equivalence of categories implicit within instrumental rationality, these thinkers did not think to epistemologically differentiate subject from object. The concept of inter-subjectivity was simply foreign to them. None was thus able to formulate what has since become common knowledge: inter-subjectivity is not reducible to the interaction of empirical subjects.

The refusal to countenance this possibility prevents many analytic Marxists from perceiving how cultural values undercut the primacy of economic rationality and manifest directly political implications. Also, thinkers as different as Husserl and Wittgenstein, Sahlins and Habermas, Freud and Bloch, all reached the conclusion that dealing with the sphere of symbolic interaction demands a notion of inter-subjectivity. There is a reason: all recognized that the *logic of cultural and ideological production and consumption is not reducible to instrumental rationality*.

Adam Przeworski, in this vein, is obviously correct when he writes that the actions of individuals cannot be mechanically derived from their class positions.[38] But, in claiming that Marx and other sociological theorists like Simmel or Durkheim cannot confront the problem, he misses the point: perhaps such a mechanistic reduction is impossible without violating the integrity of the subject or denying the unique character of historical action and the qualitatively different ways in which it becomes manifest. New Marxists, in this vein, attempt to analyze social reality with categories capable of explaining individual intentions and situations. They acknowledge that the sum of individual decisions produces a context in which the intent of individual actions becomes open to transformation.[39] But, even while they ignore the effect of rule-governed discourses on intentions, their decision to view such intentions axiomatically creates the conditions for ideological manipulation.[40]

Refusing to accept restrictions on the applicability of their middle range insights, most proponents of analytic or rational choice Marxism have not even seriously addressed the question of whether a (social) science actually needs the kind of "grounding" they seek to discover. The cost is high. Plunging into the dangerous waters of philosophical ontology, even the best thinkers of rational choice Marxism find themselves desperately grasping at an indeterminate entity – a subject that is not really a subject at all – whose motivations are imputed and then definitionally exhausted by an arbitrary mathematical game with fixed rules dependent upon a causality blind to issues of meaning, dignity, and the will to resist.

Instrumental Rationality and Political Life

"Political economy," from its very inception, was predicated on the ability of individuals to make "rational choices." Beginning with a capitalist market, and the historically conditioned inability to envision an alternative or non-exploitative mode of accumulation, its great classical exponents accorded primary emphasis to a rationality which assumed what was later termed "possessive individualism."[41] Presupposing a willingness to suspend normative, political, or long-term structural concerns, this form of rationality enabled actors to function in a world of competition by providing them with the tools to best maximize their short-term calculable economic interests.

Analytic and rational choice Marxists appropriated this most compelling aspect of political economy which recognized that people tend to act in accordance with the premises behind capitalist production in their everyday life. Accepting the assumptions of bourgeois life, they obviously tend to avoid questions regarding both the historical mutability of those socio-historical values the system seeks to render absolute as well as the critical need to *resist* them.[42] Indeed, this type of "bracketing" (Husserl) is actually the necessary prerequisite to make their actions comprehensible in game theoretical terms.

Assumptions about the trans-historical character of this "selfish" attitude remained virtually unquestioned by the most representative thinkers within the tradition of political economy. But, seeking to develop a "critique of political economy," Marx and most critical theorists refused to accept it as somehow trans-historically preordained. Instead, they saw this attitude as historically contingent and so, ultimately, as a choice rather than a necessity or an imperative.[43] It is in this way that the range of applicability for rational choice Marxism becomes apparent. The theory works to the extent that long-term normative and structural concerns are suspended in favor of short-term calculable gains and subjects choose to define themselves by the values of the "inverted world" of capitalism or, putting the matter somewhat differently, *the laws of the "object."*

Of course, certain proponents of the new tendency retain the dogmatic belief that normative and ideological goals will always be suspended and that the choices of *every* political actor are *always* open to definition according to calculable criteria – even though such a claim drastically oversimplifies reality and ignores the extent to which choices are made blindly or without adequate levels of information. Others, sensitive to such concerns, have attempted to discuss ethical norms in terms of "preferences"[44] – even though this really doesn't change matters and continues to sacrifice the historical specificity of those choices that were made. Some are willing to admit that historical "preference formation" is not susceptible to methodological individualism – even though the dualism resulting from such an admission necessarily undercuts claims about the general character of the theory. Still others emphasize that instrumentalism differs from altruism and seek to introduce a "broad notion of rationality"[45] – even though such a stance obliterates the ability to *qualitatively* distinguish between long-term and short-term, structural and incremental, incalculable and calculable, concerns and gains which underscored the power of rational choice in the first place; indeed, this last view only begs the question regarding the role of speculative rationality.[46]

A crisis thus emerges at the very heart of this new tendency and, as Adam Przeworski has recognized,[47] the simplest way out is to justify the primacy of self-interest on the basis of three pragmatic claims: 1) that the only conceptual alternative to self-interest as a foundation of analysis is altruism; 2) that strategic issues of rational choice such as "the free-rider problem" will not vanish even in an altruistic society; and 3) that the introduction of altruism will impede deductive analysis with regard to the central questions of the present. All these claims, however, are ultimately tautological.

The first merely resurrects the desire for a theory of human nature to underpin historical analysis. Here what in different ways Marx and Nietzsche both said of Bentham holds true for those who would appropriate his legacy: seeking human nature, they discover only the mind of the English shopkeeper. In reality, it is unnecessary to make a rigid or categorical choice between self-interest and altruism. The fact is that crucial historical events can have a normative component even if everyday activity is usually predicated on self-interest. The two can come together or fall apart. Analytically, then, the primacy of the one over the other is simply contingent on what events are being analyzed and how the terms are defined. Politically, furthermore, the issue is not simply whether people *are* "bad" or "good," but whether they *can* be good. If this suggests that the techniques of rational choice are relevant under certain circumstances, when people are "bad" or instrumentally calculable concerns are predominant, it is nevertheless precisely the existence of other conditions that analytic Marxism as a general theory refuses to entertain. Thus, the need for such an original choice *must* result and the decision *must* ultimately come down on the side of self-interest.

The second point pushes the discussion to a different level. It is certainly legitimate to argue that, even under a socialist or genuinely democratic order, "rationality traps" and concerns like the "free-rider" problem will not simply vanish. Once again, this merely says that people may suspend their ideological and structural interests in various everyday activities even under a new order. But, then, what makes a new order "new" can never be understood through purely formal and trans-historical categories anyway. It demands a perspective which can make qualitative distinctions and situate actions within precisely that thematized "ensemble of social relations" (Marx) which rational choice Marxists seek to fracture.

Of course, it is possible to redefine those qualitative concerns to make them meet the requirements of a formal model. But this only evades the issue, which becomes particularly evident insofar as Przeworski's last point contends that the introduction of altruism or various other norms would "impede" getting to the root of "central questions." Note that, from the outset, the assumption has already been made that the central questions are the ones which analytic and rational choice Marxism wish to ask. Indeed, given their commitment to the framework of mainstream social science, it only makes sense that they should fear introducing ethical concerns capable of rendering objective forms of inquiry "next to impossible."

But, so what? Perhaps violating historical reality and eliminating the normative dimension of social research is too high a price to pay. A theoretical perspective, which views the normative components of social action as impediments to research, will necessarily lose the texture of history as each moment turns into just another dot on a hypostatized time line. In fact, from the perspective of critical theory, the decision to squeeze qualitatively differentiated events into formal categories predicated on instrumental rationality necessarily flattens out the past even as it extinguishes the possibility for change in the future. Thus, the primacy accorded selfish attitudes becomes a self-fulfilling prophecy.

Reflecting their commitment to the truth criteria of the natural sciences, which quite legitimately allows for only a contemplation of the "object," the partisans of analytic and rational choice Marxism always find it difficult to deal with movements seeking to transform social reality. This is true even with respect to the bourgeoisie. "Possessive individualism," for example, may well describe the attitude of nascent capitalists seeking to fashion the world in their image. But, even assuming that those early bourgeois needed no normative or ideological self-justification for their revolutionary assault on the time-honored values and institutions of a religious universe, it does not suggest why that class should have been able to garner coalitional support from those it would exploit. Especially since its calculable short-term economic enticements to poorer allies were minor, the explanation of mass support for the bourgeoisie's struggle against the aristocracy necessarily demands reference to a set of normative values.[48] And these derive, not from contemplative materialism, but from the idealist tradition and the commitment to democracy.

Of course, it is possible to claim that normative "preferences" are basically no different from those *calculable* choices dictated by instrumental reason. A formal model can then be introduced to explain why people or organizations will make sacrifices for "irrational" goals which contradict their own immediate, short-term, tangible concerns.[49] Rational choice theory, however, was originally predicated on the assumption that individuals can discriminate between the tangible and certain benefits of short-term aims against the intangible and uncertain prospects of realizing long-term interests. That originally gave this theoretical stance its analytic power – a power which is liquidated once the distinction is surrendered.

Similarly, it is theoretically possible to distinguish between explaining normative motivations and providing a normative judgment. But, in practice, the explanation of a movement's ideological uniqueness itself calls for a judgment about what qualitatively distinguishes it – as well as the motivations of those who support it – from other movements. Ideology *can* color a *unique* perception of "objective" reality and so shatter those indeterminate assumptions of equivalence which underpin every game theoretical model. This is of particular importance since analytic Marxism assumes a fundamentally capitalist state of mind, while any number of movements have expressed values – whether theological, xenophobic, or anti-scientist – inimical to either a strictly bourgeois worldview or instrumental rationality. Mass movements are inherently infused with a speculative sense of purpose which differs qualitatively from one to another, and from this it only follows that a basic perversion of the historical understanding will take place when fascism is analyzed within the same game theoretical frame of reference as, say, the actions of those now nearly forgotten Chinese students in Tiananmen Square. Indeed, the refusal to delineate that difference or the ways in which divergent ideologies impact on the constitution of social reality will itself have political implications.

And it is simply impossible to "finesse" this issue. Reality becomes truncated, even as the multidimensional conditions for action are narrowed, when such issues are ignored in order to conform with the "abstract" requirements of a model. But that's not all. Beneath the learned analyses and the mathematical sophistication, a corrosive cynicism makes itself felt which undermines the need to consider the import of non-instrumental action or even articulate any particular set of ethical aims. In this way, especially when taken uncritically, rational choice Marxism turns the values of the existing logic of accumulation into a new set of "iron laws" which can only stifle future ideological or cultural attempts at building solidarity.

The collapse of Marxian teleology demands a new appreciation as well as a new investigation of the values which define the project of emancipation. Because the old guarantees are dead, a willingness to address the conditions for political judgment has become crucial. But, insofar as it denies the speculative moment, that is precisely what rational choice Marxism cannot do. Its back turned on the need to articulate any "practical criterion," which might inform socialist or progressive politics, the failure of this new trend in Marxism to serve as a critical philosophy is precisely what undermines its pretensions to provide a general theory.

Again, rational choice does have an important role to play. It would be absurd to ignore techniques which can help determine the obstacles threatening the realization of internationalist, egalitarian, and democratic aims. Neither from the perspective of rational choice or methodological individualism, however, is it possible to derive or justify a commitment to such concerns. Their insights and techniques thus only assume political value and substantive meaning within a broader social theory which can call the "inverted world" into question and foster the need to confront it. No matter how it might employ any set of mathematical techniques, such a critical theory with a positive intent presupposes an openness to the unfinished character of human experience as well the possibility of transforming existing attitudes and creating political arrangments that might better constrain the arbitrary exercise of power. Indeed, it is only with those values in mind that political choice becomes the choice for socialism, democracy, and freedom.

Notes

1　For a discussion concerning the emergence of "analytical Marxism" and its relation to "rational choice" Marxism, cf. Erik Olin Wright, "What is Analytical Marxism?" in *Socialist Review* vol. 19 no. 4 (1989), pp. 37ff.

2　Alan Carling, "Rational Choice Marxism," *New Left Review* 160 (November–December, 1986), p. 26.

3　A major philosopher of science put the matter bluntly and succinctly: "There is no compromise between science and speculative philosophy." Hans Reichenbach, *The Rise of Scientific Philosophy* (Berkeley, 1951), p. 73. In a similar vein, "the use of mathematical techniques can clarify relationships in an unambiguous way; without these techniques, only intuition can be a guide." John E. Roemer, *Analytical Foundations of Marxian Economic Theory* (Cambridge, 1981), p. 2. See also Jon Elster, *Sour Grapes: Studies in the Subversion of Rationality* (Cambridge, 1983), pp. 15–26, 33–42, 125–40, 157–66.

4　Its insights, in this way, can prove useful for critical theory. But without specifying conditions of applicability or taking into account the epistemological divide between them, their mutually exclusive truth criteria and their divergent aims, attempts at making good the "opportunity" of bringing the two together or stimulating a "productive conversation" can only prove superficial. Cf. John S. Dryzek, "How Far is it from Virginia and Rochester to Frankfurt? Public Choice as Critical Theory" in *British Journal of Political Science* vol. 22 (October, 1992), pp. 397ff; James Johnson, "Is Talk Really Cheap? Prompting Conversation Between Critical Theory and Rational Choice" in *American Political Science Review* vol. 87, no. 1 (March, 1993), pp. 74ff.

5　This narrowing becomes readily apparent in Andrew Levine, Elliot Sober, and Erik Olin Wright, "Marxism and Methodological Individualism," *New Left Review* 162 (March–April, 1987), pp. 67–84.

6　The realist conception of science, which most analytic and rational choice Marxists accept, seeks to identify the mechanisms generating empirical phenomena and opposes attempts to inductively discover truths concerning these mechanisms from empirical facts themselves; cf. Wright, "What is Analytical Marxism?," p. 40–1.

7   Note the discussion by Julius Braunthal, *History of the International 1864–1914* trans. Henry Collins and Kenneth Mitchell (New York, 1967), pp. 265–71.

8   Untranslatable except through an artificial word like "sublation," the *Aufhebung* of a stage involves its abolition, retention, and transcendence by the next. It is usually forgotten, however, that Hegel saw this "sublation" as interconnected with the teleological development of "reason," whose most essential purpose was the extension and fulfillment of freedom. Cf. Herbert Marcuse, *Reason and Revolution: Hegel and the Rise of Social Theory* (Boston, 1960), p. 9.

9   Originally written in 1845, and first published by Engels in 1888, the very first of the *Eleven Theses on Feuerbach* makes this clear. There Marx writes: "The chief defect of all existing materialism (including Feuerbach's) is that the object, actuality, sensuousness is conceived only in the form of *the object or perception (Anschauung)* but not as *sensuous human activity, practice [praxis]*, not subjectively. Hence in opposition to materialism the active side was developed by idealism – but only abstractly since idealism naturally does not know actual, sensuous activity as such." Karl Marx, *Writings of the Young Marx on Philosophy and Society*, eds Loyd D. Easton and Kurt H. Guddat (New York, 1967), p. 400.

10   This pits Marxist materialism against traditional notions of ontology. Cf. Alfred Schmidt, *The Concept of Nature in Marx* trans. Ben Fowkes (London, 1962), pp. 19ff. and 76ff.

11   This position, best argued by Gerald Cohen, is confronted once scarcity is seen as a construct of modernity. Identified with ongoing acquisition, in a society dominated by wealth rather than status derived from birth, scarcity becomes part of a disenchanted world. Part of the problem, of course, involves how the term is understood and whether it is reducible to game theoretical formulation. Nevertheless, even taking the term in the instrumental sense while granting its historical construction, it is still not the primary category in all forms of modern social activity. See Gerald Cohen, *Karl Marx's Theory of History: A Defence* (Princeton, 1978); also, Nicholas Xenos, *Scarcity and Modernity* (New York, 1989).

12   Scarcity can be defined in political terms as the continuing dependence of political on economic power. But, even in economic terms the concept contains a contingent, historical element which cannot simply be eliminated in order to justify a hypostatized abstraction. That is the real point behind the famous statement that "hunger is hunger, but the hunger gratified by cooked meat eaten with a knife and fork is a different hunger from that which bolts down raw meat with the aid of hand, nail, and tooth." From this it only follows that there are

"characteristics which all stages of production have in common, and which are established as general ones by the mind; but the so-called general preconditions of all production are nothing more than these abstract moments with which no real historical stage of production can be grasped." Karl Marx, *The Grundrisse: Introduction to the Critique of Political Economy* trans. Martin Nicolaus (New York, 1973), pp. 88, 92.

13 See the excellent discussion by Ellen Meiskins Wood, "Rational Choice Marxism: Is the Game Worth the Candle?" in New Left Review 177 (September–October, 1989), pp. 59ff.

14 Cf. Henry Pachter, "The Idea of Progress in Marxism" in *Socialism in History : Political Essays of Henry Pachter* ed. Stephen Eric Bronner (New York, 1984), pp. 65ff.

15 Cf. Theodor W. Adorno et al. *The Positivist Dispute in German Sociology* trans. Glyn Adey and David Frisby (New York, 1976).

16 For Althusser's own view of Marxism as a science, cf. Louis Althusser, *For Marx* trans. Ben Brewster (New York, 1970), pp. 87ff; 153ff; also, Louis Althusser and Etienne Balibar, *Reading Capital* trans. Ben Brewster (London, 1970), pp. 11–81, 119–94.

17 According to the many proponents of rational choice, "normative" usually connotes nothing more than a conditional or provisional judgment dealing with the enactment of pre-existing rules. This excludes the possibility of developing an ethical framework which would inform an inquiry and provide it with meaning and purposive aims. Though he does not draw the implications of this problem for a radical social theory, a fine discussion of the issue is presented by Timothy W. Luke, "Reason and Rationality in Rational Choice Theory," in *Social Research* vol. 52, no. 1 (Spring 1985), pp. 79–97.

18 Cf. Adam Przeworski, "Proletariat into a Class: The Process of Class Formation from Karl Kautsky's *The Class Struggle* to Recent Controversies" in *Politics and Society* vol. 7, no. 4 (1977).

19 Even in his later period, for example, a major commentator on Marx like Karl Korsch could reject the claim that Comte and the positivist school exerted any serious influence on the author of *Kapital*. So too, in a somewhat less satisfactory vein, even an important critical theorist like Albrecht Wellmer is content to claim that Marx's theory of history expresses only a "latent positivism." Cf. Karl Korsch, Karl Marx (New York, 1938), pp. 17–23; Albrecht Wellmer, *Critical Theory of Society* trans. John Cumming (New York, 1974), pp. 67ff.

20 Cf. Karl Kautsky, *Ethik und materialistische Geschichtsauffassung* (Stuttgart, 1906).

21 A quite well-known interpretation of Marx's theory of value – which is crucial to the tradition of "Western Marxism" – does not begin with either quantitative or instrumentalist assumptions. Unfortunately, however, it is common knowledge that this alternative tendency has never been directly confronted by the most important proponents of rational

choice Marxism. Cf. I. I. Rubin, *Essays on Marx's Theory of Value*, trans. Milos Samardzija and Fredy Perlman (Montreal, 1973); Roman Rosdolsky, *The Making of Marx's Capital*, trans. Pete Burgess (London, 1971); Paul Mattick, *Marxism: Last Refuge of the Bourgeoisie?* ed. Paul Mattick, Jr, (Armonk, NY., 1983), pp. 10–133; Lucio Colletti, "Bernstein and the Marxism of the Second International," in *From Rousseau to Lenin: Studies in Ideology and Society* trans. John Merrington and Judith White (London, 1972), pp. 45ff.

22 "Contradiction" is often actually redefined to favor a static and indeterminate notion akin to traditional sociological views of "conflict." This can easily result in the following approach to the issue: "The *economic notion of collective rationality* implies that people, by individually rational actions, bring about an outcome that is good for all, or at least not bad for all. Failure of such collective rationality may occur in one of the three ways best described: by isolation, by perverse interaction structures, and by lack of information. Elsewhere I have referred to such failures as 'social contradictions.' The *political notion of collective rationality* implies that people by concerted action are able to overcome these contradictions." Elster, *Sour Grapes*, p. 29.

23 Despite the spirited defense of "functionalism" by Gerald Cohen, the analytic critique made by Roemer and Elster is compelling. According to the latter two thinkers, functionalism exhibits a tendency to impute the "necessity" of a given phenomenon to the reproduction of a system without exposing the "mechanism" which justifies such a claim. The belief that a capitalist "system must have crises, because crisis is necessary for capitalist demise" or that educational institutions "necessarily" act in the interests of the dominant class exemplify the problems with this type of thinking. It is in overcoming such tautologies that the new linkage between the general and the particular is seen as assuming such importance. See Gerald Cohen, *Karl Marx's Theory of History*; also see his "Forces and Relations of Production," in *Analytical Marxism* ed. John Roemer (Cambridge, 1986) pp. 11–22. For the critique, see Roemer, *Analytical Foundations*, pp. 8–9. See also Jon Elster, "Further Thoughts on Marxism, Functionalism, and Game Theory," in *Analytical Marxism* pp. 202–20.

24 Here, the philosophical problem is often confused. John Roemer, for example, fully recognizes the need for a normative interest in class struggle in order to appreciate the explanatory insights of his labor theory of exploitation which seeks to present socialism as superior to capitalism. Nevertheless, if the quest is for a general theory, that normative interest must derive immanently from the central categories employed by the overriding framework. Roemer, *Analytical Foundations*, pp. 146–61; for a critique, see Wood, "Rational Choice Marxism," pp. 75ff.

25 See John Roemer, "New Directions in the Marxian Theory of Exploitation and Class" in *Analytical Marxism*, pp. 103, 109ff.

26 See Georg Lukács, *History and Class Consciousness: Studies in Marxist Dialectics* trans. Rodney Livingstone (Cambridge, Mass., 1971), pp. 5ff.

27 See G. A. Cohen, "Reconsidering Historical Materialism" in *Nomos* 26 (1983).

28 The standpoint is, of course, not at all new. The attempt to reduce a coherent and integrated view of the totality into the sum of its component parts, with respect to the various disciplines of social scientific knowledge, was already criticized in 1923 by Karl Korsch, *Marxism and Philosophy* trans. Fred Halliday (London, 1970), pp. 52–7.

29 Adam Przeworski, "Material Interests, Class Compromise, and the Transition to Socialism" in Roemer, *Analytical Marxism*, pp. 162–88.

30 See Joshua Cohen and Joel Rogers, *On Democracy: Toward a Transformation of American Society* (New York, 1983), pp. 47–87.

31 Jon Elster, *Making Sense of Marx* (Cambridge, 1985), pp. 5ff.

32 Carling, "Rational Choice Marxism," p. 28.

33 See Jon Elster, Introduction to *The Multiple Self* ed. Jon Elster (Cambridge, 1986), p. 31.

34 Duncan Foley, "Review: Making Sense of Marx by Jon Elster" in *Journal of Economic Literature* 25 (June, 1987), pp. 749–50.

35 This is a problem with all post-Hegelian ontological formulations and, ironically, becomes particularly evident in that tradition of existential phenomenology from which rational choice Marxists obviously wish to distance themselves. See Theodor W. Adorno, *The Jargon of Authenticity*, trans. Knut Tarnowski and Frederic Will (London, 1973).

36 See Adam Przeworski, "Marxism and Rational Choice" in *Politics and Society* vol. 14, no. 4 (1985), pp. 381ff, and 401.

37 Recognizing the need for a theory of ideology formation, Roemer unfortunately misses this point as well as the role of "mediation" in the constitution of subjectivity. What remains is a formal and indeterminate abstraction which, while relying on causality, is content to claim that "culture chooses a person's preferences for him. But culture can be understood as ideology, and if there are rational foundations for ideology (as I mentioned earlier) then the process of endogenous preference formation can be seen as a rational choice. The social formation of the individual can be explained while at the same time requiring that society be understood as the consequence of many individuals' action." John Roemer, "'Rational Choice' Marxism: Some Issues of Method and Substance," in *Analytical Marxism*, p. 199. Interestingly enough, for all the attention usually paid by Elster and Przeworski to Sartre, on this most crucial matter his redefinition of the entire problem in the biographies of first Genet and then Flaubert goes totally unnoticed. On the methodological issue, see Jean-Paul Sartre, *Search for a Method* trans. Hazel E. Barnes (New York, 1963), pp. 35–166.

38 Here, it is useful to consider that Roemer seeks to resolve the problem with the theorem (rather than the postulate) that "individuals act as

members of a class rather than as individuals." Roemer, *Analytic Foundations*, p. 7.

39 The social formulation of preferences can then diverge from the individual preferences on which it putatively rests. If that is the case, however, it might well follow that certain preferences enter the process and so contravene the dictates of formal rationality – which might actually prove useful in defining the role of ideology and politics. See Kenneth Arrow, *Social Choice and Individual Values* (New Haven, 1963).

40 Note the argument by Mark Warren, "Marx and Methodological Individualism" in *Philosophy and Social Science* 18 (1988), pp. 447–76.

41 Cf. C. B. Macpherson, *The Political Theory of Possessive Individualism: Hobbes to Locke* (Oxford, 1962).

42 The result is that "precommitment" discussed by Jon Elster, *Ulysses and the Sirens: Studies in Rationality and Irrationality* (London, 1979), pp. 37ff;

43 Cohen and Rogers, *On Democracy*, pp. 145ff.

44 Interestingly enough, it has generally not been Marxists, but rather left liberal exponents of rational choice who have sought to transcend egoistic desires and construct an ethic on the basis of "meta-preferences" or "primary" wants such as the commitment to community, family, ideals, etc. Unfortunately, however, the ahistorical standpoint remains along with the subsequent inability to determine qualitative differences between differing ideologies from within the new models. See eds Amatyra Sen and Bernard Williams, *Utilitarianism and Beyond* (Cambridge, 1982).

45 So long as a concept remains purely formal, an equivalence between individuated elements occurs that necessarily subverts *qualitative* differences of normative and historical content. That is what undercuts the attempt to supplant the reliance on self-interest with a type of utilitarian thermometer which "may go down as a result of an increase in other people's consumption (as in envy) or it may go up (as in altruism)." Elster, *Ulysses and the Sirens*, p. 141.

46 Ibid., p. 146.

47 Przeworski, "Marxism and Rational Choice," p. 386.

48 The complex relation is subsequently destroyed between the "objective" reality of socio-political life and the "subjective" motivations that were moments in its constitution. What is true for the revolutionary bourgeoisie holds equally for the partisans of Stalinism or any other mass movement. In fact, here, the words of a controversial historian of Germany in the 1920s – influenced by Marxian political economy as well as rational choice – are quite telling: "the dominant economic classes were aligned with the Nazi party, but that coalition was not their first choice; they entered into it because other solutions over which they would have had more direct control did not work. We leave aside the question of how the Nazi party became as strong as it did: those who voted for or joined it did so primarily for reasons other than those which led to its successful assumption of power." David Abraham, *The

Collapse of the Weimar Republic : Political Economy and Crisis 2nd edition (New York, 1986) p. 276.

49 "The power of an ideology (in the Marxist sense of the term, not in the trivial meaning assigned to it by pragmatism) is measured by the degree to which it raises men above themselves, gives them a sense of purpose, drives them to sacrifice themselves for what they conceive to be the greater good." George Lichtheim, "From Lenin to Mao Tse-Tung," in *Collected Essays* (New York, 1973), p. 262.

14

Jürgen Habermas and the Language of Politics

Critical theory has received a new and powerful formulation from, unquestionably, the most encyclopedic and prolific thinker of the postwar period: Jürgen Habermas. A student of Max Horkheimer and Theodor Adorno, who was born in 1929, he grew up under the Nazi regime and experienced the economic dislocation of reconstruction. It is thus little wonder that he was never much attracted by particularist criticisms of reason and science. There was never much room in his thought for Nietzsche. His writings were – from the very first – always firmly anchored within the tradition of Kant, Hegel, and Marx. They are often esoteric and burdened with an unnecessarily cumbersome style. Nevertheless, those who would suggest that this renders him relevant only to a small group of academics are sorely mistaken.

Habermas has become an exemplary public intellectual.[1] He has taken a position on the major issues of the time: calling for more democracy in the educational system, dealing with student protests,[2] confronting those conservatives who considered it time to wash their hands of the Nazi past in the *Historikerstreit*,[3] challenging the postmodernist advocates of relativism and experientialism, championing the contributions of the welfare state, opposing the deployment of nuclear missiles in Germany, warning against the easy optimism generated by the prospect of reunifying his country, expressing his uncertainty while supporting the war in the Persian Gulf, and rejecting the new nationalism in the name of a "constitutional patriotism" (*Verfassungspatriotismus*). The fact is that his political convictions have remained constant beyond any changes his philosophy has undergone. Nevertheless, for all the scholarly controversy his work has produced, too rarely has it been observed that Jürgen Habermas has become *the* great exponent of political liberalism in Germany.

His understanding of socialism is indebted to this tradition and the "unfinished" character of the enlightenment enterprise. Practical commitments of a political nature underpin his theory from the early works to the "linguistic turn" and "postmetaphysical" elaboration of his "discourse ethics" in his most recent efforts. A concern with the "legitimation" of the state, the rational adjudication of grievances, the public role of language, and the unfettered use of reason explain his well-founded mistrust of postmodernism. It also provides an insight into his preoccupation with providing a positive foundation for the normative claims of critical theory.

Habermas has not completely broken with its original tenets. He remains committed to reflexivity, the critique of reification, and the "emancipation" of individuals from all forms of domination. There is also no denying, however, that he has pointed critical theory in a new direction. Habermas has given it a new democratic impulse by fusing it with American pragmatism and linguistic philosophy. He has solidified its connection with liberalism and insisted upon its becoming more "reconstructive" and sensitive to the requirements of social scientific validation. But there is some question whether the original enterprise has been narrowed or, putting the matter somewhat differently, whether its critical character has been undermined. Indeed, the penchant for procedural and systematic thinking often works to the disadvantage of his emancipatory objectives.

Criticism has been directed against Habermas from almost every academic angle. The champions of orthodoxy wrote him off long ago. Habermas may have originally sought to develop an immanent "reconstruction" of historical materialism, but it is legitimate to ask whether especially his more recent forays into language philosophy have gutted the earlier attempt.[4] But, of course, Habermas remains a man of the Left. Conservatives have castigated him unmercifully. He has also been the target of postmodernists and attacked by the advocates of "identity politics," uncritical defenders of the new social movements, and communitarians. Nevertheless, substantive political criticisms have rarely been brought to bear and the preoccupation with "unrestrained" discourse has usually been accepted at face value.

Attacks on Habermas have too often centered around purely technical matters and, even when questions of social theory come into play, their explicitly political character is never brought to the forefront.[5] The problem is not, for example, that Habermas refuses to consider labor the source of all value. Nor is it the willingness of his theory to call for communication and reciprocal respect among the members of diverse groups or employ the power of critique against the fetish with tradition. It is also unfair to condemn his theory, which recognizes the danger of equating the communicative infrastructure of possible modes of existence with a single "best" form,[6] for "totalizing" ambitions or the manner in which it privileges the "intellect" and the power of the word; "as if," remembering the words of Thomas Mann, "there were the slightest danger of too much intellectualism on earth."[7]

Very different issues are at stake. There is the refusal of his democratic theory to confront the differentiated impact of the accumulation process and its inability to pierce the insular institutional sub-systems of an increasingly complex society. There are the suspect claims concerning the "postmetaphysical" character of the new linguistic philosophy;[8] its inability to move outside an anthropological framework and provide any principles of "historical specification" (Korsch) and its attempts to substitute an abstract vision of moral evolution for a philosophy of history and a theory of society. There is the paralysis of discourse ethics when forced to confront questions concerning mass mobilization, the role of violence, the structural imbalance of power, and the predominant influence exercised by intractable interests. There is the unwillingness to face the fact that its effectiveness depends upon the prior institutional realization of its liberal assumptions.

Habermas is a brilliant theorist of liberal democracy. But whether his democratic standpoint any longer offers anything more radical, let alone, socialist is questionable and to that extent a certain undermining of the critical character of critical theory has taken place. Especially criticism in the United States, however, has ignored issues of this sort. Perhaps this reflects the timidity of the academic Left, the withering of the radical imagination, in the wake of the communist collapse and the conservative triumph of the 1980s. The euphoria on the Right, however, is now beginning to fade and the time for defensiveness has passed. A certain boldness is becoming increasingly necessary.

Before the Turn

The Structural Transformation of the Public Sphere was Habermas's first book. The "public sphere" was seen as mediating between the state and the economic forces of civil society. Its components range from the free press to the town meeting, from the family to salons, from the educational system and the cheap production of books to the liberal assumptions underpinning an open exchange of views.[9] The public sphere emerged from the humanistic tendencies of the Renaissance and became part of the bourgeois response against feudalism and its hierarchy. It presupposes equality and the ability to employ "common sense" on the part of the "common man." The public sphere is the arena in which civil liberties are put into practice; its viability is the real proof of a democratic order. Indeed, with its emphasis upon free speech and universal values, the public sphere becomes the sociological starting point for what would ultimately become a philosophical preoccupation with the role of discourse in advanced industrial society.

The study was written as a habilitation. It is indebted to *Dialectic of Enlightenment* and the Marxian method.[10] The work emphasizes the increasing power of instrumental reason and the commodity form in undermining social conditions capable of protecting the individual from the arbitrary power exercised by regimes still wavering between monarchy and republicanism. The decline of the public sphere, which was marked by the growing identification between "public opinion" and "publicity,"[11] evidenced the inability of liberalism to contest the substantive impact of the commodity form. Horkheimer and Adorno were suspicious of its pretensions from the beginning and essentially maintained that "only the word coined by commerce" can prove familiar to the mass of the populace;[12] communication is thus essentially conflated with what is produced by the commodity form.

Habermas also recognized the dangers for communication implicit in the commodification process. But he was interested in contesting reification with more than "impotent rage."[13] Habermas juxtaposed the unrealized promise of liberalism against the rather gloomy implications of an increasingly centralized cultural apparatus for a present just emerging from Nazism, still burdened by Stalin, and rife with neofascist impulses. But, where his mentors were obsessed with the subjectivity of the subject, Habermas was concerned with the subject under the liberal rule of law and the possibilities of what he would later call "democratic will formation." An altered public sphere might yet contest the march of instrumental reason through "reorganization of social and political power under the mutual control of rival organizations committed to the public sphere in their internal structure as well as in their relations with the state and each other."[14]

Habermas had a different background than the original advocates of critical theory. He was the first to have grown up under a totalitarian regime. He was also the first whose work was framed by the postwar experience in a country which lacked the resistance tradition of France or Italy, and wherein Marxism was basically identified with the German Democratic Republic. It only makes sense that Habermas should have been far more "circumspect" than the early members of the Institute in appropriating even the most radical strands of Western Marxism and more inclined to take the liberal tradition seriously.[15]

The Weimar Republic, was widely known as "the republic without republicans," and suffered the consequences. Attitudes among citizens, or better what Pierre Bourdieu would call their "habitus," seemed not very different in the postwar reconstruction with its "unmastered past" (*unbewältigte Vergangenheit*). Even academics tainted by the Nazi experience like Arnold Gehlen and Martin Heidegger who helped shape his early development,[16] no less than Ernst Rothacker and Oskar Becker who had been his first teachers, refused to engage in a political and philosophical self-criticism.[17] Thus, for Habermas, the political point was to secure criticism as a moral imperative extending beyond mere self-interest.

But with the introduction of mass media, and the generation of consensus from the top down rather than through the discursive engagement of participants, the public sphere was increasingly becoming defined by the same forms of instrumental reason exhibited in the state and the economy. Its mediating character was becoming lost, its ability to project systemic criticism was becoming rationalized, through the transformation of the public sphere into institutions buttressing the existing order. A concern with counteracting this development explains the later support extended by Habermas to the "new social movements" of the 1960s and the "sub-institutional" changes in everyday life demanded by them no less than their ability to turn previously "private" issues ranging from discrimination to incest into matters of "public" concern.[18] Indeed, the belief in rationalizing power through public discussion as well as the tension between "system" and "life–world" are rooted in the concept of the public sphere.

Habermas recognized that the high point of the public sphere lay in the eighteenth century when the bourgeoisie was on the rise. He knew that it was impossible to turn back. Of importance were thus the normative underpinnings of the concept rather than the public sphere itself. The bourgeois public sphere received emancipatory definition insofar as debate took place without regard to rank and "in accord with universal rules;" its participants produced the idea of a "common" humanity in the "implicit law of the parity of all cultivated persons" even as they rejected any authority beside that of the "better argument." Consensus, achieved even from a class interest, was capable of generating a universal interest.[19]

An increasingly instrumental use of language, however, was now threatening the suppositions which had rendered this possible. The occupation of the public sphere by the non-propertied led to the increasing interconnection between state and society, which essentially eradicated the bourgeois public sphere without supplying a new one.[20] The new task was to preserve reflexivity and maintain the conditions for discourse; indeed, with the sociological constriction of the public sphere, such an undertaking could only proceed from the standpoint of "critical philosophy." Epistemology would secure in thought what practice was destroying in action. *Knowledge and Human Interests* thus sought to justify the move from "traditional" to "critical" theory.

Habermas wished to provide a new foundation for the emancipatory norms of critical theory by using the "critique of ideology" (*Ideologie-kritik*) to explore the hidden relation between theory and practice or knowledge and interest. Just as it was necessary to preserve the promise of liberalism from what liberal society had become, however, so was it necessary to employ ideology-critique against its "dissolution" first into the philosophy of history and then, more completely, into the neutral methodology of positivism and empiricism as advocated by Auguste Comte and Ernst Mach. Simply relying on historicism, according to Habermas, makes dialectical thinking as guilty as traditional theory of liquidating an "interest in reason."[21] "Historically oriented" sociological criticism must now step back behind the teleological subsumption of epistemology by Hegel and Marx in order to retrieve the insights of Kant.

A rejection of teleology and "stages of reflection" takes place. Habermas, in fact, recognizes that the attempts by positivists to reduce the theory of knowledge to the philosophy of science was interrupted by Charles Peirce and Wilhelm Dilthey who sought to defend the self-reflexive character of knowledge from the ambitions of the "natural" and "cultural" sciences. Each after his fashion begged the question concerning the "knowledge-constitutive" interest in inquiry. Neither was aware of the manner in which his methodology reflected the assumptions of "science" or the importance of defining the point at which knowledge and interest conjoin. Thus, reconstructing a "buried hermeneutic dimension," Habermas sought to emphasize that every form of knowledge with a human interest must concern itself less with "facts" than "statements about facts."[22]

His purpose was to specify the relation between theory and practice by exploring the relation between the human species as the self-constituting subject of knowledge and the interest in knowledge itself as constituted by the objective needs derived from such an enterprise.[23] The "systematic intention" of his work becomes apparent in the delineation of three different anthropological forms of interest. The first, which arises from the interaction with nature, involves prediction and control through "monological" knowledge; the second, which produces historical and hermeneutical forms of knowledge, rests on the need for consensual understanding without which cooperative work becomes impossible; while the third form of emancipatory knowledge, which involves the ability to question previous assumptions, derives from the interest in learning and becoming free from coercively induced forms of dependency.[24]

Each of these needs is always open to linguistic interpretation and symbolically affixed to potential actions.[25] They retain a social character even as they express cognitive desires. Habermas thus draws a radical separation between symbolic interaction and instrumental activity, or work. He may not have been clear about how to reunite them, but their existence was never meant to reflect a Kantian divorce between "practical" and "pure" reason. Habermas was as critical of idealist attempts to divorce symbolic action from social reality as of Marxist attempts to reduce symbolic action to labor;[26] indeed, *Knowledge and Human Interests* and *Theory and Practice* both express a marked sympathy for Fichte who rendered reason immediately practical in the original self-reflection of the subject on its own activity.[27]

Habermas defined the three variants of interest as "quasi-transcendental" insofar as each presupposed a life context in which cognition is situated.[28] The concept of interest thus becomes a "bridge" between the constitutive context of knowledge and the alternative forms its application can take.[29] Illuminating its normative content, however, involves moving from the "monological" discourse of science to "communicative competence" along with the norms it presupposes. The critical theory of society, in contrast to traditional thinking, will thus incorporate an emancipatory interest in knowledge beyond its mere practical application and employ reflexivity in order to decide how any given interest fosters autonomy. An inherently reflexive "interest in reason" contests the ways language is employed to create unrecognized forms of dependency and justify interests in domination. Coming to terms with "distorted" forms of communication is thus possible only by positing an "undistorted" mode of communication.

Psychoanalysis is a case in point.[30] Through this dialogic method, which presupposes an analyst devoid of personal interest in the outcome and an analysand willing to treat his own concerns objectively, a common interest in furthering the autonomy of the subject presents itself through self-reflection.[31] Insofar as autonomy is the goal of self-reflection, however, the "meaning of knowledge, and thus the criterion for its autonomy as well, cannot be accounted for without recourse to a connection with interest in general."[32] Any rational justification for autonomy necessarily presupposes such a connection since, without reference to the concept of reciprocity, it turns into license and the arbitrary exercise of power; indeed, from the standpoint of philosophical rationalism and political liberalism, this is precisely what reason seeks to constrain. The critique of ideology, for this reason, can "identify the normative power built into the institutional system of a society only if it starts from the model of the suppression of generalizable interests and compares normative structures existing at a given time with the hypothetical state of a system of norms formed, *ceteris paribus*, discursively."[33]

Habermas ignores how the self-interest of the analysand in relieving suffering, which every analyst consciously employs, is coherently connected with an objective rendering of his or her problems. This unnecessary divorce of interest from reflection will continue to inform his theory. Already in this early work, however, Habermas finds the root of critique no less than its object within language. Even "legitimacy" is already defined in terms of the validity accorded the claims of justice offered by any given political order.[34] Knowledge must subsequently serve as an instrument for an ongoing practice and prove capable of calling that practice into question, which suggests that it must retain the quality of formal transcendence; indeed, from the standpoint of practical discourse, democracy is unique precisely insofar as its "formal properties of justification themselves obtain legitimating force."[35] Knowledge and interest, from the perspective of self-reflection, thus become unified. But this can only occur as a historical process and, for this reason, the transcendental subject must dissolve into the natural history of the human species. Thus, the unity of knowledge and interest will become manifest in the linguistic reconstruction of what has been historically suppressed.[36]

Insofar as reason is embedded in the natural history of the human species, however, Habermas finds himself with an indeterminate foundation for the philosophy of history and a contingent justification for rationality. The connection between theory and practice remains suspect. The "philosophy of consciousness," which presupposes a subject mechanically confronting an object, cannot overcome the gap between simply positing discursive norms or generalizable interests and viewing them as empirically constructed. Nor is Habermas able to bridge the gap. For example, within the framework of *Knowledge and Human Interests*, reflection must simultaneously exist as a value-neutral determinant of thinking and as a value-laden ability to illuminate what has been suppressed. Nor does identifying interests as "quasi-transcendental" help matters; it only leaves them stranded between serving as transcendental conditions for knowledge as such, which are value-neutral, and appearing as value-laden expressions of empirical action.[37]

Habermas came to the conclusion that overcoming these inadequacies would demand a new "phenomenology of the moral domain" capable of encompassing the rigid division between instrumental and speculative reason while surmounting the need for what some came to consider an artificially created tripartite analysis of "interest."[38] Embedding a general theory of rationality in language thus became the object of construction. The philosophy of language might ultimately become epistemology by other means, but it would none the less emphasize the forms of utterance actually taken by communication in order to connect theory with practice.[39] Without reducing norms to prescriptive decisions, while seeking to elucidate both the general presuppositions of discourse along with the way in which language contributes to the reproduction of social life,[40] Habermas would subsequently concentrate on the "performative" aspect of language.[41] Pragmatism might thus yield important insights and, in developing a "universal pragmatics," Habermas believed he would finally uncover the "ground" for freedom, truth, and justice in the very structure of communication.

An Excursus on Pragmatism

The appropriation of pragmatism for the critical project by Habermas – and Karl-Otto Apel – marks probably the first time that major proponents of critical theory looked away from Europe for genuine philosophical inspiration. It was believed that pragmatism, unreservedly condemned for its utilitarian and decisionist impulses by Max Horkheimer, might prove valuable for problems connected with justifying the values of critical theory. Nevertheless, the new use of this uniquely American philosophy has actually perpetuated the very form of sterile academic theorizing that its major representatives sought to combat.

Pragmatism was originally an assault on metaphysics and the various forms of what Marx would have called "vulgar" materialism. It sought to dispense with metaphysical disputation, streamline concepts, and make philosophy participate in the world of action. Concepts like the consensual "community of investigators" postulated by Charles Peirce were embraced by Habermas. But this was done in the name of a discourse ethics encumbered by a seemingly endless set of subtle categorical distinctions, which could stand a cut from Occam's razor, and a standpoint incapable of dealing with strategic problems. Indeed, whatever the "postmetaphysical" claims, pragmatism was employed for the purpose of fashioning what is actually little more than a metatheory.

This has led Habermas and Apel, in turn, to ignore both the most progressive strain within pragmatism along with its most severe weakness. Pragmatism is seen as somehow mirroring the type of "ameliorism" supposedly indicative of the American experience, which is why

Habermas called it the "radical democratic" offshoot of Hegelianism. Such a view, however, somewhat exaggerates the pragmatist commitment to change; it forgets that the saying "if it ain't broke don't fix it" is as much in accord with the practical thrust of pragmatism as the call for change. The progressive commitments of men like Charles Peirce, William James, George Herbert Mead, and John Dewey were actually less a matter of "philosophy" than of the fact that they were fundamentally decent men with liberal instincts and an expansive intelligence seeking new combinations of communitarianism and individualism. But more conservative theorists like Sidney Hook, who studied with Karl Korsch and embraced the work of Dewey, could also employ the insights of pragmatism and its admirers in Europe included Henri Bergson and Mussolini.

Pragmatism habors vitalist and utilitarian components. Its major representatives were content to assume a liberal milieu and, for this very reason, could forthrightly embrace elements of the decisionism so understandably feared by the modern continental advocates of discourse ethics. There are important differences, of course, between them. The contrast between the philosophy of Charles Peirce and William James is particularly well known. But the "pragmaticism" of the former was never rigidly divorced from the "experientialism" of his friend with its criteria of "usefulness" and the "vital good." Even the architect of semiotic transcendentalism, in contrast to Habermas and Apel, ultimately believed that the conception of an object depends upon the clarification of its practical "effects."

Pragmatism is based on experience. The notions of consensus and participation offered by John Dewey were predicated not on categorical preconditions of language like the "life–world," but on the vision of face-to-face interactions by of citizens in the equivalents of those New England "town meetings" so well described by Tocqueville. Pragmatism never had much use for *a priori* constructs. It derived from a critique of Kant, which sought to overcome traditional dualisms like those posited by Habermas between truth and justice or theory and practice. Its original concerns had little in common with contemporary attempts to "ground" reflexivity, consensus, or emancipatory norms in the structure of "communication."

The point, in any event, was not to secure a given set of normative presuppositions. It was to make philosophy useful for issues of "public" debate and, in even more radical terms, render its academic usage irrelevant. In fact, according to the famous formulation of Peirce, the aim of pragmatism was not to "solve" problems, but to show why "supposed problems are not real problems." Instrumentalism and immediacy help unite the tradition. Doubt, for example, was always open to termination once a given approach seemed "workable" (James) and it is stretching the boundaries of the framework to maintain that pragmatism can embrace the famous phrase of Descartes that "every definition is a denial;" indeed, there is no reason to believe that pragmatism is inherently "critical."

It was always an anti-philosophy. Korsch, in particular, liked its anti-metaphysical impetus, its emphasis upon action and "concreteness" (*Diesseitigkeit*). The materialism of Horkheimer, in this vein, was also less defined by a concern with the ontological primacy of matter over consciousness than by the tasks of overcoming repression in any given historical moment. What Josiah Royce might have termed the "spirit" of pragmatism rather than its more stultifying rituals and categories can thus help lead critical theory to focus on the primacy of political analysis and the need for something other than a concept of practice derived from the structure of language.

The Linguistic Turn

But that is just what Habermas provides. His "universal pragmatics" is an important contribution to the debates internal to the philosophy of language.[42] Its attempt to define those forms evident within every possible speech situation offers a stance, which is both formal and substantive, logical and normative. Within the philosophy of language, in fact, an admirable attempt is made to overcome subject–object relations through the use of concepts like inter-subjectivity and the "life–world." His emphasis on symbolically mediated forms of interaction, which link communicative action with argumentation, make possible a "reconstruction of philosophy" (Dewey) predicated on the claim that "reaching understanding is the inherent telos of human speech."[43] Speech is seen as retaining a rational core. Only if this is the case can everyday speech, even of the most distorted sort, both anticipate and presuppose an undistorted form of communication.

"Communicative reason," writes Habermas, "operates in history as an avenging force."[44] An ideal speech situation, precisely because it must confront a counter-factual reality, grounds reflexivity in language. The problem with the argument is not its relevance for linguistics, but whether its anthropological assumptions are sound and whether they allow for translation into categories capable of clarifying the historically determinate ways in which reality is constituted. Habermas is aware of the anthropological issue at stake in the claim that language is intrinsically rational. Thus, it only makes sense that he should have begun the *Theory of Communicative Action* with a critique of Max Weber for assuming the epistemological division between subject and object in his views on rationalization and the "iron cage."[45]

Habermas has never disputed the claim of Weber concerning the progressive erosion of meaning caused by rationalization. He is aware of the manner in which Durkheim's anomie is a product of the "disenchantment of the world." But he refuses to equate science with the domination of nature; Habermas is sharply critical of the attempts by Herbert Marcuse and others to offer an alternative without specifying its character or categories.[46] The thinking of Habermas is essentially devoid of "romantic impulses."[47] He is willing to entertain the validity of scientific reason within delineated boundaries and thus, following Kant, draws a distinction between the subject-centered reason underpinning instrumental rationality and speculative reason or reflexivity. The new "pathologies of the life–world" fostered by instrumental rationality are subsequently only one aspect of modern society. An increase in moral and cognitive learning capacity also results along with potentially new forms of meaning–giving activity inspired by the democratic ethos of communicative humanism.

Weber ignored anthropological developments of this sort by identifying purposive rationality with reason as such. The "philosophy of consciousness" with its assumptions concerning the division between subject and object, according to Habermas, lay at the root of his reduction of reason to the instrumental manipulation of the object. But, insofar as critical theory also uncritically carried over its assumptions, the result was merely a transition from the positive to the negative reading of reason and its power; critical theory also became caught in the "iron cage."[48] After all, in principle, *Dialectic of Enlightenment* agreed with the belief of Weber that liberation through reason is as negative as it is positive.[49] Or putting it another way, according to Habermas, Weber and Nietzsche reinforce one another in eroding the regenerative possibilities of reason.

These are what Habermas seeks to illuminate by surmounting the subject–object division and grounding rationality within the inter-subjective structure of language. Neither subject nor object exists for Habermas in the abstract. But the "concrete" takes anthropological rather than historical form. Communicative action of any sort pre-supposes a shared "life–world" (*Lebenswelt*), which is apodictic or preconceptual, and thus implies a certain degree of consensus. Reification or the "colonization of the life–world" will occur insofar as the realm of experience is narrowed and, more importantly, there is a diminishing ability to question the consensus achieved. The speculative element within reason is thus precisely what Habermas wishes to preserve and he argues his case by claiming that language inherently makes reason regenerative. Discourse becomes the ground of critique. Indeed, even when it seeks to disturb the prevailing consensus, discourse assumes a commitment to truth whose determination will once again demand consensual validation.

This can occur in any number of ways depending on the referential domain of interaction. Validity claims can take communicative, strategic, normative, and dramaturgic form. Communication, however, must receive conceptual primacy in order to supplant the traditional reliance of critical theory on the philosophy of consciousness and ground its normative assumptions.[50] The philosophy of language, for this reason, can only appear as a theory of rationality and break with all contingent forms of strategic action pertaining to compromises or bargaining among particular interests.[51] Only from such a standpoint is it possible to argue that norms will ultimately emerge from the rational use of procedures rather than by making reference to specific outcomes.

The necessity follows, in keeping with Charles Peirce and John Dewey,[52] of presupposing what Apel termed a "communication community" (*Kommunikationsgemeinschaft*) ideally predisposed to illuminate instrumental and illegitimate forms of domination. The issue is not some equitable adjudication of interests or any given constraints on action. Theory, according to Habermas, can never directly justify political action.[53] The primary concern is the pursuit of the "best argument" and, for this reason, the central problem of democracy is not the discovery of some optimal solution or standard for ranking incommensurate values; it is instead the formation of a somewhat vaguely defined "postconventional" consensus through which everyone affected by a decision must be able to participate in reaching it.[54] Thus, norms can receive validity only insofar as all potential participants in a practical discourse will agree to them.[55]

Many proponents of discourse ethics maintain that there is nothing utopian in any of this since transcendence, or the need to project a "counter-factual" condition of undistorted communication against the particular discourses in which distortion takes place, is built into the very structure of language.[56] Utopia is, in fact, retained. It is – correctly – severed from teleology or ontology, but – unfortunately – stripped of substance.

Reflexivity and counter-factuality, in any event, are seen as taking place only insofar as the discourse is open to all, mutual respect is given to each, needs are linguistically interpreted, and the claim of every disputant is supported by an "informal logic" of argumentation predicated on a moral principle whose function is equivalent to the principle of induction in the empirical sciences: "universalizability."[57] It is impossible to transcend these presuppositions of discourse, which has led Apel to claim an "ultimate justification" (*Letztbegründung*) for the rules of discourse ethics,[58] and Albrecht Wellmer to speak about a "pluridimensional foundation" of ethics.[59] Habermas, however, has secured the middle position in noting the manner in which discursive presuppositions constitute a "weak transcendental necessity" and that there are no alternatives to them.

Habermas retains the skepticism of critical theory with respect to all ontological formulations.[60] More importantly, in keeping with critical theory, his discourse ethics makes no concession to either positivism or irrationalism. Discourse ethics, after all, insists upon the ability to decide upon ethical principles without demanding that such cognition coincide with knowledge of any given set of facts even while its emphasis upon the principle of "universal reciprocity" contests particularism, relativism, and the recourse to intuition. The normative expectations regulating ideal speech are implicit in the telos of communication as such and thus constitute a *prima facie* refutation of ethical skepticism. The theory of communicative action, building on Kant, connects three spheres of rationality: the cognitive-instrumental, the moral-practical, and the aesthetic-judgmental.

"Discourses," writes Habermas, "are islands in the sea of practice."[61] Their ethical emphasis on impartial procedures and universalized reciprocity is seen as offering a "regulative idea" for dealing with concrete situations and criticizing repression.[62] The philosophy's "post-metaphysical" character derives principally from its willingness to employ an inter-subjective framework, with the "life–world" as its referent, in which norms are made and the search for truth is generated. The theory of communicative action does not posit a self-sufficient subject confronting an object, but begins instead with a symbolically structured notion of everyday life in which reflexivity is constituted. Subjectivism and the "negative metaphysics" of Adorno no less than the neo–positivism of Karl Popper, with its inability to provide knowledge with a determinate status or foundation are surmounted by the new standpoint.[63]

Just as every hermeneutic understanding must refer to a given historical context, however, so must every moral position refer to a "shared ethos."[64] Here is the ethos of the Enlightenment. Underpinning strategic forms of discursive interaction with communicative rationality presupposes certain political forms of association, which guarantee the possibility of emancipation from dependency. The theory of communicative action, in fact, is really a "scarcely concealed translation of the requisites for ideal political democracy."[65] It is less concerned with developing a substantive notion of the "good" than affirming a procedural notion of justice.[66] The "linguistic turn" thus becomes an attempt to further the struggle for political liberalism evident in Habermas's earlier works.

Showing its practical implications, however, calls forth an encounter with the state and law. Earlier, in *Legitimation Crisis*, Habermas drew the distinction between various social and institutional spheres. Given the manner in which civil society is "patronized" by the state, however, his point was not to resurrect some new relation between the "base" and "superstructure." It was rather to develop a critique of capitalist society as an integrated whole and demonstrate how "legitimation" serves as a *sine qua non* for the proper functioning of the existing order along with its various sub-systems.[67] This work emphasized the limits of "formal" democracy and emphasized the manner in which needs generated by the system tended to undercut the motivations for economic performance. Nevertheless, whatever the various disruptive tendencies of advanced industrial society, only when effective learning within a system is no longer possible will "crisis" shake the existing order.[68]

"Consciousness," in keeping with the spirit of the Frankfurt School and the New Left, becomes the decisive factor in social transformation. Economics also plays a role insofar as it impacts upon consciousness. Politics, however, drops out or becomes a mere "reflex."[69] Habermas recognizes the role capital and private control over investment plays in the formation of policy; he stands in favor of making private investment decisions publicly accountable. Nevertheless, given the relative autonomy of institutionalized political power and its influence on the distribution of income within capitalist democracy, analyzing the state and the economy must take place without reference to the working class as a revolutionary subject intimately linked to the actual production and reproduction of the system.

Autopoesis, or the self-generating character of the system and its particular sub-systems, has also rendered anachronistic the attempt to thematize the existing order from the "macro" standpoint of class.[70] The autopoetic development of increasingly complex bureaucratic systems is a practical reality for economic growth and, for this reason, preserving them from the effects of participatory "will formation" is unavoidable.[71] Habermas, however, maintained his concern with legitimation. It became ever more apparent that rendering the legal order "positive" was increasingly leading to the *displacement* of all substantive problems beyond the purely technical concerns internal to the administration of law.[72] Thus, the original question of legitimation came to take on ever greater urgency.

A cogent argument justifying the worthiness of a given political order and the extent to which it deserves recognition would depend upon its ability to differentiate between a legitimate political order and the various claims to legitimacy forwarded by a given form of institutional association.[73] This, in turn, presupposes a connection between morality and law along with the ability of legal procedures to differentiate between particular and generalizable interests.[74] Insofar as that becomes the claim, however, Habermas must contest the instrumental theory of law developed by Max Weber who, in keeping with his attempt to develop a value-free social science, sought to divorce morality from law.[75] And this involves more than a merely academic disputation. For, if the purpose of law is less to secure justice within the society than affirm the neutral understanding of the legal system, then its interconnection with the welfare state becomes suspect.[76] Instrumental rationality, which is purely formal, inherently militates against the material rationality generated by those making particular and substantive claims on the state.

Franz Neumann and Otto Kirchheimer, who were both involved with the Institute for Social Research in the 1930s, claimed that liberal legal systems are not "fully rational" if they fail to deal with the concentrated social and economic power of particular capitalist interests.[77] Habermas, in keeping with their views, is willing to argue that the rationality and autonomy of the legal system is not guaranteed simply because extra-legal concerns are translated into the language of positive law; latent power structures can invade the seemingly self-referential legal sub-system.[78] Thus, the attempt by Habermas to redefine the ethical character of law is actually an attempt to deal with how law can remain rational even while the "juridification" (*Verrechtlichung*) of social life increases.[79]

Weber recognized how law was losing its traditional legitimating foundations in religion or custom. Identifying it with the predictability and calculability of instrumental rationality seemed the only way to prevent its descent into arbitrariness.[80] Morality, from this perspective, is reduced to an "ethical minimum" while behavior is regulated in accord with the rights individuals possess in the formation of contracts. The point of Habermas, however, is to show that neither decisionism nor scientific objectivity can provide a foundation for legal practice. His claim, in keeping with the anthropological assumptions of discourse ethics, is that procedural rationality generates the norms and values "worthy" of legitimation. The functionalist theory of law elaborated by Max Weber thus becomes open to rational justification only in the light of moral principles.[81]

Law is seen by Habermas as mediating the idea of human rights with that of popular sovereignty in such a way that the moral purpose of law becomes the extension of political autonomy. This purpose is, in turn, secured through "the communicative form of the discursive formation of will and opinion."[82] Law is thus more than the codification of injunctions or moral impulses; it is not merely a system of symbols, but a system wherein action takes place.[83] It is a form of social integration in which the moral imperatives behind the rule of law are in a constant state of tension with the various forms of instrumental activity pertaining to power and money.[84] And, precisely to that extent, the internal dynamics of law are capable of becoming embedded in those existing between communicative and strategic action.[85] The object of law converges with the implications of discourse theory;[86] the anthropological meets the ethical.

The issue for him is less the outcome of legal decisions than the manner in which they are derived. Predictability and calculability, which are seemingly embedded within the law, thus give way before the primacy of procedures capable of preventing law-making from becoming arbitrary.[87] These procedures, in turn, obviously result from particular forms of legal reasoning or discursive argumentation. They neither prescribe any given form of behavior nor a given norm; they make no identification between justice or morality and the given order, but merely provide a construct and criteria wherein the rational pursuit of justice and morality becomes possible: the procedures distributing burdens of proof, defining the requirements of justification, and setting the path of argumentative vindication.[88] Reducing law to politics, in this way, becomes illegitimate.[89] Nevertheless, the linguistic turn now provides its practical political justification.

The rationality of law becomes impossible to understand without reference to the structure of legal discourse.[90] But, where language structurally subsumes object and subject, its materialization in law enables it to "interface" between the systems identified with objective or strategic forms of interaction and the "life–world" *(Lebenswelt)* in which the apodictic experiences of subjectivity and everyday intercourse are stored.[91] The two spheres may have been "uncoupled" by the differentiation process of modernity. But law must presuppose a life–world even if its sphere of "just" regulation is confined to systems defined by power and money. It thus retains a "double function." Law must simultaneously regulate particular forms of strategic action even as it projects generalizable interests and the possibility of a critical discourse.

Given the manner in which strategic action is predicated on monological communication, and both the economy and the state apparatus presuppose an instrumentalism or an orientation towards "success," discourse is circumscribed within the life–world by definition. The extent to which law trespasses into the "life–world" is thus the extent to which reification or its "colonization" takes place. Some have emphasized, in this vein, the need to employ the "symbolic" resources of the life–world or civil society against the encroachments of the state and the economy.[92] Nevertheless, for Habermas, the aim is more concrete.

He seeks the development of institutions capable of binding systemic processes to the substantive moral implications of law. His emphasis derived from the radical tradition of critical theory and its concern with participation and democracy reflects the central concerns of the New Left; it also confronts the postmodernist counter-enlightenment and evidences certain liberal and constitutional concerns, which had such an impact on the revolutions of 1989. Habermas, however, wants to take the process a step further. His vision is not only of a public life free from arbitrary interference by the state, but also of an egalitarian society in which the poorest and the weakest can participate.

Democracy need not preclude ideology. Quite the contrary. It should foster a plethora of views.[93] The emphasis on consensus, and differentiating general from particular interests, should not interfere with either pluralism or individualism.[94] Democracy is a process by which generalizable interests are constituted and, insofar as its formal freedoms give it substantive legitimation, liberalism is seen as generating what, in considering his consensual community of scholars, Charles Peirce called "logical socialism." This type of socialism, according to Habermas, will survive: "only if it takes seriously the utopian element within democratic procedures themselves. The procedural utopia focuses on the structures and presuppositions for a radical pluralistic, largely decentralized process that produces complexity and is certainly costly, a process the content and outcomes of which no one can – or should want to – anticipate."[95]

Socialism, if it retains any possibility of realization at all, must break with the type of fatalism and economism associated with it in the past. It must now rely on democratic will formation through the public sphere and the emancipatory potential of discourse. There is thus a sense in which Habermas is not merely concerned with protecting speculative reason against the irrationalists and instrumentalists, but also in anthropologically defending "the belief in progress, in a world-historical evolution toward the realization of reason in the world."[96]

Progress is a modern concept and, in anticipation of Marxism, idealist philosophy fused it with history. Teleology, in this way, became part of the effort to develop a philosophy of history. No less than with the critical theory of society, however, Habermas seeks to ground the philosophy of history within a general anthropological vision of which the philosophy of language is the primary component. A "reconstruction" or, better, transvaluation of historical materialism thus takes place wherein the evolution of symbolic action or the structures of communication complement the development of modes of production or the "instrumental" spheres of action.[97] Work ultimately gives way, following Jean Piaget and Lawrence Kohlberg, to the "moral responsibility" and role differentiation learned within the family as the central criteria distinguishing the human from the animal. Morality is rendered autonomous and an independent anthropological dynamic presents itself in the normative orders, which appear at given historical conjunctures, and provide an "organizational principle" for all social relationships.[98]

Kingship, with its initial differentiation of roles and formal "equality" extended to the non-aristocratic, is seen as giving way before what C. B. Macpherson termed "possessive individualism" which, in turn, generates the need for a new moral order predicated on the rational or discursive adjudication of grievances. This typology is meant to serve as a substitute for the "functionalist" notion of development predicated on the tension between forces and relations of production. As with the original view of the young Marx, which becomes particularly evident in the interpretation provided by Lukács,[99] the motor of change lies in the symbolic and the communicative rather than in the instrumental and strategic spheres of action.

Universal and critical thought is seen by Piaget and Kohlberg as becoming manifest in the normal development of the mind. The typology reflects their views insofar as socialization is identified with learning to become rational and independent. Extrapolating this development upon humanity thus becomes tempting. The problem, without even considering questions of descriptive accuracy, is that it is just that: a typology. The development of given societies, if not the evolutionary process, is reversible.[100] But there is no apparent motor of development and questions arise regarding its identification with either ontogenetic or phylogenetic development.[101] Nor is there any way of deriving the manner in which events are actually constituted from the categories of what seeks to substitute for a philosophy of history. Humanity as the universal agent of moral evolution is a weak substitute for the proletariat. Idealism and the "philosophy of consciousness" lurks in the background; language might actually be serving the rehabilitation of a new universal subject. But this remains open. Only one thing is certain. Habermas refuses to juxtapose subjectivity against an order increasingly rationalized and defined by instrumental reason.

Habermas, following Talcott Parsons and Niklas Luhmann,[102] asserts that modernization involves the generation of systems with increasingly complicated sub-systems whose reproduction depends upon their capacity to secure universalistic processes of adaptation against the "life-world." If the life–world stands distinct from the instrumental logic of state and economic systems, however, it is not divorced from all integration mechanisms. New social movements,[103] which have supplanted the proletarian "macro-subject" of history by translating "latently available structures of rationality" into social practice, thus receive emancipatory definition in terms of their ability to assail the given systems-logic through their attempts to redeem the solidarity and subjectivity anthropologically embedded in the life–world.[104]

How well these movements succeed is open to determination only by employing the very concept of universalism they so often oppose in judging the cultural traditions and norms influencing their actions. This is only logical since advanced industrial society, with its strategically defined economic and state institutions, provides the material foundations for regenerating the life–world.[105] The "illegitimate" extent to which these materials are employed, of course, is the extent to which anomie and "colonization of the life–world" take place. This is obviously not open to determination *a priori*. The future, for that reason, remains open. Indeed, whatever the reliance of Habermas on systems-logic and ahistorical criteria for making social judgments, the dialectic continues on course in this most prominent contemporary representative of critical theory.

Rethinking Habermas

Habermas has been radical in emphasizing the emancipatory relevance of the enlightenment heritage. His "universal pragmatics" sought to ground its norms and cement the connection between a philosophy and a sociology of law. Habermas is justified in placing himself within the tradition of Lessing and Kant, especially insofar as he prizes the search for truth over its definition; so too, has he remained consistent in refusing to identify the socialist project with any particular form of life.[106] Nor have his critics been able to specify alternatives to his prerequisites for communicative interaction. His standpoint need not buttress the existing consensus or smother pluralism. It merely offers a framework for discourse and even solidarity among the new social movements in a period characterized by a logic of fragmentation. His desire to overcome the "philosophy of consciousness" is tempered by a healthy resistance to decisionism and irrationalism, and he is legitimately concerned with the formation of institutions capable of rationally adjudicating between conflicting claims and interests. Habermas has gone the furthest in making critical theory, once again, shoulder a sense of political responsibility. Nevertheless, for all that, the limits of the welfare state evidence the limits of his imagination and it is impossible to take at face value either the "postmetaphysical" pretensions of his new philosophy of language or his claim that "the theory of communicative action is not a metatheory but the beginning of a social theory concerned to validate its own critical standards."[107]

Liberalism is founded on the rule of law and the right to property, both of which rest on the concepts of universalism and a rational subject.

But, if the conflict between democracy and capital has been noted often enough,[108] liberal theory has never been able immanently to thematize the relation between political institutions and the capitalist accumulation process from within its own categories. Nor has it ever been able to present itself as a historical theory with categories capable of thematizing the totality or the manner in which events receive their meaning within it. The original advocates of liberalism, for these very reasons, could divide into partisans of the utilitarian and the idealist traditions. This division, in turn, gave expression to the great schisms between subject and object, fact and value, theory and practice.

It was "abstract" antinomies of this sort which Hegel sought to abolish. Nor were the concerns of Habermas very different in his attempt to supplant the "philosophy of consciousness" with universal pragmatics. But the question lingers in terms of how well he succeeded. And success cannot merely become identified with framing philosophical questions in a new way; it must involve coming to terms with the practical weaknesses of earlier arguments. The problem for Habermas, however, was never the practical implications of the "categorical imperative" or even the willingness to divorce theoretical from practical and normative from instrumental questions; it was rather the manner in which the formulation of dualisms and the emphasis on the transcendental subject precluded an emphasis on communicative interaction between individuals. The issue for Habermas was never really ethics; it was a matter of meta-ethics all along.

The same dualisms remain even if they are articulated differently. Communicative is now divorced from strategic interaction and the "life–world" is divorced from the "system." The structure of language predicated on an intersubjectively constituted "life–world" serves as the underpinning of both. But universalism remains incapable of dealing with intractable material interests. The theory of communicative action aims to overcome the relativism associated with the hermeneutics of Hans-Georg Gadamer or Hannah Arendt. Nevertheless, it offers no criteria for moving from a description of the whole to a critique of its oppressive parts.

History as the unfolding of political institutions, or even the social development of everyday life, is less subsumed within the philosophy of language or the discourse theory of law than defined out of existence through the use of static categories and questionable anthropological assumptions. This takes place in three ways. It occurs structurally by dividing the "life–world" from the "system." It occurs analytically by divorcing dialogic communication, which is confined to the life–world, from the strategic forms of monologic bargaining and compromise identified with acting in a "system." It, finally, occurs normatively insofar as liberation from "hunger and misery" is not seen as necessarily converging with liberation from "servitude and degradation."[109]

Making distinctions between concepts and levels of argument can prove useful. But, this does not justify placing them in what is often an antinomial relation to one another. Just as every moral norm can be employed for strategic purposes, which is precisely why Kant identified ethical action with intention, so are political and economic activites often inspired by morality and ideology. Habermas, however, is not content with intention. He wishes to give the norms girding communicative action a practical function without reducing theory to any form of instrumental exigency. That is why he seeks to employ the discourse ethic for resurrecting the moral foundations for a theory of law. Nevertheless, the building blocks remain the same: the "life–world," the discursive community, and the moral commitment to autonomy.

The "life–world," of course, provides an inter-subjective context for all speech situations and interpretive possibilities. But its character remains vague. The category is defined both ontologically as the apodictic construct in which values are shared and, simultaneously, as the anthropological background underpinning any given systemic or strategic forms of differentiation. Part of the problem derives from the fact that, whatever the claims concerning the manner in which strategic forms of action are grounded in genuine communication, instrumental activity always presupposes categories from the philosophy of consciousness, which the linguistic turn wished to supersede;[110] indeed, the distinction between activity oriented towards success and discourse directed towards achieving an understanding becomes undermined in this way. The problem is, furthermore, not solved merely by claiming that the "rationalization of the life–world must adjust to the extent that the rational potential for communicative action is provided and discursively set free within the structures of the life–world."[111]

Concepts like the "life–world" have an obvious relevance for phenomenological inquiry. Husserl used it in terms still indebted to the "philosophy of consciousness." Heidegger made the break and secured his category of "being-in-the-world" with the notion of "care" (*Sorge*). While rejecting the "philosophy of consciousness," however, Habermas never anchors his concept of the "life–world" in "Being" or seeks to determine the manner in which it interlocks with an existential analysis of human existence. The apodictic "background" has no grounding; it thus turns into little more than a vague anthropological postulate for the understanding of the non-institutional features of everyday life. While the existential analysis remains truncated, however, no categories are provided for unlocking the historical character or development of this "life–world" and its correlative systems. The categories of life–world and system are neither ontologically grounded nor historically articulated. Thus, it makes little sense to claim that a new interpretive position is being presented in which events and actors are no longer primary.[112]

Habermas has not supplanted the "philosophy of consciousness;" its dualisms have merely been shifted onto a different plane. The chasm, so evident when dealing with the philosophy of Martin Heidegger, also looms in the new "phenomenology of moral intention." The linguistic theory cannot perform the tasks of a critical social theory while the anthropological conception of moral evolution inherited from psychology can neither offer insights into the constitution of social reality nor the categories necessary for conceptualizing events with respect to their historically determinate quality.

The bifurcations between communicative and strategic action, system and life–world, are belied in practice. Habermas recognizes that certain spheres of communicative action exist within systems as well as the practical dominance of strategic action. But the matter must be framed more starkly. The political and economic "systems" of advanced industrial society are obviously intertwined with the myths and symbols of the market and individualism, while social movements, even if they originate in the life–world, have always been *fundamentally* inspired by strategic interests. Finally, on the apodictic level, symbolic action is open to various forms of semiotic organization and capable of influencing other strategic areas of life.[113]

"Communication" lies at the root of the undertaking. It is seen as presupposing an unrestrained discourse, the willingness of each to place himself or herself in the position of the other, the discipline to engage in a rational justification of claims, and a willingness to bracket self-interest so that the "better argument" can win out. Concretely, however, every discourse is necessarily "constrained" both in terms of the agenda and those participating in the discussion. Also, if each is able to put himself or herself in the place of the other, then, perhaps even more surely than with the "monological" forms of strategic action, there will remain very little to discuss. Finally, even if participants are sometimes willing to engage in a rational justification of claims, history suggests that there is no reason whatsoever why the "better argument" should intrinsically prove victorious without extra-discursive activities being brought into play; indeed, "better" arguments often emerge victorious for non-rational reasons.

"Postmetaphysical" claims to concreteness for the new linguistic perspective make sense only from the standpoint of academic philosophy. It is possible to argue, of course, that communicative practices are constitutive of social relations which, in turn, reveal given forms of ethical commitment. But this provides only an illusory notion of concreteness. No sooner is the question of social or historical specificity raised than the most fundamental categories lose their analytic power; "general interests" can conflict, for example, when directed to a host of issues – often unique to Western societies – like growth and environmental protection. Cutting back growth could impede not only the development of productive forces, but the "material level of culture" (Marx) within a society and the range of choice or autonomy of its members.[114]

Choosing among generalizable concerns is always a political question. The linguistic category of "universalizability" is incapable of specifying priorities among competing general concerns, and it simply makes little difference whether discourse ethics can "ground" the different rationalities behind morality, law, and politics when it cannot confront organizational questions, the conflicting material interests among the oppressed, or even their often generalizable if mutually exclusive ideological claims.[115] The problem, in this same vein, does not derive from the claim of linguistic philosophy that even strategic interaction presupposes communicative foundations. It stems rather from an inability to generate categories capable of reconstructing the reasons why "genuine" communication has shriveled or the ways in which distorted forms of speech constantly reproduce themselves.[116]

A genuinely "postmetaphysical" philosophy must begin with neither the deconstruction nor the reconstruction of "truth," but concern with the specification of those material conditions which inhibit and best foster its quest.[117] Neither the legal nor the linguistic theory of Habermas, can link the prerequisites for communicative competence or the stages of moral evolution with the reality of compromise, violence, and the structural imbalance of power. The plight of Marx's "holy family" of young Hegelians is reproduced; the "idea" of autonomy is "disgraced" since, once again, it is divorced from "interest."[118]

There is surely something ironic about the manner in which "discourse" is becoming ever more fashionable in theory just as its political effectiveness is appearing ever more questionable in practice. The influence of "public opinion" and "opinion makers" is, of course, still very real. But its implications for the extension of genuine democracy is truncated if the extraordinary "complexity" of the system closes its sub-systems to participatory impulses. Just how democracy actually applies with respect to such sub-systems, or how fragmented interests might further conditions of unity to engage in extending it, always seems absent from the agenda. And there is a reason: the emphasis on "participation" by Habermas is defined by what it opposes. The concern with extending participation and "equalizing power" in the discourse is really the philosophical expression of the practical assault on the very forms of hierarchic and bureaucratic organization, which – for better or worse – are alone capable of achieving such equality in reality, by the new social movements.

Accountability rather than *participation* or *autonomy* is the primary category for a new politics willing to recognize that the great battles of the future will take place in what are still burgeoning international and regional institutions.[119] The new standpoint of Habermas retreats from his earlier concern with the manner in which "experts" can shape the direction of argument.[120] Coming to terms with the experts demands their accountability, which itself presupposes a strategic no less than a moral or *ideological* interest on the part of those who must contest the "free-rider" problem and matters pertaining to differentiated information costs deriving from what Mancur Olson called "the logic of collective action."

Habermas has emphasized often enough since the publication of *Legitimation Crisis* the impossibility of thematizing the "totality" from the perspective of any macro-subject or structural interest like the working class.[121] Even if that is the case, however, this still does not justify its irrelevance for conceptualizing and contesting the logic of the existing accumulation process. He is certainly aware of the implications deriving from the welfare state's inability to control private investment decisions other than through activities conforming to the logic of the existing system, and he is cognizant of the opposition generated by private investors against every attempt to implement a radical social program.[122] But nowhere does this receive expression in the philosophical elaboration. Structural problems of this sort no less than the ways in which "compromises" are substantively affected by existing imbalances of power inherently stand outside the discourse ethic.[123] It is not enough for Habermas to speak of "equal treatment" as the normative bias beyond a purely contemplative notion of law.[124]

Such matters are not merely of "ontic" concern if Habermas is seriously committed to developing a "postmetaphysical" form of philosophy. Participants in a collective bargaining agreement can receive "equal treatment" in the formal terms of a discourse. They can even share a general interest in keeping a firm profitable, which will call upon the various sides to put themselves in the shoes of their adversaries even as they provide rational justifications for their particular claims in order to "reach an understanding." From within the parameters of the discourse set by the substantively disparate power of employers and employees, the "better argument" might even win out. It remains impossible, however, to consider the manner in which the dependency of workers upon the investment decisions of capitalists will affect the agenda and the ensuing discourse. Discursive rules are also surely followed, for the most part, by practitioners in the American legal system. Nevertheless, one in four Afro-American males is either in jail, waiting trial, or on probation.

Even in a system more closely approximating the perfect conditions of discourse ethics, "distortions" will enter from outside the field of argumentation. The question is whether theory will prove able to deal with them. Rigidly divorcing procedures from outcomes is simply inadequate. Real relations of power must disappear; without making reference to questions of interest, without considering institutional imbalances of power and the contradictory character of the accumulation process, external impingements on the discourse will become "invisible."[125] Theory will thus lose its critical edge, and take a step back behind Hegel and Marx in the name of its "reconstruction."

Horkheimer was correct, of course, in arguing that truth is never reducible to interest. But going to the opposite extreme is just as objectionable. Commitment to universals like the rule of law or even the discourse of psychoanalysis is always connected with a particular form of practice generated by particular interests. Critical theory, if only for this reason, cannot employ a neutral scientific notion of truth for analyzing society and its institutional sub-systems without undercutting its ability to inform the struggles of the exploited. Such a stance inherently preserves theory from the contradictory dynamics of power informing the systems it wishes to judge. Or, putting it differently, the interest in equitable judgment abstracts it from precisely those among the exploited whom one would wish to persuade.[126] Critical theory, in this way, becomes informed by precisely the type of lifeless bureaucratic thinking it originally sought to oppose: the life–world confronts the system, the crisis of the system is defined by the crises pertaining to its structurally demarcated sub-systems, while contingent interests and organizational prerequisites for action vanish within the "universal pragmatics."

Enough critics have noted the lack of motivational impulses in the theory of Habermas.[127] But the simple commitment to procedural "justice" can sometimes serve as motivation for action and, in fact, the work of his critics often suffers from the same problem. The real problem has less to do with motivation than the inability to develop a standpoint through which the efforts of disparate individuals and groups become susceptible to coordination. But few critics are willing to entertain such questions or develop positive positions of their own. There is, of course, the constant call for modern critical theory to become more sensitive to historical struggles *and* still provide the "metatheoretical self understanding" wherein the demands of solidarity *and* plurality are preserved.[128] Without making reference to organiza tional questions, the actual constraints on unity, the bureaucratic concerns with autonomy by various groups, or the regulative principles capable of uniting class interests with those of social movements, such calls become nothing more than pious phrases. There is also nothing particularly utopian in the desire to see the generalized as a concrete other with its own history and identity.[129] Suspending mere self-interest by emphasizing collective identity or common interests might take place – though the coordinating principles, structures, and character of the universal concerns cannot remain hanging in the abstract; otherwise, it all comes down to the forms of tolerance – or indifference – underpinning liberal notions of pluralism.

Emancipatory action is predicated on coming to terms with how the concerns of particular groups are raised and made relevant to the exercise of freedom and enjoyment by others. That, for Ernst Bloch, is the utopian moment. Habermas is content to shift the traditional frame of reference, however, by noting that the quality of a society depends largely upon the non-authoritarian character of its everyday mores and customs (*Sittlichkeit*).[130] His concept of the life–world is seen as projecting emancipatory resistance to its "colonization" by commodification and bureaucratic rationality: spontaneity, in keeping with the tradition of critical theory, is seen as repulsing reification. But this is spontaneity of a particular sort. Habermas knows that the life–world is not somehow "more innocent" than the bureaucratic institutions of modernity;[131] he has been consistent in confronting the remnants of *völkisch* ideology with what he has termed a "patriotism to the constitution" and, from his perspective, it is completely logical to maintain that the regressive character of such premodern prejudices becomes illuminated by the discourse ethic.

Habermas is correct in noting how the manner in which systems "colonize" the life–world tends to turn citizens into clients incapable of contesting or criticizing bureaucratic structures. This speaks to the matter of accountability. But framing the matter in this way renders concrete matters unnecessarily abstract. At issue is less the instrumental "colonization of the life–world" than the ability to make judgments concerning the types of systemic relief necessary to maintain the dignity of working people and the poor. Virtually closing sub-systems to democratic control and underestimating class oppression, however, makes this enterprise doubtful; indeed, contesting intractable interests cannot occur through conceptual recourse to an indeterminate discursive community "without definite limits, and capable of definite increase in knowledge."[132]

Critical interchange may have its own dynamics. Consensus need not stifle pluralism;[133] it is a linguistic prerequisite for the articulation of competing views. But there is nothing simply "self-generating" about either the economy, the state, or the public sphere. All are dependent on the tug of interests and ideologically motivated forms of strategic action; indeed, consensus isolated from matters of material and ideological interest offers little fascination. Remaining stuck at the level of shared assumptions without making reference to the conflicts and contradictions structurally embedded within the given system ultimately gives rise less to moral imperatives about increasing participation than truisms or communitarian platitudes. Employing abstract notions of consensus or a disembodied public sphere also tends to distort the analysis of how will formation is constituted; it can even contribute to the self-reinforcing ideology of "bipartisan" politics predicated on the national state and a liberal view of its institutions essentially devoid of class conflict.[134] Indeed, unless such issues are confronted, it becomes impossible to consider the "community of investigators" (Peirce) as anything more than yet another logical postulate devoid of practical relevance.

Habermas knows the danger in identifying a "community of investigators" with experts. But the complexity of sub-systems makes it difficult for him to talk about participatory input. There is subsequently nothing concrete about those engaged in forging a consensus. The problem is reflected in the evolution of the "public sphere" as a category of analysis. It was once seen as an arena in which it was possible to discern the development of consensual assumptions and democratic will formation and, indeed, the concept is still indispensable for developing a concrete analysis of "actually existing democracy."[135] Nevertheless, there is something strange about how what Habermas originally termed a "bourgeois" public sphere has become ever more surely identified with the public sphere per se.

Publics are generated not merely by movements concerned with issues of the life–world, but by material grievances, interests, and parties. The point is not to judge them by an abstract standard of utopian discourse, but by their actual achievements in furthering debate about the character of the existing order along with its institutions and its logic of accumulation. Habermas has himself spoken often of the "autonomous" and "multiple" publics produced by the new social movements. In highlighting such progressive developments, however, he has said little enough about the manner in which they are being undermined by the staggering decline in literacy, with its attendant impact upon newspapers and television, and swamped by the extraordinary centralization of media power.[136] The public sphere of "communication" becomes an inflated concept and the "community of investigators" little more than the "life of the scholar" writ large unless such issues are taken into account.

It is completely irrelevant whether or not this is just another example of the famous "hermeneutic circle" in which truth claims are seen as incapable of escaping the contextually generated assumptions on which they are based. The discourse ethic makes a phenomenological claim to concreteness. But, in fact, it must presuppose for both its validity and effectiveness the historically contingent conditions it claims to further. The discourse ethic is useless where democratic institutions and values are not already extant. The theory of Habermas is not one for uniting the exploited against the whip of the market or even overcoming the moral economy of the separate deal through which the the logic of fragmentation among existing social movements has been generated.

The "phenomenology of moral intention" is actually metaphysics in a new guise. But its somewhat nebulous anchoring of the emancipatory project within language by Habermas cannot justify ignoring his often trenchant political insights or extraordinary contributions to social theory and intellectual life. There is nothing illegitimate about developing the philosophical foundations for a reinvigorated public sphere in which political debate can spur an ever greater form of democratic will formation.[137] This concern is what allows him to claim that "the liberal interpretation is not wrong. It just does not see the beam in its own eye."[138] Indeed, the attempt to capture that beam is what makes Jürgen Habermas the thinker of our time.

Notes

1   Eight volumes have already appeared of his *Kleine Politische Schriften* and more will certainly follow. Much has already been translated in works like Jürgen Habermas, *The New Conservatism: Cultural Criticism and the Historians' Debate* ed. and trans. Shierry Weber Nicolson (Cambridge, 1992).

2   Cf. Robert Holub, *Jürgen Habermas: Critic in the Public Sphere* (New York, 1991), pp. 78ff.

3   Note the new translation of this important debate in its entirety by James Knowlton and Truett Cates under the title *Forever in the Shadow of Hitler?* (Atlantic Highlands, NJ., 1993).

4   Cf. Jürgen Habermas, *Zur Rekonstruktion des Historischen Materialismus* (Frankfurt, 1976), pp. 49ff and 144ff; also, for a critique, Tom Rockmore, *Habermas on Historical Materialism* (Indianapolis, 1989) and Richard Roderick, *Habermas and the Foundations of Critical Theory* (New York, 1986).

5   Note, for example, the strained attack by Alessandro Ferrara, "A Critique of Habermas's *Diskursethik*" in *Telos* 64 (Summer, 1985), pp. 45ff.

6   Cf. Jürgen Habermas, "Die Krise des Wohlfahrtsstaates und die Erschöpfung utopischer Energien" in *Die Neue Unübersichtlichkeit* (Frankfurt, 1985), pp. 141ff.

7   Thomas Mann, "The Light of Recent History" in *Last Essays* trans. Richard Winston et al. (New York, 1970), p. 162.

8   Jürgen Habermas, "Motive nachmetaphysichen Denkens" in *Nachmetaphysiches Denken; Philosophische Aufsätze* (Frankfurt, 1988), pp. 35ff; Jürgen Habermas, "An Alternative Way out of the Philosophy of the Subject" in *The Philosophical Discourse of Modernity* trans. Frederick Lawrence (Cambridge, Mass., 1987), pp. 294ff.

9   Jürgen Habermas, *Strukturwandel der Öffentlichkeit: Untersuchungen zu einer Kategorie der bürgerlichen Gesellschaft* (Darmstadt and Neuwied, 1971), pp. 46ff.

10 "*Structural Transformation* moved totally within the circle of a classical Marxian critique of ideology, at least as it was understood in the Frankfurt environment. What I meant to do was to take the liberal limitations of public opinion, publicity, the public sphere, and so on, at their worst, and then try to confront these ideas of publicness with their selective embodiments and even the change of their very meaning during the process of transformation from liberal to organized capitalism, as I described it at that time." Jürgen Habermas, "Concluding Remarks" in *Habermas and the Public Sphere* ed. Craig Calhoun (Cambridge, Mass., 1992), p. 463.

11 Ibid., pp. 211ff.

12 Max Horkheimer and Theodor W. Adorno, *Dialectic of Enlightenment* trans. John Cumming (New York, 1982), p. 256.

13 Cf. Jürgen Habermas, *The Theory of Communicative Action* trans. Thomas McCarthy (Boston, 1987) vol. 2, pp. 333ff.

14 Jürgen Habermas, "The Public Sphere: An Encyclopedia Article" in *Critical Theory and Society: A Reader* eds Stephen Eric Bronner and Douglas Kellner (New York, 1989), p. 142.

15 Martin Jay, *Marxism and Totality: The Adventures of a Concept from Lukács to Habermas* (Berkeley, 1984), p. 464.

16 His first published work was an indignant response in 1953 to the republication of Heidegger's *Introduction to Metaphysics* from 1935, which simply ignored its most compromising portions. Cf. Jürgen Habermas, "Zur Veröffentlichung von Vorlesungen aus dem Jahre 1935" in *Philosophisch-politische Profile* (Frankfurt, 1971).

17 Cf. Jürgen Habermas, *Autonomy and Solidarity* ed. Peter Dews (London, 1992), pp. 192, 43–61.

18 Habermas, *The Theory of Communicative Action* vol. 2, pp. 374ff.

19 Note the fine discussion by Neil Saccamano, "The Consolations of Ambivalence: Habermas and the Public Sphere" in *MLN* 106 (1991), pp. 685ff.

20 Cf. Oskar Negt und Alexander Klüge, *Zur Organisationsanalyse von bürgerlicher und proletarischer Öffentlichkeit* (Frankfurt, 1977), pp. 106ff; also, cf. Peter Uwe Hohendahl, "Kritische Theorie, Öffentlichkeit und Kultur. Anmerkungen zu Habermas und seinen Kritikern," *Basis*, 8 (1978), pp. 60–90.

21 Jürgen Habermas, *Knowledge and Human Interests* trans. Jeremy J. Shapiro (Boston, 1971), pp. 198ff.

22 Cf. Jürgen Habermas, *On the Logic of the Social Sciences* trans. Shierry Weber Nicholson and Jerry A. Stark (Cambridge, Mass., 1988), pp. 24, 92.

23 Habermas, *Knowledge and Human Interests*, p. 196.

24 Ibid., p. 308.

25 Ibid., p. 285.

26 cf. Richard J. Bernstein, *The Restructuring of Social and Political Theory* (New York, 1976), pp. 197ff.

27 Ibid., pp. 204ff.

28 "The transition to modernity is characterized by a differentiation of spheres of value and structures of consciousness that makes possible a critical transformation of traditional knowledge in relation to specifically given validity claims." Habermas, *Theory of Communicative Action* vol. 1, p. 340.

29 Jürgen Habermas, *Theory and Practice* trans. John Viertel (Boston, 1973), p. 9.

30 "A meaning, even if it is not intended as such, takes form in the course of communicative action and articulates itself reflectively as the experience of a life history. This is the way in which 'meaning' discloses itself in the course of a drama. But in our own self-formative process, we are at once both actor and critic. In the final instance, the meaning of the process itself must be capable of becoming part of our consciousness in a critical manner, entangled as we are in the drama of a life history. The subject must be able to relate his own history and have comprehended the inhibitions that blocked the path of self-reflection." Habermas, *Knowledge and Human Interests*, p. 260.

31 "Habermas saw [psychoanalysis] essentially as a methodological model of personal ideology critique . . . [and as] a process of heightened insight on the part of the patient, whose self-reflection helped dissolve the pseudo-otherness of his symptoms, which controlled him as if they were externally determined." Jay, *Marxism and Totality*, pp. 479–80.

32 Habermas, *Knowledge and Human Interests*, p. 289.

33 Jürgen Habermas, *Legitimation Crisis* (Boston, 1975), p. 113.

34 Jürgen Habermas, *Communication and the Evolution of Society* trans. Jeremy Shapiro (Boston, 1978) p. 178.

35 Ibid., p. 84.

36 Habermas, *Knowledge and Human Interest*, pp. 312–15.

37 Holub, *Jürgen Habermas*, pp. 8ff; also, cf. Thomas McCarthy, *The Critical Theory of Jürgen Habermas* (Cambridge, Mass., 1978).

38 Bernstein, *The Restructuring of Social and Political Theory*, pp. 219ff.

39 The theory of communicative action "is not a continuation of methodology by other means. It breaks with the primacy of epistemology and treats the presupposition of action oriented to mutual understanding

independently of the transcendental preconditions of knowledge."
Habermas, *On the Logic of the Social Sciences*, p. xiv.

40 John B. Thompson, "Rationality and Social Rationalization: An Assessment of Habermas's Theory of Communicative Action" in *Sociology* vol. 17, no. 2 (May, 1983), p. 289.

41 Martin Jay, "The Debate Over Performative Contradiction: Habermas vs. the Post-structuralists" in *Zwischenbetractungen: Im Prozess der Aufklärung* eds Axel Honneth et al. (Frankfurt, 1989), pp. 171ff.

42 Cf. John B. Thompson, "Universal Pragmatics," in *Habermas: Critical Debates* eds John B. Thompson and David Held (Cambridge, Mass., 1982), pp. 116ff.

43 Habermas, *The Theory of Communicative Action* vol. 1, p. 287.

44 Jürgen Habermas, "A Reply to My Critics" in *Habermas: Critical Debates*, p. 227.

45 Ibid., vol. 1, pp. 143ff.

46 Cf. Jürgen Habermas, "Technology and Science as 'Ideology' " in *Toward A Rational Society: Student Protest, Science, and Politics* trans. Jeremy Shapiro (Boston, 1970), pp. 81ff.

47 Jay, *Marxism and Totality*, p. 467.

48 Habermas, *The Theory of Communicative Action* vol. 1, pp. 339ff.

49 Cf. Habermas, "The Entwinement of Myth and Enlightenment: Max Horkheimer and Theodor Adorno" in *The Philosophical Discourse of Modernity*, pp. 106ff.

50 The break with Kant and subjective idealism is seen as occuring in that "instead of asking what an individual moral agent could or would will, without self-contradiction, to be a universal maxim for all, one asks: what norms or instituions would the members of an ideal or real communication agree to as representing their common interests after engaging in a special kind of argumentation or conversation?" Seyla Benhabib, "Communicative Ethics and Current Controversies in Practical Philosophy" in *The Communicative Ethics Controversy* eds Seyla Benhabib and Fred Dallmayr (Cambridge, Mass., 1991), p. 331.

51 "Whereas in strategic action one actor seeks to *influence* the behavior of another by means of the threat of sanctions or the prospect of gratification in order to *cause* the interaction to continue as the first actor desires, in communicative action one actor seeks *rationally* to *motivate* another by relying on the illocutionary binding/bonding effect (*Bindungseffekt*) of the offer contained in the speech act." Jürgen Habermas, *Moral Consciousness and Communicative Action* trans. Christian Lenhardt and Shierry Weber Nicholson (Cambridge, Mass., 1990), p. 58.

52 Cf. Jürgen Habermas, "Charles S. Peirce über Kommunikation" in *Texte und Kontexte* (Frankfurt, 1991), pp. 9ff; Robert J. Antonio and Douglas Kellner, "Communication, Modernity, and Democracy in Habermas and Dewey" in *Symbolic Interaction* (1992) vol. 15, no. 3, pp. 277ff.

53 Habermas, *Theory and Practice*, pp. 36–9.

54 James F. Bohman, "Communication, Ideology, and Democratic Theory" in *American Political Science Review* vol. 84, no. 1 (March, 1990), p. 99.

55 Cf. Jürgen Habermas, *The Tanner Lectures on Human Values* vol. 8 (Salt Lake City, 1988), p. 243.

56 Cf. Karl-Otto Apel, "Is the Ethics of the Ideal Communication Community a Utopia: On the Relationship between Ethics, Utopia, and the Critique of Utopia" in *The Communicative Ethics Controversy*, pp. 23ff.

57 Habermas, *Moral Consciousness and Communicative Action*, p. 62.

58 Cf. Dietrich Böhler, "Transcendental Pragmatics and Critical Morality: On the Possibility and Moral Significance of a Self-Enlightenment of Reason" in *The Communicative Ethics Controversy*, pp. 111ff.

59 Albrecht Wellmer, *Ethik und Dialog* (Frankfurt, 1989), pp. 10–12, 123ff.

60 Cf. Jürgen Habermas, "Discourse Ethics: Notes on a Program of Philosophical Justification" in *The Communicative Ethics Controversy*, pp. 60ff; also, cf. Jürgen Habermas, *Erläuterungen zur Diskursethik* (Frankfurt, 1992).

61 Habermas, "A Reply to My Critics," p. 235.

62 Note the schema offered in the seminal article by Joshua Cohen, "Deliberation and Democratic Legitimacy" in *The Good Polity* eds A. Hamlin and B. Petit (Oxford, 1989).

63 Cf. Jürgen Habermas, "Motive nachmetaphysichen Denkens," p. 35.

64 Seyla Benhabib, "Communicative Ethics and Current Controversies in Practical Philosophy" in *The Communicative Ethics Controversy*, p. 333.

65 Jeffrey Alexander, "Habermas's New Critical Theory: Its Promise and Problems" in *The American Journal of Sociology* vol. 91, no. 2, (1985), p. 414.

66 Ethics oriented to conceptions of the good or to specific value hierarchies single out particular *normative contents*. Their premises are too strong to serve as the foundation for universally binding decisions in a modern society characterized by the pluralism of gods and demons. Only theories of morality and justice developed in the Kantian tradition hold out the promise of an *impartial* procedure for the justification and assessment of principles." Habermas, *The Tanner Lectures*, p. 241.

67 Cf. David Held, "Crisis Tendencies, Legitimation and the State" in *Habermas: Critical Debates*, pp. 181ff.

68 Habermas, *Legitimation Crisis*, p. 7.

69 Cf. Richard Lowenthal, "Social Transformation and Democratic Legitimacy" in *Social Change and Cultural Crisis* (New York, 1984), p. 48.

70 Cf. Jürgen Habermas, "What Does Socialism Mean Today? The Revolutions of Recuperation and the Need for New Thinking" in *After*

the Fall: The Failure of Communism and the Future of Socialism ed. Robin
Blackburn (London, 1991), p. 39.

71 Habermas, *Legitimation Crisis*, pp. 36ff, 123ff; for an opposing view, in
which administrative sub-systems are seen as capable of taking the
leading role in developing society precisely because they are no longer
dependent upon profit, cf. Lowenthal, "Social Transformation and
Democratic Legitimacy," pp. 54ff.

72 Cf. Habermas, *The Theory of Communicative Action* vol. 1, p. 261.

73 Habermas, *Communication and the Evolution of Society*, p. 178.

74 Cf. Peter Koller, "Moralischer Diskurs und politische Legitimation" in
Zur Anwendung der Diskursethik in Politik, Recht, und Wissenschaft eds
Karl-Otto Apel und Matthias Kettner (Frankfurt, 1992), pp. 62ff.

75 Habermas, *The Tanner Lectures*, pp. 220ff.

76 Cf. Niklas Luhmann, *Rechtssoziologie* (Opladen, 1983).

77 Cf. Richard R. Weiner, "Retrieving Civil Society in a Postmodern
Epoch" in *The Social Science Journal* vol. 28, no. 3 (1991), pp. 313ff;
also, Axel Honneth, "Critical Theory" in *Social Theory Today* eds
Anthony Giddens and J. H. Turner (Cambridge, 1987), pp. 362ff.

78 Habermas, *The Tanner Lectures*, pp. 258–9.

79 Cf. Klaus Eder, "Critique of Habermas's Contribution to the Sociology of Law" in *Law and Society Review* vol. 22, no. 5 (1988), p. 934.

80 Still, "Weber's denial that values are logically demonstrable – Habermas would say that they are *wahrheitsfähig* – does not imply a denial
that in any historical situation a particular set of values is given and
binding . . . the cohesion of a complex society is never based on its
economic division of labor alone, but always also on the norms of
conduct that make that division possible." Lowenthal, "Social Transformation and Democratic Legitimacy," pp. 62ff.

81 Habermas, *The Tanner Lectures*, p. 226.

82 Ibid., p. 133.

83 Ibid., p. 137.

84 Ibid., p. 59.

85 Jürgen Habermas, *Faktizität und Geltung: Beitrage zur Diskurstheorie des
Rechts und des demokratischen Rechtsstaats* (Frankfurt, 1992), p. 41.

86 Ibid., p. 10.

87 "Legitimacy is possible on the basis of legality insofar as the procedures
for the production and application of legal norms are also conducted
reasonably, in the moral-practical sense of procedural rationality. The
legitimacy of legality is due to the interlocking of two types of
procedures, namely, of legal processes with processes of moral
argumentation that obey a procedural rationality of their own."
Habermas, *The Tanner Lectures*, p. 230.

88 Ibid., p. 242; on the different types of proceduralism, cf. John Rawls,
A Theory of Justice (Cambridge, Mass., 1971), pp. 85ff, 359ff.

89 Ibid., p. 267.

90 Ibid., p. 246; also, cf. Eder, "Critique of Habermas's Contribution to the Sociology of Law," p. 937.

91 Cf. Habermas, *The Theory of Communicative Action* vol. 2, pp. 113ff.

92 Cf. Claus Offe, "The New Social Movements: Challenging the Institutional Boundaries of the Political" in *Social Research* (Winter, 1985); also, Jean Cohen and Andrew Arato, "Politics and the Reconstruction of the Concept of Civil Society" in *Zwischenbetrachtungen*, pp. 482ff.

93 Bohman, "Communication, Ideology, and Democratic Theory," p. 101.

94 It is correct to suggest, in this vein, that "our communicative practices are constitutive of our forms of relationship, and our forms of relationship reveal our ethical commitments. The interest in consensus is just our commitment to recognizing the most important form of relationship – a universal moral community." Cf. Jane Braaten, "The Succession of Theories and the Recession of Practice" in *Social Theory and Practice* vol. 18, vo. 1 (Spring, 1992), p. 98; for an alternative view, which misunderstands the philosophical issues involved and thus criticizes the theory of Habermas for posing a threat to pluralism, cf. Douglas B. Rasmussen, "Political Legitimacy and Discourse Ethics" in *International Philosophical Quarterly* vol. 32, no. 1, issue no. 125 (March, 1992), pp. 17ff.

95 Jürgen Habermas, "Political Culture in Germany Since 1968: An Interview with Dr Rainer Erd for the *Frankfurter Rundschau*" in *The New Conservatism*, p. 192.

96 Randall Collins, "Habermas and the Search for Reason" in *Semiotica* 64 (1987), p. 157.

97 Note the excellent discussion by Ron Eyerman, "Social Movements and Social Theory" in *Sociology* vol. 18, no. 1 (February, 1984), pp. 75ff.

98 Habermas, *Communication and the Evolution of Society*, p. 153.

99 Habermas, *The Theory of Communicative Action* vol. 2, pp. 354ff.

100 "It is not evolutionary processes that are *irreversible* but the structural sequences that a society must run through *if* and *to the extent* that it is involved in evolution." Habermas, *Communication and the Evolution of Society*, p. 141.

101 Habermas is aware of the difficulty in linking the ontogenetic with the phylogenetic. Given that these terms are anthropological in character, however, the "principle of historical specification" still drops from the discussion. It also remains unclear how the connection between ontogenesis and the developmental logic of worldviews becomes concrete given that people of earlier social formations did not all pass through all the stages of ontogenetic development. Cf. Jürgen Habermas, "Individuierung durch Vergesellschaftung. Zu G. H. Meads Theorie der Subjektivität" in *Nachmetaphysisches Denken*, pp. 187ff; also, cf.

Michael Schmid, "Habermas's Theory of Social Evolution" in *Habermas: Critical Debates*, pp. 173ff.

102   With regard to analyzing the points of disagreement between Habermas and these more politically conservative sociologists, cf. Habermas, *The Theory of Communicative Action* vol. 2, pp. 199ff; also Jürgen Habermas and Niklas Luhmann, *Theorie der Gesellschaft oder Sozialtechnologie* (Frankfurt, 1971) and *Theorie der Gesellschaft oder Sozialtechnologie: Beitrage zur Habermas–Luhmann Diskussion* ed. Franz Maciejewski (Frankfurt, 1975).

103   Cf. Jürgen Habermas, "New Social Movements" in *Telos* 49 (Fall, 1981), pp. 33ff.

104   Cf. Kenneth H. Tucker, Jr, "Ideology and Social Movements: The Contributions of Habermas" in *Sociological Inquiry* vol. 59, no. 1 (February, 1989), pp. 30ff.

105   "The contradiction arises between, on the one hand, a rationalization of everyday communication that is tied to the structures of inter-subjectivity of the life–world, in which language counts as the genuine and irreplaceable medium of reaching an understanding, and, on the other hand, the growing complexity of sub-systems of purposive-rational action, in which actions are coordinated through steering media such as money and power." Habermas, *The Theory of Communicative Action* vol. 1, p. 342.

106   Habermas, *Faktizitä t und Geltung*, p. 12.

107   Habermas *The Theory of Communicative Action*, p. xxxix.

108   Habermas's claim that power should come into play only insofar as it furthers rather than constrains the autonomy of the citizen is anchored in the ideology of laissez faire capitalism. The autonomy of the citizen leaves him or her free to act – once again – autonomously in the market and exploit others; it is impossible to give autonomy an emancipatory connotation, which involves demonstrating its connection with solidarity and reciprocity, without explicitly confronting the existing logic of accumulation. Cf. Habermas, *Faktizität und Geltung*, p. 215.

109   Habermas, *Theory and Practice*, p. 169.

110   Cf. Gerhard Wagner and Heinz Zipprian, "Intersubjectivity and Critical Consciousness: Remarks on Habermas's Theory of Communicative Action" in *Inquiry* 34 (1990), pp. 54ff.

111   Habermas, *Faktizität und Geltung*, p. 127.

112   "With a theory of communication, there is no obligation to proceed only according to action theory, to speak only of agents and their fate, acts and consequences. It becomes possible also to speak of the characteristics of life–worlds in which agents and collectives or individual subjects move." Habermas, *Autonomy and Solidarity*, p. 113.

113   Alexander, "Habermas's New Critical Theory", p. 410.

114   "Hence Habermas's methodic fiction that a discourse that was freed from particular interests and elements of domination and oriented only toward truth – according to his own example, a discourse resembling

an ideal seminar – could never justify a social order based on structural inequality, does not rest on logically compelling arguments, but on the primacy of a utopian vision of equality in his personal order of values; and I dispute that, even in the conditions of an "ideal talking situation" as postulated by him, he could achieve consensus about his thesis – certainly not with Karl Marx." Lowenthal, "Social Transformation and Democratic Legitimacy," pp. 59–60.

115 For a different view, cf. Karl-Otto Apel, "Diskursethik vor der Problematik von Recht und Politik: Können die Rationalitätsdifferenzen zwischen Moralität, Recht und Politik selbst noch durch die Diskursethik normativ-rational referchtfertigt werden?" in *Zur Anwendung der Diskursethik in Politik, Recht und Wissenschaft*, pp. 29ff.

116 Submission to religious practices and various other premodern customs, after all, are not simply based on "coercion" – unless the term is stretched beyond recognition – and, when dealing with such issues, it is simply an evasion to maintain that all distortion in communication "can be seen as the result of the confusion of action oriented to understanding and action oriented to success, of strategic and communicative action." Habermas, *The Theory of Communicative Action* vol. 1, p. 373.

117 Cf. Schmid, "Habermas's Theory of Social Evolution," p. 180.

118 Karl Marx and Friedrich Engels, *The Holy Family or Critique of Critical Criticism: Against Bruno Bauer and Company* trans. Richard Dixon and Clemens Dutt (Moscow, 1975), p. 96.

119 Stephen Eric Bronner, *Socialism Unbound* (New York, 1990), pp. 156ff.

120 Cf. Jürgen Habermas, "The Scientization of Politics and Public Opinion" in *Toward a Rational Society: Student Protest, Science, and Politics*, pp. 62ff.

121 The state apparatus and the economy "can no longer be transformed democratically from within, that is, be switched over to a political mode of integration, without damage to their proper systemic logic and therewith their ability to function . . . The goal is no longer to supersede an economic system having a capitalist life of its own and a system of domination having a bureaucratic life of its own but to erect a democratic dam against the colonializing *encroachment* of system imperatives on areas of the life–world." Habermas, "Further Reflections on the Public Sphere" in *Habermas and the Public Sphere*, p. 444.

122 Habermas, *The New Conservatism*, pp. 55–6.

123 Cf. Cohen, "Deliberation and Democratic Legitimacy," pp. 26ff.

124 Habermas, *Faktizität und Geltung*, p. 108.

125 Ellen Meiksins Wood, "The Uses and Abuses of 'Civil Society' " in *The Retreat of the Intellectuals: Socialist Register 1990* eds Ralph Miliband and Leo Panitch (London, 1990), p. 60.

126 Habermas, *Faktizität und Geltung*, pp. 190ff.

127 Cf. Adela Cortina, "Ethik ohne Moral: Grenzen einer postkantischen

Prinzipienethik?" in *Zur Anwendung der Diskursethik in Politik, Recht, und Wissenschaft* pp. 278ff.

128   Cf. Stephen T. Leonard, *Critical Theory in Political Practice* (Princeton, 1990); for my notion of the "class ideal," which seeks to combine formal equality for all groups with the interests specific to the working people within each," note the discussion in Bronner, *Socialism Unbound*, pp. 161ff.

129   Seyla Benhabib, *Critique, Norm, Utopia* (New York, 1989), p. 248.

130   Habermas, *Autonomy and Solidarity*, p. 266.

131   Habermas, *The New Conservatism*, pp. 62–3.

132   Habermas, *Faktizität und Geltung*, p. 205.

133   Jane Braaten, "The Succession of Theories and the Recession of Practice," pp. 98ff.

134   "While class conflict is not the only form of struggle that characterizes advanced capitalist societies, it would seem imprudent to maintain, as Habermas is inclined to do, that such conflict has been 'dammed up.' Moreover, it is striking – although perhaps not surprising in view of its evolutionary emphasis – that a 'society' or a 'nation-state' remains the *pierre de touche* of Habermas's account. Nowhere does he examine in detail the international system of nation-states, the multi-national alliances which greatly affect economic development and threaten one another's survival with the accumulated means of waging war. It is at best incomplete to interpret the conflicts and protest movements of our societies from within a framework that filters out the confrontation of nation-states and the politics of mass destruction." John B. Thompson, "Rationality and Social Rationalization," p. 293.

135   Cf. Nancy Fraser, "Rethinking the Public Sphere: A Contribution to the Critique of Actually Existing Democracy" in *Habermas and the Public Sphere*, p. 57.

136   Cf. Ben H. Bagdikian, *The Media Monopoly* (Boston, 1992).

137   Habermas, "Further Reflections on the Public Sphere," p. 441.

138   Habermas, "What Does Socialism Mean Today?," p. 31.

15

Points of Departure: Sketches for a Critical Theory with Public Aims

Introduction

Critical theory began with an emancipatory promise. It offered an interdisciplinary perspective seeking to inform the struggle against oppression in all its guises; it rejected the priority accorded political economy by Marxism and subverted the "privileged position" of the proletariat. It called the domination of nature into question and any identification of the subject with existing institutional arrangements; it championed the reflexive subject against totalitarianism and the "happy consciousness." It defended hope and the concept of utopia.

The great proponents of critical theory produced works of enduring intellectual quality on a remarkable range of subjects and themes. They dared progressive intellectuals to reject the verities of positivism and teleology; they radicalized the use of psychology and anthropology; they linked Marx with Freud and Nietzsche; they proclaimed that "the whole is false" and transformed the debate over culture; they raised the banner of a "negative dialectic" and profoundly influenced the ideology of the 1960s in Europe as well as, in varying degrees, all over the world.

Horkheimer, Adorno, Benjamin, and others associated with the Institute for Social Research forged a radical tradition. Over the last decade, however, critical theory began to lose much of its allure. The triumph of conservativism was not alone to blame. Neither was the continuing lack of a universal "agent" for emancipatory change. The fact is that critical theory had become increasingly domesticated. The success of the enterprise, in good dialectical fashion, generated the conditions for its decline. Apolitical literati turned it into the subject of a deadening scholasticism and embraced its most elitist tendencies while social scientists partitioned its insights for mainstream research. Jürgen Habermas and other innovative thinkers of the "second generation" saw the warning signs. They tried to reinvigorate critical theory, place it on a new "positive" footing, and reaffirm its connection with the most progressive elements of the enlightenment legacy. Nevertheless, the "great refusal" withered.

Philosophical differences, shifting political allegiances, and personal conflicts, make it difficult to get an overall sense of what critical theory was originally meant to convey. Basically, however, it was a normative perspective generated from the traditions of philosophical idealism and historical materialism, which sought to inform empirical research and the struggles of the working class after the initial euphoria of the Russian Revolution had passed. Critical theory was a form of Marxism without organizational attachments. It emphasized the question of consciousness and the manifold threats to individual autonomy. It also sought to restore the connection between theory and practice, which had been perverted by Stalinism. That purpose has eroded and, indeed, it is somewhat difficult to agree with the famous claim of Leo Lowenthal that it was not the critical theorists who abandoned praxis, but praxis which had abandoned them.

A metaphysical veil has fallen over critical theory. Negative dialectics and discourse theory both use it to hide from the reality of conflicting interests and institutions defined by structural imbalances of power. A new identification with the disempowered can help lift this veil. Providing critical theory with a new positive direction of this sort, however, is possible only by reaffirming its forgotten materialist component and reinvesting it with a practical interest in public affairs.

Critical theory was always based on a commitment to freedom and the need for ongoing revision in order to confront new questions posed by new historical circumstances. It was never a set of fixed claims or iron-clad proscriptions. Critical theory is perhaps best understood as what Theodor Adorno termed a "force-field," a problem-complex, composed of certain intersecting concepts.

The future of critical theory depends upon their fate. This problem-complex falls under a set of rough rubrics. The first speaks to the theoretical status of the enterprise and questions concerning its foundations, its view of society, and its conception of tradition. The second deals with immanence and the categories necessary for translating theory into meaningful forms of emancipatory practice: solidarity, accountability, and autonomy. The last involves transcendence and the emancipatory concern with aesthetics, nature, and utopia. Only sketches of these concepts and their implications will be given in the following sections. Nevertheless, should they provide an insight into the possibilities of the critical method, this undertaking will have fulfilled its aims.

I

Foundations

Foundations were precisely what critical theory sought to deny. They smacked of "traditional theory" with its finished claims, fixed systems, and attempts to subsume the particular within the general. In rejecting the foundationalist concern, however, critical theory found itself torn by competing impulses: the positive and the negative, the objective and the subjective, the anthropological and the historical, the sociological and the aesthetic, the material and the metaphysical. Innovative attempts to analyze phenomena from within a determinate historical context confronted the radical projection of freedom beyond any context.

Critical theory had originally inspired radical experiments in the sociology of knowledge. Gradually, however, its focus shifted. The "negation" of society was undertaken so that potentiality might explode actuality, and the integrative power of the culture industries seemed to justify this new preoccupation with transcendence against immanence. Emphasizing the "nonidentity" between subject and object thus became a way of preserving freedom and reflection from necessity and instrumental rationality.

Every system and ideology assuming an identity between the subject and his or her world became open to critique. But the failure of the revolutionary proletariat generated concerns with its foundations. Theodor Adorno and Ernst Bloch, in keeping with the thrust of the original enterprise, sought to resist the use of analytic philosophy and traditional forms of ontology. Both the ontology of "false conditions" developed by the former and the utopian ontology of latter presupposed the existence of "latent" experiences and possibilities resisting definition by reified forms of instrumental thinking. Each called upon reflexivity to deal with "what is not." Each stressed the unfinished character of reality. Each provided an opening to the *novum*.

Categories were lacking in both cases, however, for making distinctions between traditions or translating the latent into the real. Mediations vanished, institutions too, as these critical forms of radical thought conflated the difference between utopia as an other and as a regulative idea. The philosophical attempt to define reality *a priori* became separated from the practical need for categories capable of dealing with contingent situations. Ontology rendered indeterminate the moment of resistance it promised to deliver. Distinguishing the "false" utopia or negation from the "true" thus became an ever more arbitrary exercise.

Supplanting a failed teleology and contesting the philosophical mainstream involved rejecting the positive moment of "synthesis" or the "negation of the negation" in favor of "negativity" and a new antinomial form of thinking. Antinomies, when properly set in motion, were seen as fueling the "dialectical" tension within phenomena thereby maintaining their "non-identity" and utopian potentiality. The new emphasis on negation, however, made the falsification of claims impossible and critical theory found itself simultaneously detached from the empirical sciences and in danger of creating its own form of dogmatism. Critical theory became content to identify its project with resistance to oppression. This purely negative formulation was seen as manifesting the materialist content latent within the idealist concept of reason. Nevertheless, interpreting the "materialist" impulse of idealism in this manner left justice without any historical or institutional points of reference.

The negation of injustice and the commitment to freedom became divorced from practical interests, institutions, and actual movements. Freedom and necessity, subjectivity and the objective world, no longer reciprocally defined one another. The negation was left to contemplate the world of positivity. The contestation of reality would take place without reference to the political implications of ideas. Emancipation became its own justification. But the problem was less a matter of "grounding" in the abstract than an inability to deal concretely with concepts like democracy and the rule of law, socialism and equality, internationalism and cosmopolitanism.

Critical theory had never been inspired by liberalism and social democracy was derided for its economic reductionism, cultural plebianism, and reformism. The new philosophy was influenced instead by the "dialectical" works of Karl Korsch and Georg Lukács whose "theory of praxis" reflected the "heroic phase" of the Russian Revolution. These thinkers were principally concerned with analyzing the mediations linking base and superstructure along with the various cultural and psychological impediments to radical change. Their followers in the Institute essentially saw the weakness of liberal and social democratic traditions as creating the preconditions for the rise of authoritarianism. Little speculation was wasted on their relevance for an emancipated social order. Indeed, with the exception of Erich Fromm, the "inner circle" never showed much support for the Weimar Republic.

History seemed to invalidate the original liberal vision of the bourgeoisie as well as that of its social democratic inheritors. And so, when the communist experiment turned sour, it only made sense that Horkheimer and Adorno should have placed a new emphasis on Nietzsche. Marx never vanished from critical theory. But criticism of the commodity form was now leveled in the name of an increasingly imperiled subjectivity and its incommensurability with any objective system. The "subject," once historical and determinate, now became philosophical and abstract. The attempt to explode all "systems" left it stranded beyond any particular institutional conditions capable of securing its existence.

Foundations are a matter for political and social theory rather than philosophy. Horkheimer already intuited in his youth that happiness requires no philosophical justification. But he never extended his insight to issues concerning reflection or the primacy of liberal values. It is now necessary to radicalize the original claim. Neither linguistic philosophy nor a scientific theory, neither epistemology nor a theory of moral evolution, is necessary or sufficient in order to justify accountability or the rule of law. It is enough to look back at *real systems* and see that, with few historical exceptions, the extent to which the liberal rule of law is employed is the extent to which grievances are open to consistent forms of equitable redress. It is enough to note that the extent to which reciprocity is denied is the extent to which popular sovereignty is subverted, inequality is legitimated, and the subject's security is lost. It is enough to know from the past that the arbitrary exercise of power is grounded in terror.

John Dewey would probably have agreed that these are "warranted assertions." Engaging in ontological, phenomenological, and epistemological forms of justification – or using the "grounding" problems of such philosophical approaches to justify the most nihilistic implications of postmodernism – is all nothing more than an academic exercise. The question over whether the public realm is really "better" or merely "differently" served by accountability and the rule of law as against the arbitrary exercise of power is more than a matter of abstract disputation. Refusing to make a practical judgment, in the name of resisting the "domination" supposedly implicit in such a choice, is merely an abdication of responsibility; judgment is then always exercised by others.

Critical theory is partisan, if not blindly so. It recognizes the existence of diverse constituencies with different ideological commitments. It does not speak only to the converted. But, in practical terms, it recognizes the idealism inherent in seeking to convince the oppressor about the exploitation of the oppressed or, in terms of pure theory, attempting to provide "neutral" justification of its claims before "society" as a whole. The interests of critical theory in justice and happiness are validated by those who suffer from their denial. They need not "justify" their experience of oppression, only the manner in which they seek to mitigate it – and that because, in fact, they will assuredly bear the burden for its failure. Constraining the arbitrary exercise of power and emphasizing the universal constructs underpinning the rule of law is thus legitimated not simply from the the phenomenological standpoint of linguistic rules; its justification derives from a judgment concerning the *practical* needs of the disadvantaged for equitably adjudicating their grievances, overcoming their lack of unity, and developing a sensible view of the institutional conditions capable of fostering their public well-being.

Karl Mannheim liked to speak about "styles of thought" whose internal consistency and relevance for solving practical problems might provide ways of judging between them. Ontology, epistemology, and narrowly linguistic forms of validation become irrelevant from this perspective. The extent to which power is abused becomes the extent to which the "negation" retains its determinate validity. Justifying claims of this sort can occur by reflecting on the past and, from the standpoint of the present, speculating on the practical consequences for the future of a given idea. Controversy will obviously arise on the status of such claims; the counter-factual can confront the general and conflict among various generalizable interests, or rights, will also surely occur. Politics will prove primary in reaching a decision. Such, however, is the practical reality.

Immanent criticism remains sufficient for judging the conduct of any given order in relation to the ideas most consistent in the given context with social equality, democracy, and internationalism. A critical theory with practical commitments and a public purpose will recognize that values of this sort extend beyond the purely formal. Liberalism presupposes certain substantive judgments about the character of "human dignity" and individual responsibility, socialism holds certain substantive views on the value of competition, and internationalism makes certain assumptions concerning the value of "community" and ethnic forms of solidarity. Critical theory cannot ignore substance in the name of form; it must prove willing to confront power and offer criteria for judging how one response to exploitation or oppression might work better for the exploited and oppressed than another.

Old fashioned dualisms between truth and justice or knowledge and interest have grown stale. Critical theory must anchor itself in the structural imbalances of power defining the manifold contexts wherein subjectivity is put into practice. Only then will discussions regarding the grounding of values lose their metaphysical character. Illuminating and confronting the repressed possibilities for freedom defining particular forms of ideological and material production can alone provide the critical enterprise with concreteness and the ability to anticipate the practical concerns over which future struggles will take place. Seeking to expose the interests of the exploited and the institutional constraints inhibiting their articulation, can alone – once again – render critical theory relevant for the coming century.

Society

"Society" remains the cornerstone of the critical enterprise. Conceptualizing it meant overcoming the exclusive reliance on either the empirical or the formal and, for this reason, the method of critical theory was originally seen as resting on the concept of totality. Recently, however, this category has become the object of violent criticism, and much of it is legitimate. "Totality" resonates with absolutist ambitions; it threatens the particularity with subsumption; it has been compromised by association with outmoded forms of historical teleology; it even conjures up the image of totalitarianism. But the concept also militates against reification. It situates the particular and provides it with determination; it turns history into a mutable human product; it explodes paradoxical formulations and makes irrelevant rigid distinctions between facts and value or truth and justice. Totality, in short, illuminates the dynamism of reality and makes the perception of contradictions possible.

Idealism, with its commitment to reflexivity, introduced the category into the modern discourse. Western Marxists like Lukács and Korsch then rejected its neutral epistemological status; its objective character, they maintained, was comprehensible only from the standpoint of a proletarian class subject generated by the very society it was destined to transform. A value-laden and decisionist quality became inextricably linked with the concept. The neutral truth criteria of the natural sciences, for their part, were seen as excluding the "emancipatory interest" (Habermas) in changing existing social relations. Thus, totality was conceived as an inherently social category and the critical theory of society became defined as an interdisciplinary enterprise informed by revolutionary norms.

Conceiving of "society" is still possible only from an interdisciplinary stance. This was a fundamental contention of both Western Marxism and critical theory; indeed, even Jürgen Habermas can legitimately maintain that his theory of communicative action retains a thematic connection with the whole. But the justification for an interdisciplinary stance does not merely derive from the intellectual enrichment that can occur through the interchange between scholars in different fields. More important is the recognition that neither reflection nor ethical judgment can arbitrarily grind to a halt even when disciplinary boundaries are "consensually" raised. Thus, whatever the necessary heuristic boundaries separating the various fields of scholarly endeavor, Theodor Adorno was correct in emphasizing that no *social fact* exists beyond the determinations of society as a whole.

The "whole" is opened to ethical judgment. Totality makes visible the structures of production and reproduction in which reification and commodification are generated. It makes thematizing the various contradictions of society possible and, insofar as they are always "mediated," the various factors inhibiting social transformation as well. Economic determinism is undermined and the theory of Marx becomes receptive to contributions by thinkers concerned with psychological, anthropological, cultural and a host of other issues. Inhibitions on revolutionary commitment receive articulation, ideology is recognized as a "lived experience," and repression assumes a manifold guise with the introduction of the mediated totality.

With the failure of the working class to fulfill its revolutionary mission, however, the category of totality lost its constitutive subject, its potential for transformation, and its dynamism. The integrity of distinct moments within it, no less than the contradictions defining their reproduction, became smothered by reification; the "whole" now confronted the individual it had originally subsumed. No longer could the subject receive its determination within a preformed construct. Theory and practice, subject and object, form and content, transcendence and immanence, fell asunder. It was now necessary to introduce a new category capable of recognizing this reality while keeping the subject "non-identical" with objective reality and all reified systems of thought.

The category of "constellations" sought to contest the "totalitarian" tendencies of the parent category. They would restore a sense of what had been forgotten, whether the sacrifices of the past or the repressed elements of subjectivity in the present, and dynamize the understanding of phenomena without reference to the teleological assumptions of Hegelian dialectics. They would also confront reification by continuing to insist that society is a product of human action and that the particular receives its definition only within a context. Proponents of the new category like Walter Benjamin and Theodor Adorno never relinquished the traditional concern of Western Marxism with thematizing a context. Both theorists rejected relativism and maintained a notion of truth. Indeed, the whole remained a point of reference for their respective notions of "negativity" as well as a category for analyzing history or the social reality being negated.

Systematically emphasizing the "non-identity" between subject and object, however, became the price for rejecting systematic thinking. The

notion of constellations surrendered any historical or institutional referent for freedom. Solidarity lost its concreteness; it became anchored in
art, theology, or anamnesis. Withdrawing from any positive relation to
the empirical world undermined the ability of critical theory either to
justify its status or provide determinations for what needs transformation
and why. Immanently deriving the moments of the whole or the internal
dynamics (*Eigendynamik*) animating them, in the same vein, became ever
more difficult. Concern with reconstructing the relation between theory
and practice faded and the use of constellations ever more surely became
a self-referential and aesthetic exercise.

"Society" can no longer present itself either as preconstituted like the
Hegelian totality or as an arbitrary form of construction motivated by
purely subjective concerns. Its constituent elements, its moments and
their determinations, are not open to definition *a priori*. Reification is
only reproduced when, for example, cultural inquiry is pursued through
economic categories or when the mediations affecting the dynamics of
international trade become the same as those influencing the development of modern painting. The point is to specify the constitution of the
object under consideration and the hidden dynamics defining its potential
for emancipatory transformation. *The object*, in short, *must generate its
categories of inquiry.*

Categories engaged in the task of resurrecting "society" can thus claim
neither "scientific" validity nor ontological status. They exist within a
hermeneutic frame of reference. Just as social scientific inquiry will
always retain an intepretive moment, however, hermeneutics cannot
dispense with social scientific constructs. An exclusive reliance on either
hermenutic formalism or empirical immediacy can only hinder serious
analysis. Nevertheless, the explanatory status of the interpretive construct need not diminish so long as its particular knowledge–constituitive
interests are made explicit.

"Society" will always elude the categories seeking to comprehend it.
But the need to make sense of it still remains. Grand narratives remain
necessary precisely because the economy and mass media are breaking
down national barriers, transnational institutions are on the rise, and
problems ranging from the environment to the economy are becoming
planetary in character. History is taking a global form and, for this
reason, thematizing society from a critical standpoint is less a theoretical
issue than a practical one.

Traditional relations between theory and practice, of course, have
broken down. But this does not justify withdrawing into what Goethe
called the "small world" of the self. It merely involves recognizing that
there is no philosophical or evolutionary trick with which to compensate
for the collapse of teleology. There is nothing with which to cancel the

cunning of history or overcome the contingency of progress. Critical theory, for this reason, needs to grasp freedom in the constraints and concrete alternatives making for its *practical exercise*; philosophy, in this way, remains its "epoch comprehended in thought" (Hegel) and critique the possibility of calling the age into question. Critical theory, whatever its commitment to transcendence, cannot escape immanence or the constraints of historical reality.

Tradition

Struggle is always embedded in tradition; its presence is derived from injustices inherited from the past as well as anticipation regarding their amelioration in the future. Proponents of the new are always situated in time. Tradition is, for this reason, inescapable. It becomes manifest in the values inspiring their enterprise; it appears in the questions they ask and the assumptions they make. Communitarians and conservatives maintain that actions gain their moral value only in the context of lived traditions. But tradition is not simply handed down to the present in a one-dimensional manner. It needs construction and reconstruction in order to exploit the unrealized "surplus" of the past for emancipatory ends.

Tradition provides history with coherence. With the new power of the culture industry, however, the past is ever more surely becoming a buffet from which the gourmet can select a bit of this and a touch of that. The culture industry celebrates the fad, immediacy, cynicism and the "happy consciousness;" it loosens the bonds of tradition and, in keeping with the claims of postmodern thinkers, creates juxtapositions whose arbitrariness is limited only by the dictates of profit. Liquidation of the past, or the inability to give it coherence, is a principal effect of the culture industry.

Critical theory must confront this situation with a more coherent and precise perspective capable of utilizing the seemingly limitless possibilities for signification without surrendering to relativism. Lukács once warned against attempts to pursue left-wing politics with right-wing philosophy. A new understanding of this insight has become necessary. It does not suggest that conservative traditions, and their most outstanding representatives, have nothing to teach. Ideas obviously project beyond the historical context in which they originated and the simplistic reduction of transcendence to immmance impoverishes culture. Nevertheless, even in the greatest of works, a *historical residue* remains.

Walter Benjamin was aware how every document of progress retains an element of barbarism. Traces of repression from the past, whatever the forms of symbolic and institutional mediation, never completely disappear from an idea. The emancipatory appropriation of cultural artifacts cannot occur without recognizing and judging the social and political norms inherited from their contextual origin. Considering the fluctuating connection between theory and practice, transcendence and immanence, is thus imperative for a theory seeking to make sense of the past and employ it for realizing an emancipatory future.

Difficulties arise, however, insofar as not every impulse from the past is reactionary and not every document retains traces of barbarism to the same degree. Gradations exist, freedom and repression intermingle, and a pre-existing conceptual framework is necessary for making determinations. An arbitrary assemblage of objects is easy to create and opens the door to the exercise of the imagination. But cultural artifacts do not simply speak to the present. Their *critical* meaning is illuminated only from within a tradition, whose formation is itself a constitutive act inspired by norms and interests. The question is always how well they are made explicit.

Different traditions of theory and practice will prove useful in different ways for different forms of inquiry. Each forwards a certain relation between the transcendent imperatives of theory and the historical limitations of practice on which progressive philosophical and political undertakings can build. Each also generates a multitiude of contradictions in search of resolutions. A single tradition, such as that stemming from Baudelaire and Nietzsche, can simultaneously prove progressive for modern art and regressive for dealing with social or political issues. Differentiating investigative domains, establishing the connections between knowledge–constitutive interests and unique forms of creative activity, articulating the hermeneutical framework within which a given inquiry is situated, thus become matters of paramount concern.

Clarifying the positive purposes and practical interests generated by any given tradition is a complicated undertaking. Its utopian "surplus," borrowing a term from Ernst Bloch, is never reducible to the ways in which it was employed. Other interpretations and forms of appropriation are always possible. Recognizing the "elective affinity" (Weber) harbored by any given tradition with certain modes of political or cultural practice, however, is a matter of importance.

Dialectic of Enlightenment never took this into account and, consequently, its authors were never able to deal coherently with the historical residue, the political values, and social implications of the Enlightenment. Their critique created an image of enlightenment to suit their purposes. It was, of course, undertaken from the standpoint of enlightenment itself just as the critique of Marxian orthodoxy was undertaken by Korsch from the standpoint of historical materialism itself. But there was one crucial difference. Korsch sought to maintain the connection between theory and practice or ideas and the political context in which they took shape. Horkheimer and Adorno, in bringing legitimate representatives of the Enlightenment and its critics under one roof, broke that connection and innovatively employed a questionable form of historical juxtaposition. They simply ignored the political trajectory of enlightenment philosophy along with the historical connection between republicanism and socialism.

Critical theory, for this reason, became content to elaborate a ratio of resistance by grafting the utopian element within its views on theology and aesthetics upon its theory of society and historical development. Refusing to recognize any disciplinary boundaries, unable to provide its emancipatory concerns with any institutional referents, critical theory ever more surely began to conflate philosophical with political and aesthetic with social forms of resistance. And this is where the problem arises. Critical theory can contribute further to developing a theory of modernism or a "negative" philosophy of history; it can inquire more deeply into the commodity form, deepen the critique of technology, and illuminate new forms of discourse theory. Its possibilities are unlimited. But it cannot do everything at the same time or ignore the distinctions between the manifold spheres of social action. It must take what Douglas Kellner and Steven Best have called a "multi-perspectival" form.

The negation only appears all powerful. The "inversion" of concepts and their connotations, with which critical theory began to preoccupy itself, is satisfying to the spirit of neither Marx nor Nietzsche. A new commitment to determinacy on the part of critical theory has become necessary. This means situating itself in relation to the past, identifying what it wishes to transform in the present, and making sense of its aims in the future. It means, in short, identifying critical theory with a reconstructive project grounded in concrete forms of solidarity.

II

Solidarity

Max Horkheimer once wrote that "the anonymous martyrs of the concentration camps are the symbols of a humanity that is striving to be born. The task of philosophy is to translate what they have done into language that will be heard." But, of course, there are other martyrs as well. Solidarity is just a word unless anchored in a worldview. These take different forms. The most dangerous, however, is one which breaks the connection between the universal and the particular. Indeed, solidarity is too easily manipulated when delimited in terms of purely racial or sexual as well as ethnic or national feelings and experiences.

André Schwarz-Bart recognizes this. *The Last of the Just*, for which he used the loss of his family and his own experiences in the camps, is among the greatest evocations of the holocaust and its connection with the fabric of Jewish history. After moving to Guadeloupe, however, he wrote *A Woman Named Solitude* in which he reconstructed a lost part of Caribbean history through the story of a slave who becomes a revolutionary. A recurrence of images and motifs takes place, and the novel ends with a modern tourist walking near the unmarked grave of the rebels. Thus, the author is able to note that: "If he is in the mood to salute a memory, his imagination will people the environing space, and human figures will rise up around him, just as the phantoms that wander about the humiliated ruins of the Warsaw ghetto are said to rise up before the eyes of other travelers."

The work of Schwarz-Bart, with its internationalist commitments and cosmopolitan sentiments, turns solidarity into more than an anthropological abstraction. This, however, was precisely the way in which the proponents of critical theory defined it. Following Schopenhauer, for example, the young Horkheimer rooted solidarity in empathy for human suffering. An instinctual conception of solidarity underpins Herbert Marcuse's notion of the "new sensibility," Ernst Bloch's utopian category of the "we," and the subjectivity seen by Adorno as inherent within an artwork. Empathy also plays a role in the anamnestic view of history developed by Walter Benjamin, the humanism of Erich Fromm, and all forms of "negative theology." Even Jürgen Habermas presupposes it in his theory of moral evolution and communicative action.

Empathy serves all these thinkers as a basis for moral experience. Much like the notion of "care" elaborated by Martin Heidegger, however, it is incapable of generating derivative categories for coordinating action. The point for contemporary critical theory is thus to begin contesting the variants of what Richard Rorty termed "ethno-solidarity" and finding forms of persuasion for furthering the material interests of particular groups with the universalist precepts underpinning social equality, civil liberties, and internationalism. Solidarity or empathy become matters of practical concern only when they inform a public judgment concerning conflicting interests. Anthropology no more than ontology or phenomenology, for this reason, can use purely private sentiments to generate the logical categories demanded by a public philosophy with progressive aims.

Habermas has tried. Communicative action presupposes empathy or solidarity, while justifying claims discursively serves as a precondition for overcoming injustice and curbing reification. Empathy appears in the willingness of each to place himself or herself in the position of others in the communicative discourse. Solidarity is rendered equivalent with the "generalizable interests" and universalist assumptions located in the structure of language. The "moral point of view" is predicated only on what is common to all.

Certain rules for communicative competence obviously exist; language may presuppose inter-subjectivity and make reflection possible. Simply denying this *in toto* leads only to obscurantism and irrationalism. The critique must take a different form. The problem is that the salience of these rules is dependent upon *prior commitment* to an equitable resolution of differences and, in the same vein, the issue is not whether people *can* put themselves in the place of others, but whether they *will*. The "communicative" use of language can convey little when faced with intransigent interests. The proponents of rational choice have noted, in fact, how the concern for public goods and private interests diverge in notions like the "free-rider" problem. They see the invalidation of empathy, without too much exaggeration, as part of the very logic informing collective action. Simply divorcing communication from such instrumental concerns, or positing formal equality as a precondition for discourse, is insufficient for challenging their argument concretely.

No "phenomenology of moral intuition" can make reference to the ways in which substantive issues of exploitation and the imbalances of institutional power impinge upon contingent discourses. None have been able to deal with the fact that adhering to the normative implications of discourse is a matter of political and existential *choice*. None have much to say about the possibilities for translating solidarity or reciprocity into empirical reality. Indeed, even if generalizable interests have informed every movement of the oppressed, the need to choose between often mutually exclusive universalizable demands will not disappear by simply making reference to the rules of communicative action.

Injunctions pertaining to the reciprocal identification of the other in discourse no less than concepts like what John Rawls termed the "veil of ignorance" undercut the ability to thematize the clash of interests and their effects. Idealistic categories of this sort always rest on the idealistic assumption, so sharply contested by Pierre Bourdieu and his followers, that the exploited is somehow merely the exploiter without riches or advantages. Uncritical preoccupation with what Nietzche termed the "all too human" can easily create a situation in which, identifying with the suffering of all, it becomes impossible to distinguish between the suffering of each. Reciprocity and solidarity thus become lifeless assumptions rather than *material interests in their own right* capable of being denied or advanced. Indeed, this is what creates the nagging thought that perhaps the emancipatory implications residing within communicative interaction are seriously pursued only in the breach and that discourse ethics must quietly presuppose the very institutions in which its assumptions gain validity.

Solidarity is, of course, not simply reducible to matters of social or historical interests. It always harbors an element of transcendence. Were this not the case then, according to Erich Fromm, people could never have confronted the values embedded in the dominant personality patterns of an epoch, nor could they have united for radical aims. From the standpoint of critical anthropology or discourse theory, however, solidarity loses its connection with reality. The concrete is either subsumed within the covering category or defined by the freedom it denies. Solidarity is left either hanging in the realm of metaphysical abstractions or drowning in empirical immediacy. It lacks reference to the choices informing action and, in this way, the public recedes before the private aspect of the sentiment. Critical theory must oppose this trend in the future. Solidarity becomes material only when consideration is given is given to competing views, policies, interests, and ideas, on ending misery. That is why it cannot be imposed by philosophical fiat.

Accountability

Solidarity is no guarantee against the abuse of power. Its political value is defined by the way in which it is organizationally mediated. Issues concerning liberty, for this reason, must always make reference to the institutional conditions through which interests might become tractable and social formations accountable. Empowerment is subsequently less a discursive concept than a political one. It is always the product of strategic action even if its aim involves the creation of institutions capable of reproducing norms consonant with an ongoing discourse among equals.

Accountability is the lynchpin for any institutional notion of empowerment. It connects knowledge and interest. It binds the communitarian notion of popular sovereignty with liberal ideas of individual responsibility (*Mündigkeit*). It reflects a concern not only with the production, but with the reproduction of relations empowering the disempowered. It rejects identifying democracy with the will of the majority or even participation; it tempers such concern with respect for the rights of the minority and the problems pertaining to representation. It recognizes the positive role bureaucracies can play in furthering democracy and insists on confronting their petrifying tendencies so well analyzed by Max Weber. Accountability is not merely a metaphysical or discursive concept, but the *practical fulcrum* for making judgments concerning the democratic character of existing institutions.

Empowerment is a process. It can take different forms and call for the primacy of different "standpoints" under different circumstances. New social movements have furthered equality under the law and transformed previously "private" issues like spouse abuse into matters of public concern; indeed, they have challenged and changed the realm of everyday life. Unions and labor parties have, by the same token, historically waged the battle for economic equality and republican institutions. The priority accorded social movements and interest groups in relation to unions and organized parties will, under present circumstances, vary according to the given institutional context. No single organization like the labor movement of the nineteenth century, after all, is able any longer to both extend universality in the political domain and class specific interests in the economic realm. Nevertheless, only in terms of this dual burden inherited from the labor movement is it possible for critical theory to deal with empowerment from the standpoint of both form and content.

Accountability speaks to this dual burden. Whatever the obvious contributions of the new social movements, insofar as their identity claims have been created by particular interests, they have also generated a certain logic of political fragmentation and an inability to confront the existing production process. Unions, similarly, have increasingly become preoccupied with the narrow economic concerns of their constituencies while labor parties have entered the mainstream and ignored issues dealing with identity or the quality of life under advanced capitalism.

The whole has become less than the sum of its parts. Coordination of what political scientists call "cross cutting" interests among the exploited has, for this reason, become a paramount concern. Class, of course, is what these interests "cut across." Capital and labor remain the two basic categories of the existing economic system. But they are either turned into simple interests by important pluralists like Robert Dahl, who ignore the imbalance of structural power between them, or dismissed from the political discussion entirely by theorists like Hannah Arendt.

Empowerment generates a concern with the accountability of all social, political, and economic institutions. The exclusion of capital is purely arbitrary and a class concept is necessary to contest its power as well as its ability to set different subaltern groups and organizations off against one another. Such a category must link the formal equality sought by most of the new social movements with the interests specific to the working people within each; it must also confront petrifying labor organizations with their original reason for being. Neither economics nor the "spirit" of a nation can guarantee the employment of a *class ideal*. Indeed, for this reason, politics must take precedence in the formulation of any future socialist or critical theory.

No longer is it possible to think of class in terms inherited from the nineteenth century. Working people may still serve as the *sine qua non* for any successful attempt to transform the accumulation process or restructure the political order. There is no longer a single organization capable of expressing their interests; indeed, their identities have been fractured – and undeniably broadened – in a multitude of ways. Class conflict has, certainly for the time being, been "suspended" (Habermas); it has been pushed or displaced to the margins of society. Labor is no longer identifiable with the industrial working class, and stratification has helped shatter "class consciousness." The structural, empirical, and normative elements within the concept of class are, in short, no longer unified as they were during the last quarter of the nineteenth century. And the same holds true for the values informing the proletarian class consciousness of a bygone era: republicanism, social equity, and internationalism.

These values remain necessary for developing any emancipatory project concerned with the accountability of institutions, and future forms of critical theory must seek to reconnect them in a coherent fashion. This means confronting once again the issue of class. Empirical and structural inquiries, however, are insufficient for such a task. More important is political insight and speculative judgment since the primacy accorded any constituent element of the class ideal will change from one set of contingent circumstances to another.

Formulating standards of accountability for differing institutional systems and sub-systems, illuminating repressed contradictions within the "autopoetic" processes of a complex bureaucratic society, can alone make empowement concrete. Realizing accountability is possible only through democratic institutions. Commitment to the formal and universal elements of democracy must, for this reason, serve as the precondition for realizing substantive and particular aims. Only in this way is it possible to reject the trade-off, so reminiscent of Cold War thinking, between civil rights and economic equity. A self-enforced blindness to questions of class and the structural imbalances of economic power, however, will result in an abstraction not only from the accumulation process and its differentiated effects, but from the constituting practice of various other institutional systems and sub-systems as well. Indeed, following Claus Offe and Ulrich Preuss, it becomes apparent that opening the various sub-systems of society to public pressure can only occur by contesting the various hegemonic interests embedded within them.

A critical theory with public aims must deal with issues of this sort. Such a theory, however, must content itself with generating the freest possible conditions in which individuals can reach intelligent decisions concerning the quality of their lives. A public philosophy has its limits. It can never decide on the existential "meaning" of life or a host of private issues ranging from sexual practice to euthanasia.

But this need not simply relegate ethics to matters of procedure. Ronald Dworkin was indeed correct in suggesting that the debate over euthanasia becomes confused when framed in terms of generalizable interests or the "right to live" and the "right to die." Substantive judgments concerning dignity and the integrity of the individual are crucial for rendering judgments about conflicting generalizable concerns. A public philosophy cannot simply rest on the universal character of claims, but must advance certain informed substantive positions on issues ranging from ecology to life-style and the assumptions of institutions as diverse as capital and the Catholic Church.

Ideological controversy and the clash of interests is the stuff of democracy. A public ethic is, for this reason, as little concerned with ontological questions of truth as with theological questions of grace. It is preoccupied with the institutional and ideological preconditions for democratic action: issues of power, accountability, and the equitable redress of grievances. Contingency marks the new epoch. Too much is at stake, however, for using the concept to justify some poststructuralist reduction of philosophy into "play." Confronting the triumph of uncertainty means substituting an ethics, contingent in its appeal and utility, for any form of teleology and developing a new relation between theory and practice.

There is no artificial substitute for an "agent" capable of connecting theory with practice. Theory can now only present the prerequisites for its realization. An emancipated future is no longer appearing in the present. Opposing teleology subsequently calls for tempering optimistic theories of moral evolution and discourse ethics as surely as the predictions of an outworn Marxism. The insights of an artist like Ödön von Horváth can prove useful; his major works like *Geschichte aus dem Wienerwald*, *Der Ewige Spiesser*, *Die Italienische Nacht*, and *Jugend ohne Gott* all refuse to presuppose reflexivity, conscience, or the inherent desire of people to reconcile contradictions.

New approaches in critical theory must squarely confront the reality portrayed by Horváth without resorting to abstractions concerning moral evolution, the "cunning of history," or inflexible economic laws. It is necessary to draw the consequences of teleological failure. But this means less accepting a rupture in the relation between theory and practice than a disjuncture. Arguing against any attempt concerned with developing the preconditions for judgment is useless and grounded in an outmoded metaphysic. Judgment remains a "practical" necessity; Kant, in this regard, was simply right. Theory, for this reason, still has a task. But it can now only provide what are usually considered ethical questions with a practical referent and practical questions with an ethical framework for judgment. Therein lie its limits and possibilities. Indeed, for the time being, connecting theory and practice can occur only from the standpoint of theory itself.

Autonomy

Autonomy was, for critical theory, the response to alienation and reification. It was, from the start, a reflexive concept with ethical connotations. Autonomy never had anything in common with license. Increasingly, however, the preoccupation with autonomy has begun to evidence ever stronger affinities with what the young Hegel called "bad reflection" or the fear of entering the real. It became self-referential, coterminous with the "totally other," the "great refusal," "higher praxis," or genuine "communication." Such exercises in "bad reflection" made it impossible to specify *what* tendencies were inhibiting the exercise of autonomy in *which* particular spheres. Thus, autonomy turned in upon itself.

Autonomy exhibits a material component insofar as the exercise of human faculties depends upon certain economic, political, and social preconditions. Even Kant used the concept to anchor his theory of "practical reason" and, politically, its identification with individual responsibility (*Mündigkeit*) made autonomy the core justification for republicanism. Civil liberties and the rule of law, human rights and popular sovereignty, all presuppose autonomy even as they seek to secure it universally through a public realm capable of protecting the weak from the arbitrary exercise of power by the privileged. For this reason, from the standpoint of practice, universalism and particularism do not stand in some rigidly antinomial relation with one another. The same is true of solidarity and autonomy. Following this line of thought, in fact, the partisans of democratic socialism were intent on pursuing material equality precisely so that economic "necessity" would not intrude on the exercise of "freedom." Thus, Henry Pachter could identify a genuinely socialist order with "the highest stage of individualism."

Autonomy only makes sense with reference to accountable institutional forms capable of realizing reciprocal conditions for the free play of the faculties. But critical theory has had trouble conceiving of it in these terms and part of the problem derives from identifying alienation and reification with objectification. The increasing dominance of instrumental reason was seen by various members of the Institute as creating a situation in which all forms of social and political action undermine subjectivity. Only the aesthetic or philosophical inversion of public life was seen as capable of redeeming authentic experience in the "totally administered society."

Both for Marx and Lukács, however, coming to terms with reification involved empowering the exploited and disadvantaged through political action. They may have assumed the existence of a revolutionary subject. But they assumed something else as well: the existence of responsible people with determinate political aims. Neither meant to imply that working people *are* things or that subjects *are* objects. Crucial for their understanding of the commodity form was how working people are treated by dominant institutions and treat each other, the values of the existing order and the extent to which workers are defined as a mere cost of production by capital.

Focusing on this concrete referent for reification produces the preoccupation with empowerment and the accountability of institutions. Reification projects a counter-world in which no subject is treated as an object or means to an instrumental end; indeed, this is the point on which the *critical* theories of Kant and Marx converge. Such a world is one in which the institutional space and material conditions are created for a permanent revolution and enrichment of subjectivity. Certain forms of political activity can help bring about such a world and, for this reason, reification is not interchangeable with objectification or the mere externalization of subjectivity. Indeed, for this same reason, neither concept is identifiable with alienation.

Alienation generates little interest in reforms or revolution; it lacks a determinate referent and, for this reason, creates a concern with the apocalypse and utopia. Alienation expresses the "poverty of the interior" (Benjamin); it is not concerned with externalization at all. It is existential in character and speaks to issues like loneliness, death, and the lack or source of ultimate meaning. These are real concerns and there is no sense in simply condemning them as mystical or irrational. Arguably, in fact, the emancipatory purpose of abolishing reification is so that each can come to terms with private matters of this sort in his or her own way without the intrusion of institutional dogmas like the fear of hell or the economic needs of everyday life. Indeed, there is a sense in which autonomy does involve becoming sovereign over what Martin Heidegger called "one's ownmost possibility."

"Écrasez l'infame," the famous words flung by Voltaire at the Church, must now receive a new and expanded meaning. Old prejudices and provincial beliefs, along with the institutions profiting from them, must receive a new form of criticism. Sensitivity for existential problems must combine with a commitment to broaden the public space in which autonomy is exercised. For all that, however, the proponents of critical theory cannot deceive themselves. No theory can offer magic remedies for alienation. Loneliness and death will not disappear. Dealing with them through the mores of a "new sensibility" might indirectly temper the experience of alienation. But subjectivity will always recede behind the veil of politics and the longing for utopia or the "wholly other" will remain. Thus, the danger in burdening political action with limitless expectations or viewing empowerment as a series of steps on the road to utopia.

Alienation and reification speak to different domains of existence, and dealing with the one does not invalidate the importance of the other. There are even points of overlap. Considering the commodity form, for example, qualitative differences between objects are still ever more surely being reduced to quantitative ones and the "labor power" sold by individuals on the market is ultimately still being evaluated by the employer no differently than any other resource. Nevertheless, this is all taking a new and more radical form insofar as the subversion of reflexive capacities is increasingly becoming fused with the expansion of choices.

Amid a staggering literacy crisis, and an invasion of the private sphere by mass media in ways even Flaubert could never have imagined, the subject now faces an expanding number of material decisions with existential import. Public are steadily becoming private questions. Violence, environmental decay, the difficulties in accessing masses of new information, and making choices ranging from cloning to euthanasia, obviously impinge on the existential experience of existence. Indeed, the question concerns just how well society is preparing the subject for this expanded realm of decision-making.

Autonomy means being able to choose between cultural and political options. Its public exercise thus still presupposes reflexivity, which depends upon education. For this reason, in keeping with the efforts of Henry Giroux and others, critical theory has an important role to play in developing new forms of pedagogy and contesting both the narrow ways in which "culture" is transmitted and the avoidance of questions concerning "quality" in modern education. Without making reference to education and reflexivity, in fact, it makes no sense to speak of autonomy. Indifference will then increasingly define its exercise. One choice will become the same as another even as the range of alternatives increases. Autonomy will, under these circumstances, ever more surely degenerate into cynical forms of anomie.

Inhibiting choices by which the individual might enhance the control of his or her destiny is no alternative: it only leads to the arbitrary exercise of power and resentment. The point is rather to develop categories for proceeding with ethical precepts and a sense of human possibility. Critical theory and all forms of rationalism, for this reason, will soon have to begin thinking about how new advances in parapsychology, space travel, cybernetics, and holograms might effect the phenomenological encounter of the subject with his or her world. The "end of history" and the "end of art" are metaphysical phenomena. Technology continues to develop and coming to terms with it will demand a rejection of the assumptions formed in the postmodern night where all cows are black. Indeed, conceiving of the future as unfinished is less a theoretical necessity than a practical one.

III

Aesthetics

John Dewey once said that aesthetics is the "ultimate judgment on the quality of civilization." It only makes sense then that virtually every major representative of critical theory should have produced studies on art and the ways in which given works and styles of music, poetry, film, and literature reflect certain historical and anthropological experiences. The contextual referent never entirely vanished from the cultural criticism of the Frankfurt School, and it remained dominant in the work of Leo Lowenthal. But it clearly grew less important in the aesthetic theory of Adorno, Benjamin, Marcuse, and even Siegfried Kracauer. Epecially following World War II, in keeping with philosophical developments, a preoccupation with form increasingly marked the greatest aesthetic achievements of critical theory.

Both its unequivocal allegiance to modernism and its famous analysis of the culture industry were anchored in the emphasis on form. An understanding of the one, in fact, is possible only in terms of the other. The history of modernism coincides with an elimination of the representational object in the name of color or line; consider, for example, the dynamic leading from the haystacks of Monet to the Fauves and Kandinsky as well as the road leading from Cézanne's *Mont Saint-Victoire* and *Château Noir* to the cubists and the constructivists. Subjectivity affirms its autonomy from the objective world precisely insofar as form vanquishes representation in an effort to capture a more "authentic" content.

Autonomy and the unique experience generated by modernism are, by the same token, seen as precisely what the culture industry seeks to subvert with its emphasis on the lowest common denominator and desire to assure the greatest possible profits. Classicism and realism, with their contemplative concern for the representational object and commitment to narrative, can offer no resistance. Their formal conservatism, in fact, makes their more radical elements particularly susceptible to "nullification" by the culture industry. Indeed, according to Lowenthal's interpretation of classical French drama, the "realist" critique of society is seen as occuring concommitantly with the gradual elimination of unique subjective experience.

The emancipatory elements of modernism are, of course, also open to absorption. But, with its affirmation of subjectivity and formal innovations like montage, the modernist legacy was generally seen by critical theorists as the only bulwark against the conformism generated by the extension of the commodity form into the cultural realm. Aesthetic resistance to the culture industry was thus undertaken in two ways, which essentially derived from the idealist and romantic currents of modernism.

According to Herbert Marcuse, whose views were based on a tradition extending from Friedrich Schiller to Arthur Rimbaud, aesthetic resistance would involve the projection of utopia. Cultural norms would inform a new sensibility capable of envisioning the emancipated life-world, and the "pacification of existence" would serve as the critical referent for contesting advanced industrial society and the commodity form. A confusion between political and cultural practice, however, takes place. The aesthetic projection of utopia winds up substituting for the determination of emancipatory social or political institutions even while the particular work of art and the categories for dealing with it vanish from critical inquiry.

By contrast, in keeping with a central tenet of romanticism, Theodor Adorno provides the work with primacy to the point where its inner dynamics actually generate the categories, or characteristics, making for its interpretation. Reception is no longer an important category of aesthetic understanding precisely because the culture industry has already impinged upon the autonomous exercise of subjectivity. The work with its paradoxical ability to resist the conditions of its own genesis, preserves subjectivity in an objective fashion, forges a mimetic content through reflexive means, and creates a unique inner language through technique. It resists the omnivorous culture industry only by producing an inversion of sociological categories. Thus, the identity of the artwork lies in its ability to strengthen the tensions underlying the non-identity between subject and object.

Both Marcuse and Adorno essentially begin with a metacritique of the culture industry. Its products are essentially dismissed *a priori*. Neither ever provides categories for making qualitative distinctions between different works developed within different traditions, styles and genres. Sociologically, of course, it is legitimate to forward general claims concerning the negative effects of the culture industry. Aesthetically, however, it is both mistaken and useless to deny that the culture industry has produced numerous works of high quality. Nevertheless, excepting perhaps Benjamin and Kracauer, an unyielding emphasis on aesthetic form and complex techniques combined with old-fashioned elitism has made most proponents of critical theory blind to this possibility.

A metacritique of the culture industry makes no sense if it must assume that the dove of Picasso or any other "popular" work can produce enlightenment only in the form of "mass deception." Works of popular culture deserve the same serious treatment as those generally interpreted from the perspective of high art. They too exist within a context and manifest its contradictions; they too are defined within genres and influenced by manifold traditions; indeed, they too *can* evidence critical and emancipatory elements. None of this calls for a suspension of critical judgment. Quite the contrary. Precisely because the culture industry is eradicating perceived differences in quality, which is only in keeping with the imperatives of the commodity form, aesthetics must privilege the category of judgment.

Aesthetics can only reassert its critical character and contemporary value by confronting its assumptions and applying its methods to practical problems. Old concerns about the nature of aesthetic "experience" have lost their relevance given the ability of the culture industry to create and even fulfill a variety of existential needs. Subjectivity is, furthermore, now less threatened than overwhelmed. Arguing for modernism over realism, or non-representation against representation, is simply irrelevant given the dominance of an industry capable of generating a plethora of styles in any number of genres. Nor is it any longer legitimate to maintain that "art" inherently projects freedom or a vision of emancipation. Indeed, this only assumes what interpretation must demonstrate.

Making practical differentiations between the manifold critical or utopian potential that artworks in the most diverse traditions *may or may not* evidence is the contemporary task of radical cultural criticism. Art has no predetermined purpose and neither its "meaning" nor its contribution is self-evident. Fostering resistance or reflexivity, for example, no more defines music than the limitless ways in which popular songs give rise to various dances or become associated with a limitless set of personal memories. Giving priority to either only makes sense if aesthetic inquiry enters the public arena and makes explicit its social or political presuppositions.

The point is not to simply define aesthetic inquiry in terms of politics. It is merely to recognize that the work of art does not generate the norms for either its application or appropriation. A given work, just like a particular tradition, can simultaneously offer progressive impulses for cultural production and regressive implications for politics and vice versa. Cultural criticism must respect the tensions between different spheres of activity even as it seeks to expand the alternatives of cultural experience. Nevertheless, this cannot occur by continuing to focus on the autonomy of art or the manner in which "resistance" takes place through technical complexity and the preservation of a repressed subjectivity.

"Resistance," from the standpoint of aesthetics, is meaningful only insofar as the subject is able to make meaningful choices among an increasing set of cultural products. Technical aesthetic knowledge is crucial for determining quality. But so is a certain cosmpolitan exposure to diverse cultural traditions. A genuine commitment to diversity involves judgment. It calls for contesting the fad and relativism of the culture industry in the name of imperiled classics and excluded traditions. But it also recognizes that doing so is possible only within a *public* arena and on the basis of assumptions consonant with enlightenment notions of pedagogy. There is also a place for the *private*, "purposefully purposeless" (Kant), experience of an artwork in which public judgment is simply irrelevant.

The more elitist tenets of critical theory have as little place in an emancipatory cultural criticism as the more patronizing tenets of populism. The "material level of culture" (Marx), however, is a genuine issue. Raising it will always involve the criticism of bohemians, nonconformists, and those whom reactionaries like Maurice Barrés liked to call "rootless cosmpolitans." Aesthetics will always have a special place for such people; indeed, therein lies its special power.

Nature

The harnessing of nature once seemed closely linked with the philosophical promise of the good life. Technology promised both empowerment and the transformation of dead nature into a live world of commodities. Critical theory played an important role in dispelling such illusions. Its willingness to emphasize the human price of progress, the costs of alienation and reification, the impact of scientific reason on moral capacities, and the potential "revenge of nature" were all major contributions. The increasing fear of everything associated with instrumentalism, however, sundered whatever fruitful interchange Max Horkheimer had originally envisioned between critical theory and the empirical sciences.

Nature increasingly became pitted against technology while "science" was engaged either sociologically or from a "new" utopian perspective whose categories and criteria were never fully articulated. But there was a kernel of truth to the often exaggerated criticisms of empiricism and positivism. Skepticism concerning the technological definition of progress was surely warranted and, if the proponents of critical theory generally ignored the new theoretical developments in the philosophy of science, they anticipated many contemporary concerns of the ecology movement.

Each age defines its problems. Ecology first became an issue in advanced industrial society just as "society" only appeared as an object of concern in the industrial age. Without this historical perspective, in fact, coming to terms with the effects of either becomes merely a metaphysical exercise. The institutions of modernity itself are necessary for dealing with what modernity produced. A degree of bureaucracy and planning are unavoidable in mitigating what is rapidly becoming an environmental nightmare. What makes the process so difficult, however, is that an ever more complex division of labor has seemingly bedeviled administrative decision-making.

Linear notions of scientific development have fallen before the new preoccupation with "paradigm shifts." There is also little consensus concerning what values and and political priorities are intrinsically connected with developing sustainable forms of ecologically sound production. It has become ever more apparent, without even considering purely metaphysical questions of grounding the "scientific method," that specialists in different fields of scientific endeavor increasingly find themselves unable to communicate with one another on the most advanced planes of research. All this, indeed, contributes to the creation of what Ulrich Beck has termed the "risk society."

Consequences of previously unimaginable ecological horror now seem attendant on the most routine decisions of an administrative apparatus increasingly defined by what Hannah Arendt originally called the "rule of nobody." The impact of an oil spill is incalculable. The very dynamism of modern technology, the prospect of a geometrically increasing set of unintended consequences for every technological act, fosters a growing refusal to accept responsibility which has itself become ever more difficult to assign due to the proliferation of institutional subsystems, committees, and the like. Elisabeth Beck-Gernsheim and others have even shown how technological change is transforming the existential character of decision-making by forcing individuals to deal with issues ranging from cloning to personal appearance.

Raising ecological concerns of this sort is an important contribution by theories dealing with the risk society. Its systems and sub-systems become the point of reference. Movements can raise issues and pressure existing institutions. Ultimately, however, adjustment will depend upon the ability of the very organizations generating ecological and other forms of risk to reform themselves through what has variously been described as "reflexive modernization." An often contradictory drive toward self-criticism takes hold. Critique is no longer limited to particular institutions or sub-systems; the risk society seemingly engages in an ongoing self-criticism of its own "risk" dynamics. The problem, of course, is that certain institutions profit from "risk" while others fear it. Consequently, if this actually generates new concern for a public response to newly intractable interests, it also becomes evident that even the process of adjusting will manifest the uncertainty and contingency associated with the new order.

The encounter with nature, and the pervasive character of risk, is seen as rendering irrelevant the old political distinctions between "left" and "right." An integration of the "other" – whether black, woman, proletarian, etc. – is also projected. But this will not result in a new organic form of community. The implications of the new risk society will actually intensify the anomie and moral paralysis with which critical theory originally concerned itself. The "poor" might still suffer most from its effects. But traditional assumptions will none the less fall by the wayside. The very expansion of alternatives, for example, will explode the enlightenment equation of autonomy with emancipation. Radically interpreting the hermeneutic of "risk theory" will involve recognizing that the concern for justice and procedural fairness cannot substitute for questions concerning the interaction with nature and the substantive character of the "good society." Behind the back, so to speak, happiness reasserts itself as a public issue generated by the domination of nature.

There are obvious problems regarding the abolition of the "other" in the face of unresolved "non-synchronous contradictions" like racism. Believing in the irrelevance of political worldviews ignores the manner in which ideologies inform policy choices. It is also somewhat naive to suggest that the mere recognition of future risk will cause industries like nuclear energy to "reform" themselves; indeed, a prime cause for the weakness of regulatory agencies in the United States is their dependency on the experts and information of those very industries whose excesses they are seeking to mitigate. Risk theory is missing the categories for articulating ethical judgments, understanding the accumulation process, or dealing with matters pertaining to the contradictory character of institutional or symbolic reproduction. Nevertheless, future experiments in critical theory should not ignore the serious questions raised by Ulrich Beck and other proponents of this new interpretation of modernity.

Coming to terms with them will involve dealing with the manner in which the given order structures alteratives and poses choices. These are substantive rather than purely formal concerns and Korsch's "principle of historical specification," once again, shows its relevance. Rolling back technology or offering unformulated versions of a "new science," for example, is an abstraction. The irony is that new bureaucratic institutions and new forms of technology will become necessary to constrain ecologically devastating forms of production *before they are introduced.* The issue thus becomes one of making choices about the direction of technology or the social character of science. Indeed, these will become the substantive concerns of any public philosophy committed to progressive aims.

A critical theory with public aims must begin indicating the ways government can influence ecologically sound production, provide subsidies or tax-benefits for particular industries, fund particular forms of knowledge creation, and make "risks" a matter of public debate. It must propose ways of rendering anonymous institutions and their administrative sub-systems *more* accountable and individuals *more* aware of the moral conflicts awaiting them. It will have to consider the role of political parties and intermediate forms of control linking the locality with larger institutional settings. It will also have to offer revised definitions of responsibility, "evidence," and culpability in order to meet the needs of a society whose interaction with nature is ever more defined by complex developments in science, technology, and administrative management.

Progress has always worked behind the backs of the masses. Imprisoned within the private realm of the subject, ethics could not respond to a scientific method whose extension seemed to permit of no alternatives. The complexity of "science" and its neutrality with respect to means, which seemingly justifies a closed debate among experts, became the basis for an often uncritical acceptance of purposive ends generated without reference to any democratic will formation. Focusing on internal issues pertaining to the methodological conduct of research thus actually perpetuates the reification of society. It is less a matter of the scientific method than the manner in which technology crystallizes social goals. The goal for critical theory is to prevent the scientific enteprise from remaining identified with the discourse of experts.

Progress, in emancipatory terms, will occur only insofar as the public has input into its definition. A democratic critique of technology is, following Andre Gorz, the basis for any "revolutionary reform" of society. But too much time has been spent, especially by those who lack any genuine scientific expertise, on deconstructing the "scientific method." More important are sustained critical inquiries into the institutional complexes, with their particular balance of forces, wherein the "scientific" method receives its purposive aims and social content. Retreating into the realm of procedure is too often a way of avoiding questions concerning the normative content of social choices. Dealing with such issues *critically* is impossible without a substantive interest in reasserting the lost connection between critical theory and the empirical sciences no less than with the movements and political organizations seeking to effect ecological change.

Instituting new technological priorities and ethical parameters for the human interchange with nature is inherently a "world experiment" (Bloch). Ecological concerns are the new motor for internationalism precisely because a disaster like Chernobyl is limited neither by time nor space. The very difficulty of assigning responsibility or providing compensation calls forth a cosmopolitan commitment as surely as the need to control a rapacious set of multinationals. James O'Connor may have exaggerated the case in arguing that the ongoing despoliation of the planet will ultimately bring about the final crisis of capitalism. Ecological concerns will, however, surely help set the parameters for any new progressive views on the accumulation process in a democratic polity as well as any future definition of social equity or internationalism. They raise the need to reconsider the notion of progress and human well-being. Indeed, precisely to that extent, confronting the domination of nature immanently raises the question of utopia.

Utopia

History has not been kind to utopia, perhaps because there is no way ever to deliver on what it promises. Utopia is the response to alienation and, for that very reason, it always retains an element of otherness. But that doesn't obliterate its practical importance. Utopian longing has inspired the most extraordinary sacrifices and the grandest undertakings. These have always given way to resentment following their betrayal and with every failed experiment in liberation, of which communism is only the most recent example, utopia has been buried anew. But then, with an event like Tiananmen Square, it again rises from the dead. Somehow whenever the call for "common sense" is trumpeted, whether in Eastern Europe or elsewhere, the need for "hope" makes itself felt. Utopia is "nowhere." But its traces appear every time solidarity triumphs over self-interest. Speaking about "the end of utopia," like Judith Shklar, thus simply misses the point.

Every experiment in social change presupposes a certain notion of the "best life." Each assumes, in its own way and after its own fashion, that things can be different. Glowing like the biblical "burning bush," with which Manès Sperber associated it, utopia constantly rekindles the dreams of the lowly and the insulted. It forms the underside of history, the response to alienation, and the preoccupation of critical theory with the concept was only logical. The utopian imagination opened materialism to a host of repressed and unrealized possibilities. It offered a certain standard with which to judge the repression of the present and provided the future with an emancipatory legacy from the past.

Transcendence is not inimical to immanence. Both are moments of material practice. Fantasy and happiness, beauty and wonder, have often inspired what in the moment of execution can only have appeared as inherently "anticipatory" enterprises of social or political change. Karl Mannheim was aware that the neglect of utopia constituted a serious failing of all "realistic" theories. Even a critical theory reinvigorated by the insights of pragmatism cannot afford to ignore the practical role of the *novum*.

Marx, of course, was always justifiably wary of attempting to depict the emancipated communist society of the future. He had only contempt for the "system builders" and moralists concerned with making dogmatic claims about the "good." Marx could indulge in such irony, however, because he considered his own theory capable of "objectively" explaining how an alternative to the prevailing course of history would arise within history itself. Perhaps there is still a place for such forms of "scientific" endeavor. But the teleology of times past is no longer plausible. Ernst Bloch probably has the most to offer for the development of a new philosophy of history in which transcendence is linked with immanence. His utopian theory, however, is still grounded in the ontological and teleological assumptions of an earlier time. History now makes new demands on social theory.

"Negative dialectics" breaks the connection between utopia and teleology. It interprets utopia to meet the conditions defined by the previously unimaginable horrors of the 1930s and 1940s. The proponents of negative dialectics, however, take a step back behind Bloch. Auschwitz is seen as the final and most compelling reason for the *Bilderverbot*. In projecting utopia beyond the realm of action, however, transcendence becomes reified. "Other-worldliness" (*Jenseitigkeit*) and abstraction become ends unto themselves in notions of the "totally other" and the "yearning" for God, no less than in the fleeting moment of aesthetic experience and anamnestic remembrance. Reification is ignored in favor of alienation. The *novum* loses its power no less than its appeal. Articulation becomes impossible. Utopia is a content devoid of form.

An alternative is to interpret utopia as a regulative ideal. No longer is it the other. The formal assumptions of a democracy are seen as prerequisites for an emancipated order. Utopia is thus asymptotically connected with practice as a phenomenological complex of procedural rules for communication. Conditions for the reproduction of utopia enter the analysis even while the regulative view militates against associating it, either positively or negatively, with the totality; Habermas has indeed correctly argued that, even when considering feudalism, progress made in one systemic domain can produce regression in another. He has also recognized the danger of dogmatism in venturing substantive judgments on the relative merits of one culture or set of traditions against another. Utopia, from this perspective, is immanent within "justice" rather than transcendent in its vision of the "good." Alienation is ignored in favor of reification; utopia becomes a form without content.

Relativism on all matters other than procedure, however, makes it impossible to "rub history against the grain" (Benjamin). Even relatively emancipated political institutions do not necessarily generate emancipatory culture or expressions of subjectivity. An exclusive commitment to justice leaves the culture industry, no less than most regressive mores, intact. A pure proceduralism ignores the pleas of Benjamin and Bloch to "never forget the best" even as it denies everyday experience wherein judgments regarding the superiority of one set of texts over another becomes practically necessary in the forming of curricula as surely as in making sense of what Marx called the "material level of culture." The legacy of the past can only receive an emancipatory determination when judgments make substantive reference to particular works and forms of conduct.

Utopia can conceptually illuminate repressed needs and even help provide insights into what Ernst Bloch termed the ratio of the irratio. But the concept retains practical relevance only when impulses towards the "best life" are symbolically and institutionally mediated and their inherently transcendent character is given a degree of determination. Alternatives to existing institutions and forms of cultural production are concrete only when intertwined with existing interests, some intractable and some open to compromise, which are themselves in need of judgment. Alternatives conceived without reference to interests must hang in the abstract. Future forms of critical theory thus cannot afford to ignore questions concerning the contextual specification of material interests and how they buttress structural imbalances of power within given domains of action.

Action generates its context. Different spheres of activity demand different criteria of judgment. The legal toleration of cigarette smoking, for example, should not preclude an evaluative judgment or a cultural campaign against it. A cultural critique does not necessarily imply the need for political action nor, for that matter, is every political act in need of a cultural critique. An asymmetry marks society and, *for this concrete reason*, the exercise of freedom can never prove total. The prerequisites for social change seeking to realize utopia are precisely what generate new, if often qualitatively different, forms of alienation. Utopia is the "totally other," but it inspires every struggle for justice and every theory willing to view freedom in its asymptotic relation to reality.

The absence of utopia, following Jacques Derrida, indicates its presence. Utopia is not an anthropological break. It is not merely pacification, it is also growth. It is not simply play, it is also *l'esprit sérieux*. It is not just spontaneity, but order. It is not only a higher form of intuition, but also knowledge. It is not only the future or anticipations of space travel and parapsychology, but remembrance and logic. It is not merely "mimesis" (Adorno), but reflexivity. Utopia is a juggler balancing an inherently mutuable content with a regulative form. It is the tension between freedom and license.

Perhaps that is why "the best life" is never defined by a system. It is closer to a sketch. Sketches are not paintings. Nor are they drawings. Both are complete; they integrate their diverse components, place them in motion against one another, and project beyond the context. Sketches are always incomplete. They are often little more than half-visible outlines of a seemingly indeterminate content. That is why the sketch cannot dictate how an artist *must* employ contrasts of tone, shadow, and color in a painting. Each is open to employment in a different way, in one part of the sketch or another, and each is open to being redrawn or withdrawn. Sketches, however, retain their inner logic. The best offer constructive insights into the problems internal to a particular artistic undertaking and the terms in which the struggle to resolve them will be waged. The very indeterminacy of a sketch thus provides the future work with a degree of determination. It lets the eye play and gives a sense of direction. The sketch serves as a set of coordinates. It shows the way in which a painting of the future can become visible.

Index